G.E.Hare

Newcastle

Oct 93.

French today is a profile of the French language in its social context. British and French linguists examine trends in French throughout the French-speaking world, and address issues around prescriptivism, gender and language, and regional languages and dialects. The collection includes overviews of work done in particular areas and deeper analyses of sociolinguistic questions. One theme is how to represent and interpret data relating to language varieties that have been marginalised. Another concerns the way in which French is adapting to the future, whether as a language of new technology, or as a vehicular language on another continent.

French today

French today

Language in its social context

Edited by
CAROL SANDERS
Professor of French
Department of Linguistic and International Studies, University of Surrey

 CAMBRIDGE
UNIVERSITY PRESS

Published by the Press Syndicate of the University of Cambridge
The Pitt Building, Trumpington Street, Cambridge CB2 1RP
40 West 20th Street, New York, NY 10011–4211, USA
10 Stamford Road, Oakleigh, Victoria 3166, Australia

First published 1993

Printed in Great Britain at the University Press, Cambridge

A catalogue record for this book is available from the British Library

Library of Congress cataloguing in publication data
French today: language in its social context / edited by Carol
Sanders.
    p. cm.
Includes bibliographical references and index.
ISBN 0–521–39505–4 (hc). ISBN 0–521–39695–6 (pb)
1. French language – Social aspects – France. 2. French language –
Social aspects – French-speaking countries.
PC2074.75.F74   1992
306.4′4′0944 – dc20   92-5017 CIP

ISBN 0 521 39505 4 hardback
ISBN 0 521 39695 6 paperback

TS

CONTENTS

FIGURES AND MAPS

Figures

Maps

TABLES

NOTES ON THE CONTRIBUTORS

Gertrud Aub-Buscher is Director of the Language Centre, University of Hull. She has published a book on French dialectology and articles on French Creoles and language teaching.

Michel Blanc is Emeritus Reader in Applied Linguistics and Bilingualism at the University of London. He is a former Senior Research Fellow at the International Center for Research on Bilingualism, Laval University, and the former Chair of the London Conference for Canadian Studies. He has published extensively in the field of bilingualism.

L.-J. Calvet is Professor of Linguistics at the Sorbonne. His many publications include *La guerre des langues* (Payot, 1987), and a forthcoming book on the linguistic problems of Europe.

Nina Catach is a well-known authority on French orthography and spelling reform. She leads a CNRS (*Centre National de la Recherche Scientifique*) research team in this area, and is the author of a number of books including the recent *L'orthographe en débat* (Nathan, 1991)

Jacques Durand is Professor of French and Linguistics at the University of Salford. He has written widely on machine translation, general linguistics and phonology (both theoretical and applied to French). His recent publications include *Generative and non-linear phonology* (Longman, 1990).

John Gaffney is Reader in European Politics at Aston University. Among his books are *The French Left and the Fifth Republic: the discourses of socialism and communism in contemporary France* (Macmillan, 1989) and *The language of political leadership in contemporary Britain* (Macmillan, 1991).

Ken George is Reader in French at the University of Buckingham and the author of numerous books, articles and papers on current lexical trends in French.

Marie-Marthe Gervais of the South Bank University has taught French and linguistics at a number of British universities and polytechnics. Her doctoral thesis was on women and language in France, and she is co-author, with Carol Sanders, of an advanced-level French course (*Cours de français contemporain: niveau approfondi*, Cambridge University Press).

Roger Hawkins is Senior Lecturer in French at the University of Essex. His interests range from second language acquisition to regional variation in French.

Anne Judge is Senior Lecturer in French at the University of Surrey. She is co-author of one of the most authoritative grammars of French, *A reference grammar of modern French* (E. Arnold).

Suzanne Lafage is Professor at the Sorbonne Nouvelle, and the author of major publications on French in Africa. She is director of the *Réseau des Observatoires du français contemporain en Afrique Noire* of the *Institut National de la Langue Française* (CNRS).

Foued Laroussi is a researcher in sociolinguistics for the CNRS in Rouen, and a specialist on French–Arabic code-switching, and linguistic aspects of immigration.

J.-B. Marcellesi is Professor at the University of Rouen, and director of the CNRS sociolinguistics research unit in Rouen. He is well known for his work on sociolinguistic theory, languages in conflict and minority languages.

Stephen Noreiko is lecturer in French at the University of Hull. He is a lively contributor to a number of journals on French language issues, and author of *A la tienne: French word games*.

Carol Sanders is Professor of French at the University of Surrey. She has taught French language and linguistics at various universities in Britain, Australia and the West Indies. She is the author of a book on Saussurean linguistics, and of a number of French language coursebooks.

ACKNOWLEDGEMENTS

I should like to thank Gertrud Aub-Buscher and Margaret Deuchar for commenting on parts of the manuscript, and Karen Bonstein and Patricia Thomas for help with typing. The translation of chapters 4, 5, 7 and 12 was done by Jennifer Marty, Carol Sanders, Patricia Thomas and Lucas Weschke.

I am grateful to the Australian National University, Canberra, whose funding enabled me to carry out the initial work needed for chapter 2 of this book.

Thanks are due to the following publishers, for permission to use extracts, the full sources of which are recorded in the bibliography: Association for French Language Studies, *Association pour la Recherche et l'Expérimentation sur le Fonctionnement du Français*, Bordas, *Centre International de Recherche sur le Bilinguisme*, Editions d'Acadie, Editions du Seuil, Faculté des Lettres de Mulhouse, Fayard, *Grif an tè, International Journal of the Sociology of Language, Journal Officiel*, La Découverte/Maspéro, *Les Brèves*, L'Harmattan, Leméac, *Le Monde, Le Monde de l'Education, Le Nouvel Observateur*, Robert Laffont, Routledge and Kegan Paul.

All possible efforts have been made to obtain copyright approval for all extracts that have been reproduced here.

Carol Sanders

Introduction

CAROL SANDERS

This collection seeks to present a profile of the contemporary French language in its social context, through a discussion of certain key issues relating to language in both France and the French-speaking world. The chapters, all by specialists from Britain or France, divide into two categories: some (like chapter 3) give an overview of work done in a particular area, others (like chapter 12) choose to go into greater depth about a specific aspect of what may be a vast field. A number of themes recur in the book. One is the question of how to represent, analyse and interpret data relating to language varieties that have long been marginalised, and have not been properly codified or documented (chapters 1 and 2). Another concerns the way in which French, sometimes despite a number of obstacles, is adapting to the future, whether as a language of new technology in France (chapter 9), or as a vehicular language on another continent (chapter 12).

France's linguistic history has been characterised by attempts to impose uniformity. The goal remained the same, even when the ideology varied: while the French monarchy may have seen centralism (linguistic and cultural, as well as political and administrative) as a way of extending and maintaining power, the revolutionaries appealed to democratic principles, urging that:

> Chez un peuple libre, la langue est une et la même pour tous. (Barrère 1794, quoted in Bronckart 1988)

Thus it is that for many of its speakers, the 'French language' is not only a linguistic, or cultural, phenomenon; on the one hand, it symbolises national unity and stability, and on the other, reason and democracy, with all these notions being evoked to legitimise the spread of French abroad. Moreover, it is not just one language that has been promoted, but one variety of that language, a highly regulated variety from which some of the agencies described in chapter 1 have, at various times, filtered out words coming from the *bas peuple*, or from foreign borrow-

1

ings. A limited corpus of vetted and approved structures and words came to make up *the* grammar and vocabulary of French, to the exclusion of much that is the stuff of everyday communication. This rigid prescriptivism went hand in hand with the myth of *la clarté française* (see Swiggers 1990), and with the veneration of the written language at the expense of the oral:

> la culture française est une culture puriste . . . La langue écrite y est outil de cohérence; elle nous fournit la sécurité de formes stables, fixées et normées; elle est un facteur d'unité, elle élimine les à-peu-près interlocutoires; elle seule paraît munie d'une consistance auto-réglée par un modèle intérieur, et de quelqu´un qui parle sans heurts et de façon liée, on dira qu'il parle comme un livre.   (Culioli 1983)

Indeed, any *laxisme linguistique* may be seen as symptomatic of a more general problem; as recently as 1980, a public figure could declare:

> La première des valeurs fondamentales de notre civilisation est le bon usage de notre langue. Il y a, parmi les jeunes, dans la pratique loyale du français, une vertue morale et civique.   (Raymond Barre, quoted in Beaujot 1981)

At one stage, after education became widespread, and the use of the regional languages was on the decline, it must have seemed as though the ideal of a universally observed standard was attainable. Yet just when the goal may have seemed to be within sight, it began to seem unattainable. In recent years, the languages of sub-cultures have flourished (*le français non-conventionnel, le verlan* etc., see chapter 8); the regional languages, which had been thought to have been eradicated, are so strongly represented by pressure groups that they have found a place in the education system (chapter 4). It is not surprising, perhaps, that in some circles, there is talk of 'la crise du français' (see Charmeux 1989), and the question is asked: 'la langue française est-elle gouvernable?' (Schoeni et al. 1988). There is a fear that linguistic jacobinism has bred its own brand of anarchy. If the rich flowering of alternative 'Frenches' is a concomitant of linguistic purism, in many cases the alternative forms are denied *droit de cité*. There are signs, however, that the dichotomising paradigm is changing, with, for example, the gradual admission of 'non-standard' terms in dictionaries, and now with the decision of most dictionaries either to adopt the new spellings, or to include them as variants. Indeed, the recent resolution of the long and heated debate over orthographic reform is perhaps indicative of a new spirit of compromise (see chapter 7). Although the two sides were polarised, and passions ran high (with spelling reform being dubbed as an issue as explosive as immigration by the media in 1990), it is interesting that the question was resolved firstly, with the involvement, and on the advice, of professional linguists, and, secondly, with a moderate solution, which gets rid of many anomalies, while leaving most French texts little changed and eminently readable (see Catach 1991).

In the international context, the picture is also changing. Although French does not have as many first-language speakers as the 'big five' (Chinese, English, Spanish, Russian and Hindi), it is a second language in a large number of countries, and the number of francophones in the world can be estimated at around 100,000,000. All of this of course depends on a definition of 'francophone'. As Suzanne Lafage shows, it is a non-standard variety of French which functions successfully as a vehicular language in parts of Africa, and the survival of French in that context may depend precisely on the acceptance and promotion of variants other than the standard.

Within the European context, too, the roles of various languages are changing. French may be both protected and threatened by France's membership of the European Community. It is protected in so far as it is one of the original official languages of the Community, in which French-speaking countries play an important part. Indeed, the locating of a number of international bodies in Brussels served to strengthen the presence of French in that city. On the other hand, French is forced to react to the challenge of English, in ways which are referred to in both chapters 1 and 4. Furthermore, it may be as a result of European policies that France (among other countries) will be encouraged to act positively towards its regional and migrant languages. An important phenomenon of our contemporary world is the rapid growth of multilingual urban areas; the urgent need for some sort of *glottopolitique* in France is addressed in both chapters 4 and 5. It is clear from these chapters, and from others, that the old equation of language and national identity will have to give way to a formula that includes a wider notion of identity, and allows for an understanding of the links between language and membership of a sub-group, or language and religious identity, with the realisation that an individual can belong to more than one group, just as he or she can have more than one language. It is less, in the modern world, a matter of providing freedom of access to one, dominant, language, than of how to manage linguistic pluralism in a way that allows freedom of linguistic choice.

> Aux 4000, les keum sont branchés funk. C'est des beurs – des racail-les – des reurtis qui vont voler dans le tromé pour la came. Alors que nous, on est zulus.

> (Les jeunes) n'arrivent pas à s'intégrer à un groupe qui serait porteur d'un projet large de société.

> Mon femme tu connais pidgin y a pas.

These utterances are all examples of 'French': the first two are from the article in *Le Nouvel Observateur*, 9–15 August 1990, from which the last extract in chapter 8 is taken, and the third is from chapter 12 of this book. What then do we mean by French, and what do we mean by a variety? It is of course an eloquent testimony to the lack of linguistic homogeneity that, in this century, grammarians and phoneticians have been at pains to label the selected focus of their study. Borrel and Billières (1989) trace various developments, from the early selection of *le français parisien cultivé* (i.e. a particular class and regional variant), to Léon's *français standard* (1966), which allows for the possibility that this form of French is used across regional and class boundaries. This is close to the definition which Martinet and Walter give of the French pronunciation that they are aiming to describe in their *Dictionnaire de la prononciation du français réel*, characterised as that which will not immediately identify the speaker as belonging to a particular region, class etc. Subsequently, a large number of different terms have been used, often with different nuances, such as *le français commun, le français ordinaire* (this being used in Gadet 1989 to encompass the 'everyday' usage that is often missing in grammar books). Some have used *le français standardisé* to emphasise the artificially codified and forcibly imposed nature of this variant. Unless a specific author uses another term for a particular purpose, we shall generally refer to *le français standard* in this book, to designate – as far as it is possible to do so – the variety which, though originally middle-class northern French in origin, is that used with minor modifications, in education, serious media presentations and so on in many parts of France and by an educated élite in many other French-speaking countries. In order to avoid confusion between social class and social-situational variation, *français courant* may be used to describe a register level.

It can be seen from the above that it is difficult to give even a very general definition of *le français standard*, without the need to allow for 'minor modifications'. It is quite possible, for example, to find a young and educated speaker who is proud of having a distinct Toulouse 'accent'; even more likely than this, is the speaker whose French is slightly 'marked', for example, by the pronunciation of /ɛŋ/ and not /ɛ̃/, for instance. In this case, /ɛŋ/ and /ɛ̃/ are both variants of the linguistic variable usually represented as /ɛ̃/. Of course, all sorts of questions are begged here, including the obvious one of how major the modifications need to be before one is dealing with a different language variety. Distinguishing between varieties – and indeed between languages and dialects, is only partly a linguistic matter. It may be a matter of political perception – or indeed a political ploy – to consider one language as a dialect of another: for years Occitan was dismissed as 'dialect' or even more pejoratively, as *patois* by the northern French, who would not have not have dreamt of referring to Spanish, for example, in those terms. As is seen in chapters 4 and 11, those seeking political autonomy may wish to claim 'separate status' for a variant that is more closely linked to the dominant language, than is the case of variants in other parts of the world that are considered as the 'same' language. (For further definitions and discussion of terms used above, the reader is advised to consult Wardhaugh 1986 and Crystal 1991.)

We have said that all the contributions to this book view French in its social context. This means, of course, that a number of theoretical questions concerning the nature of the relationshp between language and society are implicit in some of the chapters. Although the main aim of the collection is to focus on the current state of French, some chapters refer briefly to matters of theory relevant to that particular topic (e.g. Aub-Buscher on Creoles, Sanders on register). In addition, the chapter by Durand addresses itself to the balance-sheet, positive and negative, of Labovian-inspired work on sociolinguistic variation. For the last two decades, sociolinguistics has for many been synonymous with quantative research, correlating linguistic variables with isolatable extralinguistic variables, such as social class, age or sex. An important part of this was the formulation of variable rules which would account for variation within the framework of generative grammar. Relatively little work was done in France using Labovian variable rules, although their use was extended and refined by Cedergren, Sankoff and others, working on Quebec French. Variable rules have been criticised on a number of grounds (see chapter 14); partly by generativists who felt that they violated the premises of generative grammar. It was objected (Bickerton 1971) that speakers could not possibly carry all those probabilities in their heads. To that, some of today's researchers would reply that, whatever it is that we carry around in our heads, it has been shown to allow us to make pretty rapid and sophisticated judgements. An example of this would be the social connotations of a speaker's use of optional liaison in French (cf. Encrevé 1988), about which rapid, consistent and sensitive judgements are shown to be made by speakers in a study by Tousignant and Sankoff (Thibault 1980). If anything, then, that criticism was nearer the mark which maintained that 'the relationship between linguistic knowledge . . . and its application . . . is far too complex to be expressed in variable rules' (Butters 1972 summarised by Dittmar 1976: 146). Indeed, there were a number of respects in which Labovian sociolinguistics did not take account of the complexities of language use. For one thing, the category of 'social class' (i.e. mainly income plus profession) which dominated early Labovian work was unsatisfactory; it was to remedy this that some linguists in France, such as Encrevé, and in particular in Quebec, drew heavily on Bourdieu's

(1975) concept of the *habitus linguistique*. For another, some linguists (e.g. Romaine 1982b) have had difficulty in accepting the Labovian assumptions that the starting-point is the speech community, and that the group grammar equates with the individual's grammar. The concept of 'speech community' itself is by no means self-evident, and other researchers have worked with different concepts (e.g. 'networks' Milroy 1980). Thus Romaine (1982b: 8) suggests that it may be useful to work with a hierarchy of concepts: individual – network – social group – speech community – language. A potentially fruitful alternative to the variable rule school for the study of complex variation (e.g. socio-situational) seemed at one stage to lie in the use of implicational scaling. Decamp put forward early on (1971) a convincing case to show how the individual speaker's 'sociolinguistic competence' could be represented in this way, as did C.-J. Bailey (1973), whose term 'polylectal' competence is echoed in Berrendonner et al. (1983). Many would now agree with Fasold's judgement that 'the idea of a variable rule as part of a phonological or syntactic theory seems to contribute little to our understanding of language use in social contexts' (Fasold 1990: 252). Fasold adds, however, that the actual analyses of data made possible by the application of variable rules has been useful. Indeed, correlational studies continue, even though some of the basic problems they raise – e.g. of whether a knowledge of several varieties is part of a speaker's 'competence' – remain. Other sociolinguists have in recent years tended to concentrate their work in certain specific areas, be they multilingualism and language policies, women's language, interaction or creoles. It is of course with reference to areas such as these that we are attempting here to give a picture of the contemporary French language.

The authors who have contributed to this book have assumed a basic knowledge of the central concepts and terms of linguistics (see Yule 1985 as an introductory text). They have also assumed a reasonable degree of informedness about the French language (for overviews of the French language in its social context, see Ager 1990 and Offord 1990). All the chapters are in English, with examples and quotations in French, and a mixture of references is given in both English and French. It is hoped that for many readers, the chapters in English will be a starting-point from which to explore the field in French. To this end, one or two texts in French are given at the end of each chapter: these are either illustrative texts, or extracts from works which are recommended as further reading. It is hoped that this formula will prove accessible, useful and enjoyable to students of French, linguists and others interested in the current state of the French language.

1

French: a planned language?

ANNE JUDGE

France is famous for the degree of state interference in linguistic matters; indeed some very famous 'laws' have been passed in this area, the most famous being the *Edit de Villers-Cotterêts* in 1539. But legislative interference has varied between direct and indirect legislation and in some cases the extent to which these interferences may be considered 'legislative' is debatable because of the lack of real sanctions. The first part of this chapter examines the origins of direct linguistic legislation as symbolised by the *Edit de Villers-Cotterêts*, the second part considers the delegated legislation of the *Académie* and the third part linguistic legislation through state education; the final part deals with the present-day return to direct legislation.

The origins of direct linguistic legislation

At this point two preliminary points need to be made. The first is that for a law relating to language to be followed it must conform with general opinion: the *Edit de Villers-Cotterêts*, which established that all official and administrative documents would be in French, was possible only because this was already largely the case. The second point is that it was only one step from writing legislation in French to making French compulsory for official matters. That French came to be used for legislative matters was due to the manner in which the French legal system developed, to the gradual centralisation of power in the hands of the king and the various disasters which decimated the population leaving it short of people able to write in Latin.

Originally each ethnic group (i.e. each group of people sharing a common cultural tradition) had its own law: this was called a *système personnel* (thus in a same village it was possible to have different people coming under different laws) but with the development of the feudal system, law became territorially based and customary law developed. The judge's task was to establish whether the law invoked by a party existed or not. Uncertainty as to the existence of certain customs led to their being written down in what were termed *coutumiers*. These were often in French for the convenience of litigants who had no knowledge of Latin. Thus *Le grand coutumier de Normandie*, written in the thirteenth century, existed in three versions, one Latin, one in French prose and one in French verse (for mnemonic reasons). The most famous of all *coutumiers*, was *Les coutumes de Beauvaisis* by Philippe de Beaumanoir written directly in French *c.*1280.

Competing with customary law was canon law, which remained of course in Latin. On the other hand the documents issued from the *Chancellerie Royale* were often in French, particularly charters giving towns privileges and rights. This was because the kings were either not too well versed in Latin or because they preferred French. The tendency was for the chanceries of the *Comtés* to follow suit. At first these documents were written in the vernacular of the area but, by the second half of the thirteenth century, Acts appeared in French rather than in the dialects. The move towards French was accentuated during the four-teenth and fifteenth centuries as the increasingly centralised monarchy led to an increase in the number of legal and administrative documents.

Famines and epidemics led to a drop in the level of education, hence an increasing number of documents in French rather than in Latin: during the first famine of 1315–17, the accounts of Ypres giving the cost of burying the victims of the famine are in French. The Hundred Years War had a similar effect. Finally the Papal Schism in 1378 weakened the position of the church, and therefore of Latin, in society (although the early church had promoted the vernacular, with the Council of Tours in 813 recommending that sermons be in the vernacular, the mass had continued to be in Latin). Latin was still far from extinct, however, and the tendency was for 'national law' to be in Latin (Charles V's Ordinance of 1376 proclaiming the majority of kings at fourteen was in Latin), while local customs and regulations were in French, the *coutumiers* in parti-cular. Similarly decisions affecting the individual were more and more often in French (e.g. the *lettres de naturalité* granted by Louis XI in 1476 to three printers were in French) as were deeds, wills, receipts and official letters. On an international level, Latin was the norm but even so some treaties were in French: the Treaty of Paris of 1250 between Henry III and Saint Louis, the letter of provocation from Edward III to Philippe VI in 1340 and the Treaty of Arras between Louis XI and Maximilian, archduke of Austria in 1482.

Parallel with these accidental reasons for an increasing use of French for legal and administrative matters, there was a move in the law towards codification, and codification eventually included linguistic matters. In 1454 in the *Edit de Montil-les-Tours* Charles VII proclaimed that written customs were to have force of law. Then in 1498 the Crown ordered that the customs and usages of northern France be written down in an official form. It is in this context that the kings came across the language problem: codification meant the introduction of precision into existing law and language was an element in this search for precision.

The first king to legislate on such matters was Charles VIII who in 1490 decreed by the *Ordonnances de Moulins* that the 'dits et depositions de témoins dans les cours de justice du Languedoc seront mis ou redigés en *langage françois ou maternel,* tels que les dits témoins puissent entendre leurs depositions et on les leur puisse dire et recenser en tel langage et forme qu'ils auront dit et deposé'. This decision was clearly taken for legal reasons rather than to unify France linguistically. Continuing in this vein, Louis XII in 1510 decreed that 'tous les procès criminels et les dites enquestes en quelque maniere que ce soit seront faites *en vulgaire et langage du pays où seront faits les dits procès et enquestes'.* Then in 1535 Françqis I declared in the *Ordonnances d' Is-sur-Tille* on the reforming of justice in Provence that 'doresnavant tous les procès criminels et les enquestes seront faictz *en françoys ou tout le moins en vulgaire dudict pays'.* Here the king's preference for French appears, since the previous laws accepted any local language. Finally in 1539 by the *Ordonnances de Villers-Cotterêts,* it was French alone which won the day. Thus articles 110 and 111 state:

> (110) Et afin que il n'y ait cause de douter sur l'intelligence desdits arrests, nous voulons et ordonnons qu'ils soient faits et escrits si clairement qu'il n'y ait ne puisse avoir aucune ambiguïté ou incertitude, ne lieu de demander interprétation. (111) Et pour ce que de telles choses sont souvent advenues sur l'intelligence des mots latins conte-nus esdits arrests, nous voulons d'ores en avant que tous arrests, ensemble toutes autres procédures, soient de nos cours souveraines et autres subalternes et inférieures, soient de registres, enquestes, con-trats, commissions, sentences, testaments, et autres quelconques actes et exploicts de justice, ou qui en dépendent, soient prononcez, enregis-trez et délivrez en *langaige maternel français et non autrement.* (Caput 1972: vol. 1, p. 163–4) (my italics)

The effects of the new decree were very rapid: from 1549 there are no traces of the local vernaculars in texts, even in isolated areas. Even in meridional France, by 1550, French was the normal language for writing. Commenting on the objections which locals made to this, Ramus (1572) wrote the following about a group of elders who had come to complain to the king about the matter:

> Mais ce gentil esprit de Roy, les delayans de mois en mois, et leur faisant entendre par son Chancelier *qu'il ne prenoit point plaisir douir parler en aultre langue quen la sienne,* leur donna occasion daprendre

sogneusement le françois : puis quelques temps après ils exposerent leur charge en harangue Frãcoyse. Lors ce fut une risée de ces orateurs qui estoient venus pour combattre la langue Françoyse et neantmoins par ce combat l'avoient aprise, et par effect avoient monstre que puisquelle estoit si aysee aux personnes daage, comme ils estoient, quelle seroit encores plus facile aux jeunes gens, *et qu'il estoit bien seant, combien que le langaige demeurant à la populasse, néantmoins que les hommes plus notables estans en charge publicque eussent, comme en robbe, ainsi en parolle quelque praeeminance sur leurs inférieurs.* (Caput 1972: vol. 1, p. 164) (my italics)

From then on the aim was to spread French, but only amongst the elite. (No need was felt to extend it to the lower orders; on the contrary 'standard' French remained, for a long time, the privilege of the upper classes, the lower orders speaking either completely different languages or various dialects of French.) Thus Moulin (1500–66) developed his ideas in Latin but also wrote in French a book on contract law, dedicated to Henri II, 'pour le bien public'. By the end of the sixteenth century the codification of French law was complete. Custom and legislation were nearly always in French except in the domain of academic law.

This contrasts with the situation which prevailed previous to 1539. The three main law suits of Louis XII (1462–1515) are interesting in this respect: his divorce from Jeanne de France was in Latin, since divorce came under canon law; but in the case in which Anne de France tried to establish the validity of her marriage, the case starts in Latin, continues in French and reverts to Latin, often mixing the two, and in the trial for *lèse-majesté* against Pierre de Rohan the case was pleaded in French in front of the *Grand Conseil*, then referred to the *Parlement* of Toulouse where most of the case was in French, but the *reprise de l'instruction* was in Latin for the first two pages. The *arrêt* or decision starts with two short French paragraphs and continues in Latin. The final speech of the *procureur* was in French and six out of sixty-eight of the pieces of documentary evidence were in Latin; finally the judgement of the *Parlement* condemning the *Maréchal* was in Latin, while the sentence was in French. But royal legislation was entirely in French.

The creation of the *Académie* and delegated legislation

Other factors encouraged the spreading of French in the South: the development of Protestantism (the Reformation movement broke away from the church of Rome when Luther was excommunicated in 1520), the influence of printing and the creation by the king of the new *collèges*. Already in 1530 François I created the *Collège des Lecteurs royaux* which was to become the *Collège de France:* several professors including Ramus taught in French. Similar schools were created in different towns where the teaching was in principle in Latin but in fact in French. Then in 1570 Charles IX created an *Académie du Palais* specifically for the advancement of French in all fields, particularly those which had been the prerogative of Latin. This was very much in keeping with the spirit of the time: in 1549 Du Bellay's *Défense et illustration de la langue française* constituted an enthusiastic manifesto proclaiming for French *le droit à la Francité*; the Pléiade worked hard for this aim and in 1550 Meigret published the first grammar of French in French. This Academy ended with the death of Baïf in 1581 but it was recreated in 1625 and eventually became the *Académie française* in 1635; it was registered by Parliament in 1537, which turned it into a legal establishment capable of delegated legislative powers. This marked the first governmental interference in linguistic matters since *Villers-Cotterêts*.

The role of the *Académie française* emerged gradually. In fact it did not immediately accept the idea of becoming an official body because to acquire this power it had to give up its intellectual freedom. Pressure was brought to bear, however, and with its official status it acquired the brief to give French proper rules, to pass judgement on the language used by authors, and to write a dictionary, a grammar, a rhetoric and a treatise on poetics. The dictionary was to become the 'law' both in matters of meanings and spellings since Louis XIV gave it legal existence in 1674 (i.e. before it was completed) by forbidding all printers to publish any other dictionary. The need to adopt a standardised orthography had already been established the previous year. To quote Henriette Walter (1988) in a section entitled 'Les martyrs de l'orthographe':

> Tous les enfants qui peinent aujourd'hui pour apprendre l'orthographe du français peuvent maudire le lundi 8 mai 1673, jour funeste où *les académiciens ont pris la décision d'adopter une orthographe unique, obligatoire pour eux-mêmes et qu'ils s'efforceraient ensuite de faire accepter par le public.* Dans l'angoisse des zéros en dictée, cette orthographe, à la fois abhorrée et vénérée, continue au XXe siècle à avoir ses martyrs et ses adorateurs. (Walter 1988: 101)

Whereas codification of the law had led accidentally to linguistic legislation, codification in language under the *Académie* was an end in itself. Malherbe (1555–1628) was the first to lay down rules aimed at creating a language which could be understood by all; one aspect of this approach was the elimination of technical, scientific and especially legal terms from the language of polite society, creating a *bienséance du vocabulaire*. Then Vaugelas (1585–1650) published his *Remarques sur la langue française* in 1647 which became a linguistic Bible, the very foundation of *le bon usage*. He was greatly influenced in this by Saint François de Sales who was a friend of his father with whom he used to discuss linguistic matters when Vaugelas was a child; one of his sayings was 'dites peu, dites bien'; Vaugelas reproduced many such sayings in his *Remarques*; Saint François de Sales also recommended the removal of all vulgarity from language, as did his disciple. Since such views were widely held in the literary salons, they encountered little resistance (even Corneille and Racine meekly corrected their 'mistakes' when these were pointed out to them).

The rules of *bon usage* were not, however, enforceable by the courts. They were enforced indirectly through access to posts of influence. Whether therefore this is 'legislation' in the narrow sense of the word is debatable. And yet the power of enforcement of the *Académie* was extraordinary since its decisions were, on the whole, followed for at least two centuries by all those in positions of power and by most important writers (spelling being somewhat an exception). This general consensus was perhaps due to its conservative and often *ad hoc* approach to linguistic matters (there was a famous debate in which *ouïstes* and *non-ouïstes* were opposed, e.g. was one to say *corbeau* or *courbeau*, *forbu* or *fourbu*; in fact the decisions were all taken word by word, no attempt being made to make a general rule in such matters). Indeed the *Académie* was so much the subject of general approval (whatever the dissension within it) that it survived the Revolution: dissolved in 1793, it was reconstituted in a diminished form in 1795 and re-established in its original form in 1816, mainly because the revolutionaries too wanted a codified form of French.

To jump to the present, although the *Académie* has seen its power decline, it still retains some of its influence. It awards a large number of prizes each year for literary works which contribute to 'le rayonnement de la langue et de la culture française'. There are some 150 of these of which one is explicitly called *le prix du Rayonnement du français*. It subsidises various literary associations and literary reviews; it collaborates with various governmental bodies dealing with linguistic matters as may be seen from the wording of the decree of January 1983 establishing lists of terms to be used in the field of *l'audiovisuel et la publicité*: 'Article 1: Les expressions et termes inscrits *après avis de l'Académie française* en annexe 1 du présent arrêté sont approuvés'. Its position was strengthened in 1986 by making the *secrétaire perpétuel* of the *Académie* sit on the *Commissariat général de la langue française* and it is normally consulted by the Minister of Education on matters of linguistic reforms (see chapter 7 on orthography).

Another form of delegated legislation: linguistic legislation through post-revolutionary state education

One of the first practical problems which had to be overcome by the revolutionaries was the linguistic diversity of France, seen as an obstacle to the diffusion of revolutionary ideals. It also appeared to be an obstacle to equality and so the principle of linguistic uniformity became a matter for legislation. The first linguistic act of the revolutionaries was to organise as early as 1790 a survey of the linguistic situation in France, the first of its kind. This was one of the contributions of l'Abbé Grégoire. The results were interpreted as showing that many people wished to be 'délivrées de leur patois' and demanded that French should be taught to the whole nation. At roughly the same time, in 1791, Talleyrand presented his *Rapport à l'Assemblée Constituante* asking for the establishment of primary schools in each commune where the teaching would be in French and in which French would be taught as a subject. This was because the revolutionaries believed in the principle of equality through education. Thus Danton declared that 'après le pain, l'éducation est le premier besoin du peuple' and Condorcet declared to the *Assemblée Nationale* in 1792:

> Celui qui a besoin de recourir à un autre pour écrire ou même lire une lettre, pour faire le calcul de sa dépense ou de son impôt, pour connoître l'étendue de son champ ou le partager, pour savoir ce que la loi lui permet ou lui défend; celui qui ne parle point sa langue de manière à pouvoir exprimer ses idées, qui n'écrit pas de manière à être lu sans dégoût; celui-là est nécessairement dans une dépendance individuelle, dans une dépendance qui rend nul ou dangereux pour lui l'exercice des droits du citoyen.

The need to train teachers led to the creation of the *écoles normales* for primary school teachers, and the *Ecole normale supérieure* for secondary teaching (such a school for teaching girls was not founded until 1881). The term *normales* is in itself prescriptive since it proclaims the need to teach norms. This is therefore again delegated linguistic legislation but of a different, less consensual, nature than the *Académie*'s: in this case a state system of education is set up – and has force of law – one of its specific aims being the teaching of a particular kind of French.

L'Abbé Grégoire suggested other ways of achieving this aim in a report written in 1794. One of these was through propaganda; the other was to impose French as the language of the municipal councils. He even suggested that people wanting to get married should prove first that they could read and write French. A lack of financial resources and the subsequent arrival to power of Napoleon and the first Restoration prevented the more reasonable of these suggestions from being applied until much later: Guizot organised the primary school system in 1832 but primary education was not made compulsory until the 1880s.

Another suggestion by l'Abbé Grégoire and only recently applied was the use of French in the Catholic church. It was tried experimentally in Versailles; then the *Concile de l'Eglise Gallicane* discussed the subject in

1798; the members of the *Concile*, although not opposed to the idea, noted that there were problems, namely that in some areas such as Brittany people still did not speak much French and that Latin had the advantage of being international. Finally it was decided that prayers and the administering of the sacraments would be in French, while the Latin mass was retained, although Napoleon's *Concordat* later marked a return to Latin for the whole service.

Thus the revolutionaries tried to enforce the use of French in all domains using the power of the law but they were defeated by events on a higher plane, namely both external and civil war. The next important date was 1832 when the government, having set up a system of primary schools, decided that official orthography – the orthography of the *Dictionnaire de l'Académie* – would be compulsory for all examinations and official documents. This meant that all access to civil service posts was subject to this rule. It is important to note that 'correct' or 'official' spelling became for the first time synonymous with 'correct French'. There were of course objections to this because of the often irrational nature of the orthography imposed. There were many calls for reforms but they fell on deaf ears. Then came the *Travaux ministériels de 1900 à 1903* which led to an inventory of *tolérances*. Some of these were embodied in the *Arrêté de 1901* which stated that they were acceptable alternatives for examination purposes; they were again put forth in February 1975 and published by the *Journal Officiel* in 1977. They are, however, often not followed. It seems that the enforcement of *tolérances* is doomed to failure, the implication being that the suggested forms are less good than the original ones (but see chapter 7 on orthography and writing reform).

The return to direct legislation typical of the modern period

In recent years a new subject of concern has appeared, that of the survival of French as a world language. This has led to considerable legislation aimed both at defending the language from the influx of English terms and at ensuring its diffusion throughout the world. The problem is said to date from the Franco-Prussian war, and indeed a number of organisations were created shortly afterwards to defend the position of French, the most important of which was the *Alliance française* founded in 1833. Such organisations were also in keeping with the spirit of French colonialism and the fact that French has always played a part in foreign policy (see Gordon 1978). Whatever the reasons for the creation of such bodies, the situation of French as a world language deteriorated rapidly during the course of the twentieth century to the extent that at the San Francisco meeting of the United Nations in 1945 the French had to fight for French to be maintained as an official language. Matters improved later when the newly independent ex-colonial states gained access to the various international organisations. This added a new concept and a new dimension to the problem, that of *la francophonie*.

Some of the newly independent countries used French for pragmatic reasons, i.e. in order to communicate with the outside world and as a common language in what were usually multilingual countries. Others also wished to see the establishment of a *communauté francophone*. The leading figures were Presidents Senghor (Senegal), Bourguiba (Tunisia) and Hamani (Niger). This movement led to the setting up of a number of institutions, of which the most important was the ACCT (*Agence de Coopération Culturelle et Technique*) in 1970. Many other organisations have been created to back these aims: the CILF (*Conseil international de la langue française*), the AUPELF (*Association des universités partiellement ou entièrement de langue française*), and the AIPELF (*Association internationale des parlementaires de langue française*).

At the governmental level (and at first the French dragged their feet, fearing the accusation of cultural and economic colonialism) there was the creation by decree of the *Haut Conseil de la francophonie* in 1984. Its mission: 'il a pour but de préciser le rôle de la francophonie et de la langue française dans le monde externe. Il rassemble les données et confronte les expériences, notamment dans le domaine de l'enseigne-ment, de la communication, de la science et des techniques nouvelles'. It is presided over by the president of the Republic; its vice-president is a member of a francophone country. Its budget comes from the Ministry of Foreign Affairs. In 1988 a new decree gave it increased means of action. It cooperates very closely with the *Délégation générale de la langue française* and the *Conseil supérieur de la langue française*, which are the two governmental bodies created to ensure harmony and coherence in the development of the language (see below).

It must be said however that not everybody favours *la francophonie* which has been described as the internationalisation of Villers-Cotterêts, the *Rapport Grégoire* and the republican educational system all rolled into one, to the detriment of indigenous languages. It is this which led to a new approach in the 1980s, one which favoured pluralism rather than *francophonie* alone. The idea is that French and other languages can and should coexist, serving different and changing needs. Indeed the new philosophy in France today is that to fulfill the European ideal every-body should be given the possibility of being trilingual. Thus pluri-lingualism is seen as a way of fighting against the constantly increasing use of *l'espéranglais*; the reason (or excuse) is that the latter is a reduced form of English which can be inadequate in certain contexts such as the drawing up of legal documents, hence the preference for legal texts written in the native tongue of the country concerned, accompanied when necessary by a translation. (This new 'liberal' approach to languages has led various regionalists to demand the right to use their mother tongue in France, hence the *Projet de loi* put forward in 1985 by a group of socialist deputies, but it has remained at the 'proposal' stage and no one seems too concerned to push it through. See chapter 4 on the other languages of France.)

English has certainly been seen of recent years as representing a danger for the French language; the worry is mainly the wholesale adoption of words and expressions, without any effort to adapt them to the morphology of the language. This, it is feared, could lead to French becoming an 'incoherent' language, one in which internal harmony is no longer respected. This worry has led over the years to the creation of a number of governmental institutions to defend the integrity of French, but they tend to change name each time a new ideological slant is felt to be desirable. The first was the *Haut Comité de défense et d'expansion de la langue française* created by decree in March 1966 under the influence of Charles de Gaulle and placed directly under the prime minister's control. Its role was very similar to that of the *Académie* since it aimed at establishing the purity of the French language. The difference was that from the start terminology was the main focus of interest. This body was modified by decree in 1973 and became the *Haut Comité de la langue française*, its change of name reflecting a change in orientation. It included three commissions: one for the defence of the 'quality' of French, one responsible for cultural influence abroad and one to deal with cooperation with francophone countries. Each commission was responsible vis-à-vis the various ministries and consultative bodies such as the *Académie*.

A new decree in 1984 replaced the *Haut Comité de la langue française* by the *Comité consultatif de la langue française* and the *Commissariat général de la langue française*. The role of the *Comité consultatif de la langue française* was to examine, within a general framework defined by the president of the Republic and the government, general problems of language usage at home and abroad, francophone matters in general and French policy in relation to the teaching of foreign languages. An example of a document to emerge from this body was, in 1986, the *circulaire* or official memorandum about the 'féminisation des noms de métier, fonction, grade ou titre'. The role of the *Comité consultatif de la langue française* was therefore to set up working parties on linguistic problems and then advise the prime minister on measures to be taken or attitudes to be adopted.

The role of the *Commissariat général de la langue française* was similar to that of the *Haut Comité* but the new decree specified that it was also to encourage all public and private bodies to take measures to help defend the French language – presumably against the agressor, i.e. English. It was also given the task of coordinating the linguistic decisions taken by various competent bodies both in France and the various francophone countries: 'animer et coordonner l'action des administrations et des organismes publics et privés qui concourent à la diffusion et à la défense de la langue française'. It played a particularly important role in coordinating work done by the various terminological commissions and making it well known. It published, for example, *Avenir de la langue française* in 1986, *La terminologie française de l'économie* in 1987 and a *Dictionnaire des néologismes officiels* in 1988.

Finally, in June 1989, a decree replaced the *Commissariat général de la langue française* by the *Délégation générale à la langue française* and the *Comité consultatif de la langue française* by the *Conseil supérieur de la langue française*. The two new bodies resemble in their aims those which they are replacing, but their goals are far more specific and their brief is at the same time broader. In other words the new legislation has given the new bodies greater importance. Thus whereas the *Commissariat*'s role was 'd'animer et de coordonner' the *Délégation* is supposed to promote ('promouvoir et coordonner'); the decree establishing the Commissariat simply refers to 'la défense de la langue française', whereas the new *Délégation* refers to 'le bon usage de la langue française'. More ministries are involved in the *Délégation*. Similarly, the new *Conseil supérieur de la langue française* resembles the old *Comité consultatif* except that it is also responsible for the promotion of French abroad. There is no longer any mention, as there had been in article 2 of the 1984 decree, of 'les langues de France'. The membership of the *Comité* is slightly different in that it automatically includes, as well as the prime minister, the ministry of education and the minister for *la francophonie*. The *secrétaires perpétuels* of the *Académie française* and of the *Académie des Sciences* are also automatically members, which was not the case previously. In other words there has been a move towards prescriptivism and a more aggressive policy of implantation of linguistic directives (figure 1.1.).

It is generally agreed that the main problem facing the French language is that of developing a terminology adapted to the modern technological world. It is therefore in terminology that most advances have been made. Already in January 1970 a decree established the need for ministerial commissions on terminology; this led to the 1972 decree on the 'enrichissement de la langue française'. This established that in each ministry the minister was to see that a list of accepted terms, and a list of expressions on trial were published in the form of *arrêtés* which had the force of law once published in the *Journal Officiel*. Numerous terminological commissions were set up subsequently. Then in 1986 a decree made the general provision that all ministries were to have their own *Commissions ministerielles de terminologie* or CMT. These have been

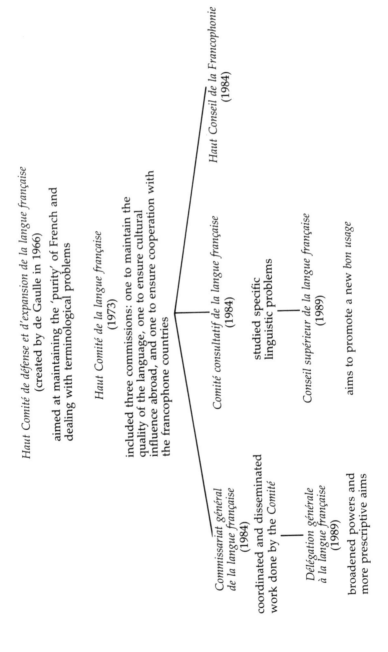

Haut Comité de défense et d'expansion de la langue française
(created by de Gaulle in 1966)

aimed at maintaining the 'purity' of French and
dealing with terminological problems

Haut Comité de la langue française
(1973)

included three commissions: one to maintain the
quality of the language, one to ensure cultural
influence abroad, and one to ensure cooperation with
the francophone countries

Haut Conseil de la Francophonie
(1984)

Comité consultatif de la langue française
(1984)

studied specific
linguistic problems

Conseil supérieur de la langue française
(1989)

aims to promote a new *bon usage*

*Commissariat général
de la langue française*
(1984)

coordinated and disseminated
work done by the *Comité*

*Délégation générale
à la langue française*
(1989)

broadened powers and
more prescriptive aims

Figure 1.1 Governmental institutions created to defend the integrity of French, 1966–89

referred to as 'petites académies spécialisées'. There are around twenty, divided up into some forty sub-groups. Since June 1990 these commissions include representatives of the Canadian Embassy, the Quebec Delegation, the Swiss Confederation, the French community in Belgium and the ACCT (*Agence de coopération culturelle et technique*). This reflects the desire mentioned above to move away from any colonial approach placing France at the epicentre. It also has the advantage of being efficient in helping the implantation of the new terms abroad since these representatives have to report back respectively to the *Secretariat d'Etat d'Ottawa*, to the *Office de la langue française du Québec*, to the *Service de la langue française de Bruxelles*, and to the *Chancellerie fédérale de la Confédération Hélvétique*.

Over the years, these commissions have been very active: no less than twenty-nine decrees establishing official terminology became law between 1970 and 1988. These deal with such varied topics as defence, telecommunications, tourism, sport, the oil industry, senior citizens and so on (so far there is no official list for words referring to fashion, clothes or music). The commissions themselves are not always made up of just one working party: the ministerial terminological commission for sport, set up in 1984, was made up of no less than eleven working parties. It takes approximately between two and six months from the time of the first meeting of the working parties to the publication of their recommendations in the *Journal officiel de néologismes*. Every so often, all decrees are regrouped in a general publication. Thus the *Commissariat* published the *Dictionnaire des néologismes officiels* and the *Délégation* published the *Dictionnaire des termes officiels*:

> La mise à jour au 31 mars 1991 du *Dictionnaire de néologismes officiels* le fait changer de nom: il devient le *Dictionnaire des termes officiels*, beaucoup des termes que contient ce dictionnaire ayant maintenant fait leurs premiers pas. L'ouvrage dresse le panorama des travaux des commissions ministérielles de terminologie, et rend disponibles les derniers 'néologismes' publiés au *Journal Officiel* . . . On notera avec interêt que ces taxtes d'arrêtés de terminologie ont été depuis 1973, date de sortie des premiers d'entre eux, grandement renouvelés et mis à jour. (publicity in *Les Brèves, ler trimestre 1991*, published by the Délégation)

These recommendations may take different forms depending on the subject matter. For example the *Ministère des Affaires Etrangères* published in 1985 a list of the official spelling for names of the world's countries and capitals which includes two possible spellings for certain Chinese place names, namely: 'la forme française consacrée par un usage constant' and 'la transcription officielle adoptée par les autorités de la République populaire de Chine dite transcription "Pin Yin" '. In contrast the terminological decree published in 1987 on computer science is a simple bilingual French–English list of words and expressions to be added to a previous list published in 1981. It was stated in this decree that the terms listed were compulsory for all governmental official documents within three months of the publication of the decree; and within six months for all civil service documents, all contracts in which public establishments were involved, and for all educational and research documents or documents emanating from any establishments receiving state subsidies. Other lists give both definitions and translation into English, for example in the decree of 1983 'relatif à l'enrichissement du vocabulaire de l'audiovisual et de la publicite' (in which the *Académie* played a part) there is a list of foreign terms and French terms the use of which is to be strongly discouraged. The layout in this case is as follows:

> ANNEXE I
> maquette, n.f.
> Domaine: Publicité
> Définition: Projet permettant de donner l'aperçu le plus juste de ce que
>   sera la réalisation.
> Anglais: advanced lay-out
>
> ANNEXE II
> Index alphabétique des termes à éviter
> TERMES A EVITER   TERMES RECOMMANDES
> advanced lay-out   maquette

The fact that these lists are made within the context of different ministries has had the advantage of highlighting the ambiguous nature of certain terms; thus 'marketing' is translated either by *commercialisation* or by *mercatique* depending on the context.

These decrees on terminological matters are headed both by the minister concerned and the *Ministre de l'Education Nationale*. This further reinforces their scope and pinpoints the importance still attached to education in terms of language planning. Indeed in 1984 terminology was even the object of a question in the paper on Advertising (*Publicité*) for the BTS (*Brevet de technicien supérieur*). The examination question was the following:

> Conformément aux recommandations ministérielles, vous souhaitez utiliser l'équivalent français des termes suivants: JINGLE, CASTING, SPOT, SPEAKER, SYNOPSIS, STORY BOARD, CAMERAMAN, SPONSOR, DRIVE IN. [Try and do this before you consult the answers at the end].[1]

Some of the commissions have also published booklets such as the one entitled *200 mots du sport olympique* published in 1986. It was published by the joint efforts of the *Secrétaire d'Etat* au sport, the *Délégation générale à la langue française* and the *Comité national Olympique et sportif français*. Non-governmental bodies have also participated in this effort. In 1985 the AFPA (*Association pour promouvoir le français des affaires*) published 700 *mots nouveaux pour les affaires* which was sent to different firms. In 1987 a survey was made of the terms used for economic matters in French firms (it is called *L'enquête STS AC 87* (STS standing for *Sections de Techniciens Supérieurs* and AC for *Action Commerciale*). It revealed that, in a third of the firms, employees often found it difficult to come up with a French equivalent of a foreign term. Half the firms in the survey used a dictionary in an effort to find French equivalents to foreign terms and three-quarters would use a terminological service if it existed on something like Minitel. IBM publishes a newsletter which is a model of correction in terms of its terminology. Indeed in 1986 IBM published a lexicon thirty pages long on the terminology to be used and the recommendations of the decrees concerning their domain are carefully reprinted in their in-house journal. Another factor backing these decrees has been the recent world-wide development of Term Banks which by definition are prescriptive. France has several of these, the most important being AFNOR, or *Association Française de Normalisation* with its term bank NORMATERM, created in 1976, and containing solely French standards. AFNOR functions within the context of ISO, the International Standards Organization, which puts the whole question on a new international basis.

It was the problem of enforcement of these decrees which originally led to the *loi Bas-Lauriol* first presented to the *Assemblée Nationale* in May 1973 and passed in a less rigid form in December 1975. It established in fact the very principle of the use of French in France. It refers to three domains in which French was to become compulsory: in commercial and advertising contexts, to protect the consumer; in work contracts, to protect the employee; and in the context of information given to consumers either by private firms or public bodies, usually in the form of leaflets. It also established that the new terminology would be compulsory in all governmental documentation, in all contracts, in education and in all other state institutions. The rule was that, where a French term existed, it had to be used. If not, the firm was liable to be fined. The aim was mainly to protect the consumer by establishing a clear terminology and the right to be informed in his/her mother tongue. The law of 1975 also legislated on a unified grammatical terminology. It was completed by the *circulaire* of March 1976, again modified by the *circulaire* of October 1982. Reasonable as this law may seem, its scope is however limited by the laws governing the Common Market (see text 1).

The actual implementation of the *loi Bas-Lauriol* is dependent on the *Direction de la consommation et de la répression des fraudes* (which comes under the *Secrétaire d'Etat à la Consommation*) and the *Direction générale de la concurrence et de la consommation* (which comes under the *Ministère de l'Economie, des Finances et du Budget*); it also is dependent on the *Service des Douanes* since the law covers imports. But these bodies have brought about very few civil actions (possibly because of the problem of clashes with Common Market law, see text 1); the *Direction de la consommation et de la répression des fraudes* has been the most successful: in 1983, for example, it obtained 174 convictions representing fines totalling 373,711 francs; the *Direction de la concurrence et de la consommation* on the other hand took up 136 cases but none led to convictions; the *Direction des Douanes* does not appear to have any figures on the subject.

It was to compensate for this shirking of obligations that the *Association générale des usagers de la langue française* (or AGULF) was created in 1976 with the aim 'd'unir sur le modèle des groupements de consommateurs, les usagers de la langue française, soucieux de défendre leur commun patrimoine linguistique et culturel et d'en assurer le rayonnement', according to M. Michel Fichet, the president of the association. Unfortunately, like most private organisations, it seems to have been constantly short of funds, and indeed nowadays it has largely faded out of existence. But it published for a while a newsletter and the one published in August/September 1986 (number 16) concentrates on the cases they had taken to court since 1981: six in 1981, four in 1982, three in 1983 (it does not give a number for later years).

To give an example of the nature of these cases, they sued the *Société Photo-Europe* in 1981 for selling photographic material with an instruction leaflet and guarantee which were not in French. The fine was of 300 francs; the same applies to the *Société Dupuy-Bazile* who had imported a 'galaxy gun' which came with an instruction leaflet entirely written in English; the fine was of 400 francs, 200 francs going to AGULF and to a consumer since this had been a joint action. In 1983 the *Théâtre national de l'Opéra de Paris* and *MGA Konzert und Theater-Agentur* were fined 160 francs and made to pay 1,300 francs to AGULF for producing a programme for the show *Bubbling Brown Sugar* entirely in English. A particularly shocking case was that of the *Société Pier-Import* which sold as a Christmas decoration what appeared to be a sweet but with a warning note stating that it was not edible printed only in English. The fine was therefore higher, 500 francs to the consumer who brought the case and 1,000 francs to the *Union féminine civique et sociale* and AGULF which shared in its cost. Such cases reveal two things: firstly that the French do indeed have the right to be defended linguistically, for it is inadmissable that instruction leaflets and warnings should not be printed in the language of the country; and secondly, that the fines are far too low to have an impact in themselves. Moreover the governmental bodies lack enthusiasm in enforcing the law in the courts. On the other hand the French have been alerted to the dangers of letting another language take over, and now this has been accepted it is likely that by national consensus matters will improve since the French have shown in the past the ability to regulate their language and its use.

Conclusion

The French pride themselves on having an extremely 'civilised' language. If by 'civilised' one means improved by conscious human effort, certainly no effort has been spared. To improve the language was not the aim of early linguistic legislation which was simply part of the legal process of codification. But the aim of the *Académie* was to have a civilising influence. Although a legally constituted body, the *Académie* only had indirect sanctions, and yet it seems to have considerable powers of persuasion founded on a mixture of idealism, elitism and liberalism. On the debit side, the codifying influence of the *Académie* also deprived the language of much of its creative energy. From the Revolution onwards linguistic policies became part of political ideologies and were implemented mainly through education and governmental establishments. The power of the *école républicaine* was remarkable: this was indirect or delegated legislation at its most effective. Today matters have changed: there is direct legislation which is, to a certain extent, difficult to enforce and indeed, at first, the results did not seem promising. Matters seem to be changing however, for example the fourth edition of the booklet published on the language of business, *700 mots d'aujourd'hui pour les affaires* has sold 24,000 copies in four years. Moreover, the new approach taken by France to *la francophonie* appears promising in terms of the world-wide implantation of a homogeneous and coherent terminology, mainly no doubt because of the new direct involvement of the francophone countries in the elaboration process.

Text 1

Législation linguistique: droit français et droit européen

En France, le texte juridique fondamental qui pose le principe même de l'emploi de la langue française est la loi du 31 décembre 1975.

Cette dernière intéresse trois domaines particulièrement sensibles, à savoir le commerce et la publicité (protection du consommateur, article 1er), la protection du salarié et du contractant (articles 4,5), et l'information du contractant et de l'usager des services publics (articles 6,8).

En 1982, une circulaire a été adoptée qui concerne notamment l'utilisation obligatoire du français pour les marchandises importées par la France, et qui s'applique également à tous le documents qui les accompagnent, dès leur passage en douane. Toutefois, et contrairement à ce texte, les documents qui accompagnent des déclarations de douane peuvent être établis dans une langue étrangère.

La loi de 1975, qui a le mérite d'exister, voit sa portée réduite dans le contexte européen. Ainsi, les règles communautaires obligent les douanes à distinguer entre marchandises européennes et marchandises en provenance du reste du monde: 'au stade de l'importation seule doivent être en conformité avec la loi les marchandises provenant de pays n'appartenant pas à la CEE'.

La Commission européenne pour sa part met en avant l'article 30 du traité de Rome lequel dispose que 'les restrictions quantitatives à l'importation ainsi que toutes mesures d'effet équivalent sont interdites entre Etats membres'.

Toutefois, à l'encontre de cette disposition, il est possible d'invoquer l'article 36 du traité, lequel contient les termes de 'civilisation nationale' et de 'patrimoine national', à condition d'estimer que la langue d'un pays fait partie de sa civilisation.

Tableau présentant les principales dispositions de la loi de 1975 ainsi que les dispositions européenes pouvant intéresser notre langue

Domaines	France Loi du 31 décembre 1975	Europe	
		Traité de Rome	Acte unique européen
		(exceptions à la libre circulation des personnes et des biens)	
Protection du consommateur *(commerce-publicité)*	Article 1er Il impose l'utilisation du français dans la présentation écrite ou parlée d'un bien ou d'un service ou dans tous les documents lors de leur vente	Article 36 Il énumère des exceptions qui relèvent notamment de valeurs de civilisation nationale, valeurs qui peuvent justifier des interdictions d'importation, d'exportation ou de transit	Paragraphe 5 de l'article 100 A Les mesures d'harmonisation comportent dans les cas appropriés une clause de sauvegarde autorisant les Etats membres à prendre, pour une ou plusieurs raisons non économiques mentionnées à l'article 36 du Traité de Rome, des mesures provisoires soumises à une procédure communautaire de contrôle
Protection du salarié et du contractant	Article 4 Il impose principalement la rédaction en français de tout contrat de travail constaté par écrit et à exécuter sur le territoire national		
Information du contractant et de l'usager des service publics	Article 6 Il rend obligatoire l'utilisation de la langue française pour les inscriptions dans les lieux publics Article 8 Les contrats conclus entre une collectivité ou un établissement public et une personne quelconque doivent, selon cet article, être rédigés en français	Rien de prévu	

(Les Breves, Lettre de la délégation générale à la langue française, no. 42, 2 ème trimestre 1991)

La clause prévue au paragraphe 5 de l'article 100 A de l'acte unique européen reprend cette disposition. Cependant sa mise en oeuvre parait difficile et dépend en grande partie du soutien des autres Etats membres quant à la préservation de l'identité culturelle de chacun des partenaires considérés.

(*Les Brèves, Lettre de la délégation générale à la langue française*, no. 42, 2 ème trimestre 1991).

Text 2

La révolution française et la politique d'unification linguistique

Les résultats de l'enquête de l'abbé Grégoire représentent les principales informations disponibles sur la situation linguistique en France au début de la Révolution. En présentant son rapport à la Convention le 6 juin 1794, Grégoire constate que le français est ignoré d'une grande partie du peuple. Pour cela, il faut, d'après lui, 'uniformer la langue' et extirper tous les 'patois'. Nourrie des idées de Grégoire, la politique linguistique de la Révolution a connu en réalité deux étapes. Dans un premier temps, la langue étant considérée comme un simple véhicule, la Constituante a décidé de faire traduire dans les diverses langues de France les principales décisions de l'assemblée. Le véto du roi a freiné la mise en pratique de cette stratégie. Dans un second temps, derrière l'abbé Grégoire, les Révolutionnaires ont identifié les langues de France aux idées que, dans la pratique, elles servaient à véhiculer et les ont déclarées ainsi contre-révolutionnaires. La stratégie s'est alors déployée sur deux plans: propagation des idées révolutionnaires et diffusion du français à travers l'école.

Nous tenterons de présenter ci-dessous, brièvement, les principales mesures qui ont fait accélérer la diffusion du français.

– le rapport Talleyrand (septembre 1791) déplore la survie des 'patois' et conclut à la nécessité d'une école primaire commune et gratuite où l'on enseignera essentiellement le français.

– le rapport de Lanthenas a l'Assemblée (le 18 décembre 1792) fait la distinction entre les 'idiomes' communs à la France et aux pays voisins et les 'idiomes' particuliers 'qui ne sont qu'un reste de barbarie des siècles passés, pour lesquels, on s'empressera de prendre tous les moyens nécessaires pour les faire disparaître le plus tôt possible' (F. Brunot 1967, IX:136).

– le décret du 27 janvier 1794 (pluviose an II) est destiné, selon Barrère qui rapporte au nom du comité du salut public, à empêcher les populations patriotes de se laisser tromper à la faveur de la différence de langage, par les prêtres en Bretagne, par les émigrés dans le Bas-Rhin, par les partisans de Paoli en Corse, par les ennemis de la liberté au Pays Basque. Selon Barrère, cité par F. Brunot (1967, IX: 213) 'le fédéralisme et la superstition parlent bas-breton; l'émigration et la haine de la République parlent allemand; la contre révolution parle italien et le fanatisme parle basque'. Ce décret instaurait dans les régions à idiomes étrangers ou particuliers 'des instituteurs de langue' pour les adultes. Ces mesures révolutionnaires ont été peu appliquées, mais l'histoire politique et militaire a été sans doute plus efficace: il semble bien que la situation linguistique de la France à la fin de la Révolution soit profondément différente de ce qu'elle était au début; la langue française a pénétré dans les couches populaires des villes et des campagnes: l'enquête de Coquebert de Montbret, en 1807, a pour but déjà d'enregistrer les parlers locaux avant qu'ils ne disparaissent.

(F. Laroussi and J.-B. Marcellesi, Text written for this volume.)

Note

1. The answers to the BTS *Publicité* exam according to AGULF are:

jingle	=	*sonal, terme obligatoire (1983)*
casting	=	*distribution artistique, terme obligatoire (1983)*
spot	=	*pas de terme officiellement proposé (Hélas!) mais 'message publicitaire' ne conviendrait-il pas?*
story board	=	*scénarimage, terme obligatoire (1983)*
cameraman	=	*opérateur de prises de vue, cadreur, terme obligatoire (1983)*
sponsor	=	*commanditaire, terme obligatoire (1982)*
drive in (cinéma)	=	*ciné-parc, terme obligatoire (1983)*
synopsis	=	*même s'il est entré dans le vocabulaire du cinéma grâce aux Américains, nul besoin de créer un équivalent à ce terme, qui a fait son apparition dans les dictionnaires en 1842 et vient du grec 'sunopsis' qui signifie 'vue d'ensemble'*
speaker	=	*aucun équivalent n'est officiellement proposé, mais pourquoi ne pas dire 'Présentateur'?*

(Quoted from nos. 3/4, 1984 of the *Bulletin de l'AGULF*). The years in parenthesis correspond to the year of the terminological decree making the use of the term given official.

2

Sociosituational variation

CAROL SANDERS

Defining and describing sociosituational variation

> Les théories linguistiques définissent toutes un objet réduit par rapport
> à l'usage qui est fait d'une langue; elles rejettent donc hors du champ
> des faits que d'aucuns considèrent comme primordiaux; citons, en
> vrac, les aspects paraverbaux et non verbaux qui accompagnent la
> parole, la variation des usages (phonologique, morphologique, syntaxi-
> que, sémantique et pragmatique) en fonction de facteurs individuels,
> sociaux, situationnels. Cet élargissement de l'objet peut-il se faire dans
> le cadre des théories que l'on peut considérer aujourd'hui comme
> classiques, du fonctionnalisme par exemple? Nombreux sont ceux qui
> essaient de créer, d'aménager de nouveaux modèles descriptifs au sein
> de la théorie; d'autres, en développant et modifiant certaines
> définitions, comme celle de la communication, vont accroître le champ;
> d'autres enfin vont modifier la théorie afin de la rendre plus adéquate,
> de leur point de vue, à l'objet.   (Lefebvre and Morsley 1990)

A major difference between English and French is the way in which
spoken French has come to diverge from written French. Related to
this – though not identical with it – is the distinction between 'informal'
and 'formal' usage, which is much greater in French than it is in British
English. Although for many years the majority of descriptive and
reference works failed to take account of either 'oral' or 'informal'
language use, except to censure it as a deviation from the 'standard',
there has for the last few decades been a recognition by some that
register (i.e. sociosituational variation, or variation dependent on setting
and relationship between interlocutors) is an important phenomenon in
French. This does not mean that we are anywhere near having a
complete description of it, nor indeed even an adequate theoretical
framework within which to describe it. While a good deal of work has
been done in recent years in certain areas of which we shall be giving an
overview later in this chapter, much that is currently written on French,
whether with a theoretical or a pedagogical orientation, still fails to

address this issue, and it is possible for a major work to be published which fails to state clearly which variant of the language it is dealing with (e.g. Adamczewski 1991). It is not surprising, then, that those linguists who perceive the need for work on variation still lament the situation, such as Blanche-Benveniste speaking about the lack of serious studies of spoken French:

> Mais qui s'intéresse au français parlé? Par certains côtés, tout le monde s'y intéresse; mais peu de gens y voient un objet légitime d'étude, même chez les linguistes. C'est un domaine où foisonnent les malentendus, les préjugés et les mythes.   (Blanche-Benveniste 1987: 1)

A few examples will suffice to demonstrate that we are talking about a form of variation which cannot be reduced to social class, or age, or text type, even though it may be linked to all of these. Only in some cases can you rapidly identify their region or sex from the way someone speaks in France; you can far more frequently deduce from it something about their relationship with their interlocutor. In other words, all speakers use some sort of range of registers, and yet relatively little research has been done in this area. Consider the following sentences (for which you will have to imagine the contexts, even the recently recorded oral corpora failing to provide much contextual information, a fact lamented in Culioli 1983, from whom sentence 2a is taken):

(1)a.   – Tu peux aller me chercher le bouquin cet aprem?
         – J'sais pas encore, j'suis tellement crevé!
   b.   – Est-ce que vous pourriez aller me chercher le livre cet après-midi?
         – Je ne sais pas encore, je suis tellement fatigué!
(2)a.   Moi, mon père, sa voiture, les freins i'déconnent!
   b.   Les freins de la voiture de mon père fonctionnent mal.

The exchanges given in (1a) and (1b) are typical of the sorts of sentences often used to illustrate different register levels. Though invented, they sound like plausible examples of everyday utterances, and it is on examples like these that the usual description of register is based. That is, the most easily identifiable differences are said to be lexical: *bouquin*, *crevé* and *aprem* are all listed as *familier* (e.g. in *Le Petit Robert*), the latter being an example of lexical truncation which is often found in colloquial French. An attempt may be made to represent pronunciation, e.g. *ne* deletion causes the dropping of /ə/ plus assimilation, to give *je ne sais pas – je sais pas – chsais pas* = [ʃsɛpɑ]. At the levels of morphology and syntax, there is an accepted check-list of items which indicate register level, such as the absence or presence of *ne*. The various forms of the interrogative are often used to illustrate register differences, along the lines shown in table 2.1.

Table 2.1 *Register differences*

Populaire:	Interrogative particle *-ti* *tu viens- ti?*
Familier:	No inversion *tu peux?*
Courant:	*Est-ce que* + subject + verb *est-ce que tu peux?*
Soutenu:	Inversion of subject + verb *peux-tu?*
Académique/Littéraire:	Certain other formulae e.g. *puis-je . . . ?*

It is not unusual to find the (perhaps unexceptionable) division into *familier/courant/soutenu* extended in both directions, to illustrate other levels such as *populaire* or *littéraire* which are felt to exist. Unfortunately, such a table does not inform us as to the very limited use of *-ti* in France (restricted to certain verbs, indicates social class and geographical origin) and of *puis-je* (restricted to certain contexts, may have an affected connotation). Nor does it give us any clue about likely or unlikely collocations, e.g. while no one would (seriously) use *puis-je* and *bouquin* in the same sentence, either *livre* or *bouquin* may quite well be used in conjunction with a *familier* structure. Most importantly, perhaps, sufficient attention has not been paid to the role of intonation, and other prosodic features, which may perform a syntactic function in spoken French.

Certainly, there is nothing in the usual description of *français familier* which prepares us to describe or analyse sentence (2a). First of all, the sentence may strike the hearer as *très familier*, yet there is only one lexical item that fits into that category (*déconner* = vulg. in *Le Petit Robert*) (*familier* equivalents for *voiture* and even *père* could have been used, but were not).

Secondly, the syntax does not resemble anything that we have come to expect of French: the subject occurs very late in the utterance, and we may find it difficult to know how to describe the association between the elements. Presumably, when spoken, the groups *moi* to *les freins* were bound by a repeatedly rising intonation pattern, designating a relationship of possession, which radiates from the speaker outwards, and which, it is interesting to note, is in exactly the reverse order from (2b). There may be a rhetorical reason for this, but we do not have the context (were the others talking about *their* fathers' car?). Indeed, it is likely that the syntax of colloquial French is here being used to fulfil a textual function (linking or contrasting with a previous utterance? changing topic?) which it is impossible to establish without the context. Hence, it is noticeably more difficult to give an 'equivalent' sentence for (2a) than it is for (1a); maybe it should rather be 'Mon père a une voiture mais les freins sont cassés', or perhaps 'Ce qui s'est passé, c'est que les freins de la voiture de mon père ne marchent pas'? In any event, the authentic sentence (2a) is much more dependent for its interpretation on both suprasegmentals and on context. This is just one example of many patterns which are common in everyday French, but rarely feature in the grammar books, some of which force us to ask whether French is necessarily an SVO language, and whether such categories as subject – verb inversion are those most needed to describe it, in much the same way as the writer Raymond Queneau asked about fifty years ago whether a sentence like 'Il l'a-t-i jamais attrapé le gendarme son voleur?' was not closer to structures of the American Indian Language Chinook than to those of other European languages.

It has become apparent that one major factor in determining the form of an utterance is whether it is spoken or written. We have just looked at the output, or the linguistic characteristics of various registers; let us now return to the input which determines register use. The authors quoted earlier mentioned a number of factors, and all we will do at this stage is to list them, and comment on them briefly. There are various possible classifications, but for the moment we can conveniently group the various factors involved under context of communication, context of situation and interlocutors, although there may be some overlap between them.

A main division under context of communication will be between spoken and written, but these can be further sub-divided, for example into face-to-face or distance communication, and then according to degree of permanence of the medium, and the nature and degree of mechanical intervention. We can see the sorts of questions that we are asking: does the use of a VDU as opposed to a pencil affect the register we use? is radio commentary the same as television commentary, and so on. To this, we can perhaps add the question as to whether our utterance is intended for an individual, or a large audience, which brings us close to talking about the interlocutors. Context of situation covers event type (formal meeting or family gathering, lecture, seminar or café discussion), physical location (would you speak about someone in the same way if the conversation took place in a church, or in a pub?), and subject matter. It also includes the social role being fulfilled at the the time of utterance (if your father is also your class teacher, you will use a different register to address him in each capacity).

Finally, the all-important matter of the speaker/writer and the addressee. So far, it has been mentioned that sociosituational variation may reflect the social class, age, sex and regional (and possibly ethnic) affiliations of the speaker. The speaker will also take into account these factors as they relate to the addressee(s). It is thus the relationshp between both sides, in other words, the relative age, social class etc. of the interlocutors that is as crucial as the class or age of either of them taken in isolation. Finally, the relationship between interlocutors needs defining in terms of degree of formality (which can of course be linked to several of the factors we have just listed): it is seen by some in terms of length of acquaintance, or intimacy, by others as degree of 'solidarity' often studied in relation to *tu/vous* usage (see Brown and Gilman 1960; Lambert and Tucker 1976).

It must be stressed here, that it is the *interaction* of some or all of these factors that determines register use. For example, while you might never use 'familiar' items with someone 'superior' to you in the occupational hierarchy at work, the way you speak to him/her may be *courant* or more or less *soutenu* depending on whether the communication is oral or written, takes place alone in an office, or at a board meeting. And of course different people occupying that slot at work will elicit a different linguistic reaction from you, depending on relative age, social class, shared background, and so on. Secondly, of the various factors that we have provisionally listed above, some obviously play a more important part than others. Between interlocutors, for example, relative social class and occupational standing will be more important than regional provenance in many contexts. Overall, the most important factor is probably whether we are dealing with written or spoken communication. This does not mean that the written/spoken division should be confused with register, as some have done: even if there will be more written than oral examples of *français soutenu* (and vice versa), both written and oral will nevertheless occur in a range of registers.

Having begun to see what some of the ingredients are for register differences, and what a complex and important issue it is, let us see how it has been presented in a range of books about the French language in the last fifteen years or so. One of the first to give it proper mention was Caput (1975). Caput represents register levels on a five-point scale with some sub-divisions and extensions (see figure 2.1). He avoids the common mistake of assuming that *familier/populaire* is only spoken, and *littéraire* is only written. Others who propose a similar grid may stop at *langue soutenue*, and it could indeed be argued that *littéraire* relates to a particular genre rather than to a regularly used register. Despite any criticisms we may have, this is an early, and a full, attempt to give proper mention of register.

Désirat and Hordé's *La langue française au 20e siècle* (1976) begins with a section on variation, but pays much more attention to geographical than to sociosituational differences. Apart from the inconsistency of labelling register in dictionary entries, the only mention of the 'lower' registers is to the exotic (*argot*), reflecting the prejudices usually shown by non-linguists ('la "richesse" du langage populaire, son caractère "vivant", "savage" . . . ' Désirat and Hordé 1976: 46).

Plan oral : exemples	Registre de langue	Plan écrit : exemples
Conversation (*cf.* 4.2.1, 3ᵉ texte cité.)	POPULAIRE	Lettres populaires à l'Administration (Sécurité sociale, etc).
	LANGUE COURANTE	
Conversation (*cf.* 4.2.1, 1ᵉʳ texte cité). Conversation de type mondain sur des sujets plutôt culturels.	— familière — soignée	Lettre à un 'copain'. Lettre amicale pour une occasion particulière (fête, distinction, requête, . . .
Exposé public.	LANGUE SOIGNÉE HOMOGÈNE	Lettre à un supérieur.

AFFECTATIONS A PARTIR DE LA LANGUE SOIGNÉE HOMOGÈNE
(= volonté de se distinguer des autres par appui sur un critère défini)

- tendance précieuse
  (critère : raffinement, délicatesse)

- tendance 'snob'
  (critère : la mode)

- tendance pédante
  (critère : les connaissances)

Conférence.	LANGUE SOUTENUE	Dissertation.
Discours académique (bien qu'il soit d'abord écrit, puis lu)	LANGUE LITTÉRAIRE	Article ou livre.

AFFECTATIONS A PARTIR DE LA LANGUE LITTÉRAIRE
- le pompeux (emphase excessive)
- l'ampoulé (ornementation excessive)
- l'ésotérique (obscurité)

(affecté et) soutenu	langue courante	très familier	populaire
je puis	je peux	–	–
fussiez-vous malade	même si vous étiez malade	–	même si (ou : que) vous seriez malade
encore qu'il soit bien tard	quoi qu'il soit bien tard	–	malgré qu'il est très tard
n'est-ce pas une erreur?	(est-ce que) ce n'est pas une erreur?	c'est pas une erreur?	y a pas erreur?
qu'est-ce	qu'est-ce que c'est?	c'est quoi?	c'est quoi?

Figure 2.1   Register levels according to Caput (1975)

The two previously mentioned works are intended for a specialist audience, linguists or students. Bonnard, in an introduction to his advanced textbook (for *seconde*, *première* and *terminale*, but also used in teaching French as a foreign language), uses the notion of different codes, in an attempt to placate both purists and progressives. 'S'il y a deux façons, ou dix, d'exprimer en français telle ou telle pensée, nous n'imposerons pas l'une aux dépens de tout autre', he claims. But he goes on to explain that the first book, *Code du français courant* (1981), will deal with the sort of French that 'personne ne jugera incorrect', which will be taken as a benchmark by which other registers can be gauged, the latter being hived off into a different volume, *Procédés annexes d'expression*. He defines *français courant* as

> la langue comprise de tous les Français, pratiquée à la fois par le journaliste de la télévision, le représentant de commerce, le médecin, l'instituteur, celle des règles de jeux, des notices de fonctionnement des machines.

Unfortunately, this definition begs more questions than it answers (the doctor addressing a patient? a fellow doctor?), and ignores the enormous amount of variability that exists even in the speech of doctors and teachers!

In a book that deals in some detail with aspects of variation in contemporary French, Muller (1985) combines the ideas of both continuum and standard, by placing a *norme* somewhere between *cultivé* and *courant* on a five-point scale (figure 2.2). He illustrates four of these levels in relation to the likely occurrence of optional liaisons, adding that the variant used will depend on both the 'situation de communication', and on certain 'facteurs sociolinguistiques'.

> Les liaisons sont moins fréquentes à Paris qu'en province; les jeunes en font moins que les générations plus âgées; les personnes que leur profession ne met pas en contact avec le public en font moins que les locuteurs que leur professeur amène á s'exprimer en public . . .
> (Muller 1985: 229)

It is striking that social class is missing from Muller's list of 'facteurs sociolinguistiques'. Indeed he goes on to suggest that social class variation has given way to situational variation (see the first sentence of the quotation from Muller below).

This seems at first to be an extraordinary claim, since we know that both social class and situational variation existed in the past and continue to do so. What Muller is trying to say is that parameters of variation shift over time; in other words, the points of intersection between social class and register may vary at different periods, some linguistic phenomena which are considered colloquial may become

français cultivé	le premier avril, après un long hiver			
···············				
– – – NORME – – –	fr. cultivé	ɛr	z	k
···············	fr. courant	(ɛr)	|	(k)
français courant	fr. familier	|	|	|
– – – – – – – –	fr. populaire	|	|	|
français familier				

français populaire	ils ont fait un grand effort pour retrouver leur ami trop indulgent				
– – – – – – – –					
français vulgaire	fr. cultivé	z	t	t	ɔp
	fr. courant	z	|	t	|
	fr. familier	z	|	(t)	|
	fr. populaire	z	|	|	|

Figure 2.2   Muller's five-point scale of variation in contemporary French

accepted as part of the *norme*, and so on. However, given the lack of documentation on non-standard varieties, such an assertion is hard to substantiate. Indeed, Muller does not refer to any research, such as that by Ashby (1981) which argues that a high frequency of *ne* deletion among younger informants indicates change in progress. Against this, it can be argued that the young make more use of a colloquial register, and what little evidence we have shows that *ne* deletion has characterised *français familier* for centuries. (For references and a further counterargument, see Ashby 1991.)

In general, it is symptomatic that Muller's book, excellent as it is in other areas, is confused over the question of register. The extract below, while describing well the need for situational appropriateness, has not resolved the problem of the relationship between register and social class, between colloquial and 'incorrect' French, and still presents register as being a question of lexis, which are all issues to which we shall return. (For lexical difference in register, see chapter 8.)

> Dans la seconde moitié du XXᵉ siècle, les niveaux qualitatifs ne font plus fonction de caractéristiques sociales, mais avant tout d'*obligations socioculturelles*, adaptées aux – très différentes – *situations de communication*. Chaque situation exige en effet un niveau bien défini, c'est-à-dire celui qui lui convient. Ceci signifie donc qu'il existe à côté d'une hiérarchie absolue des niveaux linguistiques, une échelle de valeurs relative, adaptée aux conditions de l'acte de communication. Le 'bon' niveau n'est pas automatiquement et exclusivement la norme ou, dans certains cas, la surpernorme; le 'bon' niveau c'est tout autant le français populaire quand on bavarde avec sa concierge ou le français familier quand on s'entretient de choses et d'autres avec des amis; mais s'il s'agit d'un discours officiel, la limite se déplace à nouveau vers le haut,

car le 'bon' niveau est alors le français cultivé, puisqu'il est adapté à la situation.

On ne se 'déclasse' plus quand on délaisse 'son' niveau de langue; mais on contrevient aux règles de la parole quand on choisit des niveaux qui ne conviennent pas à une situation donnée. Des phrases comme:

'Comment va Mademoiselle votre sœur?' ou *'Chère Madame, j'aurais voulu une baguette qui fût plus croustillante'* sont effectivement du 'très bon' français, en l'occurrence du français cultivé, mais elles sont déplacées quand on se croise en toute hâte à un coin de rue ou que l'on va acheter son pain à la boulangerie – et, du coup, elles font sourire.

Ce que la norme et le style littéraire désignent par *le livre* ou *l'ouvrage*, l'auteur lui-même, en train de dédicacer ses œuvres dans une librairie, choisira peut-être de l'appeler *'mon bouquin'*, expression plus modeste et plus désinvolte, sans que, pour autant, on soit toujours en droit (c'est à-dire dans le ton demandé par la situation) d'utiliser *'votre bouquin'* dans la réponse.   (Muller 1985:230–1)

The lively book by Walter, *Le français dans tous les sens* (1988), could take as its motto one of its section headings 'On peut pas dire *le* français'. Yet it fails to deal satisfactorily with register. The various aspects that go to make up 'non-standard' French are fragmented and discussed briefly under a variety of headings. Grammatical variants are mentioned mainly under regional differences, and what could have been the interesting issue of the use of the vocabulary of *le français non-conventionnel* by respected public figures is relegated to an (amusing) paragraph that is no longer than the one devoted to that contemporary but less widespread phenomenon *le verlan* (Walter 1988: 292).

Three recent books that have been published in Britain differ on the amount of importance that they attach to register. Ager (1990) deals separately with a number of the factors that are central to sociosituational variation (e.g. formality levels), and then briefly refers to the difficulty of describing the way in which these factors interact to result in the use of a particular level of register:

Different factors such as age, social category, spoken/written differences, regional and interactive characteristics often lead to a very similar overall selection of items, and it is the number and interplay of these, rather than them as individual items, which contribute to establishing the indexical information conveyed by the text . . . For practical purposes the three-part differentiation presented by Batchelor and Offord is sufficient.   (Ager 1990: 214)

Offord (1990) devotes considerably more space to register, using the Hallidayan categories of field, mode and tenor (Halliday 1978; Gregory and Carroll 1978). He sums up the factors determining register choice as:

> the age, sex and socioeconomic status, of the addressee, the degree of intimacy between the participants in the conversation or speech – event and the formality of the situation.   (Offord 1990: 119)

The list obviously omits certain factors (e.g. the age, sex etc. of the *speaker*; regional provenance), some of which are covered in the course of the same chapter. For his illustrations, Offord too uses the classification of examples given in Batchelor and Offord (1982), which are unfortunately open to a number of criticisms.

In Batchelor and Offord, 'register' is used, confusingly, to mean *both* a language variety (R1, R2 and R3), *and* an extralinguistic factor, 'the relationship of formality/informality existing between speakers'. Register 3 (formal, literary, etc.) is said to be reluctant to admit new terms, whereas it is probably at this level that many of the foreign loan words, learned neologisms and so on occur. Register 1 is characterised as incorrect grammatically and including vulgarisms, which leaves one wondering how the many speakers who eschew ungrammaticality and vulgarity manage to engage in an informal conversation! Moreover, the listing of 'R1' words in a book intended for learners of French brings home the need for a sub-division of the *familier* category: it is misleading for the foreign learner to find *embêter* and *emmerder* under the same heading, as if they can be used interchangeably. The pages illustrating register in grammar contain some useful examples; in general, a telling exercise is to consult pages 13–19, in order to discuss the difficulties of assigning linguistic items to register categories. The reader should beware, however, of confusing incorrect usage, and informality: the most educated French speakers have informal register at their disposal: they may drop a *ne* or use a word like *bouquin* but they would be unlikely – apart from slips of the tongue – to use the wrong gender as in *une avion* (Batchelor and Offord 1982: 19).

Battye and Hintze (1992) conclude their book with a section on register. Here also, it is unclear exactly what is meant by register, that is, what differentiates it from 'stylistic variation' dealt with in their previous section. Battye and Hintze distinguish only three register levels: *soigné* e.g. *comment dirais-je, familier* [ʒãvøpy], and *non-standard* (*argot, vulgaire*), thus giving the impression that there is nothing between *Qu'est-ce que tu penses de ma bagnole?* and *Que penses-tu de mon automobile?* (Battye and Hintze 1992: 347)

To conclude this overview of what has been written about register, we can say that the field has been opened up, and that there is agreement on a number of points. Register is best envisaged as a continuum, with, for the sake of descriptive convenience, the identification of a number of levels, which must include at least *soutenu, courant* and *familier,* but which can be further subdivided. The question of the relationship between register and other sorts of variation is of course a difficult one: some linguists have tended to see register in isolation (as uniquely some sort of formality/informality indicator), others have confused register and social class. In the case of these two, it is important to realise that they impinge on each other, but need to be considered separately. For this reason, perhaps *populaire,* which already has a social class connotation, should not be used as a classification in talking about register. Similarly, we need an understanding of the interaction between sociosituational variation and spoken/written differences, but we do not want to confuse the two issues. Finally, we need some way of describing, or at least representing, the interplay between all these factors.

As we shall see, a certain amount of work has been done on correlating linguistic differences with social class, or age. But work on 'real' spoken French has only begun relatively recently. Why is it that we are surprised by an utterance like the one cited in (2a), the sort of sentence we perhaps use several times a day in French? One answer is to be found in the prestige of the written language (see chapter 7), taken as a symbol of both social and political unity, and cultural superiority.

Hence what Culioli (1983) calls 'le poids de la prestigieuse tradition philologique':

> un bon texte est donc un texte attesté, . . . un texte de poids qui fait partie d'un trésor et non une de ces productions éphémères et volatiles.

It is only recently that researchers have begun to come to terms with 'ces productions éphémères et volatiles', and, because of its importance for the study of register, we shall review their work later in this chapter. First of all, however, let us look briefly at the history of the study of register, how it is that it took so long before it came to be recognised as a phenomenon worthy of attention, and why the study of register developed in the way that it did.

The background

We have said that, for several centuries (in particular from the sixteenth to nineteenth centuries), the emphasis was on the written language, and on a sort of idealised 'norm'. Thus the only way in which any variants on this could be conceptualised was in terms of deviation, deficiency and error. It is only relatively recently that it has been recognised that there is a need to study the way people actually use the French language, what Gadet (1989) calls 'le français ordinaire'.

The first phase which interests us is therefore one in which the study of the 'non-standard' began with the polarisation of *le français populaire* and *le français standard*. There are a number of works which serve as landmarks. The first attempt to make a systematic description of the speech of the urban proletariat, as opposed to rural '*patois* speakers', was C. Nisard's *Etude sur le langage populaire* in 1872. In 1920, Bauche published a very full study of 'le langage populaire', and in 1921, the linguist Vendryes exposed his thesis that French was splitting into two languages, classical and vernacular, in a way similar to that of Arabic or Greek. Frei's *Grammaire des fautes* (1929), based on the letters of servicemen written in the First World War, took, in part, a positive attitude to *fautes*, seeing them as serving to fill gaps in the expressivity of the 'standard'. Concurrently, work done in phonetics began to give a picture of the phonemes – as opposed to the graphemes – of French.

The next period that interests us is that of Structuralist linguistics, and its legacy. The Structuralist concern with providing a 'scientific' descripton of phonological and morphological systems, and its recognition of the importance of the spoken language, led to descriptions being made of the morphology of spoken French, an early example being Träger (1944). Studies followed by Martinet (1958), Dubois (1965 and 1967), Mok (1968), among others. Dubois' volumes clearly juxtaposed the morphologies of spoken and written French, revealing the vast gap between them, and showing for example, that while written French is a language marked for number and gender, this is not always true of the spoken language, as in this example:

leurs	livres	étaient	ouverts	[lœr	livr	zetɛ	uvɛr]
+	+	+	+	–	–	+	–

(Dubois 1965: 20)

These studies, largely done in the 1950s and 60s, still presented variation in terms of two opposing, monolithic systems, rather than in terms of a continuum, although at this stage it is less an opposition between *français standard* and *français populaire* then between *français écrit* and *français parlé*.

In the 1970s, we can identify several strands of research which are of interest to us. These follow on partly from the French Structuralist and Functionalist traditions, and partly from sociolinguistic work done elsewhere. Analysis of the phonology and morphology of spoken French continued, often using a corpus of broadcast material, e.g. Ågren (1973) on liaison. This work was extended to cover syntax as well as phonology and morphology: see for example Allaire (1973) and Lamérand (1970).

At around this time also, models were beginning to be proposed for the study of register (e.g. Stoudzé and Collet-Hasan 1969), and both *la norme* and *l'oral* were becoming the object of serious study (see Guenier et al. 1978 and Peytard 1970 respectively). Dictionaries were starting to classify words according to register level – and many were including 'colloquial' vocabulary for the first time. A number of studies were published showing how subjective and how inconsistent the labels were (Muller 1985: 232), but at least lexicographers were acknowledging the need to mark different levels.

Elsewhere, the foundations were being established for the new discipline of sociolinguistics, by Hymes' work on communicative competence on the one hand (Hymes 1971) and Labov's work on language and social class on the other (Labov 1972). Both these linguists broadened the scope of the theoretical (generative) paradigm. Hymes demonstrated how producing an 'acceptable' utterance is as much a part of a speaker's competence as producing a grammatical one, a position which has obvious implications for the study of register. Labov pioneered research into correlating social factors and linguistic features, which led him to formulate rules to account for variation. It took some time for the work of Labov to have much impact in France (see Encrevé's introduction to Labov 1976). However, it is noticeable that researchers in France did begin to take account of the social class of their informants.

François, in a study entitled *Le français parlé* (D. François 1974), worked on a phonological and morphological description of the working-class speech of Argenteuil, while Mettas (1979) worked on aspects of the less-studied pronunciation of upper- and upper-middle-class Parisians.

On the syntactic level, the frequency of four different interrogative types was examined in two sociocultural groups in a study by Behnstedt (1973). The speech of the 'lower' sociocultural group was designated as *français populaire*, and the so-called *français standard* speakers were divided into *soutenu* and *familier*. (The results are reported in Valdman (1982) which is more easily available than Behnstedt's study.) As might be expected intuitively, *français populaire* and the *français familier* of the 'standard' speakers were similar in having a higher frequency of the structures *où tu vas?* and *où est-ce que tu vas?*, against a higher frequency of inversion for *français soutenu*. However, *français familier* and *soutenu* share frequent use of *Tu vas où?* We have seen that there is some convergence between *français populaire* and *français familier*; how then do they differ? In this case, besides the use of the *Tu vas où?* pattern, they differ in the pleonastic interrogatives used in the *français populaire* (*Où c'est que tu vas?*). Obviously both François' and Behnstedt's studies raise questions about the definition of *français populaire* (for a full discussion of this see Guiraud 1965), and about the need to separate out class variants, register variants and code (spoken/written) variants. Behnstedt's investigation, while trying to take into account both class and register, makes the at least questionable assumption that register variation exists only for 'higher' sociocultural groups.

It can be seen that researchers had begun to use authentic corpora for the study of social class variation and of register differences, albeit generally on a small scale. There were certain drawbacks with the corpora used, and the whole problem of recording and interpreting oral data, which is so central to the study of register, was to become such a hotly debated question in French research that we shall review some of the issues here. Firstly, broadcast material was available in abundance, but represented only one very specific type of spoken language, often scripted (sometimes called *français parlé écrit*) Secondly, when recording 'authentic' speech it is not necessarily easy to get a range of registers. For one thing, an enormous corpus is needed to cover a variety of situations and register usage; for another, it is by definition difficult to get unselfconscious recordings in a relaxed or even intimate setting! In the case of Lindenfeld's study (1972), where she sets out explicitly to control for register variables, her method of eliciting them is to tell informants 'Imagine you are in an informal setting . . . '. Moreover, the main emphasis for most of the work we have just described was phonological. In order to investigate the specific characteristics of the spoken in longer units, e.g. at the levels of syntax, or of discourse, then larger corpora were needed. Hence, while individual researchers continued to analyse recordings they had collected, or radio material (we could cite here Malécot 1972, Lucci 1983), a certain number of larger projects got underway. We shall be referring to the work of teams at Crédif ('Le français des années quatre-vingts'), the University of Paris III (*Centre de recherche en morphosyntaxe du français contemporain*; see Morel ed. 1991) and , particularly, the University of Aix (*Groupe Aixois de Recherche en Syntaxe* or GARS). (See Blanche-Benveniste et al. 1990.)

The work done by these teams first of all had to grapple with the difficulties inherent in recording and transcribing oral language in all its authenticity. Written language is by its very nature already recorded according to agreed conventions, easy to store, ready for analysis, often intended for distance communication and less linked to a specific setting. In speech, the reverse is true: it is reinforced by paralinguistic phenomena and modified by interaction. Problems arise with the presence of an interviewer (the Crédif group have written on the problems of the recorded interview situation – see Mochet 1986) or a machine (sometimes with attendant recording difficulties, e.g. in a market-place, Lindenfeld 1978).

Once some (reasonably authentic) samples of spoken French have been recorded, they have to be listened to, transcribed and then analysed. First of all, listening is not the simple business we assume it to be. As Blanche-Benveniste (1987) puts it, you soon realise that 'l'oreille est un traître'. As with all perception, psychologists have shown that one hears what one expects, or wants to hear. Listening is an active process and one may interpret what one hears according to one's own linguistic system (hence learners can often not 'hear' the difference between certain sounds in a foreign language); the listener also strives to 'make sense' of what he or she hears, and may unconsciously modify things in order to be able to assign a meaning to them. Blanche-Benveniste (1987: 106) describes how several highly trained linguists listened and relistened to a high quality tape, on which each was sure he or she heard variously:

> j'étais en train de (soumettre) les tracts.
> (souligner)
> (signer)

Moreover, there is what Gadet (1989) calls an 'attente idéologique', whereby we expect to hear certain speakers (according to educational level etc.) say certain things. Blanche-Benveniste lists a number of highly unexpected 'errors' (gender, agreement etc.) attested in recordings of highly educated informants, Quebec researchers Sankoff and Vincent (1977) report that, in their study of the use of *ne*, they had to guard against the problem of transcribers putting *ne* down for speakers they thought deserved it! The main thing is for the researcher to take account of this problem. Hence Blanche-Benveniste is cautious abut Ashby's (1985) findings that younger speakers pronounce /i/ more often, and his generalisation that in time *il* will become /i/ in French, given the difficulty of distinguishing /i/ from /il/ on a tape. Indeed, a number of people have pointed out that it is often just at the *points faibles* of language that these auditory difficulties occur, such as the occurrence or not of *ne* (e.g. particularly after *on*). Other examples would be the difference between /e/ and /ə/, making it difficult to say whether the speaker has said *sans faire de fautes* or *sans faire des fautes*, and *je dis* or *j'ai dit*, both of which may lead to comments (possibly erroneously) about the deviation from *le français standard*.

French offers its own particular oral comprehension teasers. While it is fairly clear in the written language where word boundaries occur, this is less obvious in spoken French for a number of reasons. As opposed to the word-based stress of English, French stress usually falls quite regularly on each syllable, until the end of each meaning-unit. Elision, liaison, enchaînement and assimilation all tend to blur the distinctions between words. How then to distinguish between the following sentences (Blanche-Benveniste 1987: 105):

> Le dernier service est froid.
> Le dernier servi c'est froid.

French is known to be a language with a relatively high percentage of homophones, for example:

son (3 meanings)   [sɔ̃]
sang cent sans   [sɑ]

You could try to think of a pair of sentences in which the context may not necessarily make it clear which of these words is involved. You may also like to try and find two possible transliterations of this sentence, over which the researchers of the GARS team hesitated (as a clue, the informant is a southern French speaker who does not necessarily distinguish /ɛ/ and /e/.)

[la patri sa ne pɑ tuʒur lɑ̃drwa u lɔ̃ ne]

This obviously leads us on to problems of transcription. As Gadet says, 'la notation de l'oral par l'écrit constitue une contradiction irréductible: l'écrit ne présentera jamais qu'une image approximative de la réalité linguistique orale . . . '. Apart from the problem of the lack of correspondence between phoneme and grapheme (see chapter 7), written characters are discontinuous and linear, and exclude most prosodic features. The International Phonetic Alphabet is good for an accurate rendering of small segments, but in a lengthy corpus it is difficult to read through fast or feed into a computer. (Hence large corpora such as the Sankoff–Cedergren Quebec corpus, or the GARS corpus in Aix used conventional orthography.) A compromise is to use a mixture of IPA and orthography, or a modified orthography. In order to better represent the movement of oral syntax, the GARS team has worked out a system of non-linear configurations, where essentially paradigmatic elements which add to the utterance but do not move it forward (repetitions, corrections, paraphrases) are positioned vertically, in contrast to the horizontal representation of the advancing syntactic chain (Blanche-Benveniste 1990: 177–83).

Because of the aforementioned difficulties, and precisely because as we transcribe, we interpret, Blanche-Benveniste (1987) cautions against assuming too quickly that a speaker has used a form that deviates from the standard. She advises opting for 'la forme la plus normative' with 'multi-transcription', i.e. noting also the other possibilities. As an illustration of how easy it is to interpret an utterance as more 'deviant' than it necessarily is, she takes an example from Guiraud's list of the features which characterise le français populaire (Guiraud 1966), among which is the sentence Vous me demandez ce que ça me ferait plaisir. Here, the sequence [sk sa] is being interpreted as a deviant relative, unknown in standard French. Had it, however, been interpreted as a hastily pronounced [(ɛ)sk], the phrase would be the more usual Vous me demandez, est-ce que ça me ferait plaisir! Whatever the arguments in favour of each 'reading', the point is made that even a morpho-syntactic description of a system, or sub-system, may vary according to initial choices made in transcribing the data.

> P. Guiraud choisit la moins normative, et bâtit toute une doctrine à partir de ce choix de transcription. Nous aurions choisi la seconde, plus normative; on peut proposer une solution moyenne, qui consiste à mentionner les deux. (Blanche-Benveniste 1987: 145)

Some examples

Let us now look at two specific areas which have not always been adequately dealt with in descriptions of French, either because they belong to the spoken language, or the non-standard, or both, and see whether recent research sheds any light on register use, and on the interactions between register and other sociolinguistic phenomena. We have deliberately chosen not to look at those examples whose implications for register are immediately obvious and relatively well documented (e.g. negation, interrogation, optional liaison, vocabulary). Instead, we shall report on recent work on, firstly, the vocalic system of French, and secondly, the relative *que*.

Traditionally, the French vocalic system has been represented as having twelve oral vowels, three semi-vowels, and four nasal vowels, spread over four degrees of aperture.

Among the oral vowels, while / i, y, u/ remain stable, the status of the mid-vowels /ɛ, e, ɔ, o, œ, ø, ə/ as well as of /a/ and /ɑ/ has been for some time a subject for debate. That these oppositions were not maintained in the way in which they had traditionally been described was first documented by Martinet in his study of prisoners-of-war (published in 1945), and confirmed by Reichstein (1960) and Deyhime (1967). Since then, these vowels have been investigated a number of times, although not always with sociosituational variation in mind.

The /A/ vowels have gone through a number of fascinating changes. When Martinet conducted his study, there were still those speakers for whom the maintenance of the posterior /ɑ/ in words such as *las* was considered a sign of educated and *soigné* speech. At the same time a long ('drawled') back /ɑ:/ had come to be considered typical of working-class Paris suburban speech. Mettas (1970 and 1979), in an enquiry with two groups of young female speakers (group I – *haute bourgeoisie*, group II – *bourgeoisie*) notes a generation gap between older speakers, who have kept the /a ɑ/ distinction and whom she compares with her own, younger, informants. Groups I and II had both kept the distinction in words traditionally considered to have an /ɑ/ preceding a pause, although for group II the sound was often slightly more fronted. They had both lost it elsewhere (i.e. in non-final position in a word or sense group). However, a new velar 'a' was being used by group I to replace a front /a/ especially before a pause. Mettas observed of the velar 'a':

> (Cet A) . . . c'est l'un des éléments de la prononciation distinguée pour les sujets de la jeune génération. . . Mais si un allongement, un peu plus important que la durée habituelle des finales, vient s'ajouter à cet A, la prononciation prend aussitôt un caractère affecté. (Mettas 1970: 102)

Lenning, also researching in Paris in the 1970s, but among informants from a wider range of social class backgrounds, concluded that 'les deux A sont en train de se fusionner dans toutes les classes sociales à l'exception possible des ouvriers de sexe masculin' (Lenning 1979: 32).

It is true that the picture is a complicated and shifting one, and that different sets of vocalic oppositions will be obtained, depending on the age, social class and sex of the informant, and on the context – and therefore the register – of the utterance. Northern French has been considered as having a uniquely rich and complex vowel system, with its oppositions between half-open and half-closed mid-vowels, but some would now maintain that many speakers' systems use only three degrees of aperture. Lefebvre (1988) compares the pronunciation of mid-vowels by a heterogeneous group of speakers on twelve hours of broadcast radio material in 1978–9, with the pronunciation given in the Martinet and Walter *Dictionnaire* (1973). Lefebvre finds greater use of /e/, in positions where Martinet and Walter found /ɛ/. The only words in which /ɛ/ is used in even slightly more than half the occurrences are nouns ending in -ès, -ay, -aix and the trio *très, après, près*. In the imperfect (-ais, -ait, -aient), a closed /e/ is more common: except after 'r', which has an opening influence. Over 66 per cent of occurrences are with /e/, only 14 per cent with /ɛ/, and the rest with an intermediate sound. Also, where speakers do use /ɛ/, its occurrences are very variable. Lefebvre began her study with the assumption that by analysing broadcast material she would be able to isolate features which speakers consider to be *du bon français*:

> Les personnes qui parlent à la radio choisissent généralement, que cela soit conscient ou non, un registre plus soigné que dans la conversation courante.

However, these results that differ (albeit slightly) from those of Walter–Martinet leave us wondering if the explanation lies in the method of data collection (as well as broadcast materials, Walter and Martinet used questionnaire and reading, which may elicit a more *soigné* pronunciation), in the less homogeneous nature of her informants, or in the nature of media language.

In another study, Baraduc and others in Tours recorded 21 school children aged between eight and eleven, and did a four-way analysis according to sex and social class (*classe moyenne/populaire*). In general, this study follows the others in finding a good deal of fluctuation in mid-vowel oppositions. In the central /œ, ø/ and back /o, ɔ/ vowels, there is a trend towards greater vowel aperture: [sɔt] for *saute* in informal contexts, but with neutralisation of the [o] [ɔ] distinction leading to unexpected results eg. [is promɛn] for *ils se promènent*. However, while the children from the *classes populaires* tend also to open /ɛ/, there is marked contrary movement in the middle class, where the researchers found evidence of the 'fermeture linguistique de la bourgeoisie – Giscard tel qu'on l'imite en étant le paragon', but which was manifest particularly in words belonging to a school context (e.g. *exemple, question*). Overall, they hazard a hypothesis about the future of two registers:

> Un modèle du français scolaire (reproduit par ceux que l'excellence a déjà reconnus), fondé sur un principe de fermeture, . . . que l'on peut opposer sommairement à une langue orale, liée aux situations concrètes, plus percutante: celle de l'apostrophe, ouvrant les 'o' des prénoms, et même de "saute!" quand il est crié comme un défi. (Baraduc et al. 1989)

Moreover, their results show a contrast between the more conservative speech of the working-class boys, and that of the middle-class children who infringe the opposition 'rules' more frequently.

> Tout se passe comme si le changement, longtemps assimilé aux 'prononciations vicieuses' et aux classes populaires, se révélait pour ce qu'il est: une stratégie de distinction associée à l'aisance à l'oral, marquée entre autres par la reproduction des réalisations scolaires.

Baraduc et al.'s quantitative data bear out other studies. Their broader interpretations are only tentative, of course, and raise the problematic relationship between variation and change. However, they are not the only ones to have commented on the middle-class closure of 'e', nor indeed on the idea that the middle classes, whom occupational and demographic trends (growth of service sector, rural exodus etc.) have made more prominent than ever, hold the key to the future 'norm'. (On the preceding points, see for example Gueunier et al. 1978, Borrell and Billières 1989.) A lot more research is needed before we know what the current 'norm' really is, and what its place is on a sociosituational continuum. The research done on age, sex and class differences all feeds into any consideration of register. Even more interestingly, perhaps, researchers are beginning to comment on the importance of the context of situation, and on the connotation that certain linguistic features have for the French listener. Understandably, the empirical evidence is still scant. To the difficulties mentioned earlier which obtain in the collection of any oral data, are added the complexities of taking a number of variables into account at once. The same – or a similar – subtle difference in vowel sound may connote age or class or region, depending on the overall phonological systems used by speakers. Thus, the length distinction of *mettre* versus *maître* was found by Peretz (1977) in upper-class women of an older age group, but it is also maintained in certain regions e.g. Alsace; the maintenance of the /œ̃ ɛ̃/ distinction (*brun/brin*) may indicate the *soigné* pronunciation of an older Parisian, or the 'provincial' pronunciation of someone of an altogether different social class and age group, and so on. There has for a long time been intuitive recognition that the vowel system of French is a vehicle for a multitude of connotations. Bennett (1991) quotes the sixteenth-century Geoffrey Tory:

> Les dames de Paris, au lieu de *a* prononcent *e* bien souvent, quant elles disent: 'Mon mery est a la porte de Peris où il se fait peier.'

And Mettas (1970), describes one informant's awareness of the connotations of her accent, and of the way in which it shifts according to the company she keeps:

> BRL (22 ans) – Ma mère trouve que j'ai une prononciation très snob parce que 'j'accentue' sur les A, depuis que je vais à Lubeck surtout.

Let us hope that this may be the beginning of more systematic research focusing specifically on these questions.

Secondly, let us take an example from syntax. The area of relatives and of *que* clauses in general is rich, complex and unsatisfactorily described in French. Traditionally, grammarians drew a rigid distinction between those forms which belonged to *le bon usage* or standard French, and those which were considered non-standard and beyond the pale of description. The result was an incomplete picture, with many frequently occurring forms being either ignored or relegated to a sanctioning footnote. Examples of neglected or even proscribed forms, of which others will be given later, might be:

(1)   Donnes-moi la boîte *que* je vois ce qu'il y a dedans.
       (Not covered by the categories into which 'correct' forms are usually divided, but very common.)

(2)   Voilà Pierre *qui* fait démarrer sa voiture. (Labelled 'relatives déictiques' by Cadiot 1976, their importance in the spoken language is not reflected by their treatment in grammars.)

(3)   Nous avions déjà quitté Cambrai depuis longtemps et la ville avait disparu *que* restés seuls à l'horizon à nous regarder fuir les deux

clochers agitaient encore en signe d'adieu leur cîme ensoleillée. (Proust) (There are abundant literary examples of a range of coordinating and subordinating uses of *que*, which are accepted in an 'archaïc' text, but rarely given full treatment in a description of contemporary French.)

One approach is not to exclude so-called 'non-standard' forms, but to consider them in the context of social class variation. In fact, as Deulofeu (1981) points out, the relative has become a stereotype in the Labovian sense that: 'elle permet de classer rapidement un locuteur'. The problem is that while certain forms may correlate with social class, in general the use of the so-called *relatives du français populaire* or of coordinating *que*, is far more common outside of working-class speech than was previously assumed. There is ample evidence of this in recently assembled oral corpora, such as that described in Gadet (1989), or the GARS corpus, of which Deulofeu (1986) says:

> La situation me semble complexe: certains locuteurs emploient plus de *que* 'marginaux' que d'autres, sans que l'on puisse associer cette fréquence à des caractéristiques externes stables: en situation de conversation non surveillée, tous les locuteurs sont susceptibles de produire tel ou tel de ces emplois de *que*.

This would indicate a sociosituational dimension i.e. some speakers have the full range of, for example, relatives, and use one form or the other for stylistic effect, or according to context. Apparently, this is true for some forms and some speakers; for other 'non-standard' forms, it appears as though they may embody a semantic difference, rather than being in free variation with the 'standard' form. 'L'étude sociolinguistique des *que* "marginaux" reste à faire', comments Deulofeu. Obviously this is something we need to know more about. Let us look at the position so far. In the case of relatives, let us (following Gadet 1989) take the following examples:

(4)   La femme dont je te parle (*standard*)

(5)   La femme que je t'en parle (*relatives du français populaire* – RFP)

(6)   La femme que je te parle d'elle (*relative défective*)

It had already been suggested by Guiraud (1965) that standard French relatives bear too heavy a syntactic load (i.e. fulfill a number of functions), and that the system in *français populaire* represents a *décumul du relatif*. Gadet goes along with this, suggesting that the RFP fulfills only the delimitative function (i.e. *que* indicates the boundary of the relative clause), shifting both the job of representing a preceding noun (to a pronoun *en* in (5) and *elle* in (6)) and the functional role of indicating syntagmatic relationship/parts of speech (here *en* in (5) and *d'* in (6)).

As far as the 'defective relative' goes, most grammarians have dismissed it as ambiguous. Gadet points out that grammatical theories in the past have been predicated on the use of snippets of illustrative data out of context. For oral language, it is generally unsatisfactory to leave the *contexte énonciatif* out of account, and once in context, the *que* of *la femme que je te parle* ceases to be ambiguous.

In terms of social class variation, Gadet states that in her corpus, ' . . . une partie non négligeable des RFP a été relevée dans la bouche d'universitaires. Par contre, toutes les défectives ont été relevées chez des locuteurs des classes populaires.' If we assume that these are used by 'universitaires' in *français familier*, which looks likely from the examples given, then we have the beginning of a distinction between social class and sociosituational variation.

Turning now to the wide range of functions which *que* has, beside its use as a relative, we find that these rarely receive adequate treatment in grammars or descriptions of French. Deulofeu (1986) writes:

> Les grammairiens ont en fait adopté une solution pragmatique: ils voient bien que ces exemples remettent profondément en cause un certain nombre de distinctions sur lesquelles leur modèle d'analyse est fondé (principale/subordonnée, subordination/coordination) mais ils n'en tirent pas la conséquence qu'il faut la remanier. Il n'est pas rentable de bouleverser un cadre de présentation reconnu par tous pour récupérer des emplois ressentis comme marginaux.

But how marginal are they? These are just a few examples of *que* usages which are given in Gadet (1989) ((7–15) from her corpus; (16–18) from the GARS corpus):

(7)   donnes-moi du tabac que je fume

(8)   quatre degrés à Lamoura le matin qu'il a dit le boucher

(9)   – t'as l'air furieuse
        – y a de quoi que je sois furieuse

(10)   – je l'aime bien quand même
        – quand même que quoi?

(11)   heureusement qu'il a réussi

(12)   éreintant qu'il est mon métier (Queneau)

(13)   t'as besoin de rien que je monte (= est-ce que je monte quelque chose?)

(14)   tu sais à qui tu n'as pas téléphoné depuis longtemps et que c'est pas sympa?

(15)   j'ai fait un cours qu'on aurait entendu une mouche voler

(16)   il dansait qu'on pouvait pas mieux

(17)   il me le demanderait que je ne lui dirais pas

(18)   je vais voir les enfants qu'ils font beaucoup de bruit

Although generally marginalised or ignored in the grammar, some of these examples will seem less 'non-standard' than others. Some, of course, contain morphological or lexical features belonging to *le français familier* (*t'as* in (13), *sympa* in (14)); others, however, may be considered to belong to standard oral French ((11)? (7)? (16)? – the reader may like to try the examples out on a variety of native speakers). Apart from the possible stylistic/sociosituational function of these usages, some of these examples are not syntactically equivalent to their (so-called) standard counterparts. The structure in (7), for example, is not just an inaccurate replacement or lazy abbreviation of *pour que*, but it functions differently from it as the following sentences from Deulofeu (1986) show:

(19)   descendez ici que je vous embrasse

(20)   descendez ici pour que je vous embrasse

(21)   pour que je vous embrasse descendez ici

(22)   * que je vous embrasse descendez ici

(23)   descendez ici non pas pour que je vous embrasse mais pour prendre la valise

(24)   * descendez ici non pas que je vous embrasse mais que vous preniez la valise

Apart from the 'normal' subordinating function that every grammar documents, what then may be the functions of *que*? Some of the patterns which Gadet (1989) suggests emerge from her corpus involve the following uses of *que*:

i)   as 'une incise d'énonciation', frequent in spoken French, and accompanied by a particular intonation pattern; (8)

ii)   to indicate a 'reprise de dialogue'; (9) (10)

iii)   as an 'introducteur de prédicat' (called a 'séparatif' in Frei 1929); (11) (12)

iv)   'télescopage'; (13)

v)   general, vague subordinating role; (14)–(18)

This last is sometimes described by those grammarians who mention such examples as *subordination universelle*, a sort of *fourre-tout* category, occasionally further refined, e.g. into *subordination inversée*, (16), and *subordination à valeur coordonnante*, (14)?, (18)?.

It is obvious that category (v) is particularly interesting for it contains a wealth of examples of *que* used to join clauses in one way or another. It is in the admission that *que* has a 'valeur coordonnante' that we begin to see a blurring of the old distinction between subordination and coordination: long considered as a quintessential 'subordinator', *que*, to many researchers, now seems to have a variety of important coordinating roles.

It is because of the inadequacy of previous analyses that Deulofeu (1986) applies a different framework (of 'government' and 'association') developed by GARS, to examples (16)–(18) above. Without going into this here, we can see that in (16), for example, the *que* clause has a *comme cela/comment* sort of relation to the main verb (cf. also (15)?), and that a straight analysis of *que* introducing subordination is not satisfactory.

Indeed, for GARS, the absolute coordination/subordination distinction is also challenged by a number of other structures e.g. 'le processus de répétition-hésitation' in spoken language is seen by Blanche-Benveniste and by Bilger (in *Recherches sur le français parlé* 1987) to fulfill a particular syntactic role which is close to that of coordination.

Finally, another factor that we should mention briefly is the interaction between syntax and prosodic features. It may well be that, in spoken uses of some of the examples given, intonation helps to identify the various uses of *que*. The intersecting roles of intonation and syntax have been investigated by the *Centre de Morphosyntaxe du Français Contemporain, Université de Paris III* under A.-M., Morel (see Morel 1991).

In the case of *que* relative, Delomier (1985) demonstrates the role of intonation in distinguishing between explicative and descriptive relatives. Traditionally the comma of the written language was said to be present in a pause in the spoken language (Bally 1965). Delomier finds in general that the pause is a less reliable indicator of the 'relative explicative' than a particular intonation pattern, which is characterised by a break in intonation and a lowering of pitch, followed by a gradually increasing in pace and ending on an abrupt high-rise. In the case of what the GARS calls 'macro-syntaxe' (which deals with elements whose 'togetherness' is not governed by noun or verb dependency), intonation plays a determining role in assigning meaning; as in the following example of *préfixe + noyau*, in GARS's terms:

> plus d'argent, plus de travail . . . (série)
>
> plus d'argent, plus de sorties (hypothèse, conséquence)   (see Blanche-Benveniste et al. 1991: chs. 3 and 4)

To sum up, we can see that the adherence to an artifically predetermined, largely written, 'standard' has resulted in a biased and incomplete description of French. The points that we have made with respect to certain items, for example *que*, could be made for others (another example would be the neglect of the ubiquitous pseudo-clef construction; see Valli 1981). The differences between spoken and written French are crucial for an understanding of sociosituational variation, and it is in this area that a good deal of research is currently underway. Often, but not always, there is also an overlap – or an interaction between situational and other factors (age, social class), about which we need to know more. In order to represent this interaction, it may be helpful if we get away from the 'layered' representation of register in two or more columns, either horizontal or vertical, and attempt to portray the way in which it is the interaction of a number of factors which determines the choice and combination of linguistic items that we call register, or sociosituational variation, as depicted in figure 2.3.

Text 1

Ah! qu'il est trou, ce bonbon!

'Polo, le bonbon le plus trou!', prononce la dame en se pâmant, très Marie-Chantal. Une pub au demeurant très réussie. Derrière l'inanité, le non-sens du slogan, se cache quelque chose qui fait sens.

    Qu'est-ce que c'est qu'être trou, pour un bonbon ou pour tout autre objet, d'ailleurs? Ah! ce qu'il est trou ce bonbon! Plus trou que moi, tu meurs . . . Impossible de répondre, bien entendu, sinon que la phrase fonctionne comme une phrase française incontestable. Après tout, on dit bien d'une robe qu'elle est *chic*, d'une cravate qu'elle est *classe*, d'une voiture qu'elle est *tarte*, d'une montre qu'elle est *toc*, d'une idée qu'elle est *béton* ou *bidon*, d'une musique qu'elle est *flan*, d'un enfant qu'il est *trognon*, d'un chapeau qu'il est *chou*, d'un copain qu'il est *chouette* ou bien *con*, de vacances qu'elles furent *galère*.

    L'emploi de *trou* dans l'expression *le bonbon le plus trou* s'insère ainsi sans peine dans une classe de qualificatifs du français familier. Ces qualificatifs sont fortement polarisés; ils peuvent être laudatifs, ou au contraire péjoratifs. Dans le cas de *trou*, l'interprétation est de toute évidence positive. Être trou, pour un bonbon, c'est une qualité. On peut distinguer parmi ces termes ceux dont l'emploi adjectival détruit le sens nominal (*chouette, con, tarte, béton, bidon, chou, trognon, flan*), et qui paraissent peu motivés, et ceux qui conservent le même sens (*classe, chic, toc*), et peuvent être para-phrasés par *avoir + substantif* – par exemple: 'avoir du chic'. *Être trou, peut-être est-ce tout simplement* 'avoir du trou' (à supposer que 'avoir du trou' soit un avantage sur 'ne pas en avoir').

    Il existe un autre cas assez proche, c'est celui de l'emploi qualificatif des 'labels' (très souvent empruntés à l'anglais) comme *new-wave, new-look, modern*

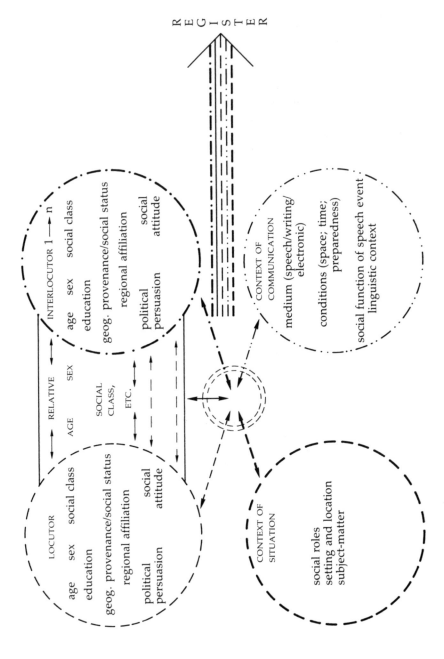

Figure 2.3   Interaction of factors which determine register or sociosituational variation

style, fifties, art déco, Nouvelle Vague, BCBG, baba-cool, skinhead. Il s'agit là aussi d'expressions nominales employées de manière adjectivale. On dit:

> *Une robe new-look*
> *Un chanteur new-wave*
> *Un look BCBG*
> *Un décor fifties*, etc.

On citera aussi quelques noms à référent humain comme *plouc, minet, putain, chameau* ou *beauf*, dont l'emploi semble être indifféremment nominal ou adjectival.

Quoi qu'il en soit, tous ces mots ont un point commun: ce sont des substantifs détournés de leur classe d'origine pour assumer un rôle adjectival. L'appartenance d'un mot à une classe grammaticale donnée est déterminée par sa 'distribution', c'est-à-dire par les positions qu'il peut occuper dans une phrase bien formée et identifiée comme telle par n'importe quel locuteur natif. Il nous faut donc accepter *trou* comme adjectif du simple fait de son emploi en position épithète et au superlatif. Mais *trou, classe, tarte, chouette, con, galère*, etc., sont-ils pour autant des adjectifs à part entière?

(From Yaguello 1991)

Text 2
Le registre dans les dictionnaires

A vous de faire de même, avec un échantillon de dictionnaires contemporains (français, et français–anglais),
pour comparer les résultats!

	1	2	3	4	5	6	7	8
	Littré 1863	*Lar.* *XIXe siècle* 1867	*PL* 1910	*Bauche* 1920	*GR* 1953	*DFC* 1966	*PL* 1970	*PR* 1972
ouvrer	=	=	=	ø	vx ou dial.	ø	=	vx ou dial.
œuvrer	=	VX	ø	ø	↗ mot noble	soi.	=	litt.
besogner	=	ATF	=	ø	=	ø	=	=
travailler	=	=	=	ø	=	=	=	=
piocher	(écolier)	FAM	FAM	ø	FAM	FAM	FAM	=
bricoler	ø	POP	FAM	= POP	=	FAM	FAM	=
trimer	ø	POP	POP	= POP	=	FAM	ARG/FAM	=
bûcher	POP	POP	POP	= POP	FAM	FAM	FAM	FAM
gratter	ø	ø	ø	= POP	POP	FAM	POP	POP
boulonner	ø	ø	ø	= POP	POP	POP	POP	FAM
bosser	ø	ø	ø	= POP	POP	POP	POP	POP
turbiner	ø	ø	ø	= POP	ARG/POP	POP	POP	ARG/POP

(From Désirat and Hordé 1976:44)

3

Regional variation in France

ROGER HAWKINS

'Géographiquement délimitable' telle est la définition de l'écart de langage qui constitue un régionalisme linguistique. Quelques exemples permettront de préciser cette définition claire mais un peu courte. Le mot *plumard* au sens de 'lit' ne peut pas être considéré comme un régionalisme, même si on l'entend souvent dans le français parlé à tel endroit. *Plumard* est un mot commun à tous les locuteurs qui pratiquent un français populaire ou argotique; ce mot s'entend dans toutes les régions et à Paris: ce n'est pas un régionalisme. Dans *Si j'aurais su, je serais pas venu*, on peut relever deux écarts grammaticaux: le conditionnel après *si* et la négation réduite à *pas*. Cela s'observe partout: ces deux écarts ne sont pas des régionalismes. Mais si j'emploie le mot *une gipe* pour dire une 'cloison entre deux pièces de la maison', je ne serai compris que par les Français originaires d'une fraction du Dauphiné. Si je dis: *Ça, j'y trouve pas beau, j'y achèterai jamais*, je me ferai comprendre, sans doute, de tous les Français, mais ma grammaire paraîtra étrange à tous les Français sauf à ceux de la région située autour de Lyon, Grenoble, Chambéry, Mâcon. *Gipe* au sens de 'cloison' et le pronom *y* en fonction d'objet direct neutre sont de véritables régionalismes, car ils ne s'observent que dans une aire linguistique délimitable. (Tuaillon 1983: 227–8)

Introduction

There is a great deal of linguistic variety within the borders of France, the 'hexagon', just as there is in most speech communities with a long settlement history which occupy a relatively large geographical space. There is, of course, standard French, which is referred to by a number of names in French: *français standard, français institutionnel, français normalisé, français commun, français universel*. Standard French is the official language of France; its grammatical forms, vocabulary and pronunciation are described in textbooks (grammars, dictionaries and manuals of phonetics); it is the linguistic variety taught in French schools, and the variety which native speakers of other languages usually learn when they learn French as a foreign language. Standard French exists in two media: it has a spoken form and a written form. It is also 'pan-regional'; that is, it is spoken by people living throughout the hexagon, and it is impossible to tell, simply from listening to a speaker of standard French, with a standard accent, which region that speaker comes from.

There are, in addition to standard French, a number of regional varieties of French spoken within the hexagon: *les français régionaux*. Regional varieties of French have many features in common with standard spoken French in terms of grammatical forms and vocabulary. Characteristically, however, they differ in pronunciation, and they also display some grammatical forms and some items of vocabulary which are specific to the region where they are spoken. Tuaillon, in the quotation cited at the head of this chapter, gives an example of a grammatical difference and a lexical difference between standard French and the regional French of eastern France: respectively *Ça j'y trouve pas beau* 'I don't like it', for the standard spoken French *Ça, je le trouve pas beau* (in standard written French: *(Cela), je ne le trouve pas beau*), and the vocabulary item *une gipe* 'a partition' for the standard French *une cloison*.

Speakers of regional varieties of French have little or no difficulty in communicating both with speakers of standard French and with speakers of other regional varieties of French. However, whereas it is impossible to guess where a speaker of standard French, with a standard accent, comes from, speakers of regional varieties of French signal their regional origin as soon as they start speaking, largely as a result of the specifically regional features of their accent.

In the written medium, speakers of regional varieties of French are usually indistinguisable from other literate French speakers, because they normally use standard written French. This is not just because the written language is acquired in school, and the written form promoted exclusively within the French educational system is standard written French, but also because regional varieties of French usually have no stable, recognised orthography for representing regional pronunciations.

Alongside standard French and the regional varieties of French, a number of other languages are spoken in certain regions of France: Basque, Breton, Flemish, German, Catalan, Occitan and Corsican. Although these languages are not 'official' languages of France, they have been spoken in the regions in question for centuries, and they can currently be taught and studied (optionally) within the state educational system in those regions. See chapter 4 for discussion of the 'other languages' of France.

The extent of linguistic variation within France does not stop there, however. There are also the dialects:

Il suffit de parcourir la France pour s'apercevoir qu'il n'existe pas 'un' mais 'des' français. A côté de ce que nous appellerons 'langue standard' ou 'langue normalisée', celle des manuels scolaires par exemple, il existe d'une part de nombreux 'français régionaux' et d'autre part des parlers dialectaux, d'origine romane ou autre, dont la vitalité est plus ou moins grande. (Hadjadj 1981: 71)

In general the term 'dialect' refers to a 'shared set of speech habits'. When speakers use the same lexical items, the same grammatical constructions and the same features of pronunciation, they are 'speaking the same dialect', and as a group they are in contrast to other groups of speakers who share different speech habits, who 'speak different dialects'.

On this definition 'standard French' is a dialect, and so is 'standard English', 'standard German', 'standard Spanish', and so on. Of course, French, English, German and Spanish are also referred to as 'languages'. This is because they have acquired the status of the 'official dialect' in the countries where they are spoken: they have become the 'standard languages' of those countries. These days many people living in Britain, France, Germany and Spain speak the dialect which is the standard language (although they may continue to speak other dialects as well). In the past, when education was not universal, when communications were less easy than they are today, and when social mobility was more restricted, the numbers speaking the standard language were much smaller, and the numbers speaking non-standard dialects much greater.

Commonly people oppose the terms 'dialect' and 'language', implying that dialects are in some way 'corrupt' versions of languages. This is a misconception. Standard languages are as much dialects as any other sets of shared speech habits. Standard French was once a geographically localised dialect spoken in central northern France; this region happened to become prestigious because the kings of France fixed their residence there; a consequence of this was that the speech habits of those living in the region also became prestigious. Standard English has a similar history, being once a dialect limited geographically to the London area. (For more on the rise of French as a standard language see chapter 1.)

The difference between a non-standard dialect and a standard dialect, then, is not a linguistic one, but has to do with social status. A dialect which acts as the standard language for a given speech community is one which has, for purely accidental historical reasons, become prestigious within that speech community: 'As a social norm, . . . a dialect is a language that is excluded from polite society' (Haugen 1966: 924–5).

Sometimes when a dialect has fallen from social grace as the result of another one becoming the standard it is referred to pejoratively as a *patois*, implying that it is an inferior form of communication, even though objectively it is capable of the same range of linguistic expression as other dialects, including the standard. Dauzat (1927: 30) defines a *patois* as follows:

> Est patois tout idiome, langue ou dialecte, socialement déchu en tant qu'il n'est plus parlé par l'élite intellectuelle, et, subsidiairement, en tant qu'il n'a plus de littérature. La distinction n'est pas d'ordre linguistique, mais social.

The non-standard dialects which exist within the hexagon (excluding the 'other languages' of France), together with standard French, have all evolved from the same basic source: the Latin of the Roman Empire – Vulgar Latin – which was spoken when the country which is today called France belonged to that Empire, roughly from 1 BC to AD 5. The dialects of France developed when factors external to the language (the collapse of the Roman Empire and the invasion of the hexagon by Germanic-speaking peoples) caused the division of the country and the severing of communication between groups of speakers of Vulgar Latin for periods long enough for the shared speech habits of those speakers to diverge. The result was the development of the three broad dialect areas indicated by the solid lines in map 1, and within those broad dialect areas the development of sub-dialect areas (indicated by broken lines).

Each of the three areas represent major linguistic divergences, particularly between the north and the south. By the Middle Ages the dialects of the north had become as different from the dialects of the south as, say, modern French is from modern Spanish or Italian, and one imagines that speakers of northern dialects would have found it difficult to understand speakers of southern dialects, and vice versa. The northern dialects have been given the collective name *langue d'oïl* (pronounced 'oyle'), the southern dialects the name *langue d'oc* (pronounced 'ock'), or more commonly Occitan (pronounced 'Oksitan'), and the eastern dialects, which form something of a transition zone between Occitan dialects and the dialects of *langue d'oïl*, the collective name Franco-Provençal. (The names *oïl* and *oc* come from the word for 'yes' in the northern and southern medieval dialects respectively, both words coming from the Latin expression *hoc ille*. In the north, phonetic changes led to the form *oïl* (which subsequently became modern standard French *oui*), while in the south phonetic evolution led to the form *oc*.) The regional or sub-dialects within each of these broad dialect areas also diverged one from another, but less dramatically, and one imagines that speakers of different dialects within the same speech area were mutually comprehensible to varying degrees.

As recently as one hundred and fifty years ago there were many people living in the north of France who would have spoken a

———— language boundary
– – – dialect boundary
—·—·— political (national) boundary

Adapted from Guiraud (1968:29)

Map 1 Dialect areas of France

non-standard *langue d'oïl* dialect as their normal medium of everyday communication. Some of those speakers would have been monolingual non-standard dialect speakers; i.e. they would not have known standard French. In the south of France, one need go back no further than a hundred years to find a great many monolingual speakers of Occitan dialects.

The numbers speaking the non-standard dialects began to decline dramatically in the nineteenth century, particularly in the north of

France, to the point where, realistically, today there are very few
surviving speakers of northern non-standard dialects, and not all that
many speakers of Occitan dialects. This rapid disappearance can be
gauged from reading the work of dialectologists writing in the early part
of this century, and those writing more recently. Albert Dauzat, writing
in the 1920s, tells us that monolingual non-standard dialect speakers
could still be found at that period, albeit in remote parts of France:

> A l'heure actuelle [i.e. 1920s], pour ne parler que de la France romane
> [i.e. excluding Basque, Breton, Flemish and German speakers], il faut
> aller dans les coins les plus reculés des Alpes-Maritimes . . . ou du
> Roussillon . . . pour trouver quelques vieillards qui ignorent encore
> notre langue [i.e. French].   (Dauzat 1927: 28)

However, by the 1970s, not only have monolingual non-standard
dialect speakers disappeared (those remaining speakers of non-standard
dialects being bilingual in French and the non-standard dialect), but the
contexts in which the non-standard dialect is used have become highly
restricted:

> En réalité la diffusion du français standard a été si poussée qu'en pays
> d'oïl l'usage cohérent des anciens dialectes a été souvent réduit à des
> îlots de peu d'importance.   (Marcellesi 1979: 64)

And those speaking dialects of Occitan in the south are to be found
mainly in rural areas:

> Cette longue pression [du français standard sur l'occitan] aboutit
> aujourd'hui à la disparition à peu près totale du monolinguisme
> occitan, à un monolinguisme français majoritaire en milieu urbain (avec
> usage fort général d'un français régional à substrat occitan).   (Lafont
> 1971: 93)

While the non-standard regional dialects may be disappearing as
French becomes the single first language for most people in France, they
have nevertheless left their mark on the French of many speakers living
in the regions, as Lafont suggests, in the form of regionalisms: pronunciation features, lexical items and grammatical constructions which can
be directly attributed to the regional dialect, and which have been
transferred into French.

In this chapter we shall be concerned specifically with regional
varieties of French, *les français régionaux*, how they are related to
standard French and the non-standard dialects, what their current
status is, and what people's attitudes to variation are.

Linguistic properties of the regional varieties of French

There are numerous articles, monographs and books about particular regional varieties of French, giving details of features of regional accents, listing items of regional vocabulary, and commenting on regional grammatical constructions. One should be aware that such collections do not necessarily represent what any individual speaker of a regional variety of French is likely to produce himself or herself. The authors of such works tend to aim for comprehensiveness, and present all items of non-standard pronunciation, vocabulary and grammar which they have come across in the productions of many speakers living in the region in question, and often collected over a number of years. Individual speakers of regional varieties of French may themselves use only a fraction of the regionalisms listed in works on regional varieties of French. Indeed, as we shall see later in the chapter, whether a speaker uses a greater or smaller number of regionalisms when speaking French is dependent on a number of factors, like the age, social class, level of education and place of residence (urban or rural) of the speaker in question, and the context in which he or she is speaking.

Some features of the sound systems of regional varieties of French

'Le Franchiman *parle pointu*, tandis que le Méridional à l'accent accusé *parle plat.*'

Définition:

Franchiman: 'Français d'oïl [i.e. an inhabitant of the northern half of France] qui parle le français avec l'accent de son pays; Méridional [i.e. an inhabitant of the southern half of France] qui s'essaie à prendre cet accent (péjoratif), ou qui écorche le français. (Séguy 1951: 68)

Vowels

Standard French is usually held to distinguish the vowel sounds in pairs of words like the following:

(1)	couch**é**	[e] 'slept'	couch**ait**	[ɛ] 'was sleeping'
(2)	s**au**le	[o] 'willow'	s**o**l	[ɔ] 'ground'
(3)	p**a**tte	[a] 'paw'	p**â**te	[ɑ] 'pastry'

In many regional varieties of French, however, the distribution of vowel sounds in such pairs of words is different. In some varieties only one vowel sound is found in each pair. For example, most regional varieties in the south of France pronounce -*é* and -*ait* identically as [e]. On the other hand, speakers of the regional French of Normandy do distinguish pairs of words like (1), but do so the other way round from standard French:

(4)   couché   [kuʃɛ]   couchait   [kuʃe]

The regional French of Normandy also makes a distinction between short and long vowels (which standard French does not) in pairs of words like:

(5)   couché   [kuʃɛ]   couchée   [kuʃɛ:]
        joli   [ʒɔli]   jolis   [ʒɔli:]

That is, the regional French of Normandy marks an acoustically audible difference between the masculine and feminine forms, and the singular and plural forms of some words (Lepelley 1975).

The regional French of the Haute-Marne (a region to the east of Paris) also distinguishes vowel length in pairs of words like:

(6)   couché   [kuʃe]   couchée   [kuʃe:]

(The vowel quality here is [e], like standard French, and unlike the regional French of Normandy.)

This regional variety also distinguishes length where the round vowel [ø] is involved, as in examples like:

(7)   bleu   [blø]   bleue   [blø:]
        lieu   [ljø]   lieue   [ljø:]
        peu   [pø]   queue   [kø:]
        (Bourcelot 1973)

For the vowel sounds in pairs of words like (2) – *saule* [o]/*sol* [ɔ] – again regional varieties of French tend to diverge. In the Languedoc region (central southern France) when the vowel is in word-final position in an open syllable (i.e. there is no following consonant in the spoken language), the vowel is a half close rounded vowel [o], as it is in standard French:

(8)   mot 'word', pot 'pot', seau 'bucket'   [mo], [po], [so]

When the syllable is closed by a pronounced consonant, however, standard French has two vowel sounds: [o] in some words, but [ɔ] in others:

(9)   saule 'willow' [sol]   sol 'ground'   [sɔl]
        gauche 'clumsy' [goʃ]   cloche 'bell'   [klɔʃ]
        côte 'coast' [kot]   cote 'value'   [kɔt]

In the regional French of the Languedoc, by contrast, there is a strong tendency for all of these words to have the vowel [ɔ], as Séguy (1951) notes. Séguy suggests that the reason for this lies in the fact that the regional French of the Languedoc operates on a binary opposition: close vowels, like [o], [e] and [ø], in open syllables, and open vowels, like [ɔ], [ɛ] and [œ], in closed syllables – an opposition which does not operate in standard French. Interestingly, between the 1950s, when Séguy was writing, and the 1980s, there appears to have been an innovation in the regional French of the Languedoc. Carton et al. (1983: 56) indicate that there is a strong tendency these days in Languedoc French to produce close vowels everywhere, whether in open or closed syllables, so that words like *saule* and *sol* are both being pronounced [sol], *fête* is coming to be pronounced as [fet] (standard French [fɛt]), and *fleur* is coming to be pronounced as [flør] (standard French [flœr]).

In pairs of words like (3), standard French traditionally distinguishes between a front of the mouth [a] in words like *patte*, and a back of the mouth [ɑ] in words like *pâte* (the latter sound usually being signalled in the written language by *â*, or an *a* followed by a written *s*, as in *raser* 'to shave' [rɑze], *passer* 'to pass' [pɑse], *ras* 'close shaven' [rɑ] – there is also a small number of other words containing the vowel [ɑ] which are not so signalled: *fable*, *sable*, *nation*, etc.).

Many regional varities of French display only one type of vowel corresponding to written *a*. In most of them it is the front vowel [a]; an exception is the regional French of Normandy, where there is a strong tendency to use [ɑ] universally, so that a word like *garage*, which in standard French and most regional varieties of French is pronounced [gɑrɑʒ], in the regional French of Normandy is pronounced [gɑrɑʒ] (Carton et al., 1983: 29).

Nasal vowels are characteristic of standard French, in which there are four, illustrated by the words: *bien* [bjɛ̃], *brun* [brœ̃], *bon* [bɔ̃], *banc* [bɑ̃]. In regional varieties of French of the south of France these vowels are much less nasalised than they are in standard French, and in addition the vowels are followed by nasal consonants: often a velar nasal [ŋ] (the sound represented by written *ng* in English: *sing* [siŋ]) when the word occurs before a pause, and [n] or [m] when it is before another word beginning with a consonant. Compare the typical difference in pronunciation between a speaker of French with a standard accent, and a speaker with a southern accent saying the following (admittedly somewhat bizarre) sentence:

(10)   Il est bien bon, ce banc.   'That's a nice bench.'
        [il ɛ bjɛ̃ bɔ̃//sə bɑ̃]   (standard accent of French)
        [il ɛ bjɛ̃m bɔ̃ŋ//sə bɑ̃ŋ]   (southern accent of French)
        (∞ = denasalisation, // = pause)

In other regional varieties, there are fully nasalised vowels, but fewer than the four of standard French. In the regional French of the

Haute-Marne, the vowel [ɔ̃] apparently does not exist: *blanc/blond* are both pronounced [blɑ̃] (Bourcelot 1973). By contrast, in the regional French of the north of France, around the town of Lille, the vowel [ɑ̃] apparently does not exist, so that *blanc/blond* are both pronounced [blɔ̃] (Carton 1973). In the regional French of the Jura in eastern France, [ɑ̃] is replaced by [ɛ̃], so that *des fins/défend* both sound like [defɛ̃] (Carton et al. 1983). (One should perhaps add that standard French itself is rapidly losing the vowel [ɑ̃], whose functions are being taken over by [ɛ̃], so that many speakers of French with a standard accent now pronounce *brun/brin* identically as [brɛ̃].)

The unstressed central vowel [ə] (which has a name – schwa – and is often signalled in the written language by an *e* without a (grave, acute or circumflex) accent: e.g. *je̱ me̱ suis rendu compte̱; la grande̱ fenêtre̱ était ouverte*), is only pronounced in certain environments in standard French. For example, while it is often pronounced in the first syllable of a speech group, it is always deleted before a vowel and before pause; and elsewhere it is often also deleted providing that a cluster of no more than two consonants is the result. Thus in a sentence such as (11), schwa is likely to be deleted in standard accents of French in the cases indicated by the bar: notice that in those cases where it is not deleted – *je, que* and *fenêtre* – the first two are the first syllables of speech groups, and deletion in the latter case would result in a cluster of three consonants:

(11)   Je me̸ suis rendu compte̸//que la grande̸ fenêtre̸ était ouverte̸.

(The facts concerning the deletion of schwa in standard French are complex, and beyond the scope of the present chapter. For further details see for example Léon 1966; Martinet 1969; Bazylko 1981; Spence 1982; Tranel 1987.)

In regional varieties of French the facts can be different. In many southern varieties schwa is only regularly deleted before another word beginning with a vowel, but not before words beginning with a consonant, nor at the end of speech groups. Contrasting the typical standard pronunciation of a sentence like (11) with, say, the regional pronunciation of the Languedoc, one would find the pattern of (12):

(12)   a. [ʒə m sɥi rɑ̃dy kɔ̃t kə la grɑ̃d fənɛtr etɛ uvɛrt] (standard French)
        b. [ʒə mə sɥi rɑ̃ndy kɔ̃ntə kə la grɑ̃ndə fənɛtr ete uvɛrtə] (regional French of the Languedoc)

Carton et al. (1983: 51) have even noted a tendency in the regional pronunciation of Provence to extend word-final pronunciation of schwa to words which in standard French never have been candidates for the retention or deletion of a central vowel, like *avec* and *alors*, which in Provence can be pronounced [avɛkə] and [alorə]. The retention of schwa in cases where the standard accent would not retain it is one of the stereotypical features that the French associate with an *accent méridional*, *méridional*, 'a southern accent'. And this stereotyping appears to be felt by speakers with southern accents themselves. According to Séguy (1951: 43), when speakers from Toulouse wish to conceal their regional origins, they suppress [ə]:

> En français de Toulouse . . . on ne le supprime [i.e. [ə]] que lorsqu' on affecte de 'parler pointu' (c'est d'ailleurs la seule modification consciente que les Toulousains du peuple soient capables d'apporter à leur accent).

The other stereotypical feature associated with the *accent méridional* is the denasalisation and addition of nasal consonants to what are nasal vowels in standard French. We shall return to the question of stereotypes in regional variation below, in the discussion of attitudes to variation.

Consonants

Consonants, too, vary from regional variety to regional variety. Here are just a few examples.

The *r* sound of standard French is produced at the back of the mouth by vibrating the tongue against the tip of the soft palate – the uvula – hence a uvular r (*r grasseyé* in French). Some regional varieties, however, have a tip-of-the-tongue *r*, produced by rolling or tapping the tip of the tongue against the alveolar ridge behind the upper front teeth, hence an alveolar r (*r apical* or *r roulé* in French). This pronunciation, although still widespread, particularly in southern varieties of French, is decreasing because it has become somewhat stigmatised as 'rural and backward'.

Although standard French has no [h] sound – words like *histoire*, *hache, héros* begin with a vowel in standard spoken French: [istwar], [aʃ], [ero] – some regional varieties of French do. For example, speakers with non-standard accents in Normandy in the north-west, and Alsace in the north-east, pronounce words like *dehors* and *là-haut* as [dəhɔr] and [laho] (Carton et al. 1983). In the regional French of the Haute-Marne, [h] replaces the sounds [ʃ], [ʒ] of standard French in words like:

		Standard French	*Haute-Marne*
(13)	marcher	[marʃe]	[marhe]
	jeudi	[ʒødi]	[hø:di]
			(Bourcelot 1973)

In the regional French of the Languedoc, one finds double nasal consonants:

		Standard French	*Languedoc*
(14)	année	[ane]	[aɲne]
	ennui	[ãnɥi]	[ãɲnɥi]

There are even pairs of words in the regional French of the Languedoc which contrast minimally on the basis of whether they contain a single or double nasal consonant:

		Standard French	Languedoc
(15)	Anne	[an]	[aɲnə]
	âne	[ɑn]	[anə]

(Séguy 1951: 36)

Still in the south, a number of word-final consonants which are no longer pronounced in standard French (although they were pronounced in earlier periods) are pronounced in southern varieties of French:

		Standard French	Southern French
(16)	gens	[ʒã]	[ʒãns]
	plus	[ply]	[plys]
	tandis que	[tãdikə]	[tãndiskə]
	aspect	[aspɛ]	[aspek]
	estomac	[ɛstɔma]	ɛstomak]

In the regional French of Alsace, final consonants which are voiced in standard French – [b], [d], [g], [z] – are voiceless. Pairs of words like the following differ in Alsace French on the basis of vowel length, and not on the voicing of the final consonant:

(17)	vide	[viːt]	vite	[vit]
	bague	[baːk]	bac	[bak]
	cause	[koːs]	fausse	[fos]

(Philipp 1985; 20)

Some features of the lexicons of regional varieties of French

buffer (vb. intrans) (régionalisme de l'Ouest) 'reprendre son souffle'.

Anecdote vécue:
La scène se passe il y a quelques années, dans une ville de l'Ouest (exactement Saintes). Un jour d'examen du brevet élémentaire. C'est l'épreuve d'orthographe. On termine la dictée . . . empruntée à Buffon. Le texte dicté, l'examinateur vient de dire, sans aucune précision, le nom de l'auteur: Buffon.
– C'est pas trop tôt, s'exclame un candidat.
(Bulletin de la société d'études folkloriques du Centre-Ouest, 1966; 139; cited in Rézeau 1984: 82)

Mon godin a écuissé le petit blôchier – 'My little (male) calf has uprooted the little plum-tree' (français régional de la Haute-Marne, Bourcelot 1973: 224)

Regional varieties of French are rich in lexical items specific to the region in which they are spoken, although it is debatable whether the majority of speakers of regional varieties of French would use or even know more than a fraction of those words found in glossaries and dictionaries of regional French. Presenting a vast list of regional words here would serve little purpose. It is possible, however, to isolate different categories of lexical regionalism and this will be done here, with a few examples to illustrate each case.

One category of lexical regionalism is that of words which refer to entities, activities or traditions of specifically regional origin. A classic example is the case of the annual village fair which, while common to most regions of France, tends to be a focus of local interest, and not surprisingly varies in name from region to region. The word in standard French is *fête*, but in the north of France along the Franco-Belgian border the words *ducasse* and *kermesse* are used; in the north-west (in Picardy and Normandy) the term is *assemblée*; *pardon* is found in Brittany; *préveil* and *frairie* are words used in the south-west; *baloche* is the term used in Toulouse and the surrounding villages; *vogue* is a word used in eastern France. And even this does not exhaust the range of regional terms that can be found (Dauzat 1927: 102–6; Guiraud 1968: 16; Rézeau 1984: 10).

The range of climates, terrain, plant and animal life, and (in bygone days) types of agricultural and artisanal activity and techniques found in the various regions of France are often signalled by vocabulary items specific to the varieties of French spoken in those regions. A few representative examples only are cited here.

Bourcelot (1973: 224) in his study of the regional French of the Haute-Marne notes that:

> il y a plusieurs milliers de mots [dans le français régional haut-marnais] qui sont ainsi restés concernant le temps, la terre, les plantes, les animaux et l'homme, en général ce qui se rapporte à la vie rurale,

and he cites words like:

(18)   la verne   'north-west wind'
       les chevris   'April showers'
       le tafon   'clayey soil'
       le fumeron   'a small heap of manure'
       le trouble   'white clover'
       le godin   'male calf'

Rézeau (1984: 12) in his study of regionalisms of the west of France provides examples like:

(19)   une borderie   'small farm (5–15 hectares)'
       une guignette   'grape-harvester's hook'
       une loubine   'bass, sea-perch'
       un marrochon   'hoe'

un pocheteau   'skate (fish)'
un rollon   'rung (of ladder), crossbar (of gate)'

Sometimes such lexical regionalisms refer to entities which have no counterpart in standard French. For example, in the regional French of Toulouse can be found words like:

(20)   Franchiman   'a Frenchman from northern France with a northern accent, or a southerner trying to put on a northern accent'

cacarot   'Spanish or Pyrenean labourer who hires himself out for work during the grape-harvest in Languedoc'

pipine   'open-air theatre in Toulouse'

faire juntet   'to eat bread and chocolate or sausage in such a manner as to make the pleasure last, and not finish the chocolate/sausage before the bread'

(Séguy 1951: 68–71)

Mostly, however, lexical regionalisms exist side by side in the regional variety of French with a word of standard French. One can speculate why a regional variety of French should need to have two terms where standard French has only one. Rézeau's (1984: 10–11) view is that a regional term continues to be used:

> parce qu'il semble plus évocateur, ou tout simplement en vertu de la force de l'habitude . . . On sait fort bien dans l'Ouest ce que sont les *haricots*, on connait aussi les *fayots* et les *flageolets*, mais ce qu'on sème, ce qu'on récolte et ce qu'on mange, c'est la *mogette*.

However, in a sense such doubling of words for the same referent is not surprising. Synonymy is a feature of all languages. Standard French itself offers many examples of synonymy. Mostly such synonyms are not really synonyms because although they might *refer* to the same entity, they are not *used* in the same set of contexts. Think of the words *ami* and *copain*. While both words refer to the same sort of notion, a social relationship marked by a certain degree of intimacy, the former is generally usable in all contexts and is used by most speakers, but the latter tends to be used in informal contexts of utterance, and by younger and/or working-class speakers. In the example cited by Rézeau, standard French has the two words *haricot* 'bean', which is the 'usable in all contexts' term, and *fayot* which is the 'informal contexts' term. The regional French of the west of France has simply added a further synonym *mogette*, whose context of use, as Rézeau makes admirably clear, is the regional one.

The majority of lexical regionalisms are borrowings from the regional dialect/language which is, or was, spoken in the region where the regional variety of French is now spoken. Such items usually become 'francofied'; that is, they are made to conform to the phonological patterns of French. This often means that speakers of regional varieties of French are sometimes unaware that particular words are regionalisms and are not to be found in standard French. Rézeau (1984: 20) offers two examples of this phenomenon, where speakers of a regional variety of French suddenly discover that a word they had always thought to be in the lexicon of standard French turns out to be a regionalism. The first involves a dialectologist colleague of Rézeau's, Jacques Pignon, and the second Rézeau himself, who made the discovery while writing his book on regionalisms of the west of France:

> 'Personnellement, j'ai découvert que le mot *rimer* ['to stick to the bottom of the pan' (of foods, when cooking)] n'était pas français (i.e. du français général) seulement à l'âge de dix-neuf ans, quand je suis venu faire mes études à Paris' . . . Chacun peut faire pour sa part l'expérience de telles découvertes, qui causent toujours une certaine surprise: j'avoue que c'est en faisant ce travaile que je me suis aperçu que par exemple *parler sur la grosse dent* ['to kick up a fuss' – standard French: *se gendarmer*] . . . ou *tout pendant que* ['as long as' – standard French: *aussi longtemps que*] ne faisaient pas partie du français officiel.

Sometimes regional lexical items becomes more widely known to the French-speaking community, and are 'borrowed' by standard French. This usually happens where the word refers to a regional product which becomes popular beyond the region of its origin. Here are a few examples:

(21) chai   'wine and spirit store'
      cognac   'brandy'   (Rézeau 1984: West)

      olive   'olive'
      bouillabaisse   'fish soup'
      pétanque   'petanque, bowls'   (Guiraud 1968: Provence)

      houille   'coal'
      *rescapé   'survivor'
                      (Guiraud 1968: Picardy, Wallonia (Belgium))

      turbot   'turbot'
      homard   'lobster'
      crevette   'prawn'   (Guiraud 1968: Normandy)

* La terrible catastrophe [minière] de Courrières en 1906 est à l'origine de *rescapé*, forme wallonne de *réchappé*, reprise par les journalistes de la bouche des sauveteurs (Guiraud 1971: 98).

On the other hand, lexical regionalisms can also be items which were at one time current in standard French, but are no longer so, and yet have remained current in regional varieties of French. These can either be phonological forms which have completely disappeared from standard French, for example:

(22)   basselle   'a girl' (st. Fr. 'jeune fille')
        maton   'curdled milk' (st. Fr. 'lait caillé')
                                                (Lanly 1973: Lorraine)

        aubue   'chalky soil' (st. Fr. 'sol calcaire')
        buffer   'to get one's breath back' (st. Fr. 'reprendre son souffle')
        porée   'leek' (st. Fr. 'poireau')
        métive   'harvest' (st. Fr. 'moisson')   (Rézeau 1984: West)

or meanings which have been lost from standard French: in this case the phonological form remains in standard French, but with a different meaning, for example:

(23)   *Regional French of the west*   *Standard French*
        affligé   'unwell, sick'   'afflicted, cursed with'
        chancre   'crab'   'canker'
        s'écarter   'to stray, get lost'   'to step back, move away'
        (Rézeau 1984)

   Finally, another category of lexical regionalism concerns innovations in a regional variety of French; that is, items which appear not to have been derived either from other varieties, or from the French of earlier periods. The following have all been given by the various authors cited as examples of innovation:

(24)   *Lyon*   *Standard French*
        allée   'front door and hall (of   'avenue, path'
                        a house)'
        tantôt   'afternoon'   'shortly'
        (Groupe des Atlas 1978)

                        Haute-Marne
        différent   'unpleasant'   'different'
        épier   'to hesitate'   'to watch closely, spy on'
        herbages   'weeds'   'pasture'
        assortir qqn   'to work at the same rate   'to match one colour with
                        as someone'   another'
        (Bourcelot, 1973)

(25)   *Regional French of:*
                        St-Etienne
        peinable   'tiresome, tedious'   pénible
        amiteux   'affectionate'   affectueux
        regretteux   'tricky'   délicat, difficile
        (Escoffier 1976)

Alsace
gréver   'to go on strike'   faire grève
(Groupe des Atlas 1978)

Dauphiné/Toulouse/West
trempe   'soaked'   trempé
arrête   'stopped'   arrêté
gonfle   'swollen'   gonflé
(Séguy 1951; Tuaillon 1983; Rézeau 1984)

Some features of the morphology and syntax of regional varieties of French

The numbers of morphological forms or syntactic constructions which diverge between standard French and regional varieties of French in the domains of morphology and syntax are usually quite small, although they may recur frequently in speech. Consider, for example, the case of gender marking of nouns. Although this is a single grammatical feature, a difference in the distribution of gender marking between standard French and a regional variety of French would be evident in almost every utterance. In the regional French of Picardy, for example, the definite article *le* is regularly used as the only form of the definite article with nouns, while in standard French there is an opposition between the masculine/feminine forms *le/la*. Or again, consider the order of unstressed object pronouns before verbs. In standard French, when two third-person object pronouns occur before a verb, the direct object always precedes the indirect object: *je le lui donne*. In the regional French of eastern France, the indirect object comes first: *je lui le donne* (Tuaillon 1983). Again, this is a single point of grammatical divergence between standard French and a regional variety, and yet it is likely to be a frequent feature of utterances.

The grammatical differences between standard French and regional varieties of French are usually attributable to two factors. Either grammatical patterns which exist(ed) in the regional dialect/language spoken in the area before the diffusion of French took place have at some point been transferred (unconsciously) into French by speakers of the regional dialect/language who became bilingual (speaking the regional dialect/language and French). Or they are the result of innovations in the regional variety of French itself: the generalisation of a grammatical pattern already existing in standard French to grammatical environments where that pattern is not found in standard French. In the former category one could cite cases like:

(26)   *Standard French*   *Regional variety*
        Je le veux   J'y veux
        J'ai vu personne   J'ai personne vu

Il est en train de travailler   Il est toujours après travailler
(Eastern France. Tuaillon 1983; Groupe des Atlas 1978)

Pour qu'il mange   Pour lui manger
(Northern France. Carton 1973)

Tu l'as vu, ton père?   Tu l'as vu, à ton père
Il prend une orange   Il se prend une orange
et il la mange   et il se la mange
(Languedoc. Séguy 1951)

And in the second category cases like:

(27)   Standard French expresses possession in two ways:
(a) Il s'est cassé la jambe.
(b) Il met son chapeau.
Construction (a) involving a reflexive pronoun and a definite article is restricted to parts of the body. Construction (b) is used in the case of all other possessed items. The regional French of the Languedoc has generalised construction (a) to all cases of possession:
(c) Il s'est perdu la montre. (Séguy 1951)

(28)   In subordinate clauses in standard French there are a set of contexts in which the indicative form of verbs is used, and a set of contexts in which the subjunctive form of verbs is used. To take just two examples:
(a) Elle croit qu'il vient.
(b) Il faut qu'il vienne.
The regional French of the north of France has generalised the indicative to all subordinate contexts:
(c) Il faut qu'il vient. (Carton 1973)

(29)   Standard French has three main ways of marking the link between a tensed verb and a following infinitive: *de, à* and *ø*:
(a) Elle a décidé de partir.
(b) Nous les encourageons à venir.
(c) Je crois ø préférer ø manger à sept heures.
The regional French spoken around the town of St-Etienne in eastern France has generalised the use of *de* to many cases which in standard French are marked by *à* or *ø*:
(d) Je croyais de partir.
(e) Si je savais de pouvoir le faire, je le ferais. (Escoffier 1976)

Degrees of 'regionality' in regional varieties of French

This is a good moment to point out that the notion 'regional variety of French' is something of an idealisation. In reality it is not possible to say that a particular variety of French is a 'regional variety of French' because it differs from standard French in x phonetic features, y lexical items, and z grammatical forms (where x, y, and z are specific quantities). Different speakers of French will display regional features to varying degrees. When one looks at particular regions, and the French speakers living there, as a whole, one finds a continuum of speech habits, ranging from speakers who have only features of standard French at one extreme, to speakers who have a high proportion of regionalisms at the other, to the extent that their particular variety (their idiolect) may in a sense be closer to the regional dialect that is/was spoken in the region than it is to standard French. In between these two extremes there will be a range of speakers displaying regional features in their French to a greater or lesser degree. Carton (1973), Carton et al. (1983) have illustrated this phenomenon well by setting side by side transcripts of the utterances of French speakers living in the Picardy region, in the north of France. The following three examples (adapted from Carton et al. 1983) are classed by Carton as *français régional*, *français dialectal*, and *patois*, and show different degrees of divergence from standard French:

Français régional (Mme J T, 74 ans, Flers)
I sont v'nus dîner l'jour de l'enterrement |j'ai du bouillon | j'avais lavé mes pommes de terre | la fille à Catherine [standard French: *la fille de Catherine*] elle était là aussi | vlà que j'dis | j'vais pas en avoir assez | bin non | i-z-ont pluqué [standard French: *manger très peu*] tu sais | i n'avaient pas faim.

Français dialectal (Mme V N, 59 ans, Armentières)
Elle a v'nu s'semain' passée | et alors euh | bin tombé qu' j'avos fait m'vaisselle | et ch'fais tout l'temps in p'tit cop d'vassinque après qu' j'ai fini m'vaisselle hein | Elle rinte | j'avos pos acor eu l'temps de f'faire.

(St. Fr.: Elle est venue la semaine dernière et alors heureusement que j'avais fini ma vaisselle! Et je fais toujours un petit coup de wassingue ['floor cloth'] après avoir fini ma vaisselle, hein. Elle rentre je n'avais pas encore eu le temps de le faire.)

Patois (Mme M B, 81 ans, Aubers-en-Weppes)
Avant quatorsse | eh bé ch'tot cor pus pir qu'achteur | in parlot politique | y-allot fort | eh bé | Emile i dit | y-a qu'az élections | i dit | qu'in est libe | et pis y-a c'minchi à canteuer | voter cont' el gouvernemint.

(St. Fr.: Avant 1914, eh bien, c'était encore pis que maintenant: quand on parlait politique, ça allait fort oh là là! Emile dit 'Il n'y a qu'aux élections qu'on est libre!' Et puis il a commencé à chanter 'Voter contre le gouvernement'.)

What determines whether one speaker of French uses more regionalisms than another is generally a combination of the factors: age, level of education, whether the speaker lives in an urban or rural environment, and the context in which the speaker is speaking. An older speaker (60+), who left school at the minimum leaving age, living in the country and talking informally with relatives or friends is likely to display a large number of regionalisms. The regional features of such a speaker would decrease, however, were he or she to be talking in a more formal setting, say in contact with strangers, in dealings with representatives of commercial and state organisations, and so on. Older speakers living in towns tend to display fewer regionalisms in their speech than those living in the country, as do older speakers generally who had the opportunity of continuing their education beyond the minimum school-leaving age. Younger speakers on the whole display far fewer regional-isms in their French than older speakers, and particularly if they live in towns and have continued in education beyond the minimum leaving age.

To illustrate the point in a concrete way, consider a study undertaken by Rindler-Schjerve (1985) on the regional French of Alsace. Rindler-Schjerve was interested in determining the extent to which the use of Alsatian regionalisms can be correlated with age and with level of education of the speaker. To examine this question, she looked at the use of regionalisms by eighty French speakers in the town of Schilti-gheim. For our purposes, we shall consider her results for only three of the regionalisms which she investigated, and which are illustrated below:

(30)   a. Devine quoi je vais lui offrir.
            (St. Fr.: Devine ce que je vais lui offrir.)
        b. Nous cessons de travailler jusqu'à ce qu'il va revenir.
            (St. Fr.: Nous cessons de travailler jusqu'à ce qu'il revienne.)
        c. J'achète tout ce que j'ai besoin.
            (St. Fr.: J'achète tout ce dont j'ai besoin.)

On the basis of two tasks – a close (gap-filling) task, and an oral translation into French from a text written in Alsatian dialect – Rindler-Schjerve found that the percentage of use of the three regionalisms in

Table 3.1 *Use of regionalisms (%) in the French of Alsace by younger and older speakers*

Age	14–34 %	70–85 %
Regionalism		
(30a)	0	36.8
(30b)	10.5	68.4
(30c)	26.3	84.2

(30) was greater for the older speakers in her study than for the younger speakers (table 3.1), and greater overall for those speakers who had left school at the minimum leaving age than for those speakers who had continued study up to the level of the *baccalauréat* (table 3.2). Here we see that in Alsace the French of younger, late school-leavers is likely to be more 'standard-like' than the French of older, early school-leavers.

Table 3.2 *Use of regionalisms (%) in the French of Alsace by speakers who left school at the minimum leaving age and speakers who continued study to the baccalauréat*

Level of education	Baccalauréat %	Minimum %
Regionalism		
(30a)	6.3	33.3
(30b)	18.8	73.3
(30c)	25.0	80.0

(Adapted from Rindler-Schjerve 1985.)

Attitudes to regional variation

Unfavourable attitudes to variation

There is a myth that the 'best', the 'purest' French is spoken by those living in Tours and its surrounding region (Touraine). The myth goes back at least to the sixteenth century, and is still widely expressed both within and outside France. It is unfounded for two reasons. Firstly, the very idea that there are 'better' and 'less good' varieties of language is a nonsense. Varieties of language simply diverge. Where one dialect has linguistic feature x, another dialect will have linguistic feature y; but there is nothing inherently 'better' about feature x than feature y. When people describe one dialect as 'better' than another, what has happened is that they have taken a social value judgement about the dialect – the social standing of the group using that dialect – and transferred that value judgement (in a presumably unconscious way) onto linguistic form: 'if a dialect is spoken by a prestigious social group within the community, then that dialect must be superior to other dialects'.

Why Touraine should have been singled out for such social acclaim is probably the result of several factors. Gueunier et al. (1978: 167–73), in an attempt to explain the origins of the myth, ascribe it to the following: the fact that in the fifteenth and sixteenth centuries the royal court spent long periods of residence in the châteaux of the Loire; that the Loire valley has traditionally been a region frequented by foreign students learning French, with the result that it has gained a favourable reputation abroad in linguistic matters; and that the prestige of the region's architecture (e.g. the châteaux) and cultural life (with culturally active university towns like Orléans, Tours and Angers) has promoted linguistic prestige.

The second reason why the myth is a nonsense is that even on the level of social value judgements it is no longer the case, if it ever were the case, that Touraine is *the* place in France where the socially prestigious sections of the community live. Perhaps in the fifteenth and sixteenth centuries, when the kings of France spent long periods in the region this was temporarily true, but the real centre of prestige in France from the Middle Ages up to the twentieth century has been Paris and the Ile-de-France; although this pattern has been changing in the twentieth century as the result of universal education, rapid and easy communications, increased social mobility, and a general climate of decentralisation of social activity. The linguistic consequence of this has been that the most prestigious dialect – standard French – is now no longer geographically localisable, but is spoken throughout the hexagon.

The actual linguistic situation in Touraine is very much like it is in any other region of France where there is a large centre of population, and surrounding rural communities. In the city of Tours itself there are speakers of standard French. These are largely middle-class speakers, usually educated to the baccalauréat and beyond. Working-class speakers in Tours, particularly older working-class speakers who left school at the minimum leaving age, are likely to display Touraine regionalisms in their French: features like the pronunciation of *moi* as [mwɛj], of *combien* as [kõbẽ], and the use of an alveolar /r/ (*r roulé*), rather than a uvular /r/ (*r grasseyé*) (Carton et al. 1983: 37–40). And as one leaves the city and goes out into the surrounding rural communities, Touraine regionalisms are likely to be more common. In fact, just the situation to be found in any region of France. Where Touraine is perhaps different from some other regions is in being close to Paris, so that historically the diffusion of French from the Ile-de-France affected Tours earlier than it did other regions.

Whatever the origins of the Touraine myth, it is a revealing instance of the way that linguistic variation is assigned a social value by members of a speech community. While there is no objective linguistic basis to the view that one dialect is 'better' than another, if enough people believe that it is better this can and does lead to the promotion and diffusion of the 'better' dialect, and the contraction and disappearance of the 'less good' dialect. The attitudes of speakers in a speech community play an important role in determining the way that linguistic varieties evolve in that community.

One of the consequences of the rise in prestige of one particular dialect over others in the community, from the social-psychological perspective, is that people come to regard it as a linguistic yardstick, against which other dialects are then measured (mostly adversely):

> . . . the standard is often not called a dialect at all, but is regarded as the language itself. One consequence is that all other varieties become related to that standard in some way, and may be regarded as dialects of that standard. (Wardhaugh 1986: 36)

Dialects other than the standard cease to be perceived as merely different and are felt to be 'corrupt' versions of the standard, the result of the 'ignorance', the 'stupidity' or whatever of those who speak the non-standard dialects.

One might imagine that this perception is one-sided, being the view of speakers of the standard about those who do not happen to share the same speech habits. In fact, it is a perception often shared by non-standard speakers themselves, that the standard dialect is the 'natural' form of language, and that their own dialect is a deformed version of the standard:

> Le parler régional ou local . . . fait figure de sous-catégorie incorrecte, déformée, sans intérêt. 'On l'dit mais on sait bien qu'ça n'est pas comme ça . . . Le *vrai mot* c'est le mot français et il n'en existe qu'un . . . Il n'y a aucun doute, *sureau* ['elder tree'], *noisetier* ['hazel tree'] sont les *vrais noms: sui* . . . et *coeur* . . . font partie du langage de celui qui *parle mal*. Et ce langage c'est du *français à coups de trique*, du *français à coups de pioche*, ou encore du *français ferlapé*, c'est-à-dire grossièrement 'avale'. (Chaurand 1968: 10)

The differential perceptions of the status of the standard and non-standard varieties is nowhere more clearly reflected than in the way people talk about pronunciation. Speakers of standard French with a standard pronunciation are not said to have a 'standard accent', but to have 'no accent': 'She speaks French with no accent'; 'He comes from the south of France but he has lost his accent'; etc. Conversely, people who do not have a standard pronunciation are said to 'have an accent', which is often then described in derogatory terms:

> 'Les gens du Midi, ils ont un accent impossible.'
> 'Le bourguignon est un accent rocailleux, paysan.'
> 'Des personnalités politiques qui parlent à la télévision, ça me gêne si elles roulent les r et si elles ont un accent du terroir, ça me gêne.'
> (Comments by informants recorded in a study by Gueunier et al. 1978: 103–5)

Objectively this is nonsense, just as the myth that the 'best' French is spoken in Touraine is nonsense. All speakers of whatever variety of language 'have an accent'. 'Accent' is simply the production of a certain set of speech sounds. When people talk about a particular variety of language as having 'no accent', they have unconsciously converted their perception of the social prestige of the variety in question into the belief that that variety is a 'natural' form of speech, and that others are not.

Labov (1972) has suggested that, in terms of speaker perceptions about linguistic variation, there are three kinds of divergence. There are indicators, which are objective differences between the speech habits of a speaker A and another speaker B, but which appear to play little or no role in the perception that these two varieties are different. Often people are not even aware that there is a divergence. For example, standard French has no vowel-length distinction, but in the regional French of Normandy pairs of words like *chanté/chantée*, *joli/jolis* are distinguished by vowel length:

(31)   a. [ʃɑ̃te]   [ʃɑ̃te:]
        b. [ʒɔli]   [ʒɔli:]   (Lepelley 1975)

This objective difference between standard and regional French appears to have low perceptual salience, and speakers who produce long and short vowels are often surprised to find that they do (Lepelley 1975: 10).

There are also markers, which are linguistic differences between speakers with apparently higher perceptual salience than indicators, and which allow people to determine a speaker's social or regional origin. For example, a speaker producing [h] in words like *dehors* and *là-haut* might easily be determined as coming from the north-east or north-west of France on the basis of this feature; or a speaker producing final consonants in words like *gens* [ʒɑ̃s] and *estomac* [ɛstomak], might give away southern origins on the basis of this feature.

A third kind of perceived difference between varieties, which in truth is not always easy to distinguish from a marker, involves a divergent feature which has come to be associated so frequently with a particular group of speakers that it has become a stereotype:

> [a stereotype] is a popular and, therefore, conscious characterisation of the speech of a particular group: New York *boid* for *bird* or *Toitytoid Street* for 33rd Street; Texas 'drawling' or *Howdy Pardner*. (Wardhaugh 1986: 137)

Three examples of stereotypical characteristics of the regional French of France are: alveolar /r/, which is associated with 'general rurality'; denasalisation of standard French nasal vowels, together with the addition of a following nasal consonant, associated with southern French; and a generalised use of /ə/ in contexts where standard French deletes /ə/, also associated with southern French.

Stereotypes, because of their high perceptual salience, tend to be features which are liable to change in the speech community. Where a stereotypical feature of a non-prestigious dialect is concerned, people will tend to eradicate that feature from their speech precisely because they are aware of its stigmatised status (for example, recall the tendency noted by Séguy (1951) in connection with /ə/ for speakers of the regional French of Toulouse to eliminate this feature when they are affecting to *parler pointu*). Where a stereotypical feature of a prestigious dialect is concerned, that feature will be imitated by speakers of other dialects.

Favourable attitudes to variation

> There has traditionally been some antipathy between the Northerner, who is supposed to be cold and industrious, and the Southerner, who is pictured as warm and spontaneous. (Jochnowitz 1973: 19)

While perceptions of the standard dialect are almost always favourable, attitudes to non-standard varieties of language need not always be unfavourable. It is true that until quite recently the prevailing attitude towards non-standard varieties within France was generally unfavourable. The passages cited so far in this section would support this view. In the last thirty years or so, however, there has been something of a shift in attitude on the part of many speakers living in the regions to a greater tolerance of local divergence from the standard, and even, in some quarters, the promotion of linguistic variation as a symbol of individuality in an increasingly standardised world. While standard French continues to be regarded as the prestigious dialect, the language used for all matters of socio-economic importance, a significant 'solidarity factor' has entered perceptions of local varieties of speech, which are now seen as representative of positive values to do with interpersonal relationships: values like 'friendliness', 'helpfulness', 'relaxation'. A study by Paltridge and Giles (1984) examined the attitudes of 244 native speakers of French to standard French speech recorded with the following four accents: Parisian (standard), Provençal, Breton, Alsatian. By asking their subjects to rate the accents along a number of affective dimensions they found that while their subjects rated the Parisian accent highest on characteristics like 'hard-working', 'trustworthy', 'serious', 'ambitious', on characteristics like 'hospitability', 'obligingness', 'likeability' and 'sociability' subjects rated the Provençal and Breton accents as highly as the Parisian accent (although not the Alsatian accent, which Paltridge and Giles suggest may be the result of its Germanic connections).

Indeed, the view within France that northerners are hardworking, but reserved, while southerners are open, and yet may not always rush to get things done, can probably be traced precisely to this divergence in perception of the standard and non-standard varieties of language.

The 'solidarity factor' associated with non-standard varieties appears to have been increasing in strength in France in recent decades, to the point where the tendency to convergence by the regional varieties of French on standard French has slowed down. And in some cases there is even a tendency towards *divergence*. That is, some speakers of regional varieties of French may actually emphasise those features of their speech styles which differ from standard French.

A classic example of this phenomenon in an English-speaking community is provided by Labov (1972). Labov investigated the speech habits of the inhabitants of an island called Martha's Vineyard, off the coast of Massachusetts, which becomes a resort for mainland New England holidaymakers during the summer. Labov looked in particular at the pronunciation by inhabitants of words like *right* and *house*. In mainland New England English the vowels in these words are pronounced [aɪ] and [aʊ]. What Labov found was that among the permanent inhabitants of Martha's Vineyard there was a tendency to centralise the first vowel in the diphthong to [ə]: [əɪ] and [əʊ], and that this tendency had been increasing since the 1930s. Labov's explanation was that residents of the island who identified strongly with the island were exaggerating linguistic differences between themselves and the summer visitors:

> When a man says [rəɪt] or [həʊs], he is unconsciously establishing the fact that he belongs to the island: that he is one of the natives to whom the island really belongs. (Labov 1972: 36)

Similar instances have been reported in France. Bouvier (1973: 232) observes among young speakers in the Drôme region (Provence) what he calls 'une sorte de méridionalisation croissante', and he provides an example comparable to Labov's from Saint-Tropez:

> . . . des signes manifestes d'une situation nouvelle des parlers locaux apparaissent ici et là en Provence. Le plus éclatant est celui qu'on observe dans le *village* le plus célèbre de la Côte d'Azur, le plus envahi et le plus dénaturé, semble-t-il, par le tourisme: Saint-Tropez. L'enquête faite récemment dans cette commune par Madame Martel pour l'*Atlas Linguistique de Provence* a révélé que, contrairement à ce qu'on pouvait craindre, le parler local et aussi les coutumes locales y étaient encore très vivants, plus vivants même que dans d'autres localités de la côte au nom moins prestigieux. Il n'y a pas de doute qu'en se cramponnant à leur langue, à leurs particularités, leurs usages, les Tropéziens éprouvent le besoin de sauver leur identité que l'ouragan touristique de l'été risque de balayer. (Bouvier 1973: 232–3)

Carton (1973: 240) notes a similar trend in attitudes to local dialects in the north of France:

> [Aujourd'hui] les notables ou la moyenne bourgeoisie répètent volontiers que le patois n'est pas un français vulgaire, qu'il vient du latin, etc . . . Un enseignant me signale qu'il trouve actuellement des mots patois dans les copies de lycéens lillois et que ce fait est nouveau. Les réactions à l'égard des patois ont changé dans l'arrondissement de Lille au cours de ces dernières années, qui précisément ont vu s'accélérer le recul des anciens parlers locaux.

It seems that, in terms of the social-psychological perception of linguistic variation within France, a point has been reached where the benefits of knowing and using standard French are coming into conflict with a certain desire for a more local identity. What Wandruszka (1973: 112) describes as a 'real social need for diversity':

> Si, d'un côté, la tendance générale est incontestablement à l'uniformité toujours plus grande de nos langues, de l'autre nous constatons au contraire un foisonnement de diversifications socioculturelles toujours nouvelles, réaction dictée, semble-t-il, par un véritable besoin social de polymorphie.

Conclusion

> Il est vrai qu'une éducation grammaticale à la française rend le seuil d'acceptation des écarts linguistiques particulièrement bas. Depuis, la dialectologie m'a guéri.   (Tuaillon, 1983: 235)

Geographically determined linguistic variation in a speech community is the result of linguistic changes taking place at different rates in different regions. Over the last 2,000 years, the community living in the territory occupied by modern France has moved from a situation of relative linguistic unity (when a Romance dialect of the Roman Empire was spoken in Gaul) to a linguistically divergent situation in the Middle Ages, and back to a relatively unified linguistic situation in the twentieth century. From the seventeenth century until quite recently there has been strong pressure, both institutional (as Tuaillon suggests) and psychological (reflected in the attitudes of non-standard speakers to their own idiolects), for speech habits to converge on standard French. However, attitudes have been changing recently, and it appears that today people are generally more willing to accept regional linguistic variation than they used to be. It is perhaps ironic that this change in attitude occurs at a time when most of the non-French dialects of France have disappeared or are on the point of disappearing.

Text 1

Les français régionaux

Dire qu'en France on 'parle français' pourrait laisser penser qu'il s'agit d'un phénomène unitaire; or, en observant le 'français' que parlent les 55.3 millions d'habitants de la France métropolitaine on constate qu'il y a toute une gamme de variations linguistiques que recouvre le terme 'français'

Il y a bien sûr le **français standard**, la langue officielle de la France, la variété que l'on trouve décrite le plus souvent dans les grammaires et les dictionnaires; celle (sous sa forme écrite) que les petits Français apprennent à l'école; celle qu'on apprend comme français langue étrangère.

Mais le français standard n'est pas forcément la langue de tous les jours de tous les Français. Les Français habitant les régions autres que l'Ile-de-France (Paris et ses environs) peuvent parler 'avec un accent', peuvent se servir de mots, d'expressions, de constructions syntaxiques et morphologiques qui ne font pas partie du français standard. Pour la plupart les différences entre ces **français régionaux** et le français standard n'empêchent pas les gens de se comprendre: dans les deux cas on 'parle français'. Parfois, cependant, les différences sont si accusées qu'un Français 'parlant français' peut avoir des difficultés à comprendre son compatriote. Dans ce cas-là on est en droit de distinguer un **dialecte français**.

La division qui vient d'être établie entre français standard, français régional et dialecte français appelle certaines clarifications. On entend souvent dire que les variétés non-standard (les français régionaux et les dialectes) sont des variantes 'corrompues' ou 'dégradées' du standard. Cette vue ne s'appuie ni sur le plan historique ni sur le plan contemporain. Le français standard, les français régionaux et les dialectes français, en ce qui concerne leur statut linguistique, sont tout simplement des variétés de langue *différentes*. Mais, et il faut le reconnaître, il y a une importante différence dans leur **statut socio-culturel**. Le français standard est de beaucoup la plus prestigieuse des trois variétés de langue, et il jouit de ce prestige depuis plusieurs siècles. Les dialectes sont les moins prestigieux, les français régionaux occupent une place entre les deux.

En fait, le prestige du français standard (et l'avancement social dans la société française offert à celui qui le parle) a exercé une telle pression sur les autres variétés de langue à travers les siècles, et surtout au cours des cent dernières années, qu'il ne reste presque personne en France qui ne connaisse le français standard, et très peu de personnes qui se servent activement d'un dialecte. Cette pression a été tellement forte que même les français régionaux ont eu tendance à converger vers le français standard.

Depuis quelque temps, cependant, il y a des signes indiquant que cette convergence se ralentit. Il y a même, paraît-il, une tendance chez certains locuteurs dans certaines régions françaises d'*accentuer* les différences entre leur parler régional et le français standard, pour se démarquer et pour faire preuve de leur régionalité. Dans un monde qui devient de plus en plus conforme il semble qu'on commerce à ressentir un véritable besoin de diversité.

(R. Hawkins, Text written for this volume).

Text 2

La perception des variétés de langue

La géographie d'abord

Il ne faut pas se lasser d'insister sur cette place primordiale qu'on doit accorder à la géographie linguistique dans notre pays car, aux premiers mots qu'il prononce, on reconnaît un habitant de Toulouse ou de Strasbourg par rapport à un habitant de Paris, sans pouvoir toujours identifier le milieu social auquel il appartient. Un grand banquier parisien parle et surtout prononce différemment de son confrère toulousain ou alsacien, alors que la prononciation de chacun d'entre eux ressemble beaucoup à celle de son employé le plus modeste, originaire de la même région que lui.

Rappelons-nous que la fragmentation dialectale du latin sur notre territoire a précédé la généralisation du français et que son empreinte dure depuis des siècles: l'existence de ce long passé permet de comprendre pourquoi c'est dans le cadre géographique qu'il faut tout d'abord envisager la variété des usages de cette langue.

Les différences que l'on constate sur le plan de l'âge, du milieu social, du niveau de scolarisation ou de la situation de communication apparaissent toujours comme un renforcement ou une atténuation des caractéristiques d'abord bien identifiées sur le plan régional.

Remettre Paris à sa juste place

Décrire le français dans sa diversité contemporaine, c'est donc tout d'abord tenir compte du facteur géographique, mais c'est aussi prendre conscience – malgré qu'on en ait – du rôle joué par la langue qui se parle à Paris, là où se concentrent la plupart des activités économiques, politiques et culturelles du pays tout entier. Qu'ils habitent Paris ou la province, qu'ils soient ouvriers ou paysans, techniciens, intellectuels ou artistes, et qu'ils le veuillent ou non, tous nos contemporains subissent l'influence de la capitale.

Le phénomène est ancien. On a déjà vu comment, depuis le xe siècle, avec l'élection d'Hugues Capet comme roi de France en 987 – il y a tout juste mille ans – Paris n'a cessé de prendre de l'importance, sur le plan politique, bien sûr, mais aussi sur le plan de la langue. Aujourd'hui encore, Paris est plus que jamais le lieu de rencontre privilégié où communiquent, en français, des gens venus des six coins de l'Hexagone et des quatre coins du monde, chacun avec ses particularités régionales: c'est dans cette espèce de creuset que cohabitent divers usages du français, en se mêlant et en s'influençant réciproquement.

Il résulte de tous ces contacts que, pour la langue française, le plus juste représentant des usages dynamiques n'est ni le provincial resté dans son terroir, ni le Parisien d'origine, lui-même marqué par sa 'province', mais cet être hybride qu'est le 'Parisien d'adoption', qu'un linguiste a appelé sans crainte du paradoxe le 'Parisien de province'. Ce Parisien type finit par parler une langue difficile à identifier sur le plan régional, au point que l'on peut considérer son usage du français comme 'moyen': né de l'amalgame des différents apports venus de partout dans le creuset parisien, il est à la fois tout Paris et toute la province.

Au grand regret de beaucoup d'entre nous, cette situation, qui arrondit les angles et gomme les différences, risque bien entendu d'aboutir, à plus ou moins longue échéance, à une sorte d'uniformisation insipide de tout ce qui faisait encore naguère la spécificité piquante de chacune des provinces de langue française. Néanmoins, et malgré les effets de 'rouleau compresseur' des médias, qui répercutent et amplifient avec constance le parler du Parisien type, nous n'en sommes pas encore là.

Cette diversité se révèle tout d'abord dans le choix des mots.

(From Walter 1988).

4

The other languages of France: towards a multilingual policy

F. LAROUSSI and J.-B. MARCELLESI

The apparent linguistic unity of France hides a rather different reality of considerable linguistic diversity. Among the countries of Western Europe, France has the most varied linguistic profile. Yet it becomes quickly apparent, when one attempts to define in detail the historical stages involved in the process of the spreading of the French language, that linguistic variety in France has often not been recognised for what it is, a truly multilingual situation. Neither the linguistic conflicts resulting from this situation, nor the political implications of these conflicts, have been adequately dealt with. The ideology of French as a national language developed in conditions which repressed the regional languages which are still spoken in France. But, in spite of this desire to promote French as the one and only language of France, the goal of a monolingual situation has not been achieved. The problem of those languages often described as regional is still an issue today, as is shown by the recent publication of two studies on the question, one by Vermes and Boutet (1987) and one by Vermes (ed.1988), both in two volumes, which refer also to the presence of languages of migrant peoples. The question of the 'other' languages of France is not only of interest to speakers of 'indigenous' French languages. It is also of direct relevance to young people from immigrant backgrounds, who often find themselves in very complex linguistic and sociocultural situations, to teachers faced with cultural and linguistic diversity among their pupils, and finally to all those working in the social services, who regularly have to cope with situations involving linguistic diversity. Hence, alongside the problems of 'regional' languages, languages of migrant peoples will also be discussed, since politicians in France are currently asking whether – and how – to bring about the integration of immigrants into French life and culture.

Situation

Multilingual origins: the indigenous languages

The indigenous languages of France are usually defined as those which were already spoken during the Middle Ages in more or less the same areas as today. Standard French and other northern French dialects, such as Picard, are excluded from this definition. Any choice of label implies a certain point of view. Thus, Basque, Breton, Catalan, Corsican, Occitan, Alsatian and Flemish are generally referred to as 'regional' (or 'minority' or 'lesser') languages. We shall go through the 'regional' languages, but without making any mention of the linguistic situation of the *départements d'Outre-Mer* and the *territoires d'Outre-Mer*. Drawing on our own work (see Madray and Marcellesi 1981; Marcellesi 1985, 1986 and 1989 and Guespin and Marcellesi 1986) and that of Vermes (ed. 1988), we shall attempt to give some figures for these languages as they are spoken in metropolitan France. A virtual conspiracy of silence about France's multilingual origins means that figures concerning the use of regional languages are either inadequate or even completely non-existent. The current census does not ask questions about languages spoken any more than its predecessors did. P. Denetz (1988: 106, 107), writing about Breton, says

> l'affirmation, par la République, de son unité linguistique idéologique, s'accordait mal avec un décompte régulier des citoyens non conformes au modèle. On est donc réduit, en ce qui concerne la pratique du breton, à des conjectures, des évaluations qui, bien souvent, sont la projection, parfois non consciente, sur la réalité, du choix culturel du descripteur.

These remarks are doubtless applicable not only to Breton but to the other regional languages as well. A second factor which makes it difficult to quote precise figures is the problem of deciding what level of proficiency makes someone a 'speaker' of a language, whether passive knowledge is sufficient, and so on. Almost all of the contributors to *Vingt-cinq communautés linguistiques de la France* emphasise the approximate nature of the figures. These figures nevertheless allow us to perceive certain trends.

Apart from the penury of figures, there are some other general points which apply to the regional languages. Firstly, because of attempts to suppress them, and banish them from 'high register' usage where a standard would have emerged, these languages are often fragmented into a number of dialects, which sometimes put forward rival claims as to the standard, or orthography, that should be used. This is a phenomenon held against the regional languages by those who have no wish to promote their diffusion.

Secondly, while the survival of a language is sometimes said to depend on its having a nucleus of monolingual speakers, this is hard to ascertain – and certainly increasingly rare for the regional languages of France. Essentially, each of the languages – in its own different way – coexists with French in a state of diglossia. While there are some differences, there are also trends in the use of regional languages that are common to a number of them, such as their greater use by the older generation, rural communities and men (for conflicting evidence on the latter see Hadjadj and Maurard in Tabouret-Keller 1981). Where there has been a revival of the language among the young, mainly urban, population, the question arises as to whether this is enough to reverse the failures of the language, and, if not, whether you can have a cultural revival which does not depend on a linguistic one.

The perception by the state and other French speakers, has not been the same for each language. Some groups have been more vociferous than others at certain points in the recent past; whether or not greater militancy has led to more action has depended on a number of other factors, for example, whether the language demands were seen to be linked to demands for political autonomy. The groups' self-perceptions will also vary, for example, with respect to speakers of the same language in another country. For speakers of Catalan, for instance, given the weight of numbers on the Spanish side, there has been little choice but to adopt the standards proposed there, particularly since the liberalisation of attitudes by the Spanish government. Speakers of Alsatian, on the other hand, have sometimes, for historical reasons, preferred not to stress their links with Germany. Indeed, the Loi Deixonne, to which we shall refer later, was restricted to those languages which existed only or almost only on French soil (Breton, Occitan) and to those which were prohibited in Franco's Spain (Basque and Catalan), but not to those which were considered to be the language of a foreign power, e.g. Flemish (see Giacomo 1975).

Basque
>Agur bero bat
>'Avec mes meilleurs sentiments'

Split unevenly over both sides of the western part of the border between France and Spain, with a small area in France and a much larger area in Spain, Basque or 'l'Euskara' appears to be an isolated pocket in Western Europe. The language does not belong to the Indo-European family (which links all other 'autochthonous' languages in France), but to the 'Euskaro-Caucasian' family. One theory suggests links between Basque and certain Caucasian languages, although it has yet to convince a good many specialists.

Although the figures are extremely hard to find, specialists estimate that the use of Basque is in decline, even in areas most resistant to this trend (Haritschelhar 1988: 92). According to Haritschelhar, nobody is in a position to say how many bascophones there are on the French side of the border, although he suggests a tentative figure of some 80,000 speakers. Thus, 'l'Euskara' remains a daily language of communication for a good many speakers, perhaps partly due to the 'ikastola', schools founded to promote Basque language and culture, in 1969 at the pre-school level, 1975 for primary and 1980 at the secondary level. At university level, it is possible to study Basque in Bayonne, Pau and Toulouse, and there is a Chair of Basque in Bordeaux. Notwithstanding all this, it is schooling in French that has largely accelerated the process of *débasquisation*.

Breton

> Me blijfe din e teufe ma bugabe da zeskin brezhoneg
> 'J'aimerais que mes enfants apprennent le breton'

According to an estimate made by P. Denetz (1988: 107), there are between 500,000 and 700,000 Breton speakers. The first of these two figures is generally used by *Radio Bretagne Ouest*, following audience surveys conducted in 1985. As with all minority communities, the increasing control of the state in all aspects of their everyday lives has subjected the Breton community to a process of linguistic and cultural assimilation into the mainstream of French society. Although the number of Breton speakers is 'in steady decline' according to Denetz (1988: 132), the importance of Breton culture is widely recognised in the life of the region, and 'l'affirmation de la bretonnité est aujourd'hui générale'. As with Basque, nursery schools have been set up in which Breton is the medium of instruction (*les divans*, from 1977 on). At the other end of the educational cycle, it is possible to train to become a qualified teacher of Breton (by doing a 'CAPES de breton'). Efforts to agree on a common orthography for Breton were for some time hampered by the existence of two distinct dialects, one in the south (*le vannetais*) and the other spoken in the north and west, although a compromise has now been reached, and activist *bretonnant* movements use a form which is accessible to both sets of dialect speakers.

Catalan

> Els meus avis parlaven català entre ells pero a mi em francès. En vaig tenir un sentiment d'injusticia.
> 'Mes grands-parents parlaient entre eux catalan mais à moi en français. J'ai eu un sentiment d'injustice.'

Catalan is a Romance language which exists in France and in Spain, where it is the official language along with Spanish (Castilian) in most of Catalonia. The Catalan area, with a small part in France and a larger part in Spain, covers approximately 60,000 square km, with a total population of nearly ten million inhabitants, according to Bernardo (1988: 133), of whom only a portion are Catalan speakers. Furthermore, the rather patchily organised resistance to assimilation seems to be merely passive and the peripheral nature of French Catalonia means that the most one can assume is that the process of substitution, whereby the dominant language totally replaces the minority language, is being slowed down. At the same time, Bernardo reports a stable bilingualism in both town and country. He estimates that there are approximately 185,000 Catalan speakers in France.

Corsican

> So corsu è ni so fieru.
> 'Je suis corse et j'en suis fier.'

Corsican is one of the 'new' Romance languages. Its recognition only came recently (after a complex series of events), and is linked to a more general trend. On a linguistic level there is no doubt that it forms part of the Italic group. The form of Latin used on the island was subsequently affected by the regular use of specific local phrases and borrowings from other language systems, particularly from the Italian Peninsula and Sardinia. Corsica lived for more than five hundred years with Corsican–Tuscan diglossia, Corsican being used by the whole of the population as their everyday language and Tuscan being used for writing. This diglossia was replaced by the Corsican–French combination imposed by the French Government. Demands for recognition of the Corsican language go back approximately one hundred years and state recognition of the language, as a subject to be taught even if not as a medium of instruction, dates from 1974. In 1983 the *Conseil Régional* voted in favour of bilingualism in Corsica, but the government of Mauroy reversed this decision. A Corsican CAPES has been created, which is unusual in that it states of the dialects that 'aucune variété ne sera privilégiée'. It is difficult to estimate the number of Corsican speakers. Without doubt more than half of the population of the island itself (which has 240,000 inhabitants) speak Corsican, and to this number must be added as many again living away from the island. Of all the languages other than French which are used in France, Corsican, together with Alsatian, is doubtless the one which most strongly resists the process of 'substitution', whereby an attempt is made to replace bilingualism with French monolingualism. Corsican is taught in many *collèges* and *lycées* on the island as well as at Corte University, where it is taught up to DEA level (i.e. the *Diplôme d'Etudes Approfondies*, a post-graduate diploma taken before completing a PhD). In contrast, the problem is less straightforward in primary schools, bearing in mind the current system, which pays little attention to linguistic diversity. State radio (*Radio Corsa Frequenza Mora*) and television (FR3) broadcast some news and other programmes in Corsican. The former gives an annual prize for the best short story in Corsican; indeed there has recently been a wealth of creative and artistic activity, as in the novels of Rinatu Coti, for example, the poets Thiers or Geronimi, and the *Teatru Masonu*. Since the publication of a brochure entitled 'Pour une politique démocratique de la langue' (Marcellesi 1985), the issue of getting Corsican accepted as a second official language alongside French has taken priority over the issue of bilingual education.

Occitan

> Aviai vergonha de mon accent solament saviai pas que d'effieit prononciavi tot simplament lo francès ambe l'accent d'una autra lengo.
> 'J'avais honte de mon accent mais j'ignorais qu'en fait je prononçais tout simplement le français avec l'accent d'une autre langue.'

For a long time Occitan was the vehicle for a richer literature than that of the *langue d'oil* (northern French). The latter prevailed because of its status as the national language of the state. This did not prevent a resurgence in the use of the *langue d'oc* (southern French) during the nineteenth century, particularly in the writings of Mistral. the 'Occitan' area covers thirty-one departments in France, and extends into Andorra and Italy.

Any attempt to estimate the number of speakers of Occitan clearly illustrates the difficulty of making an accurate assessment of the real use of a regional language. Sauzet (1988: 215) cites previous researchers who all estimated the Occitan-speaking population as numbering between ten and twelve million, such as Anglade and Tesnière in the 1920s and Ronjat in the 1940s. Bec (1973) writes:

> on peut fixer à une douzaine de millions les gens qui, s'ils ne parlent pas coutumièrement la langue d'oc, en sont du moins assez imprégnés pour la comprendre aisément et la réapprendre dans un minimum de temps (Sauzet: 215).

However, taking into account the 'substitution' policy which resulted in *désoccitanisation* the same estimates cannot be advanced today. In the absence of any survey put forward, the question remains unanswered. Increasing demands regarding the future of Occitan have been provoked by factors such as its prestigious past and even its literary use today, its numerous admirers and the possibility of studying it while attending a *lycée* and at the universities of Toulouse and Montpellier though as yet there is no CAPES (Gardy 1985: 60–3). However, these factors do not prevent either the language from being infiltrated by French, or the considerable decline in its spontaneous use on a daily basis. There are those who even believe that, apart from a few exceptional cases, there are now no more than a few small 'pockets' of Occitan to be found. As is pertinently shown by Robert Lafont in his various works, many believe that the policies of the French government in this area have led to the destruction of an entire culture. Other researchers make the point that Occitan 'n'existe que par rapport au français' and analyse this specific type of diglossia (Gardy and Lafont 1981, and see text 2 below).

Occitan is usually divided into three main dialect groups (Nord, Sud, Gascon). Within southern Occitan, there are differences between 'Langdocien' and 'Provençal'. While the latter was the variant promoted by Mistral and the 'Félibrige' in the nineteenth century, it is the variant of the Languedoc that has been the object of more militant promotion – and of linguistic research – in recent years.

Flemish

> M'hen egaen in heberge en't waren daer vele joens.
> 'Dans un cafe il y a beaucoup d'enfants.'

The Flemish spoken in north-eastern France is a Germanic language, close to Dutch and, like Dutch, linguistically derived from 'Low-German'. It is recognised by its speakers as a variety of Belgian Flemish, which is the official language of the Flemish-speaking part of Belgium. For various reasons, both historical and geographical, the regional identity of the Flemish-speaking community is still the least recognised in France. In fact, whether on a geographical, historical or even demographic level, the terms used about it are surrounded by an ideological vagueness. There is no unanimous agreement regarding the limits of 'Flanders' in France, and the Flemish language is currently only spoken in the part of the *département du Nord* which corresponds roughly to the administrative area of Dunkerque. This comprises at present some 380,000 inhabitants (Sansen 1988: 183), according to the 1982 census. (One assumes that a small portion of these people must be able to speak and understand Flemish.) According to Sansen (p. 184), since no data has been made available more recently, the two studies made in 1970 and 1975 by two students from Brussels are all we have to go on. It emerges that, in the Flemish-speaking part of France, 60 per cent of the population is monolingual in French, 29 per cent have only a passive knowledge of Flemish and 11 per cent are truly bilingual. Of course, these results vary according to the age of the population group being sampled.

Alsatian
> Do wird oi elsassisch gredd.
> 'Ici on parle alsacien.'

The name 'Alsatian' is being used increasingly, since it usefully emphasises the shared destiny of different Germanic languages (Alemannic in the south, Frankish in the north and in Lorraine).

The fate of 'Alsatian' is analogous to that of Corsican. For a long time considered as 'German', the languages spoken in Alsace and in German-speaking Lorraine were subjected between periods of *francisation* to the policy of *germanisation* (the tendency being to substitute German for the local language during the periods 1871 to 1920 and 1940 to 1944). These languages were recognised very late in education since post-1944 schools have fluctuated between teaching French alone, teaching French and German (with the latter based on the local variant forms), and the teaching of three languages. Everyday use of Alsatian still remains widespread, but the surveys conducted bring out the difficulties involved.

In their book *Le déclin du dialecte alsacien* (1989), Denis and Veltman refer to a survey conducted in 1979 by the INSEE (*Institut national de la statistique et des études économiques*) in Strasbourg. This was the first to have provided quantitative results concerning linguistic practices in Alsace. It shows that Alsatian remains an important language in the region, but that it is undergoing the same changes as the other languages of France: they are more often spoken at home than elsewhere, and less used in administration than in any other public domain. The agricultural environment is where they are preserved and their decline is principally due to the division of labour between men and women, the latter being mainly employed in the service sector, where the pressure to use French is strongest. By speaking French more often than Alsatian, Alsatian speakers ensure their upward social mobility insofar as this is dependent on their command of French. In all cases, examination of these various studies seems to point to a slow but steady decline in the languages of France.

Thus, plans for a monoglot country at the cost of eradicating minority languages have characterised the policies of the French government. Indeed, the absence of any questions concerning the use of regional languages in censuses (and this is true again for the census of March 1990) illustrates this policy of diminution. It is doubtless considered that, insofar as no minority language should rival French in terms of institutions, and educational institutions particularly, there is no point in giving them the beginnings of recognition and legitimacy by including them in the census.

'Non-territorial' languages: a new multilingualism

Based on information provided by Vermes (1988), it can be maintained that there are today in excess of fifteen languages used in France as a result of immigration, namely: languages used by the different peoples and ethnic groups of Africa south of the Sahara; Maghreb languages; Asiatic languages; Eastern European or Mediterranean languages; and lastly other Romance languages from within the EEC. Finally, to the group of 'non-territorial' languages must be added the presence in France of Yiddish (c.f. Weber 1987), Tzigane (Romany) and Creole. Extremely varied as they are, the presence of these languages helps make up the linguistic and cultural profile of France today. Since a specific example of the coexistence of French and the migrant languages is the subject of chapter 5, we shall limit ourselves here to a brief general overview.

The languages of Africa south of the Sahara

The settlement in France of African peoples from south of the Sahara is relatively recent, arriving as they did after the independence of the countries in question (around 1960) and mainly after 1970. The great majority of nationals in this category come from Western Africa (Mauritania, Mali, Senegal, Guinea, the Ivory Coast, Guinea-Bissau, Niger, Cameroon, etc.). In general, this is a heterogeneous population, comprising a multiplicity of ethnic groups, each one possessing its own language and culture. Among the most common of the African languages from south of the Sahara found in France are Wolof, Peul and Duala. According to estimates, this population currently numbers approximately 100,000 people, living mainly in and around Paris.

Arabic

The Arab community currently represents the main foreign community in France. Arabic is the official language of all Maghreb countries. According to the latest census taken by the Ministry of the Interior in 1982, there are approximately 1,550,050 people from Arab countries, of which 1,510,933 come from three countries: Algeria, Morocco and Tunisia (Jerab 1988: 35). The allegedly common language is the official language, that is the standard, literary Arabic, which is not the mother tongue in any of these countries. With the exception of Berber speakers (see below), 'dialectal' Arabic is spoken and used for everyday communication within each of the communities.

Studies which have touched on this issue describe the everyday experience of young Arabs descended from immigrants, who are torn in different directions. On the one hand, these young people are living in France in a non-Arab environment and generally have a knowledge of literary Arabic which is too superficial to allow them to carry on a conversation in their respective mother tongues. On the other hand, the literary Arabic they do learn is generally unknown to their parents, who only know 'dialectal' Arabic. In these communities then, the French language retains the function it served in Maghreb literature written in French during the colonial era. It is a language which they are obliged to adopt, since they cannot express themselves in their own language. For these reasons therefore, it is not in the least surprising to see these young Arabs move from switching between languages to the use of French alone. The crucial question remains: which language should be taught to these young people from immigrant backgrounds? It is not easy to answer. The position currently adopted therefore consists of offering two options. The first option would be training solely in literary Arabic, and in this case we know that such training does not take account of the linguistic reality and the diglossia involved, and therefore runs the risk of failing to achieve the desired objective. The second option would be to improvise training in the spoken language, which would be difficult to implement given the lack of a suitable or supportive infrastructure, even in the countries of origin, where the dominant ideology continues to ignore or even condemn the use of the 'vernacular' language.

Berber
This language was used in North Africa prior to Arabic. Most Berber speakers are found in Algeria and Morocco (20 per cent and 45 per cent respectively). Moreover, it is these two countries which supplied the majority of the Maghreb population in France. Numbering some 510,000 (an approximate figure from Chaker 1988: 150), Berber-speaking people represent one of the largest communities of foreign extraction, though its existence and its separate identity are rarely recognised by the French population. Generally confused with Maghreb immigrants, Berber speakers are perceived as part of the so-called 'Arab population' (Chaker 1988: 147). These people very often use Berber at home, and avoid or have no experience of Arabic except for religion. Finally, it should be noted that Berber is a language refused recognition in Maghreb countries and in France alike. It is doubtless as a result of this situation that Berber speakers seem to switch to French more quickly than do Arabic speakers.

Asiatic languages
'Chinese' (a term which covers a number of very different spoken languages) occupies a relatively important position in certain districts of large towns and cities. This is also true for the languages of what was formerly Indochina (Vietnam, Laos, Cambodia). The number of nationals

from these three countries can be estimated at 114,000. An estimated 28 per cent or 32,000 of these people are Vietnamese, most of whom speak Vietnamese, with the others speaking the minority languages of Vietnam (mainly Hmong). Today they are spread throughout French territory, the majority being found in the regions of Paris and Provence–Côte d'Azur.

Latin languages
Estimates set the number of Spaniards at more than 300,000 (of whom some are Catalan speakers), the number of Italians at 470,000 and the number of Portuguese at 900,000, according to Ministry of the Interior sources in 1982. In terms of numbers, this immigration is one of the largest. Immigration of EEC nationals is labelled 'sans problème', and is of interest here to neither the researchers nor the public authorities. Today, Spaniards, Italians and Portuguese seem to adapt quickly (which has not always been the case) and integrate easily as a result. However, the question of language arises in a different way: the languages of these three countries have an official place as languages on degree courses (particularly Spanish and Italian). The proximity of these countries allows return trips and justifies the study and upkeep of the language of origin. As in the case of Arabic, teachers are available for these languages (particularly for Portuguese). Use of these teachers is relatively more efficient here because the dialectal distinctions are not so great as those which exist between 'classical' and 'dialectal' Arabic.

Linguistic ideology and the 'regional' languages

We know that the *Ordonnance de Villers-Cotterêts* of 1539 served to eliminate from the legal and administrative systems the languages of France other then French (see chapter 1). This situation was reinforced in the seventeenth century by the increased use of French, which became dominant in science and philosophy, areas which had hitherto been the preserve of Latin. In 1789, the French Revolution systematically introduced the policy of linguistic unification which has been followed until today. Schooling has obviously played an important part in this process. Under the Third Republic, the state accelerated the spreading of the French language because it needed a large number of junior administrators of a certain educational and linguistic level who could occupy posts both at home and in the colonies. A central plank of French colonial policy was to 'civilise' other peoples by imposing French monolingualism on them. In practice, the provision of schooling in occupied countries meant the suppression of local languages and cultures (cf. Gordon 1978). In France itself, the education system was a major promoter of the idea that regional languages created a barrier to understanding French and had to be eradicated. By the use of the *signum* – an object forced on any pupil found using a language other than French for which they would be punished – the children's mother tongues were belittled and prohibited. The emphasis was on a literary and normative education, accessible only to an intellectual minority (see Vermes and Boutet 1987, Poche 1987, and *Repères* nos. 61, 67 and 72). Overall, the linguistic policy of France has been to follow a controlled course of ideological and educational repression in order to eradicate languages other than French. This is in contrast to the police-enforced repression used by other European governments (for example in Spain under Franco). It is now clear that the imposition of French as the language of the state, of 'prestige' and of renown, along with the repression of regional and minority languages, was possible thanks to a national consensus. This process continues today insofar as French is still the only language which enables *la promotion sociale*.

Because of this, and because it has been instrumental in spreading a national language based on a single, unchangeable norm which does not recognise variation, the school has been the focus of demands made by 'minority' groups. Thus it came to be acknowledged as desirable that regional and minority languages should be given due recognition. In this spirit, the *loi Deixonne* (passed on 11 January 1951 – see chapter 5) concerning the teaching of certain regional languages is one of the very few governmental concessions made thus far. The laws promised in 1981 did not really get off the ground. Regional languages are apportioned a few teaching hours in derisory conditions and with no concerted policy which would allow those involved to preside over the fate of their own languages and cultures. Nevertheless, the *loi Deixonne* has one advantage at least: it represents a stage in the history of the dominant ideology and its educational policy. As Gardin (1975: 36) puts it, 'elle manifeste la faillite du jacobinisme linguistique'.

Separate consideration of the regional languages should not obscure the fact that 'French' itself is not a simple or uncomplex notion. Account should really also be taken of 'picard', 'normand' and 'gallo', which are all languages with a long history and literature, and still in use today. In addition, there are the 'accents' of those who speak southern French, and the sociolects of particular social classes (see chapters 2, 3, 6). It is for the speakers of these variants in particular that we must question a norm which is necessary in a functional sense, but disastrous when it is used in a reductive, and discriminatory way. Contrary to what is still widespread belief, making people feel guilty about the languages they speak, and destroying them, in an attempt to promote a single language, does not make for progress. It is the existence of a *common* language that is a necessary condition, but this need not mean the devaluing or wiping out of other languages.

Linguistic policy and the Giordan report

Let us now look at linguistic policy in recent years. As we have seen, of all the countries in Western Europe, France has one of the most heterogeneous linguistic profiles. More than half of metropolitan France is made up of linguistic areas which originally used languages other than French. However, in contrast to this reality of multiple languages, state policy has never moved towards the recognition or legitimatisation of linguistic and cultural differences.

Many of the studies concerned with the birth and the propagation of the French language have concluded that there is a necessary connection between the building of a national language and linguistic exclusivity, which has made of French not only a common language but also the only language. Indeed, there is nothing surprising in the fact that this coercive policy with regard to linguistic differences was able to establish itself thanks to a national consensus, which started with the Villers-Cotterêts ordinance of 1539 and which continues today. However, it is worth noting that this very policy hides a *processus de minoration*, on which we shall elaborate. What has been put in place is a hierarchy of linguistic practices, opposing a 'prestigious', 'superior', national language which has come to be considered as the only possible vehicle for recognised values, and the regional languages which can supposedly be sacrificed with no great loss. Thus, if territorial languages (as distinct from migrant languages) are today experiencing this *processus de minoration*, in a country which is becoming almost exclusively francophone, it is not because they are spoken less but because they lack power in a society in which there is strong central control over education and culture.

This linguistic policy has always tried to impose an elitist culture, that of 'culturally hegemonic groups', which alone monitor the dominant code and impose it as a common code. Under these conditions, the other languages of France have often withdrawn into traditional functions, confining themselves to activities aimed at developing and popularising the arts by emphasising their marginal and folkloric nature. Because it has consistently continued to marginalise and to devalue regional languages, France has been one of the last Western European countries to recognise that all its citizens should have le droit à la différence.

During his election campaign in 1981, François Mitterand placed emphasis on cultural democracy and respect for linguistic diversity. It was also in this spirit that the 1982 Giordan report to the Ministry of Culture was designed. In it, the author proposes

> d'indiquer les grands choix qui permettront de faire entrer dans la réalité de la vie nationale, le principe de la démocratie culturelle d'une

part, et le respect des différences linguistiques et culturelles d'autre part. (Giordan 1982: 17)

In this report, the author constantly emphasises the necessity for discussion and dialogue between minority and majority cultures, and proposes that the main danger facing any culture is 'le repli sur soi' (p. 48). Giordan concludes the report with an attempt to define the principles or guidelines which must be followed if a real promotion of regional languages is sought, namely:

> – il ne faut pas que la prise en compte des langues régionales débouche sur l'installation de 'nouveaux ghettos culturels' (p.22)
> – pour que cette prise en compte puisse contribuer efficacement au développement d'ensemble de la culture en France, il faut qu'elle soit munie des moyens qui permettront de l'insérer dans un nouveau modèle de développement culturel régional fondé sur la dialectique de l'un et du multiple. Cela revient à dire que l'Etat doit accorder aux langues régionales une reconnaissance 'franche' sans arrière-pensée et sans timidité. Bien entendu, reconnaître les différences linguistiques nécessite qu'on les désigne sans ambiguité et que l'on définisse clairement une nouvelle politique d'intervention.

Unfortunately, ten years have passed since the Giordan proposals in this field, and nothing much has been done to move towards cultural democracy. There are some exceptions, the most important being those concerning the creation of the Breton and Corsican CAPES qualifications, but these changes are not far-reaching enough to have a profound impact on a highly complex sociolinguistic situation.

The need for a democratically drawn up language policy

Any language policy for a multilingual society (*une glottopolitique*) has to be founded on the corollary that human society depends on language and that language is social in nature. Only then can the policy act meaningfully not only on the status of the various languages in a given community, but also on language use in its social context. The term *glottopolitique* covers both practice and an analysis of that practice.

In fact, in order to ensure free expression of the language needs of all and to guarantee that the citizen is protected from authoritarian decisions, the drawing up of a language policy must be a democratic process which operates in two directions:

1.   Those with political power, *les décideurs*, must be fully informed. The ignorance, contempt or condescension of the 'decision makers' with regard to the work of sociolinguists (for example at the outset of the 'bilingual education' experiment) lead in some instances to a deadlock. All specialists in the problems of language, sociolinguists, psycholingu-

ists and others, must bring the decision makers up to date with the conditions and the process of linguistic change. The decision makers must be informed about the real forces at work, in other words the dynamism and the continual transformation of linguistic practices. However, the vital question is whether what specialists say is taken into consideration by the politicians who decide the status and promotion of languages. So it must be borne in mind that, unlike other places such as Quebec for example, glottopolitical decisions in France are taken without the involvement of the very linguistic communities whose languages are at issue. It is regrettable to see that the results of academic research in France do not contribute to glottopolitical decisions.

2.   The users must be helped and encouraged to set down clearly their real linguistic 'problems'. Policies of dialogue and sociolinguistic surveys with the interested parties should allow them to choose freely and to decide the fate of their languages. To this end, it is necessary to fight against the 'common sense' notion that language is immutable and must be respected by everyone as though it were exempt from variation. In the same way, it is also necessary to guard against purist attitudes, which tend to confuse unity and uniformity, a common code and an imposed code, and do not realise that what they see as an inviolate universal norm is in fact socially and historically determined.

In its consideration of the languages of France, a 'glottopolicy' must distinguish between defending and promoting a language, and defending and promoting a language system which dominates all other systems with which it competes. An innovative glottopolicy also has to include the promotion of awareness among language minorities, including the immigrant populations, living in French territory. Via an often ill-defined linguistic undercurrent, these minorities are continually modifying and influencing linguistic practices in France. Until now, these populations have been excluded from having any legitimate voice in discussions on language. French does not exist in a social vacuum; it has to be placed in the context of the links, both complementary and contradictory, that it entertains with the other languages around it, as well as in the context of the relationship between a national norm and the range of actual language use. So a democratic glottopolicy is linked to political self-management and to economic decentralisation, just as the belittling and destroying of languages, the attempt to reduce everything to a *single* language, went hand in hand with the destruction of the regional fabric and with the movement of manpower in the interests of capitalism. The cost is known, even if the final balance sheet has yet to be drawn up.

A democratic glottopolicy must encourage the dialogue which is needed so that the concrete experiences of minority groups can be put into words, and that research can draw on real life. Anxieties about a future plurilingual France often have some basis in fact, which must be taken into account. These issues are much debated by the Council of Europe and the EC, with some governments only too aware of the possible spin-offs in terms of *l'Europe des régions*. Besides which, the promotion of 'bilingual education' (i.e. French plus another EC language) may increase the reluctance of some people to envisage the teaching of the regional or migrant languages. It is unfortunate if the right to one's mother tongue, recognised by the EC and the Council of Europe, were to be for the export market only, especially since a time may come when French itself is a *langue dominée* and may need protecting.

Text 1

Visite à Mulhouse

Entrons, à Riedisheim, dans un de ces cafés à la fois très fermés et d'abord chaleureux, mais où n'ira sans doute pas l'homme d'affaires. Cela sent trop l'intimité familiale. Il faut gravir le perron, pénétrer chez les gens, ayant tenté en vain de percer le mystère des fenêtres aux vitres opaques. Un macaron auto-collant apposé sur la porte aurait prévenu l'observateur attentif: 'Do wird oi elsassisch gredd' affiche ostensiblement la 'Schweissdissi Confrerie Mulhusa' en un message informatif que ceignent les fières paroles 'Ben i was i ben. Was i ben blib'. L'accueil égal fait aux très rares et très occasionnels consommateurs francophones monolingues montre, si besoin était, qu'il n'y a point là phénomène de coterie, pas plus qu'il ne s'agit d'ailleurs d'attirer ou de rassurer une nouvelle clientèle alsacophone, même si le cimetière voisin amène croque-morts, famille et amis des nouveaux défunts. Le café a en fait ses habitués, sûrs d'y pouvoir toujours parler alsacien. On serait donc tenté de voir, dans le macaron qui nous intéresse, un signe d'entité, une marque d'identité, si ce même autocollant ne fleurissait rapidement en ville, insigne manifeste d'une guilde ou association de commerçants plus que proclamation fière de spécificité ethnique, culturelle ou linguistique.

Quittons le café pour Mulhouse afin de faire un tour en ville. Quelles traces écrites du dialecte, insensiblement offertes aux yeux de tous, francophones et alsacophones, trouvons-nous vraiment? Peu de choses à dire vrai, et dont beaucoup sont de nature gastronomique, par nature intraduisibles: – 'Poulet provençal, Fleisch-snacken, Tripes façon traiteur, Leberknoepla' annonce un charcutier; – 'Pulpe d'églantines Buttenmus journellement frais' affiche un épicier; – 'Fleischschnaka, Surlawerla (foie sauté à l'Alsacienne), Lawerknäpfla (quenelles de foie), Schiffala sur choucroute' porte sur sa carte un restaurateur variablement soucieux de traduction et qui, sur sa devanture, appose encore: 'Cochonailles Schachtasse dimanche le 15 novembre'; – 'Frites, merguez, knacks, pizza' arbore en lettres lumineuses la roulotte d'un fastfood artisanal, témoin et acteur d'un merveilleux salmigondis en même temps que d'une efficiente intégration linguistique; – 'erika' font savoir les fleuristes de la ville en cette veille de Toussaint, sauf quelques commerçants soucieux de leur image de marque qui facturent au prix fort la traduction française'; – 'Neier siasser. Vin bourru. Assiette alsacienne (Schieffala, collet, lard paysan, lawerwurst, mettwurst)' a peint sur sa devanture un cafetier; – 'Berawecka, Lekerle' fait savoir un pâtissier; – 'hasch a gummi' a tracé un papetier près de sa caisse enregistreuse; – 'Liawer a wisteï im maga als a wassersteï' porte en vitrine une assiette décorative que vend un marchand de porcelaines; etc.

Si les mots gastronomiques et autres rencontrés sont plus de l'alsacien intégré dans le français régional d'Alsace que du dialecte alsacien, il en va différemment avec les deux derniers exemples cités à l'instant comme avec ce calendrier alsacien qui place chaque jour de l'année sous le patronage d'un savoureux et percutant juron alsacien. On devrait s'attarder aussi sur le monde des jeunes éditeurs qui, reprenant une tradition établie, s'initient et initient à la langue dialectale écrite, mais avec les moyens du temps, ceux de la bande dessinée en alsacien, bien représentée chez les libraires mulhousiens.

Faute de temps, dirigeons-nous vers le marché. Avenue Aristide Briand, notre regard est à plusieurs reprises sollicité par plusieurs affiches de représentations théâtrales apposées sur les portes des magasins et qui attestent bien qu'il y a à Mulhouse comme ailleurs en Alsace un culte et un public pour le théâtre dialectal. Ce ne sont pas moins de trois affiches différentes qui nous convient au double plaisir de voir une pièce en dialecte alsacien et de savourer ledit dialecte. Prenons connaissance des trois: – 'Papa a Magd muess her ! Lustspiel in 3 Akte vu André Furling (auteur mulhousien)' annonce pour les 8 et 15 novembre 1987 la première affiche de 'théâtre en dialecte alsacien'; – 'Dr Bourgeois gentilhomme oder Dr adelsischtiga Tuechhandler. Comédie-ballet de Molière et Lully' annonce pour sa part le 'Théâtre alsacien de Mulhouse' pour six représentations mulhousiennes au même mois de novembre – 'D'r Grossvater macht dummheite. Schwank in 3 Akte vu Franz Schaurer. En's elsàssische ewersetzt un bearweite zu André Ziegler, Dimanche 6 décembre' prévient le 'Cercle théâtral alsacien' qui en est à sa soixante-cinquième saison.

Ces trois affiches rencontrées sur le chemin du marché et que nous aurions cherchées en vain à la Faculté des Lettres de Mulhouse comme en beaucoup d'autres lieux culturels rappellent à propos l'existence d'une importante minorité bilingue qui peut, sait et veut goûter intentionnellement au dialecte, fût-il institutionnalisé comme fait de culture populaire.

(From Salmon (ed.) 1991)

Text 2
Complémentarité fonctionnelle des deux langues

La mise en rapport du choix de langue avec les différentes composantes du statut familial, et plus généralement du statut social des locuteurs a fait apparaître de nombreuses régularités: à telle ou telle relation de rôle correspond prioritairement telle ou telle langue. Toutefois le catalogue des emplois de l'une et l'autre langue, étape nécessaire de l'analyse, ne suffit pas à rendre compte de la véritable fonction de chacune. Celle-ci se dégage au niveau des domaines qui sont des catégories plus larges que les rôles et premières par rapport à eux. Les résultats des enquêtes sur les situations de communication et sur le discours franco-occitan confirment les données de l'enquête sur le comportement linguistique de 150 personnes (question 5.1 à 5.8): la langue occitane est attachée au domaine du travail agricole, tandis que la langue française et attachée au domaine de l'institution officielle. C'est à partir de ces deux fonctions fondamentales que s'organisent et s'expliquent les emplois ou fonctions dérivées de chaque langue. Pour dresser la hiérarchie des fonctions et expliciter leur engendrement, nous avons mené une enquête sur les fonctions respectives des deux langues auprès de – ou plutôt sous la direction de – nos informateurs (cf. Annexe: un fragment de discours sur l'utilité du français et l'emploi du 'patois'). La présentation que nous donnons par la figure 7, n'est qu'une synthèse des opinions émises par eux. Nous nous sommes contenté d'adapter la terminologie et de tirer des inférences. Par exemple, d'une phrase comme 'Il parle patois, c'est un paysan', nous inférons que l'occitan (= le 'patois') est la langue du travail agricole, ou encore, d'une affirmation comme 'Ils sont obligés de se présenter dans les bureaux et ils parlent français', nous inférons que le français est la langue de l'institution officielle (= 'des bureaux').

Au niveau des fonctions fondamentales, la relation entre langue et domaine est, comme l'indiquent les statistiques (cf. 3.3.3), moins contraignante dans un cas que dans l'autre: tandis que l'occitan est la langue majoritaire, mais non unique du travail agricole, le français est la langue exclusive de l'institution officielle, autrement dit imposée par l'institution, et d'abord par l'institution scolaire qui stigmatise l'occitan appelé pour la circonstance 'patois'. C'est dans ce sens que le français a statut de langue dominante et l'occitan celui de langue dominée.

Au niveau des fonctions dérivées, il est aisé de constater le plus souvent non seulement un rapport de complémentarité, mais aussi une relation de contradiction entre les emplois respectifs du français et de l'occitan. En d'autres termes, la distribution des deux langues obéit à un principe d'organisation dialectique. C'est ce que nous avons essayé de représenter sur la figure 7.

Son statut de langue de l'institution officielle prédétermine la français à être la langue de la promotion sociale, condamnant par le fait même l'occitan à être la langue du handicap social. Langue du travail agricole, l'occitan est prédisposé à être la langue du monde rural, comme le français, langue de l'institution officielle est prédisposé à être la langue du monde urbain. C'est en tant que langue de la promotion sociale que le français s'impose comme langue des jeunes, des personnes instruites et des femmes, à qui incombe pour la plus grande part, l'éducation des enfants. L'occitan assume inversement les fonctions de langue des vieux, des non-instruits et des hommes, cette dernière fonction dérive aussi, bien sûr, de la fonction fondamentale de l'occitan, langue du travail agricole: c'est parce que le travail de la terre est en majeure partie l'affaire des hommes, que les agriculteurs sont les plus nombreux à avoir l'occitan comme langue première; dans tous les cas où les femmes participent aux activités agricoles, l'occitan devient aussi chez elles langue première. La fonction de la langue de la communauté proche, qui dérive directement pour l'occitan de la

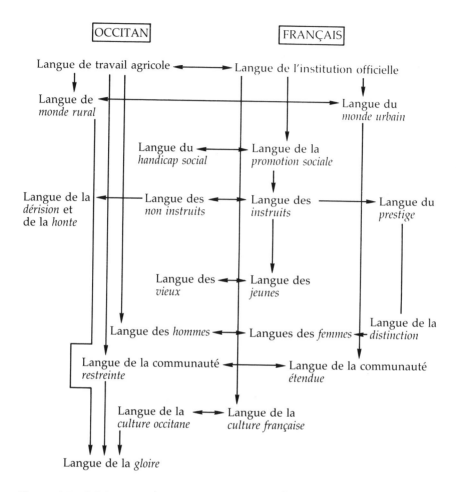

Figure 4.1 Schéma des fonctions de l'occitan et du français

fonction fondamentale de langue du travail agricole s'oppose directement à la fonction contradictoire exercée par le français, langue de la communauté étendue, elle-même dérivée de la fonction fondamentale du français, langue des institutions officielles.

Parallèlement à ces fonctions sociologiques, nos deux langues ont des fonctions psychologiques, elles aussi à la fois complémentaires et contradictoires. Langue des institutions officielles et du monde urbain, le français est reçu comme la langue de prestige qui séduit les jeunes et la langue de la distinction qui séduit les femmes; à l'inverse l'occitan est marqué au sceau de la dérision et de la honte: 'Ne parle pas patois, on se moquera de toi' est une formule que nous avons surprise des dizaines de fois dans la bouche des mères. C'est enfin la fonction de nostalgie qui explique – au dire même des agriculteurs – le goût manifesté pour l'occitan par quelques citadins d'origine rurale.

... L'Occitan est choisi comme épreuve optionnelle au baccalauréat de préférence à une langue vivante étrangère, les instituteurs et les maîtres ne le pourchassent plus comme avant, quelques-uns de nos informateurs le revendiquent comme leur 'vraie' langue. Caractéristique de ce retour à l'occitan est le comportement linguistique, déja relevé des jeunes agricultrices du groupe 2 (20 à 40 ans) qui sont plus nombreuses proportionnellement à parler l'occitan comme langue première que celles du groupe 3 (40 à 60 ans). A travers cette prise de conscience de l'appartenance à un peuple et à une culture, se manifeste une nouvelle fonction: langue du travail agricole, l'occitan tend à devenir la langue de la culture occitane. Un nouveau rapport de complémentarité est amorcé: le français n'est plus perçu par quelques-uns comme la seule langue de l'instruction et de la culture, mais seulement comme la langue de la culture française. Cette dernière fonction a pour corollaire sur le plan purement psychologique, une fonction de gloire: 'Les jeunes se font une gloire de parler patois à leur tour'. Mais en 1977, dans une communauté rurale située en domaine occitan, cette recherche d'un nouvel équilibre diglossique n'est encore qu'une amorce.

(From Maurand 1981)

5

The migrant languages of Paris

L.-J. CALVET

The situation of the languages of migrants in Paris is not solely a sociolinguistic problem. To understand present-day multilingualism in the capital, we need to reflect a little on the past. Clearly it is impossible to retrace the great migratory movements of each of the groups which have led to the current situation, but it is interesting to review briefly a century of history in order to understand the present. Paris has always been the focal point of people coming to seek work from the four corners of the country, attracting those who spoke Occitan, Breton, Basque – or even French! – and who often specialised in certain domains (for example, those from the Auvergne selling charcoal); they sometimes lived in specific quarters (e.g. Montparnasse for the Bretons). In a few generations they were assimilated linguistically and culturally and merged into the population of Paris: Corsican and Breton are not often heard in the capital today; on the other hand, as we will see, many other languages can be heard.

External economic and political migrations

This internal migration was slowly replaced by migration from outside France, which was first triggered by World War I. To replace the workforce engaged at the front, France took in 100,000 Chinese workers between 1916 and 1918, mostly metal workers. Originating from the province of Zhejiang, in the south-east of China, they spoke different dialects among themselves which were not mutually comprehensible. Most of them returned to China after the war, but those who remained in Paris are the originators of the first 'Chinese quarters' in the capital, around the Gare de Lyon and in the third arrondissement (the former area is now destroyed).

The second wave of economic migration from outside only slightly affected the capital: in 1919 France and Poland signed an agreement on immigration and Polish workers settled in the north, particularly in the coalmining areas: 309,000 in 1926, 507,000 in 1931. This differed from the immigration of the Armenians who, in 1915, left Turkey for the Near East to escape genocide. Then, between 1922 and 1926, some of them settled in France, in Marseilles, Lyons and Paris: 30,000 in 1925. The economic crisis in 1932 gave rise to high unemployment in factories and forced them to become integrated into French society by becoming craftsmen and small shopkeepers. They were joined after the war by those who had originally chosen the Near East (leaving Lebanon or Syria for France) and today there are about 300,000 people of French nationality who have an Armenian background.

Portugal has always been a great purveyor of migrants. At the end of the fifteenth century the Portuguese began to settle in Brazil where the Portuguese language, as is well known, enjoyed a period of rapid expansion. Then, at the beginning of the twentieth century, there was Portuguese migration to the USA and, after World War II, to Venezuela. In the second half of the twentieth century, Portuguese migrants changed their destination to other countries in Europe. So in 1969, 72 per cent of workers leaving Portugal settled in France where they worked particularly in the service and building industries, a characteristic feature being that they frequently lived on two salaries. In Portuguese homes, in fact, it is usual for the wife to work. An estimated 42.1 per cent of migrant Portuguese women were working in 1983 (the rate was 35.5 per cent for French women and 23 per cent for the total of foreign women) (Villanova 1988).

In France there are about 2.6 million people of North African origin (of whom 1.1 million have French nationality). Of these, 600,000 speak Berber and 2 million speak Arabic. Some of them settled in France before World War II, but it is particularly in the immediate post-war era that this movement increased: in the fifties, for example, 75 per cent of migrant workers who settled in France came from Tunisia, Algeria and Morocco, and this trend continued until 1974, when France passed a law limiting economic migration.

Also during the fifties, another migratory movement appeared. Migration from Spain had been taking place for a long time. In 1851, 30,000 Spaniards were already living in France and 255,000 by 1921, but it was after the war, when they were fleeing the Franco regime or looking for better economic conditions, that the Spanish began to settle en masse in the south west of France and in the Paris region, coming primarily from Andalusia and Galicia. There were about 600,000 at the beginning of the seventies, but only 300,000 have remained since the political changes following Franco's death, a third of whom live in the Paris region.

In addition to the Chinese migration of World War I, Vietnamese and Cambodian migrants began to settle in France from the beginning of the twentieth century, during the colonial era. These are the people who most often set up 'Chinese' restaurants (which are usually Vietnamese). But today Paris is seeing a new wave of Asian migrants, whose parents had left China in 1949 to settle in Vietnam, Thailand or Cambodia. Originally from the south of China, they generally spoke 'Chaozhou' (a south-eastern dialect) and Cantonese. Their children, who began to leave their adopted countries for France at the beginning of the seventies had inherited these languages but had also learnt Mandarin and the language of their birthplace, Khmer, Thai or Cambodian. They settled in Paris in the thirteenth arrondissement (Porte de Choisy) or in the twentieth (Belleville).

To this brief résumé, other communities can be added: for example, workers from the west of Africa (Senegal, Mali, Ivory Coast), Greeks, Turks, Yugoslavs, Italians, all migrants for economic reasons, as well as Russians who left their country after 1917 for political reasons.

Migrants among the population of Paris

The population of the Paris region and the twenty arrondissements of Paris (Paris *intra muros*) in 1982 was as follows:

Paris region: 8,707,000 inhabitantss
Paris *intra muros*: 2,176,000 inhabitants

The last figure, for Paris proper, is constantly decreasing. For example, between 1968 and 1975, Paris *intra muros* lost 290,000 inhabitants. But in the same period, the number of foreigners living there increased by 138,000, i.e. the proportion of foreigners in Paris is increasing whereas the total population is falling. In 1982 the Paris region had 1.1 million foreigners, i.e. 12 per cent of the population (the national average is 6.8 per cent of whom 39 per cent are non-EC). These figures do not include those who have acquired French nationality, who of course are of interest to us from a linguistic point of view.

Table 5.1 shows in percentages the distribution of the principal groups of foreigners in the population of Paris. These census data are only concerned with the nationality of the inhabitants and do not always give

Table 5.1 *Distribution of principal groups of foreigners in Paris (%)*

	Algerians	Spaniards	Italians	Moroccans	Portuguese	Tunisians	Turks
1975	2.1	2.4	0.7	0.8	1.9	1.1	0.1
1982	2.4	1.7	0.6	1.1	2.4	1.5	0.3

Source: *Atlas des Parisiens* (1984)

us information about the languages they speak. So, a Spaniard might only speak Castilian or he might also speak Basque, Catalan or Galician. A Moroccan may be an arabophone or a berberophone, and so on. In addition, the censuses of 1975 and 1982 have curiously classed Asians, whose number is increasing, under the heading 'diverse'; these 'diverse' people comprise a quarter of the total population of migrants (in 1982, the evaluation gave 0.9 per cent of the population of Paris as coming from south-east Asia (Atelier 1984)).

The principal groups of migrants are Algerians, Portuguese, Tunisians, Moroccans, Spaniards and 'Asians'. In 1982 in Paris there were 53,400 Portuguese, 52,360 Algerians, 36,600 Spaniards, 31,780 Tunisians, 24,020 Moroccans and 22,896 Asians (i.e. people calling themselves Chinese, Laotian, Cambodian or Vietnamese). But to this last figure should be added tens of thousands of Asians who have become French by naturalisation. These 'Asians' come from Cambodia (67 per cent), Laos (18 per cent), Vietnam (12 per cent), Taiwan, Malaya, Hong Kong and the People's Republic of China (Guillon and Taboada-Leonetti 1986: 41).

These figures are however a gross underestimate: the number of languages spoken in Paris is far greater than the few nationalities given above. One estimate, in the title of a collective work published a few years ago (Vermes 1988) is that there are twenty-five linguistic communities. A study by questionnaire among primary school children shows that the number of different mother tongues may reach a hundred or more.

> Un premier dépouillement des 500 questionnaires réalisés indique déjà qu'il y plus d'une soixantaine de langues en présence à Paris. Mais ce chiffre est assurément trop faible encore. Une enquête statistique de type démographique en ferait découvrir probablement plus d'une centaine et donnerait une estimation utile du nombre de leurs locuteurs. (Heredia 1989: 73)

Thus, the languages represented in Paris, apart of course from French, include the regional languages of France, French Creoles (from Réunion, Martinique, Guadeloupe and Guyane), non-territorial languages (Yiddish, Judo-Arabic, Judo-Spanish, Manouche) and the scores of languages of migrants, some of which are widely spoken (Arabic, English and Chinese) and others which are very limited (Wolof and Soninké). But, as the above figures show, only about ten of these migrant languges are spoken by more than 0.1 per cent of the population of Paris, and it is to these languages that we shall refer in this chapter.

Geographical distribution and the marking of territory

Foreigners are unevenly distributed throughout the city and some *quartiers* are dominated to a greater or lesser degree by one or other of the principal migrant groups. The most remarkable concentrations are those of the Spaniards and Portuguese to the west of Paris (sixteenth arrondissement), Asians in the south (thirteenth arrondissement) and north-east (Belleville) and Algerians in the north-east (la Goutte d'Or, Belleville). This uneven distribution is historical as far as the Algerians are concerned (they settled in a quarter which has always traditionally welcomed provincials or foreigners), economic for the Spaniards and Portuguese (the womenfolk often work as concierges or cleaners in the *beaux quartiers* and therefore live either in the maid's room or in the concierge's lodge). But these communities also vary in the way in which they have marked 'their territory'. Thus the Asian presence is immediately seen graphically: shop signs, restaurants, notices in Chinese, Vietnamese, Thai, Khmer, etc. In the same way, at Belleville, Moslem butchers advertise their wares in Arabic and indicate that the meat is slaughtered according to Islamic law, while Israeli businesses often carry the Star of David and the three Hebrew consonants of the word 'kosher'. In contrast, the Spaniards and Portuguese of the sixteenth arrondissement have not marked the environment with any visible, or legible, signs of their presence.

The graphic environment gives us in addition some interesting indications of the social function of language. In the *quartier* of the Opéra, for example, in the centre of Paris, there are many signs in English, Japanese or Arabic. The typeface is clear and the content varies little, indicating banks or luxury boutiques in which tourists can make their tax-free purchases. In contrast, at Belleville, whereas the Asian languages are always well written, the inscriptions in Arabic are often roughly traced, sometimes with spelling mistakes. We can learn two things from this sort of linguistic environment: on the one hand the different types of presentation of the same language and on the other, the different standing of the speakers of different languages. For example, between a sign in Arabic denoting a *bureau de change*, avenue de l'Opéra, and a sketchy sign advertising an Islamic butcher in Belleville, there is a wide social difference, separating the tourists who come from the Persian Gulf and the migrants who came from North Africa. In the same way, the content of the inscriptions throws light on the various types of migration: in contrast with the limited number of Arabic signs (butchers, Islamic bookshops, restaurants), those in Chinese or Vietnamese advertise a great variety of services (insurance brokers, doctors, lawyers, travel agents, supermarkets), thus providing further evidence of the difference in social and cultural status between the political migrants of south-east Asia who came from reasonably well-off backgrounds, and those who fled poverty in North Africa.

In Paris, this marking of territory, which is one of the means by which we can get an insight into a foreign presence, is a reflection of individual initiative. This is not always the case: for example in Soho, street names are in English and Chinese, in the same way as some street names are bilingual in the old town of Nice (French and Provençal) or in Algeria where road signs are bilingual (Arabic and French). In all three cases this bilingualism is due to the initiative of the municipality or of the state. Nothing similar is found in Paris where the sole official language is French. The walls of the capital, signs and posters tell us of the multilingualism of the town, but no official notice is taken of it.

Absence of linguistic policy

This leads us to the more general problem of linguistic policy – and politics. There are multilingual cities throughout the world (e.g. in very different ways, Brussels and Singapore) where the management of multilingualism is carefully regulated by the constitution. French legislation, however, barely mentions minority languages and remains completely silent on the question of migrant languages. The *loi Deixonne* (1951) gives the right of teaching optionally in 'local languages and dialects' in schools and *lycées* in France. The following extracts give an idea of the spirit of this law.

> Art. 3.   Tout instituteur qui en fera la demande pourra être autorisé à consacrer, chaque semaine, une heure d'activités dirigées à l'enseignement de notions élémentaires de lecture et d'écriture du parler local . . .

> Art. 6.   Dans les lycées et collèges, l'enseignement facultatif de toutes les langues et dialectes locaux, ainsi que du folklore, de la littérature et des arts populaires locaux, pourra prendre place dans le cadre des activités dirigées.

> Art. 9.   Dans les universités où il est possible d'adjoindre au jury un examinateur compétent, une épreuve facultative sera inscrite au programme du baccalauréat. Les points obtenus au-dessus de la moyenne entreront en ligne de compte pour l'attribution des mentions autres que la mention 'passable'.

More than a hundred years earlier, in 1851, a circular concerning the *loi Falloux* on national education had stipulated that French should be the sole language used in schools: from this point of view the *loi Deixonne* represented some progress for minority languages in France. But this law only concerns local languages and dialects and the sole 'local language' in Paris being French, it in no way constitutes a linguistic policy for the capital. Furthermore, the projects of the Council of Europe, in the form of a resolution proposed to the twenty-three member states concerning regional or minority languages in Europe (*Conseil de l'Europe*, 1988), as the name suggests, only take European languages into account and say nothing about migrant languages, some of which nevertheless have considerable statistical importance (e.g. Turkish in Germany, Arabic in France, Indian languages or Greek in the UK). This means that the action which the resolution asks the member states to take does not impinge on the languages which interest us here, and no real linguistic policy has been developed for the migrant languages of Paris. (The only exceptions concern official attempts to ban all monolingual signs in languages other than French, as in the case of a mayor of the thirteenth arrondissement, rather than any interest in the future of other languages.) We shall see, therefore, that the maintenance and protection of multilingualism among migrant communities is left up to families, with the occasional backing by schools. In other words, the only model entertained in France is that of the assimilation by migrants (and especially by the children of migrants) of French language and culture.

What of the future?

In the absence of a proper linguistic policy, we have to look elsewhere, and particularly at the languages of the home, in order to get some idea of what the future of these languages may be.

To what extent are the languages of migrants passed on from parents to children? The situation differs according to the community. The *beurs* for example, second-generation North Africans, speak Arabic or Berber to a lesser degree than the Chinese speak the language of their parents. A recent enquiry conducted in a school in the thirteenth arrondissement among children of Chinese origin showed that 26 out of 32 pupils had Chinese as their first langugae; 29 had learned to read in French but not in Chinese (Pang 1989: 51–2). Another enquiry, through questionnaires and interviews carried out with more than 300 children whose parents spoke Arabic, Creole, Kabyle (or Berber), Portuguese and Serbo-Croat (Heredia 1989) showed that these languages were transmitted in an equal manner (between 70 and 80 per cent) when the father and mother spoke the same language: 236 out of 268 in this situation (children of couples who are linguistically 'homogeneous') say they understand the language of their parents 'well' or 'very well':

Serbo-Croat	100%
Portuguese	95%

Creole	90%
Kabyle	86%
Arabic	81%

202 out of 268 say they speak this language 'well' or 'very well':

Kabyle	86%
Portuguese	81%
Serbo-Croat	80%
Creole	75%
Arabic	69%

and only 5 out of 268 declare that they do not understand the language of their parents. However, we should not be over-optimistic about this relatively high rate of language transmission: if we just imagine that the same percentages are repeated over two or three generations, we are in fact looking at a very bleak future for these languages. If 80 per cent of the children of the 80 per cent of Yugoslav children who speak Serbo-Croat speak it in their turn, this would give 64 per cent of the current population, 51 per cent in the next generation, and so on. It is of course difficult to predict this, but if the children of migrants are mostly bilingual today, the trend nevertheless does not favour the continuation of bilingualism, except in certain specific circumstances. Such cases might be those whose country of origin is nearby and who go there frequently on holiday (as do the Portuguese), or those who have grouped in particular quarters with a strong cultural life (like the Chinese) or those who learn the language for religious reasons (as in the case of Arabic for the Muslims, although it is a different language from the 'dialect' spoken by the parents). Yiddish, Armenian and Polish are languages which are already tending to disappear in Paris, and a good number of others appear threatened.

There is, of course, another place where languages are transmitted and that is in the classes given in primary schools in *les cours de langue d'origine*. These classes were first created in 1973 for the Portuguese (attendance was optional, and by written request from parents), and have subsequently been extended through bilateral agreements signed between France and the countries of origin, Italy, Tunisia, Spain, Morocco, Yugoslavia, Turkey and Algeria. (The presence of the three countries of North Africa in this list shows us that there is no course in Arabic, but separate courses in Tunisian Arabic, Moroccan Arabic, Algerian Arabic, normally reserved for the children of nationals of those countries.) When these children were asked whether they are following, or would like to follow, such courses, the following replies were received:

	are following	would like to follow
Portuguese	54%	16%
Arabic	33%	36%
Kabyle	29%	32%
Serbo-Croat	47%	40%
Creole	4%	33%

(Heredia 1989: 74–5 and 82)

However, even if they are sometimes taught at school in the language of their parents, the young usually speak French at home, as is illustrated in a number of studies.

Jerab (1988: 46) reports that young North Africans state clearly that their parents use their mother tongue, but that they usually reply to their parents in French. A similar situation is reported for children of Portuguese and Spanish origin.

> Dans certains cas, les parents s'adressent en portugais à leurs enfants, ceux-ci répondent en français. Néanmoins le portugais sera la première langue parlée à l'enfant avant sa scolarité et pendant celle-ci par les parents dans la majorité des cas. Si dans certains cas, le français va devenir progressivement la langue la plus utilisée, les attitudes des enfants face à la langue maternelle ne seront pas du tout homogènes pour une même génération dans une même famille, elles marqueront des degrés d'intérêt et d'investissement différenciés.   (Villanova 1987: 128)

Despite the apparent optimism of the text cited above, the children do not on the whole speak the language of their parents to each other:

> La langue d'origine elle-même est loin d'être exclue de la communication entre enfants, meme si le français lui est nettement préféré: elle est attestée dans 55% des cas pour le kabyle
> 40% des cas pour l'arabe
> 40% des cas pour le portugais.   (Heredia 1989: 81)

The *langues d'origine*, which are therefore taught optionally at primary school, mostly disappear at secondary level, where children can choose their first foreign language from English, German, Spanish or Arabic (later they will be able to choose a second foreign language out of eleven languages). In 1986–7, in the whole of France, languages chosen by pupils (first and second language) were as follows:

English	4,899,000	pupils
German	1,306,000	
Spanish	1,219,000	
Italian	168,000	
Russian	25,000	
Portuguese	14,600	

Arabic   13,560
Chinese   2,050

It can be seen that it is not the migrant languages of France (Arabic, Chinese, Serbo-Croat, Portuguese, Wolof, Bambara etc.) which are for the most part chosen, but rather the major international languages. This leads us to the problem of the type of multilingualism which is to be found in Paris.

What type of plurilingualism?

Anyone who observes multilingual African or Asian towns finds one important feature. Town life naturally acts as a catalyst for unification, and 'carrier' languages appear there which may become the languages of tomorrow: Wolof in Dakar, Bambara in Bamako, Lingala and Munukutuba in Brazzaville (cf. Calvet 1987). But at the same time what takes place is a sort of sharing or exchange of languages. African citizens not only speak their first language and the language of the town but they also very often acquire the language of their neighbour, the language of their playmates or of the quarter: multilingualism is widely shared, among the adults as well as the children (cf. the case of Dakar, Dreyfus 1986, and see chapter 12). Nothing similar has occurred in Paris. In a *quartier* such as Belleville, for example, where Africans live side-by-side with *maghrébins* and Asians, no one learns the language of the other and French is the sole unifying language. Furthermore, although the *quartier* is linguistically and ethnically the most diversified in Paris, there is very little contact between the different groups. The numerous restaurants (principally Asian and North African) are frequented by the French but one never sees Asians going to eat a couscous or North Africans a *canard laqué*, and each community has its own grocers, butchers and so on. Socially as well as linguistically the coexistence of these different communities is governed by a principle of reciprocal ignorance.

Piet Van de Craen and Hugo Baetens Beardsmore, in an article on urban linguistic phenomena, emphasise that:

> It is becoming ever more apparent that a city is not necessarily an urban melting pot in which code and variety differences get smoothed out in a unique urban vernacular but that a host of language varieties co-exist both in terms of social stratification and in terms of geographical dispersion.   (Van de Craen and Baetens Beardsmore 1987: 579)

From this point of view, Paris is a good illustration of the co-existence of numerous languages which share the same social and geographic territory without ever meeting. The main linguistic spin-off from urban

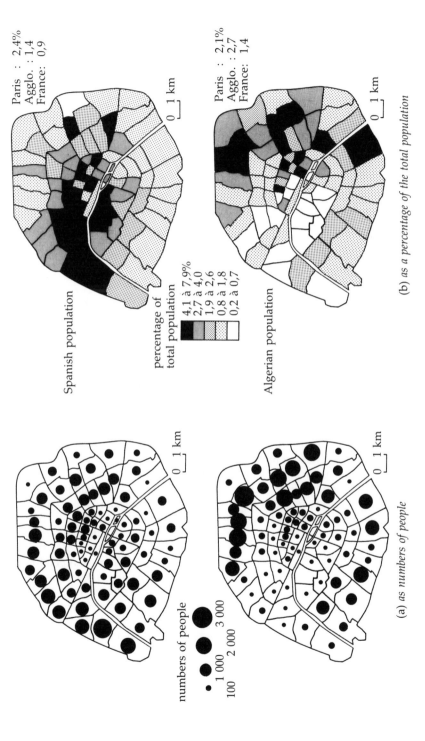

Paris : 2,4%
Agglo. : 1,4
France: 0,9

0 1 km

Spanish population

percentage of
total population

4,1 à 7,9%
2,7 à 4,0
1,9 à 2,6
0,8 à 1,8
0,2 à 0,7

Paris : 2,1%
Agglo. : 2,7
France: 1,4

0 1 km

Algerian population

(b) *as a percentage of the total population*

0 1 km

0 1 km

numbers of people

100 1 000 2 000 3 000

(a) *as numbers of people*

Figure 5.1   Two ways of representing the Spanish and Algerian population of Paris

115

life here is a slow assimilation to the dominant language, French, with only marginal borrowings from other languages. A strong monolingual vision of the state, culture and communication, a centralised administration and the standardisation of French, all militate against any sharing of languages. There is no socially valued model of bi- or multilingualism in Paris and the future of migrant languages remains for the time being solely an individual and family matter.

Text 1

Les parlers français des migrants

CHRISTINE DE HEREDIA

Les déplacements de population ont toujours été un facteur important dans l'évolution des langues, qu'il s'agisse d'invasions, de colonisation ou simplement de migrations économiques.

A l'intérieur de nos frontières vivent plus de quatre millions de personnes dites étrangères, de nationalités et de langues d'origine très diverses: Algériens, Portugais, Espagnols, Marocains, Yougoslaves, Tunisiens, Turcs, Sénégalais, Maliens, Vietnamiens, Chiliens, etc., qui s'installent en France temporairement ou définitivement au gré des événements économiques, diplomatiques et politiques. Certains y cherchent un travail, d'autres un asile. Ils forment une composante numériquement stable de la population française: 8 à 8.5%, pourcentage qui n'a pas changé depuis cinquante ans, et, de nos jours, un Français sur cinq trouve un ascendant étranger s'il remonte seulement à ses arrière-grands-parents. Ce sont donc des participants à part entière de la communauté économique, sociale et linguistique nationale.

Vivant en France, tous sont amenés, sauf cas d'extrême isolement ou de personnes très âgées, à parler plus ou moins français, ou plutôt un certain français, variété de notre langue que nous côtoyons quotidiennement dans les grandes villes. Variété que nous reconnaissons facilement et à laquelle petit à petit nous nous habituons. A tel point que, face à un étranger, nous adaptons notre compréhension à sa façon de parler (nous rétablissons automatiquement les 'u' prononcés 'ou' par exemple) et nous modifions aussi la nôtre: débit plus lent, gestes accentués, choix de mots simples, phrases plus courtes, répétitions, etc., caractérisent ce qu'on a appelé le 'foreigner talk' (le parler pour étranger).[1]

Ces variétés propres aux migrants, longtemps ignorées ou méprisées comme la plupart des variétés non prestigieuses de notre langue, sont pourtant en train de gagner un certain statut. De nombreuses études leur sont actuellement consacrées en Europe,[2] car elles constituent un terrain tout à fait privilégié pour étudier l'acquisition spontanée d'une langue étrangère, les usages sociaux des variétés et l'évolution des systèmes linguistiques.

Ces parlers trouvent aussi un résonateur dans les media: interviews télévisées de responsables syndicaux, reportages sur les immigrés, livres (récits de vie, témoignages), bandes dessinées et surtout radios libres (Radio-Afrique, Radio-

Eglantine, Radio-Immigrés, etc.) Les émissons s'adressent aux différentes communautés tantôt dans leur langue, tantôt en français avec de nombreux entretiens téléphoniques en direct avec les auditeurs.

Les chansonniers, les imitateurs s'en servent dans leurs spectacles – et, somme toute, l'imitation est une façon de reconnaître l'existence – et le théâtre lui donne ses lettres de noblesse (l'émission télévisée *Le Théâtre de Bouvard* et, par exemple, la pièce d'A. Mnouchkine *L'Age d'or*).

Mais, d'un autre côté, la parole étrangère, identificatrice de l'étranger, prête le flanc aux attaques puristes et racistes. Elle fait l'objet, tout comme ses locuteurs, d'attitudes négatives, de rejets, qui se manifestent par une incompréhension exagérée dans certaines situations: 'il n'cause même pas français' ou 'il ne sait même pas causer'. Les termes de *charabia*, de *petit-nègre* sont fréquemment employés pour le désigner. Des commentaires comme 'je comprends rien à ce qu'il me raconte', 'pourtant il vit en France depuis quinze ans', 'elle parle très mal, avec un très fort accent', 'il parle portugais avec des mots français', 'ils parlent trop vite ou trop fort', 'il baragouine le français' ou 'il parle très bien pour un Arabe' s'entendent couramment et sont révélateurs des différentes attitudes de la part des interlocuteurs français.

[1] Une étude très précise de ces modifications a été faite à Amsterdam auprès des personnels administratifs (poste, SS, etc.) en contact fréquent avec les travailleurs migrants.

[2] Notamment la recherche *Ecology of adult language acquisition* de la Fondation européene pour la science.

(From Francois (ed.) 1983)

Text 2
L'enseignement de l'arabe à l'école élémentaire

Avec l'entrée des enfants d'immigrés à l'école, on a parlé de 'langue de la famille' et 'langue de l'école', en alléguant souvent que la première empêchait l'acquisition de la seconde. Certains éducateurs et psychologues ont considéré les langues maternelles de leurs élèves comme étant 'handicapantes'. Ils 'confondent' à cause d'elle la prononciation du "i" et du "u", la distinction entre "sur", "sous" et "dans" (cet exemple a été cité pour l'espagnol et le portugais), du "ou", du "u" pour l'arabe, etc. Le mot "jambe" chez le petits Algériens comprend la "cuisse" et le "pied" et il s'applique même aux objets: "la jambe de la table"', et il en est conclu pour l'arabe qu'il est une 'langue pauvre, très approximative, peu rigoureuse, d'un niveau généralement bas'.[22]

[22] Extrait d'un rapport de psychologue sur des enfants algériens suivis dans Groupe d'Aide Psycho-pédagogique (cité par Léontine Gripois (linguiste). 'Enfants immigrés et échecs scolaires', in *Politique Aujourd'hui*, août-septembre 1974, p. 81–86).

Face à ces difficultés dites handicap langagier, on a réglé la problème en multipliant les formules d'apprentissage rapide du français en 'classe d'initiation', d' 'adaptation', puis de 'perfectionnement', l'orientation vers des 'Sections d'Education Spécialisée' . . . Les Sections d'Education Spécialisée accueillent les plus résistants à un apprentissage 'normal' (ces classes reçoivent un pourcentage trop important d'enfants étrangers (cf. Zirotti, in *France, Pays Multilingue*), souligne l'Education Nationale). Certes, elles sont aussi remplies de petits Français, généralement de milieux défavorisés . . .

L'attitude initiale de l'école face à l'arrivé d'enfants non francophones était de les classer selon leurs compétences à apprendre le français. L'objectif était donc par là-même de renforcer et de préparer la convergence linguistique. Il fallait pour apprendre une langue en désapprendre une autre.

L'enseignement des langues maternelles pour les enfants d'immigrés, autorisé depuis 1929, avec le statut d'une activité scolaire marginale: susceptible d'être organisée en dehors du temps scolaire et à la charge des autorités du pays fournisseur d'immigrés, n'a jusqu'à nos jours presque pas changé d'état. Cet enseignement a connu toutefois un tournant considéré comme une grande innovation avec la publication de la circulaire du 9 avril 1975.

Avant cette date, en ce qui concerne l'arabe, il semble que seule l'Amicale des Algériens avait organisé des cours d'arabe. C'est dans les années 1973–74 que des négociations entre la France et les pays du Maghreb ont amené le ministère de l'Education à autoriser l'enseignement de l'arabe dans le cadre de l'horaire scolaire. Les représentants officiels des trois pays du Maghreb tiennent à rappeler que cette nouveauté appelée 'enseignement intégré' est le résultat de leur propre initiative, comme le mentionne d'ailleurs le texte de la circulaire. Le titre de cette circulaire étant 'Enseignement des langues nationales', on en déduit pour l'arabe que c'est l'arabe classique en tant que langue nationale, langue officielle, qui est enseigné; pourtant le discours de l'institution scolaire française parle de 'langue et culture d'origine', 'langues maternelles'. Or, étant donné que les accords se font entre les gouvernements français et maghrébins, il semble bien logique qu'il s'agisse de fait de la langue officielle.

Pour l'enfant d'immigrés arabes, eux-mêmes ignorant la langue arabe classique la plupart du temps, cette langue est pour lui 'un peu' étrangère. L'idéologie de légitimation de cette langue est absente de son environnement. Les discours officiels, les médias, l'idéologie religieuse ou politique qui participent à la création d'un sentiment d'appartenance panarabique favorisant la légitimation de cette langue n'existe pas ici. Le mythe de l'unité arabe ne fait pas partie des principales préoccupations de l'enfant immigré né en France et souvent décidé d'y rester, comme le soulignent les sondages sur la question du retour au pays d'origine. Ce qui risque de le troubler, c'est *sa méconnaissance de 'sa' langue*. Les manuels ont pour titre: 'L'arabe, ma langue.' La couverture du manuel tunisien comporte la carte territoriale du Monde Arabe.

Lorsque l'enfant vient à apprendre 'sa langue', il apprendra d'abord qu'il ne la connaît pas. On lui découvre qu'il ne sait bien parler ni le français, ni l'arabe. Il est alors étranger, même en sa langue. Alors que parmi les justifications de cet enseignement figure en bonne place l'argument de l'enracinement nécessaire dans la langue maternelle, grâce à la communication dans cette langue avec sa famille. Or, pourra-t-il communiquer avec ses parents dans cette forme de langue qui n'est pas la leur? Ou bien pensera-t-il que ses parents ne parlent pas bien l'arabe? Les expressions utilisées à la maison sont des fautes: on lui apprend à nommer les choses autrement. Le passage à l'écrit de cette seule forme constitue la consécration de cette forme comme langue, celle qu'il parle avec sa famille ne s'écrit pas. Ainsi, pour l'enfant, son parler arabe, celui de ses parents, de son entourage est une faute. Pour la France aussi: c'est la communauté nationale qui a exporté ces hommes qui doit seule payer pour eux la légitimation de l'acte d'élocution dans leur langue. Ces cours sont financés par le budget des Etats tunisien, algérien et marocain, ce qui constitue pour eux une lourde charge.

(From Jerab 1988)

6

Gender and language in French

MARIE-MARTHE GERVAIS

Definition of gender as a grammatical category

The origin of gender, as a grammatical category, has given rise to a variety of theories and suppositions. It was thought that the distinction between the sexes led to the division between genders in grammars. This hypothesis does not, of course, account for the gender of a multitude of nouns which are inanimate and cannot in any way be linked to one sex or another. It is still currently admitted that grammatical gender is rather arbitrary and is not a static category: for example nouns like *doute* were feminine at first, and from sixteenth century its gender started fluctuating and became masculine only at the beginning of the seventeenth century. Yet, this arbitrary nature of gender in French was challenged by Bidot (1925), by Mel'cuk and, more recently by Tucker, Lambert and Rigault (1977) who established that the proportion of nouns covered by assignment rules is very high. The semantic assignment rules take precedence over the morphological rules but the major assignment rules are phonological. This led G. Corbett (1991: 61) to conclude that 'French, often quoted as a case for proving that gender is irrational, has a system of gender assignment rules.'

Most Indo-European languages have a classification in two or three genders. Many have three genders: feminine, masculine and neuter, for example, German, Slavic languages, Greek and Latin. Others distinguish between the common gender (i.e. masculine–feminine) and the neuter, as in Swedish and Danish. In Welsh, all nouns have a grammatical gender, all dogs being masculine and all cats being feminine, whatever their sex. In German, one word for 'woman' (*das Weib*) is neuter as is the word for 'girl' (*das Mädchen*). Many languages do not have grammatical gender at all, for example: Eskimo, Hungarian, Turkish, some American Indian languages, paleosiberian languages and some African languages. In Swahili, for example, there are seven 'classes' of nouns, which divide them according to various criteria, a system of classification which is sometimes referred to as 'primitive'! With inanimates there is no link between reality and gender as grammatical gender is merely a convention. It is a question of usage and as such it varies from language to language. There is no reason why *la lune* should be feminine but *le soleil* masculine and the other way around in German! Some languages have almost completely eliminated grammatical gender. For example, English has only retained 'she', 'he', 'hers', 'his' and a few morphological markers.

French distinguishes between two grammatical genders: masculine and feminine, which do not always correspond to the natural gender distinction between male and female. When there is a correlation between grammatical gender and natural gender (sex), grammarians talk about motivated gender. Gender may be motivated by morphological analogy. Thus, *armoire* and *écritoire* became feminine because most words ending in *-oire* are feminine. Gender may also be motivated by semantic analogy, thus *alarme* became feminine in the seventeenth century because of *arme*; *minuit* was influenced by *midi* and, after a period of hesitation in the sixteenth and seventeenth centuries, became masculine. Sometimes ellipsis causes a change of gender: *le (bateau à) vapeur, un (fiacre de) remise, le (vin de) Champagne, le (périodique) Marie-Claire*, etc. This metonymic use of nouns constitutes another type of motivation.

Even for animates, gender is often conventional rather than correlating with natural gender. One can cite feminine substantives which have a (+ male) referent. For instance: *une sentinelle, une ordonnance, une estafette, une recrue, une vigie, une vedette (soldat de cavalerie), une clarinette solo* and other words referring to army life, as well as nouns with a pejorative connotation: *une gouape, une crapule, une canaille, une fripouille.* Similarly, some masculine forms refer to a (female) noun, for example: *un chameau, un trumeau, un vieux tibi, un laideron, un souillon, un bas-bleu, un trottin, un tendron, un mannequin.* Some of these nouns take both genders, e.g. *un/une souillon, un/une laideron.* Some refer to either a woman or a man, e.g. *un trottin, un souillon,* whereas others like *un bas-bleu* can only have a (+ female) referent. Most of the words cited in this list are not common nowadays. Some animal names in French designate the species and a qualifier has to be added to indicate gender e.g.: *un éléphant femelle, une souris mâle.* In colloquial French, some hypocoristic nouns are used in the masculine form to denote a feminine referent, e.g.: *mon poulet, mon chéri, mon petit,* whereas the reverse is much less common, e.g. *ma vieille* to refer to a man.

The distribution of French nouns between the feminine and the masculine is an inheritance from Latin. Ninety per cent of French nouns derived from Latin have retained their Latin gender. All traces of the

Latin neuter have disappeared in French, as nearly all the Latin neuters became masculine. Thus, in contemporary French, words like *ce, cela, tout, rien, il* (in its so-called 'impersonal' use), which have a masculine form, are supposedly neuters and are better called genderless since there is no neuter category as such in French. Thus, *personne* when used as an indefinite negative pronoun is genderless (masculine in practice) and one would write *personne n'est venu*. The same applies to *chose* when used with a neuter meaning in conjunction with *quelque* or *autre*, e.g. *quelque chose s'est passé*. So, semantically, the neuter in contemporary French still exists e.g.: *il pleut, je te le dis, le vrai, que faites-vous?*, although they have the masculine.

The morphological characteristics of gender

Many determiners, in French, are morphologically marked for gender, at least in the singular. Thus we have: *la/le, un/une, ce/cet/cette, son/sa*. The information denoting gender can be redundant since the gender is often morphologically marked in the noun as well, e.g. *la chanteuse*. Gender can be neutralised by the morphological system, e.g. *lui, l', des, ces, ses, leur*, etc. Unlike English, subject-personal pronouns are marked for gender in the third-person plural as well as in the third-person singular: *il/elle*, and *elles/ils*. Object pronouns, when used directly, are marked for gender in the singular, e.g. *la/le (je la regarde)* but not in the plural. When used indirectly, they are not marked for gender, e.g. *lui, leur*. In the case of *lui*, the context usually enables one to discern whether it means 'to her' or 'to him'.

In the spoken language, it is sometimes only the article which enables the learner to ascertain the gender, for example if he or she hears a word like *Moyen Age* which sounds like / n /, i.e. it sounds exactly as if it were feminine (i.e. *moyenne*), due to the *liaison*. The same would apply to *bon élève*, which orally is identical to *bonne élève*: [bɔnelɛv].

Suffixation in French is a common morphological process to obtain a change of gender. The most common type of suffixation to obtain a feminine form is to add an 'e' to a masculine form, e.g. *une amie, une commerçante*. In the first example the pronunciation remains the same as in the singular, whereas in the second example the consonant 't' does not remain mute. The addition of 'e' entails modifications to both the pronunciation and the spelling, e.g. [ami] versus [cɔmɛrsât].

The gender agreement is sometimes only relevant in the grammar of written French, e.g. *elle est allée, les lettres qu'elle a lues*. In both these examples, the gender is not marked in spoken French, whereas it would have been in the case of e.g. *les lettres qu'elle a ouvertes*.

The traditional teaching of gender

Both in linguistic descriptions of French, and in the teaching of French, the masculine form is traditionally taken as the base form. Thus textbooks and dictionaries have sections devoted to 'la formation du féminin'. Learners discover that the feminine form is derived from the masculine one to which an 'e' has been adjuncted. To this simple rule, they have to add the learning of the phonetic and orthographic changes which ensue and all the attendant exceptions.

Given the shift of emphasis from the written to the spoken language in language teaching and, more recently, to the communicative approach, it would appear more logical to some to adopt the reverse process in the teaching of gender and to posit the feminine form as the starting point, in a number of cases (see table 6.1).

Table 6.1 *The formation of the masculine in French*

1. Words terminated by a mute 'e' in the feminine, lose the 'e' in the written form.	*aiguë* [ɛgy]	→	*aigu*
	vue [vy]	→	*vu*
	grecque [grɛk]	→	*grec*
2. Words terminated by an audible consonant in the feminine form in spoken French, lose this consonant in the spoken form, with or without a vowel change.	*dernière* [dɛrnjɛr]	→ →	*dernier* [dɛrnje]
	morte [mɔrt]	→ →	*mort* [mɔr]
	fausse [fos]	→ →	*faux* [fo]
3. Feminine words ending in a vowel + a nasal consonant lose this consonant and are terminated by a nasal vowel in the masculine form.	*blanche* [blãʃ]	→ →	*blan* [blã]
	brune [bryn]	→ →	*brun* [brõẽ]
	bénigne [beniɲ]	→ →	*bénin* [benẽ]

In a number of cases, it is immaterial whether the base form is the masculine or the feminine one, e.g.:

juive	→	*juif*	or	*sèche* → *sec*
[ʒɥiv]	→	[ʒɥif]		[sɛʃ] → [sɛk]

Generations of French school children have learned the slogan 'le masculin l'emporte sur le féminin', e.g. *Jean et ses sœurs sont allés au théâtre; Elle a étudié des questions et aspects importants*. However, this is not always the case. When the adjective is juxtaposed to a feminine noun, for example, the rule known as 'attraction' prevails and the adjective takes the feminine form, as witnessed by the famous example quoted in numerous grammar books: *Armez-vous d'un courage et d'une foi nouvelle.* There has, however, been a tolerance since 1901 and one is permitted to write, for example: *les mots et expressions usuels.*

It is commonly thought that French native speakers can instinctively indicate the gender of a French word. Albeit true for most commonly used nouns, it is the case that French people hesitate over the gender of some less frequently used substantives, for example *orbite, alluvion, élastique, enzyme, glucose, lignite, fructose, saccharose, hémisphère* (the first three of these are feminine). Many prescriptive grammars list these grey areas (cf. Grévisse 1987: 206–7). Grévisse notes that *Le Larousse* may even make a mistake, making *agrume* feminine in one edition in the 1930s.

There are further complexities attached to gender, for example:

le manche, la manche
le mémoire, la mémoire
le mode, la mode
le voile, la voile

These words now have different meanings and different genders, but originally stem from the same root, e.g. *manche* comes from the Latin adjective *manicum, manucam* derived from *manus* which means 'hand'. Others, like *tour*, have different origins. *Le tour* originates from the Latin *tornare* whereas *la tour* comes from the Latin *turrem.*

In these examples gender enables one to differentiate the meaning of the two words. Some words change gender when they are used in the plural. For example, in literary French, the word *amour* becomes feminine in the plural, example: *de folles amours.* Similarly, in literary French, the word *délice* is also feminine in the plural, e.g. *les délices de la vie*; the word *orgues* (feminine plural) refers to one instrument only, e.g. *les grandes orgues de Notre-Dame*, but when one refers to several instruments, one uses the masculine plural, e.g. *les deux orgues de cette église ont été réparés.* The word *Pâques* (Easter) is masculine and is followed by a verb in the singular, e.g. *Pâques tombe en avril cette année* but when used with an adjective it becomes feminine plural, e.g. *joyeuses pâques* (normally written without a capital 'p'). It is also used in the feminine plural in the following expressions: *Pâques fleuries, Pâques closes* and *faire ses pâques.* However it is feminine singular in the following connotations: *la pâque russe, la pâque juive, manger la pâque.*

The word *gens* is somewhat problematic; it is a masculine noun but the adjective which immediately precedes it is feminine, e.g. *de vieilles gens*; when *gens* is followed by *de* then the adjective remains masculine, e.g. *de durs gens de mer.* Furthermore, when the adjective which immediately precedes *gens* is terminated in the masculine by a mute 'e' (e.g. *brave, honnête, habile*), this adjective remains masculine as well as those that precede it, e.g. *tous les braves gens*. The word *jeunes gens* has a generic meaning but it is more commonly understood as the plural of *jeune homme* nowadays ('Jeunes gens: personnes jeunes et célibataires, garçons et filles', *Le dictionnaire de notre temps*, 1990: Hachette).

The situation regarding gender in French is further complicated by the fact that a number of words do not yet have a well-established, recognised form in the feminine. Grévisse states that certain nouns do not have a feminine form, e.g. *un assassin, un yogi, un bandit, un intercesseur, un gourmet, un zouave, un précurseur* appear in most dictionaries as 'nom masculin' and have no feminine form. Others, like *amateur*, have had a feminine form which has fallen into disuse. Such words are commented on in a recent book by M. Yaguello: 'Gourmète. On a le droit d'être gourmande mais être gourmet est réservé aux hommes' (Yaguello 1989: 83). 'Zouave. On n'est pas près de voir une zouavesse sous le pont de l'Alma' (Yaguello 1989: 165).

The feminine form *amatrice* first appeared in 1488 and was used currently in the literature of the seventeenth and eighteenth centuries. The *Robert* dictionary says 'Amateur se dit d'une femme car amatrice, employé par Rousseau et recommandé par Littré, n'est point entré dans l'usage.' As early as 1810 the question of the feminine as an issue. 'Ce mot a-t-il un féminin? Fault-il dire une femme amateur ou une amatrice? Il me semble que l'analogie nous autorise à donner un féminin à ce mot; on dit une spectatrice, une actrice . . . ; pourquoi ne dirait-on pas une amatrice? . . . On objectera peut-être qu'on ne dit pas autrice . . . ' (E. Molard, *Le mauvais langage corrigé*, 1810).

Some words cannot have a masculine form because their referent can only be [+ female], being thus semantically bound by the natural gender, e.g. *nourrice* (in the sense of a woman who breastfeeds a baby), *parturiente, mère-porteuse* or the adjective *enceinte*. These words are slightly different from words which also appear only in the feminine form in dictionaries, e.g. *nonne, nonnette, amazone, douairière* which could conceivably have a masculine equivalent although there is not one in the language.

Similarly, some words do not have a feminine form because their referent can only be [+ male], e.g. *eunuque, donneur de sperme, castrat*. These are different from words like *chevalier servant, mandarin, syndic, torero, témoin, zombi*, etc. which could also feasibly have a feminine form, i.e. a feminine referent is a possibility.

Some words have recently acquired a masculine form which has not yet been accepted in everyday usage. Thus the masculine of *sage-femme* is not **sage-homme* but a *maïeuticien*, a newish coinage from the Greek *maieutiké* meaning the art of delivering. The feminine form *jardinière* *d'enfants* has not yet led to the form *jardinier d'enfants*. The same is true of *puéricultrice* and its masculine counterpart *puériculteur*. The word *père célibataire* is used but not yet recorded in the dictionaries whereas *mère célibataire* is.

Gender constitutes a specific problem area for learners of French as a foreign language. Masculine words ending in 'e' are often perceived as feminine by students, for example *manque*, which is invariably mistaken for a feminine.

Certain words are known as the feminine generic nouns, e.g. *personne, victime, connaissance, vedette, star*. The generic masculine is usually a word which first and foremost connotes male beings. When used generically, the masculine subsumes the feminine. Feminine words used generically tend to neutralise the sex.

Just as man can be [+ male], the word *personne* can be marked [+ female], for example, in expressions like *les belles personnes, une jolie personne, les personnes du sexe*, etc. Whereas the noun *personne* is feminine, the indefinite pronoun is masculine, e.g. *personne n'est venu ce matin*.

Prescriptive grammars offer guidelines to enable students to determine the gender of nouns in French. However, there are so many exceptions to the rules that govern gender that this question was described as 'le Désordre généralisé' (Sauvageot 1978: 66).

Contemporary usage

The fact that women have penetrated into professions hitherto reserved for men has caused considerable linguistic turmoil in France, though this did not become really noticeable until the 1980s. As late as 1976, in the *Grand Larousse du vingtième siècle*, a qualified pharmacist was always *un pharmacien*, irrespective of whether it referred to a woman or a man. In 1983, in the *Reference Grammar of Modern French*, Judge and Healey wrote: 'The opening up to women of professions previously exclusively reserved for men is causing linguistic problems' (p. 7).

It may be causing problems to students of French but it seems fair to point out that the problem is not new: words like *professeur* do not have a feminine and yet 60 per cent of secondary school teachers in France are women, and the problem is not intrinsically linguistic but social in nature. It might be more accurate to posit that this new phenomenon is increasing the area of hesitation and confusion (Grévisse 1987: 247).

In the United States of America, an awareness of this linguistic issue began to emerge in the early 1970s. Until then, a woman who presided over a meeting used to be called 'chairman' but this then became 'chairwoman', later 'chairperson' and finally the epicene term 'chair' denoting either sex. The debate did not limit itself to the lexis and some suggestions were put forward to revise this sacrosanct closed set: the pronominal system. 'Nigerians have only one pronoun for him and her and I think this is the direction we'll go some day. Ultimately people won't be distinguished by sex or gender with any more import than we give eye colour.' (Varda One 1971: 15). The promotion of a third-person singular pronoun to replace 'she' and 'he' did not succeed.

In the lexical field, changes were proposed at grassroots level and they reached publishing houses which issued guidelines for their authors. In 1975, a book entitled 'Job Title Revisions to Eliminate Sex-and-Age-Reference Language from the Dictionary of Occupational Titles' was published by the Ministry for Labor in the USA. It proposed among other things, to replace the following words by an epiceneous alternative:

charwoman	→ charworker
fisherman	→ fisher
foreman, forelady	→ supervisor
office boy, girl	→ office helper
salesman, saleswoman	→ sales agent

In each case, one notices that the resulting neologism does not 'feminise' the masculine form but neutralises the gender distinction.

Even in Switzerland, where women were only given the federal vote in 1972, a motion relative to non-sexist terminology was heard at the *Grand Conseil* and terms like *Conseillère Régionale, Conseillère Fédérale* and *députée* were adopted before there had been any kind of official recognition in France that the supposedly generic term was perceived as gender specific.

In the United States of America, the revolt against the linguistic status quo had political undertones as witnessed by the incisive titles of articles published at that time. For example, 'Women's speech: separate but unequal?', 'The semantic derogation of woman', 'The politics of linguistic sexism', 'Words that oppress'.

It was common to see 'Women's Lib People', 'The Third World People', 'The Blacks', and 'The Chicanos' associated in their protest marches. Language was denounced as an instrument which enabled those in power to impose their will on the weak and the oppressed. Sexism began to be associated with racism – being partly determined and reinforced by language, and consciously or not, by words. In the words of H. A. Bosmajian 'The blacks who have no longer allowed themselves to be defined by the whites are a freer people. Women need to do the same.'

In France, when Yvette Roudy became *Ministre des Droits de la Femme*, she raised the linguistic *question* of the feminisation of job titles in social and political terms. The absence of some feminine forms in French was seen as an obstacle to social change, it was not merely a language question but also *un problème de société*.

Yvette Roudy stated that her action did not limit itself to language but was part of a general political project aimed at reducing inequalities between men and women. In July 1983, a law concerning 'l'égalité professionnelle entre les femmes et les hommes' was passed. One of the stipulations made was that no mention of a preferred sex should appear in any job advertisement. This law was easily applied when both masculine and feminine forms were available, e.g. *Société recherche vendeurs/vendeuses, groupe international recherche employé(e)s* but certain titles did not have a feminine form, e.g. *professeur, chef, entrepreneur, magistrat, huissier, commissaire-priseur, ingénieur, croupier, sapeur-pompier.* It was clearly contradictory to encourage women to enter the professions when there could be no linguistic recognition of their success in entering jobs which had been traditionally male preserves.

Yvette Roudy thought this constituted a handicap for women which was all the more scandalous because the lacunae in the language were found in the higher echelons of the social hierarchy; women who reached these heights were still perceived as anomalies to be at best tolerated. From a diachronic point of view, it seemed odd that the evaluation of language was not concomitant with social change. Yvette Roudy argued that this was profoundly anachronistic and constituted an injustice to women: it was as if language were precluding women from gaining access to certain jobs. Although a number of feminine forms were then not found in dictionaries, they were used currently in colloquial spoken French, e.g. *la toubib, une prof, une chauffeuse (de taxi), la maire, la factrice, une voyoute, la chéfesse, la chirurgienne,* etc.

In the spring of 1983, on her initiative, a preliminary committee was set up, with the following aims:

a) To establish acceptable rules for the formation of the feminine and to determine the linguistic constraints of it;
b) To identify problem areas;
c) To propose neologisms where necessary.

For Anne-Marie Houdebine, the Commission's task is at the confluence between language and politics; it refuses to see language as fossilised and it refutes any kind of absolute prescriptivism; Houdebine sees the linguistic policy of the Commission in terms of reclaiming language, something A. Leclerc had tried to do earlier (1974).

> On peut agir, dans les potentialités d'une langue, en la traitant comme vivante et non comme figée, en lui redonnant ses capacités d'innovations et ainsi en les rendant à les locuteur(e)s . . . redonner à chacune/ chacun sa parole, sa langue, sa voix. (Houdebine 1984)

To support this argument, one can cite numerous feminine words which were in common use in the Middle Ages, for example: *barbière, chirurgienne, bourrelle, abbesse, diaconesse, chasseresse, avocate, ministresse*. Many feminine forms have fallen into disuse: *successrice, vainqueresse, chanteresse, clergesse, possesseuse, mirgesse* (cf. Yaguello 1989). The Commission was made up of representatives of government ministries, sociologists, lecturers, educationists and grammarians as well as one representative of the *Académie française*. Benoîte Groult, the French *écrivaine*, as she calls herself, was made president of the Commission. The Commission continued its work along the lines of the provisional committee set up earlier.

It is interesting to point out that in other francophone countries this question reached the forefront of national awareness before it did in France. A law passed on 4 August 1978, in Belgium, forbids the use of discriminatory terminology in job advertisements and this leads to more feminine titles being used in the press. In Canada (other than Quebec), it was not until 1983 that official action was taken (see *L'Actualité terminologique*, 1983). It recommended the use of feminine titles and published a list of four hundred masculine titles with their feminine equivalents. The impact of this measure remained patchy, as even two years later the publicity campaign produced by the Immigration Employment Office was still couched in sexist language. Although women were urged by the *Office* to apply for jobs which in the past had not been open to them, they could read in the publicity: 'Vous pourriez devenir . . . électricien . . . réparateur'.

In Quebec, the question of feminisation gathered momentum earlier. As early as 1976, Madame Louise Cuerrier, vice-president of the National Assembly, declared that she would only call herself *présidente* when feminine forms had been found for all the job titles within the National Assembly. On 28 July 1979, the *Gazette officielle du Québec* published the first set of recommendations regarding feminine forms for titles. This proved useful but insufficient, as it did not resolve the most tricky cases. The recommendations were straightforward and four methods were proposed for using a feminine form whenever possible:

1. The use of a feminine form which already exists in the language, e.g. *avocate, infirmière;*

2. The use of the epicene term preceded by a feminine determiner, as gender indicator, e.g. *une ministre, une architecte;*

3. The creation of a feminine form which does not contravene French morphological rules, e.g. *la députée; la praticienne;*

4. The adjunction of the word: *femme*, e.g. *femme-ingénieur, femme-chef d'entreprise, femme-magistrat.*

At this point one is entitled to ask why use *avocate* but not *magistrate*, why *députée* but not *ingénieure*, why *femme-chef d'entreprise* rather than *une chef d'entreprise*?

A committee was set up in the autumn of 1982 to resolve such contradictions and it produced a report in the spring of 1983, mentioning possible feminine forms for about two hundred typical cases as well as enunciating general principles. This report was entitled *La féminisation des titres; énoncé de principes et étude de cas-types*. The working party included representatives from the *Conseil du statut de la femme*, a very dynamic body which was particularly active in the struggle against linguistic sexism. It declared that:

> Parallèlement à la francisation des entreprises, la désexisation de la langue française s'impose et devrait être un objectif de l'office de la langue française. (avant propos, p. xxi)

In the spring of 1983 the *Académie canadienne-française* organised debates on this topic. Some participants felt that the feminisation of job titles was slowed down by 'le fixisme des locuteurs français' (as reported in *Presse* 19 February 1983, p. 3), especially in France, and not because of the French morphological system itself. One member of the *Académie canadienne-française* wished to move fast, 'qu'on aille en tout cas plus vite que les Français (et certaines Françaises)'. Some warned against the mentality of the 'colonisés' and the danger of waiting for a *licet* from France. Following the report in 1983, the president of the *Office de la langue française* asked for a survey to be carried out to assess people's views on this controversial question. This led to the publication of a detailed document based on 79 persons referred to as 'leaders d'opinion', 47 women and 32 men. It is significant that 67.8 per cent of the informants were of the opinion that Quebec should play a leading role in the process of feminisation, vis-à-vis France and other francophone countries (Martin and Dupuis 1985).

Finally, on 4 April 1986, the *Office de la langue française* approved a text pertaining to these changes entitled *Titres et fonctions au féminin: essai d'orientation de l'usage*. It was decided not to impose the new linguistic forms but merely to 'privilégier certaines formes'. It is not possible to quote them all here, but, *à titre d'exemple*, one can cite the following:

> *une cadre, une juge* (epicene forms);
> *une contremaîtresse, une mairesse* (although the office also accepts *une contremaître* and *une maire*);
> *une ministre, une notaire, une peintre;*
> *une poète;*
> *une conseil-juridique;*
> *une consule;*

une chirurgienne;
une écrivaine;
une mannequin;
une marin;
une médecin;
une batonnière, une pompière;
une arpenteuse, une chercheuse, une régisseuse;
une gouverneure;
une ingénieure;
une professeure;
une amatrice, une rectrice;
une auteure;
une docteure;
une sculpteure;
une soldate, une coopérante;
une matelot, une camelot;
une substitut;
une chargée de, une députée;
une chef;
une commis.

On the whole, one observes that the use of epicene terms is limited, that the OLF rejects the use of *femme* followed by a masculine noun (e.g. *femme-policier*) and that the form of feminisation that prevails is that which is marked phonetically and morphologically. The salient feature which departs from the 'norm' in terms of normative suffixation is the fashionable coinage of the form in *eure* reserved primarily for a handful of professions such as those quoted above (i.e. mainly *haut de gamme*).

This publication was followed, in 1988, by another: *Pour un genre à part entière: guide pour la rédaction de textes non sexistes*, published by the Ministry of Education, under the aegis of the *coordonnatrice à la condition féminine*.

This guide is significant, as it takes the question a step further: how are these feminine forms to be integrated in discourse, since in French, gender also affects determiners, adjectives, past participles, etc. For example, the guidelines suggest: les premiers électeurs et électrices; la cégépienne ou le cégépien qui sont inscrits (agreement in the masculine plural, as there is an idea of conjunction), whereas: *le premier ministre ou la gouverneure générale . . . présidera* (agrement in the masculine singular as there is an idea of disjunction here) (Dumais, Violette et al. 1988: 10–11).

Whereas in Quebec the work done by the OLF found support in the media and among the population, in France there was a general outcry when the Commission was set up. Although it was established legally and it came in the wake of numerous other such *commissions de terminologie* since 1972 (these commissions were instituted under the aegis of the *Comité de Défense de la langue française* in 1972 when George Pompidou was prime minister), it provoked violent reactions in the media, particularly in the press and even in parliament (see *Journal Officiel*, 17 December 1984). Members of the Commission felt that there was a conspiracy between reactionary forces in matters of language and sexist ideology. Attacks against the Commission were scathing and often crudely expressed; its members were ridiculed as: 'des folles qui ne doutent de rien'; '[des] précieuses futiles'; '[des] dames pomponnées; '[se] réunissant à l'heure du thé'; '[pour] enjuponner le vocabulaire'.

The *Académie française* even sent an *avertissement* to the Commission and a former education minister, A. Peyrefitte, saw it as threat to the existence of this venerable institution: 'Jamais aucun des 17 régimes qui se sont succédés depuis la monarchie absolue n'avait remis en cause cette mission de l'Académie. L'actuel gouvernement l'avait jusqu'à présent respectée . . . Il semble aller plus loin dans la voie du dessaisissement et peut-être – comme on lui en a prêté l'intention – de l'étouffement de l'Académie' (*Le Figaro*, 23 June 1984).

Whereas the *Académie* perceived the intervention of the Commission as destructive, debasing the French language, the Commission saw its role in terms of 'revivification' which had, in certain respects, become fossilised.

The intention of the Commission was to fill the semantic gaps in the language but without disregarding the morphological structures of French. As it turned out, the main difficulty which the committee had to contend with was not the lack of possible feminine forms but the plethora of possibilities which they had to consider and choose from. They were at pains to emphasise that the stumbling block was not linguistic in nature but social. It is worth mentioning that feminisation was already well established for the so-called 'petits métiers' (e.g. *lingère, institutrice, coiffeuse*) and for those professions which have been followed by women for a considerable time (e.g. *vendeuse, secrétaire*). However, up until recently, one had no answers to give to students when they asked what was the feminine form of: *chauffeur de taxi; censeur; maçon; magistrat; maître-assistant, professeur, ingénieur; précurseur* and members of many more professions.

The Commission did some preliminary work consulting dictionaries and examining written and oral production in the media. Surveys were carried out both to find out what people say and how they feel about various neologisms: 'enquêtes de production et d'attitudes'. In the latter, linguists noticed that resistance to feminisation was marked in professions which had excluded women up until recently: the army, magistrature, the law, the stock exchange and even the medical profession. However, the reluctance to accept forms like: *magistrate, avocate, officière, lieutenante, chirurgienne, médecine, une dermatologue,* etc. does not simply come from people in those professions but also from respondents working in other fields.

The only real linguistic problems encountered by the Commission were with isolated lexical items like *témoin. Témoin* meant *témoinage* originally and is not primarily an agent. Apparently people were influenced by the Falklands war and suggested *témouine* derived from *Malouines!* Marina Yaguello suggested *tésmoing* as the 'g' appears in the old form *tesmoing* and remains in the verb *témoigner.* The Commission opted for the *féminisation minimale* with *la témoin.*

The Commission finished its work on 26 January 1986 and the *Journal Officiel* published its recommendations on 16 March 1986 (see text at the end of the chapter).

The Commission has concluded that it was necessary to let 'les usages trancher' but this was felt to be too much of a sociolinguistic approach incompatible with a legislative text. The final wording remains muted, the word 'recommendation' is the key one and there is no hint of prescriptivism. Some years later we know that some newspapers have taken on board these proposals and others still display a marked aversion towards changes or have no editorial policy on this matter. It is also interesting to note that the French Commission, like the OLF, excluded the possibility of adding *femme* to an existing noun.

This proves that Joseph Hanse's predictions were wrong. In 1983 he expressed the opinion that it would be difficult to adopt feminine forms and that compounds like *femme auteur* and *femme écrivain* would continue to be used. He was also to be proved wrong when he wrote 'tout évoluerait plus vite si les femmes le voulaient ou seulement y consentaient' (Hanse 1983: 447).

The Commission put the emphasis on the use of the feminine determiner *une/la* (i.e. the *féminisation minimale*) and in the use of the derivational suffix. But it did not go so far as suggesting the *-eure* suffix which is now used in Quebec. This cautious approach is the result of the criticisms that the Commission was subjected to or perhaps it emanates from a desire not to be seen to emulate other francophone countries where linguistic matters tend to evolve more rapidly and are less constrained by institutions like the *Académie française.* Perhaps also because it was thought that it would have a greater impact if it was not perceived as a policy of feminist linguistic reformism.

It is also interesting to note the divergent path taken by the francophone countries and by the English speaking ones. Whereas neutralised forms tend to prevail nowadays in English (the chair, the students, etc.), the French have emphasised the sexual difference through language:

the Canadian French even more so than the French in France, cf. *-eure/-eur*, which are phonologically identical.

It is significant that the first dictionary of French for French-speaking people in America has recently been published: *Dictionnaire du français plus, à l'usage des francophones d'Amérique* (1988), taking on board the recommendations of the OLF.

At another level, women intellectuals in France have been active in extending the debate beyond the question of professional designations and gender endings. There has been considerable discussion as to whether there is, or should be, a *parler-femme*, a particularly female form of speech reflecting women's mode of being, and giving expression to hitherto repressed feelings and experiences; a form of speech enabling women to reclaim their identity, their *féminitude*, and freeing them from the *langage masculin*. As one woman put it: 'J'ai souvent le sentiment de me sentir coincée, enfin, ancrée dans un, dans un mode d'expression qui est pas moi, enfin qui est, qu'on peut appeler masculin' (Aebischer 1983: 186).

Early feminist writers argued on behalf on such a language (Leclerc 1974; Cardinal 1975), in which rebelling against traditional syntax, fragmentation and the ebb and flow of unpunctuated sentences would represent the overthrow of 'male logocentrism' and would (supposedly) reflect female rhythms.

Some critics – with the approval of the author at one stage – saw M. Duras' style as an illustration of this 'écriture féminine'. Other contemporary women writers have experimented with new ways of foregrounding women in their writing. Monique Wittig, for example, experiments with getting rid of the generic *il* narrator, using *on* in *L'Opoponax* (1964), and *elles* in *Les Guérillères* (1969).

Conclusion

The battle against the suppression of women through language has been fierce. It could be argued that linguistic interventionism in France has never been successful and on this occasion it provoked extraordinarily prejudiced reactions and has only resulted in very moderate suggestions. Further surveys and analyses of linguistic corpora will be necessary to assess to what extent these recommendations have been absorbed in the French language and by whom.

Gender is an issue which is often too conveniently omitted from books on French sociolinguistics, thus further contributing to the obliteration of women through language. No learner of French would wish to be 'un perroquet anonyme mimant une langue quasi morte' (Houdebine-Gravaud 1989: 132). In learning French one could hope that 'chaque une, chaque un, peut redevenir créateur de la langue et faire advenir en elle d'autres paroles, et qui sait? peut-être d'autres mentalités . . . Ethique (linguistique) de chaque jour' (ibid. 133).

Text 1
Les règles de la féminisation des noms de métiers

**Circulaire du 11 mars 1986 relative a la féminisation
des noms de métier, fonction, grade ou titre**
Paris, le 11 mars 1986

Le Premier ministre, à Mesdames et Messieurs les ministres et secrétaires d'Etat

L'accession des femmes, de plus en plus nombreuses à des fonctions de plus en plus diverses, est une réalité qui doit trouver sa traduction dans le vocabulaire.

Pour adapter la langue à cette évolution sociale, Mme Yvette Roudy, ministre des droits de la femme, a mis en place, en 1984, une commission de terminologie chargée de la féminisation des noms de métier et de fonction, présidée par Mme Benoîte Groult.

Cette commission vient d'achever ses travaux et a remis ses conclusions. Elle a dégagé un ensemble de règles permettant la féminisation de la plupart des noms de métier, grade, fonction ou titre.

Ces règles sont définies en annexe à la présente circulaire.

Je vous demande de veiller à l'utilisation de ces termes:

– dans les décrets, arrêtés, circulaires, instructions et directives ministériels;

– dans les correspondances et documents qui émanent des administrations, services ou établissements publics de l'Etat;

– dans les textes des marchés et contrats auxquels l'Etat ou les établissements publics de l'Etat sont parties;

– dans les ouvrages d'enseignement, de formation ou de recherche utilisés dans les établissements, institutions ou organismes dépendant de l'Etat, placés sous son autorité, ou soumis à son contrôle, ou bénéficiant de son concours financier.

Pour ce qui concerne les différents secteurs d'activités économiques et sociales dont vous avez la charge, il vous appartient de prendre les contacts nécessaires avec les organisations socio-professionnelles concernées afin d'étudier les modalités spécifiques de mise en œuvre de ces dispositions.

LAURENT FABIUS

ANNEXE

**Règles de féminisation des noms de métier,
fonction, grade ou titre**

Les féminins des noms de métier, fonction, grade ou titre sont formés par application des règles suivantes:

1. L'emploi d'un déterminant féminin: une, la, cette.

2. *a*) Les noms terminés à l'écrit par un 'e' muet ont un masculin et un féminin identiques: une architecte, une comptable . . .

Remarque – On notera que le suffixe féminin 'esse' n'est plus employé en français moderne: une poétesse . . .

b) Les noms masculins terminés à l'écrit par une voyelle autre que le 'e' muet ont un féminin en 'e': une chargée de mission, un déléguée . . .

c) Les noms masculins terminés à l'écrit par une consonne, à l'exception des noms se terminant par 'eur', ont:
– un féminin identique au masculin; une médecin . . . ;
– ou un féminin en 'e' avec éventuellement l'ajout d'un accent sur la dernière voyelle ou le doublement de la dernière consonne: une agente, une huissière, une mécanicienne . . .

d) Les noms masculins terminés en 'tour' ont:
– si le 't' appartient au verbe de base, un féminin en 'teuse': une acheteuse . . . ;
– si le 't' n'appartient pas au verbe de base, un féminin en 'trice': une animatrice . . .

Remarques:
– l'usage actuel a tendance à donner un féminin en 'trice', même à des noms dans lesquels le 't' appartient au verbe de base: une éditrice . . . ;
– dans certains cas, la formes en 'trice' n'est pas aujourd'hui acceptée dans ce cas, on emploiera un féminin identique au masculin: une auteur . . .

e) Les autres noms masculins terminés en 'eur' ont, si le verbe de base est reconnaissable, un féminin en 'euse': une vendeuse, une danseuse . . .

Remarque – Le suffixe féminin 'esse' n'est plus employé en français moderne: une demanderesse . . .

Si le verbe de base n'est pas reconnaissable, que ce soit pour la forme ou le sens, il est recommandé, faute de règle acceptée, d'utiliser un masculin et un féminin identiques: une proviseur, une ingénieur, une professeur . . .

(*Journal Officiel* 16 March 1986, p. 4267)

Text 2
L'élargissement du capitaine Prieur

Le vendredi 6 mai 1988, la France entière apprenait que le capitaine Prieur, agent secret compromis dans l'affaire du *Rainbow Warrior* et assigné à résidence sur un atoll de Polynésie, était rapatrié.

Le motif, selon le communiqué du Premier ministre, Jacques Chirac, était le suivant: '[. . .] Le capitaine Prieur est actuellement *enceinte* et l'accord prévoyait que, dans ces circonstances, *elle* pouvait être rapatriée à Paris.' Le caractère incongru (linguistiquement parlant, naturellement) de cette déclaration ne semble pas avoir troublé M. Chirac. En revanche, certains des journalistes chargés de rendre compte de l'événement ont manifestement été embarrassés d'avoir à utiliser dans une même phrase *Le capitaine Prieur* et l'expression *elle est enceinte*. D'où différentes stratégies d'évitement (*Le Monde, Libération*) ou au contraire de mise en relief (*Le Canard enchaîné*) du problème.

Trois informations devaient être transmises au public:

1) le capitaine Prieur (dont tout les lecteurs savent que c'est une femme) est rentré en France;

2) la personne en question est enceinte;

3) la personne en question est accompagnée de son mari.

Normalement, ces trois informations devraient pouvoir être regroupées en une seule phrase. Par exemple, s'il s'agissait d'une simple citoyenne: 'Mme Prieur, qui est enceinte, est rentrée en France accompagnée de son mari.'

Le rédacteur du *Monde* répartit l'information dans trois phrases distinctes:

(1) '*Le* capitaine Prieur, *un* des deux agents français impliqués dans l'attentat contre le *Rainbow Warrior*, a quitté l'atoll de Hao, où *elle* vivait depuis 1986';

(2) '[. . .] la décision de rapatrier *Mme Prieur* a été prise sur la base d'un "dossier précis"; en fait Mme Prieur serait enceinte';

(3) '[. . .] M. David Lange avait affirmé dans une déclaration que Paris lui avait fait connaître, vendredi matin, sa décision de rapatrier "immédiatement" Mme Prieur, qui est attendue en France avec son mari samedi'.

Il y a de la part du rédacteur de ces lignes un effort louable pour sauvegarder la cohérence grammaticale, à ceci près que, dans la première phrase, *Le capitaine* est repris par *elle*. Ici, le pronom personnel représente directement la personne dont il est question (emploi référentiel) plutôt que de reprendre anaphoriquement un syntagme nominal antécédent – *Le capitaine Prieur*. La cohérence sémantique l'emporte sur les contraintes d'accord grammatical. Si l'accord grammatical avait été respecté (*Le capitaine . . . il*), pour un lecteur non averti, la compréhension n'aurait pas été assurée . . .

Libération adopte une stratégie d'évitement absolu; il titre: 'Le retour opportun et controversé du capitaine Prieur' et sous-titre: 'Assignée à résidence sur l'atoll de Hao depuis sa participation au sabotage du *Rainbow Warrior*, l'ex-épouse Turenge est sur le chemin du retour. Pour cause de grossesse.'

Le problème est ainsi totalement contourné par le recours au pseudonyme mais l'information n'est compréhensible que pour un public qui est au courant des différentes identités du capitaine.

Le rédacteur du *Canard enchaîné* met carrément les pieds dans le plat: il parle dans un premier temps de 'la grossesse rapatriée de *la* capitaine Prieur' puis, un peu plus loin: '"*le*" capitaine Prieur est effectivement enceinte', signalant par des guillemets l'inadéquation de l'article masculin.

. . . Claude Sarraute, mélange sans complexe le féminin et le masculin dans son billet paru dans le même numéro du *Monde*: 'Dominique Prieur, vous savez, Mme ex-Turenge, l'agent secret mêlé à l'attentat du *Rainbow Warrior*, eh ben, elle rapplique. [. . .] d'autant qu'elle attend un bébé, le capitaine Prieur. C'est une future maman.'

Le parti adopté par Claude Sarraute et par *Le Canard enchaîné* reflète (c'est bien entendu l'effet recherché) l'usage oral le plus courant. Dans la pratique, confrontés à cet imbroglio, les locuteurs se débrouillent comme ils peuvent, sans consulter l'arrêté cité ci-dessus (dont peu de gens connaissent l'existence), inspirés par une seule règle: se faire comprendre.

Le cas du capitaine Prieur est rare mais non exceptionnel. En 1990, le Premier ministre du Pakistan, Mme Benazir Bhutto, a posé le même type de problème à la presse en devenant le premier chef de gouvernement en exercice à mettre au monde un enfant.

Évidemment, ce qui simplifierait tout, ça serait de pouvoir féminiser tous les noms d'agent et d'oser dire *la capitaine*. Il faudra sans doute attendre le vingt et unième siècle.

(From Yaguello 1991)

7

The reform of the writing system
NINA CATACH

French spelling as seen by the French

How the French regard their spelling

Even the most 'enlightened' people in France (such as professionals, teachers, the middle and upper classes) talk about French spelling in terms which reflect a strange mixture of curiosity and fear, confidence and ignorance. Historically, we can summarise attitudes towards orthography under three headings:
- a long period of subservience to the written word, the power of which continues to this day;
- from the sixteenth century on, periodic attempts to take up the cause of the spoken language against the written, generally led by grammarians and linguists, with their claims couched in exaggerated language which still colours today's debate.
- more recently, on the part of a minority, a more conciliatory approach which tries to take account of the needs of both the written and the spoken language, and of social realities, and attempts to reconcile the arguments presented by both sides.

Subservience to the written word

Since the Middle Ages, generations of schoolchildren in France have been imbued with the idea that their national language was something noble, or almost sacred. It was impressed upon them that French had to retain its link with Latin, the 'father' of languages and of the humanities, and fount of religion and knowledge. This was further reinforced by royal patronage (Philippe le Bel in the twelfth and thirteenth centuries), promoting the speech of the Ile-de-France, which was as far removed from the local speech of Brittany or Provence as Latin was from French.

In those days, the small number of people who could write (mainly the clerks) possessed a secret treasure of which everyone else was in awe.

Throughout the centuries, certain ideas have come to be associated in France (more than anywhere else in the world, with the possible exception of China) in such a way that the written language has assumed the prestige of Latin; the French schoolchild is taught that spelling is as venerable and essential a part of language, as language is of nationhood.

The Revolution changed nothing. On the contrary, the role of the school as an element of national cohesion was reinforced by the Republicans in the nineteenth century. Knowing how to write was of real social value and the little 'writers', as those children who knew how to write were called, were taken on as lawyer's clerks. Various institutions such as the *Académie* (see chapter 1) were set up as guardians of 'good language', and the presses, with their large centralised workshops which dealt with newspapers, administrative documents, school textbooks and everything which needed printing, ruled supreme over the writing system.

Thus, with the introduction of compulsory schooling in the J. Ferry laws of 1882–5, it could be said that the primary schoolteacher came to regard spelling rather as the priest regarded the catechism, something to be passed on as it was, without a single letter being altered. These deep-seated social beliefs were bound to be reflected in ideas about language, giving rise to constant confusion between the written word and speech, 'grammar' and spelling: hence it has been said in recent discussions that, 'to change the spelling is to change the language itself'.

The revolt against the written word

Less than a decade after the founding of state education, these traditional ideas were, however, shaken by a cultural revolt of momentous proportions. Because of the open and dogmatic fashion in which opposing views are aired in France, the period around 1900 has been dubbed *la bataille de l'orthographe* (Catach 1985). This struggle against the tyrannical power of the written word, and for the promotion of a written form which was nearer to the spoken word, did not suddenly materialise out of thin air; its origins are in fact as old as the French language itself. But, at this point it took on new dimensions and became a veritable mass movement, comparable in importance to the 'Dreyfus Affair' which was taking place at the same time.

The movement amounted to a rejection of traditional spelling and the rigid way in which it was taught. Characteristically, it was academics at all levels, including linguists, who were in the vanguard of the movement, although its appeal was much broader. A contributing factor was unprecedented industrial expansion, along with some scientific and technical developments, such as speech-recording devices, in themselves precursors of media as we know it today. But the main motivating force in 1900 was an aspiration towards cultural democracy which was felt right across Europe. This led to substantial spelling reforms in a number of places (such as Germany, Portugal, the Netherlands and, later, the Soviet Union) with the significant exceptions of France, the UK and the US. Their reform movements did not succeed, despite considerable effort, petitions, national and international meetings, and the support of trade unions and political movements.

Since then, nothing much has changed, despite the efforts and projects of A. Dauzat (1939), the Langevin-Wallon commission (1948), Charles Beaulieux (1927 and 1952), A. Beslais (1951 and 1965), R. Thomonnier (1970), J. Hanse, president of the International Council for the French Language (1973), as well as a timid proposal outlined by the *Académie* itself (1976) but not followed up. It is important to try to understand the real reasons for this resistance to spelling reform.

Today's new national awareness

The position of the reformers

There are still those today who are in favour of a 'phonetic' spelling for French (though exactly what this means has to be defined). It is the view of certain linguists, for example, that it has become impossible to modify our very complicated writing system and that it would be better to create alongside it a much simpler writing system for everyday use. Such was the opinion of Claude Blanche-Benveniste and A. Chervel whose book *L'orthographe* (1983) created a great stir. This was also essentially the view of the great linguist A. Martinet, author of l'Alfonic, a learning alphabet simplified for the use of beginners. Their arguments should not be dismissed out of hand, for they are based on the claim that the spoken language is the real language. As Voltaire said before them, 'l'écriture est la peinture de la voix, plus elle est ressemblante, meilleure elle est'. They point to the examples of other Romance and European languages whose spellings are much simpler than those of French or English. They maintain that the spelling mistakes made because of the absurdities of French orthography, and the educational failures brought about as a consequence, prove that the current system does not serve the interests of democracy, and they conclude that better use should be made of that potentially most logical of tools at our disposal, the alphabet.

Unfortunately, people in a position to change things, who are by definition those who have mastered the rules of spelling, are not to be convinced by this logic. In the wake of numerous failures, supporters of radical reform have become less vociferous and extreme, and are now prepared to rally to the current moderate proposals, as being at least a step in the right direction.

The position of the 'conservatives'

The traditionalists wield some mighty arguments. 'We want to preserve our children's heritage. We are defending standards. Our writing system may be difficult, but it is laden with meaning, and with history; every letter tells a story. Beside which, who knows to what lengths you will go in destroying it? You can't even agree among yourselves.'

Of course, those who have benefitted from the system can be expected to defend it. However, it is not as simple as that. It is true that French spelling has its good points. It is difficult to learn and to reproduce, but efficient for the good reader to whom it offers a remarkable quantity of information. Reading plays a larger part in our lives than writing; moreover, those in a position to take decisions are adults who have left the trauma of spelling tests behind long ago. All of which makes it difficult to see how any progress can be made.

None the less, progress is being made, mainly because people's educational level has risen, and their approach to the question is changing. People have begun to realise that if only minor alterations are being proposed then there is not really any need to oppose them. They have also begun to understand why there is such deeply felt resistance. Writing is a form of distance communication, endowed with an incredible force of inertia. The written language constitutes the memory of nations. It is like an immense library, meant for storing information and the greater the amount of information in time and space, the more difficult it is to modify any part of it. These realisations have made it possible for a new consensus to emerge over the last two or three years.

The recent campaign for spelling reform

In the last few years, then, a number of groups have come round to the side of moderate reform. Alerted to changes in public opinion, particularly by ALROE (*Association pour l'information et la recherche sur les orthographes et les systèmes d'écriture*) which has been campaigning for some years, the media, primary school teachers (as shown in an opinion poll *L'Ecole libératrice* no. 88), linguists (statement in *Le Monde* 7 February 1989–text no. 2), the government (declaration by the prime minister and by the *ministre de la francophonie, Lire,* March 1989) have one after another taken a stand in favour of a plan to 'correct anomalies'. The aim of this is to modernise the spelling of French, without threatening the foundation upon which it is built. The *Lire* poll showed that 76 per cent of the French were in agreement.

During the summer of 1989 two books appeared which gave rise to a lot of debate; one, sponsored by a powerful teachers' union, the *Syndicat National des Instituteurs,* was entitled *Que vive l'orthographe,* and the other was entitled *Les délires de l'orthographe* (Catach 1989). Even before they appeared, an extremely virulent press campaign, such as had not been known since 1965, was launched against them by *Le Figaro* and other publications. The national secretary of the SNI, for example, was called 'Pol Pot' by a centre-party deputy. But, interestingly enough, the public did not follow suit and everything died down very quickly. Let us hope that this is the last furore of this type, and that from now on we shall be able to broach these very French questions without the risk of civil war.

It became evident that there was a legal vacuum. The *Académie,* when appealed to, claimed that since 1900 its role had simply been to record changes in usage as they occur. (Its feigned ignorance of the fact that its authority is used as an argument against change has led us around and around in a vicious circle for years and years.) Nor did the Ministry of Education or the big dictionary publishers, or any other organisation, deem themselves to have any rights or responsibilities in this area.

In order to fill this gap, therefore, in 1989 the government set up a whole series of organisations with expertise in these domains, such as the *Conseil Supérieur de la langue française* (vice-president Bernard Quémada, the president being the prime minister himself) and the new *Délégation à la langue française* (general delegate: Bernard Cerquiglini). These organisations were founded with the precise mandate to look at, among other things, the five points of spelling reform that I shall outline later. The *Académie,* with its permanent secretary Maurice Druon, was from the onset closely linked with these initiatives. A working party and a group of specialists worked full tilt for several months and handed in their report in spring 1990. This was approved with a few minor changes by the *Académie française* in May. On 19 June, the *Conseil Supérieur* met and recommended its adoption. This was approved by the prime minister in person and then presented to the press. Six months later, after a number of comments sent in by specialists in the field had been incorporated, the Report was published in the *Journal Officiel.*

This might have been the end of the matter, but around then a new campaign was unleashed, in only a few Parisian newspapers, but even more virulent than before. A strange mixture of writers and politicians, who seemed not to have read the text properly, and who did not realise that only a few dozen words would be affected in daily usage, got up in arms about crimes being committed against the French language, and tried to persuade the *Académie* to go back on its decision. There was nothing new about all this. Exactly one hundred years ago, a group of aristocrats ('le parti des ducs') managed to make the *Académie* withdraw its support for a project then underway. But this time the opposition lost: on 17 January 1991, the *Académie* reconfirmed its position with the sole proviso that the modifications should be recommended rather than imposed.

The question of language reform

At no time before has the public been so favourably disposed towards the question of linguistic reform, and in particular writing reform, so that, through systematic legislation in this domain, new problems which crop up can be properly dealt with.

The world today

Having summarised opinions on both sides, let us now look at the facts concerning the role of writing in today's world.

The twenty-first century, it is said, will be the century of information and communication. The importance of written communication has by no means lessened; quite the reverse. While its percentage share may have dropped, because of the positive expansion of other types of media (e.g. audio-visual), there is no doubt that written language flourishes and will continue to do so.

Certain traditional sectors have lost ground, such as strictly 'literary' writing: only 0.3 per cent of translations in Europe are 'literary', as opposed to 36 per cent of industrial and commercial texts. Terminology commissions are working flat out around the world, dealing with loan-words, and scientific and technical vocabulary. With every edition, sometimes annually, the well-known dictionaries are obliged to process several hundred new entries and several thousand new meanings, which inevitably means taking a decision on how these new words are spelt.

The pace has certainly accelerated during the last few decades, but these realities have always existed. Historically, there is an unrelenting trend for writing systems to follow the changes in the spoken language, albeit at a slower pace. The spelling of French, like that of English, has undergone several changes, some of them radical (cf. Catach et al., *Dictionnaire historique de l'Orthographe française*, forthcoming). No one writes nowadays as people did in the Middle Ages, even if a great number of words which appear not to have changed recur, surprisingly, over the years. It is of great interest to look at how and why these systems evolve.

In France, the transition from Old to Middle French, the invention of the printing press, the Renaissance, the great era of seventeenth-century French Classicism, the Enlightenment, then the 1900s, were all periods of great change, not only in economic and social life, but also in culture and in forms of writing. So it comes as no surprise if such problems rear their heads again today, as we approach the third millennium and the era of information processing.

What is a 'good' writing system?

A serious study of writing systems should also take human factors into account. For example, peoples speaking languages with an oral tradition (Africa, South America) do not necessarily want the so-called 'scientific' systems, the phonetic spelling, introduced by linguists. The strength of a linguistic system does not reside in a simple correspondence between oral and written. Indeed, if it did, it would be hard to understand how French, reputedly so difficult, has for such a long time, from the eighteenth to the twentieth century, been the diplomatic language of Europe, while English is today by far the most frequently used language of science and technology. It would also be difficult to understand why made-up, 'universal' languages, which vie with each other in their search for simplicity, have never met with much success. Or why creoles and regional languages (e.g. the written form of Occitan elaborated by Frédéric Mistral) so often take up the habits and usage of the national language with all its 'weaknesses'. The writing system is much more: it needs to have prestige and power, and its own history (as also does the spoken language, in its own way). The written language is enmeshed in emotive factors, and it is at the hub of many social, psychological, and even aesthetic issues, which at first sight seem totally irrelevant to it.

Moreover, for a code of this importance, a balance must be found between the past and the future, continuity and change, between its oral and visual aspects, reading and writing, the needs of adult and child alike, and between form and meaning. The main feature of a 'good' writing system is that it will be adapted – as nearly as it can be – to a particular language in a particular society. So often a system is inherited from a neighbour, for one reason or another. Then it is inflected, modified (as the Akkadians did for Sumerian cuneiform which they made syllabic, the Japanese with Chinese ideograms, and Europeans with the alphabets that they inherited), and it serves its purpose to a greater or lesser extent, over a very long period. Occasionally, as with Turkish, there is a complete change. But on the whole, we adapt to our systems, and they to us. The best way forward now is therefore to proceed rather as the Chinese have done: they touch up here and there, getting rid of a line of an ideogram, simplifying without throwing everything overboard. In other words, a revolutionary overthrow of the whole system does not now seem likely.

Writing systems and written French

The phonetic illusion

Looked at from a linguistic perspective, a number of long-standing prejudices need examining. For example, what would a completely 'phonetic' spelling be like? It would change from one person to the next, from one day to the next and from one word to another, for phonetic and morphological forms constantly change as we speak.

Take the alphabetical systems of Greek and Latin, which have not stopped evolving. It is known that as early as 4BC, the Greek 'koinè' was no longer the language spoken and written by the Athenians, any more than the Latin of the Empire from the first century AD on had much to do do with the Latin of Cicero. Nowadays we have most of the remaining ancient manuscripts of the great classical Latin texts in data banks. The range of spelling they display is enormous, and as instructive on the written uses of Latin, as such a comparative study would be if we had a data bank of manuscripts and works of the best-known modern authors in their uncorrected form. We need to develop such a data bank which would then give us an authentic picture of current writing.

We do not find it easy to formulate our thoughts about the written word. One of our problems is our reluctance to think of writing in terms of *variation* and *evolution*, and *slow* evolution at that. Paradoxically, the *fixistes* and the *phonéticistes* are alike in believing that a 'transparent' writing system would remain the same for ever, the former because they believe that our ancestors used to write as we do and the latter that our grandchildren will speak as we do, and therefore will recognise themselves in what we write today. Arguments based on variation and evolution provide as much evidence against a rigid, unchanging spelling system as they do against a system which is constantly altering. Both points of view are mistaken.

The alphabetic ideal

A second prejudice resulting from the first, and just as damaging, is that of the continuing absolute superiority of the Greco-Latin alphabet. As with the belief in 'phonetic transparency', this idea of superiority (linked to an untenable but lingering conviction of European superiority) does not hold, either for the past or for today.

Alphabetic writing has existed for 5,000 years. The ancient Egyptians had signs for consonants from the earliest times. Then came the Phoenicians, who copied from the Egyptians, and then the Greeks. If the Phoenicians did not note certain vowels, that is not because they were incompetent, but because they did not find it useful to do so. If the Greeks invented symbols for these vowels (although they did not have distinctive length signs for all of them), that is because they found a need to do so. Generally, only what is deemed necessary is incorporated into the writing system (which is why one should talk of phonological, rather than phonetic, spelling). Apart from which, it may be found necessary to add extra symbols, as grammatical markers or as disambiguators, which is normal practice in most languages.

Half of humanity does not use an alphabet, simply because they do not need one. A syllabic system is much more suited to the languages of India, Ethiopia, Korea or Japan, for example, which are made up of a few, well-structured, syllables. Such a system could also have worked well for certain African languages, but was of course considered too 'primitive'. Yet these systems can be considered at the same time more 'natural' (for what is a sound isolated orally?) and easier, more economic and more visually informative. It can be argued that Chinese has the best writing system in the world, because it can be understood across languages (there are at least sixty different languages in China, not including dialects!). A similar case can be made for Arabic.

In the case of our own languages, perhaps we should stop thinking of everything which does not directly conform to a non-existent ideal as an aberration, as a relic to be consigned to the rubbish heap of history. Each system has its advantages and disadvantages, which should be examined with an open mind.

The alphabet pure and simple is not good as a *writing system* for all languages; it is good for *transcription* which is not at all the same thing. On the other hand, for languages without a complex morphology, with many monosyllabic words and possible ambiguities such as Chinese, English or even French, it may be necessary to represent *words*, at least to some extent.

The French writing system

It is important to grasp the general point that written French has formed a pluralist system and has forged a sort of complex network, sometimes contradictory, but which finds coherence in this very complexity. This way of advancing by trial and error, common to the great writing systems, seems to me to go some way towards meeting, and more adequately representing, speech which is itself complex and pluralist.

Another general consideration is that speech is doubly articulated. When we speak, we use both 'empty' and 'full' units of meaning, phonemes and morphemes. The written, like spoken language, proceeds by analogy and by difference. 'Empty' units are more economical but they generate numerous ambiguities. By combining and reinforcing them, even at the expense of simplicity, we contrive to find a way through the innumerable meanderings of speech and sense (see Catach 1988). Why, in any case, should simplicity be our primary goal? As Aesop pointed out, language can also be used to hide behind, to deceive or in self-defence. As Chomsky has noted, for example, English does not always mark phonetic changes which intervene between radicals and derived forms: *serene/serenity* and *extreme/extremity* (Chomsky and Halle 1968). The rule which operates here, while it does not satisfy the strict criterion of phonetic accuracy nevertheless retains the meaning link. The first law of writing might thus be said to be the *permanence visuelle du mot*, which extends here to its derivatives. French has different examples of this, e.g. masculine examples which in the feminine or derivatives have a letter pronounced (*petit*, with silent final *t*, which is pronounced in *petite, petitesse*).

A similarity between French and English is therefore that they both use a 'deep' phonological notation, which does not became bogged down in the numerous and diverse details of individual or regional variation. English does not systematically record vowel timbre or length. French has the written variants *o, au* and *eau*, whose principal function lies elsewhere, and it has accents to go on *e*. In other words, French has developed the use of diacritics, which are economical and efficient, while English uses other means, such as the final *e* in *win/wine, hat/hate*.

The big difference between the two systems is the use in French of a veritable 'written grammar', which English does not have to the same degree. All those feminine *e* endings, and the verbal inflections which cause both foreigners and native speakers so much trouble, because you can neither memorise them nor easily look them up in the dictionary, are in fact very useful for reading and give French a certain syntactic flexibility, as also does punctuation. All in all, English and French must be given their due for preserving the word as the main unit of the written language, and for having developed coherent and integrated systems. Their spelling does not deserve the opprobium that has been heaped on it – which does not mean that nothing needs changing.

The five points

People no longer speak of spelling reform in France, but of *modifications graphiques*. Modifications have been adopted in five areas, and it is to be hoped that these positive decisions will be backed up by action.

The first concerns the circumflex accent: a vestige of the well-known Latin *s*, with prestigious medieval connotations. It has been a long time dying, as it gradually disappeared from words like *fenestre, hostel, forest, connoistre*; it is of little use today, except of course to ensure that a goodly proportion of candidates fail our exams (about half of all spelling mistakes are due to the circumflex)! It has only one real function, that of distinguishing the written form of *lâche* from *lache, côte* from *cote, sûr,* from *sur, fût* from (*qu'il*) *fût* etc., which can be kept, without retaining numerous circumflexes which have outlived their usefulness.

The second point concerns double consonants. To deal with all of them at once would have been too much of a shock to the sytem, so we have decided to start with two well-defined, mini-series, which cause problems. The first is the group of 144 verbs in -*eler/-eter* which behave eccentrically in doubling the consonant after an open *e* instead of borrowing a grave accent like everything else: *je jette*, as compared with *j'achète, j'appelle*, compared with *je gèle* etc. At one point in time, this feature had its justification. But no one remembers what it is any more and we can well do without it. The second mini-series is still more awkward to remember, and I think that it plays a large part in the alleged dyslexia of 8 per cent of our children. Just imagine that French allows itself the luxury of ninety series having suffixes which follow words in -*on* (*fonctionnel/-alisme championnat/patronat, sermonner/ramoner, tonner/détoner, donner/donation, thonier/poissonnier*, etc.), half of them being supposed to double the consonant, the other half not doubling it, with no apparent consistency within the same series. How do we explain this disaster area to children, when no one any longer re-members its origins (an old problem of vowel nasalisation). And how can one expect them to spell correctly when no normal person is capable of coping with it without recourse to a dictionary? The report recom-mends a single consonant throughout, and this should be implemented immediately with new words.

The third point concerns compound words, with their awful hyphen and even more awful plurals. These have been systematised to a degree, mainly by joining the parts together. I will quote just one example, out of several hundred innocents like *un casse-pieds, un cale-pied, un chauffe-pieds, un chausse-pied, un gratte-pieds, un marchepied, un couvre-pieds ou pied* and so on. That is, for about 85 per cent of all compounds formed from verbal base plus noun, the form is unpredictable and they have to be looked up one by one in a dictionary (but if you look in two dictionaries, you're sure to find two different spellings!).

The fourth point concerns the simplification of the agreement of the past participle with pronominal verbs, an agreement which is so difficult that no one really knows how to apply it, although we are supposed to abide by rules which means you have to write 'Elles se sont *ri* de nous et nous nous sommes moqués d'elles; elles se sont *plu* à nous taquiner et nous ne nous sommes pas *souciés* de leurs railleries.' The report recommends that the past participle *laissé* should always be invariable before an infinitive: 'Les chanteuses qu'elles ont *laissé* chanter' and 'les airs qu'elles ont *laissé* chanter'. It is worth pointing out in this context that the *tolérances* of 1977 (*Arrêté Haby*) had already recommended that non-agreement of the past participle before an infinitive should not be counted as a mistake. On this point, and on the hyphen and the circumflex, a proper application of the *Arrêté Haby* would nicely complement the recent proposals.

The fifth point, finally, groups together quite a long list of anomalies, such as the spelling of *oignon* and *pognon*, *événement* and *avènement* etc., and a certain Frenchification of borrowed words, a procedure which should be carried out rather like the naturalisation process, on an on-going basis.

Overall, the modifications affect 2,000 words, including 500 new forms which have already been adopted in dictionaries, 800 accents, 800 compound words and 600 plurals (the same word sometimes being affected by more than one change). This is no small undertaking, but it is to be hoped that it will bring a fresh, new impetus to the language debate, and to language use. In actual fact, in terms of frequency lists, only 69 words are affected, and the real list is probably shorter, including mainly such forms as the third-person singular of verbs ending in *-aître* (*il parait*, *connait*, in the new spelling). However, it is a beginning. Finally, it may be salutory to compare French and English spelling, the turn-of-the-century reform movements in both countries, and to ask why the movement has fizzled out in English-speaking countries, when it has gained recent momentum in France.

Text 1

Un appel de linguistes sur l'orthographe: 'Moderniser l'écriture du français'

Dix linguistes éminents professeurs d'université et au Collège de France et chercheurs au CNRS, publient un appel en faveur d'une 'modernisation de l'écriture du français'. Ils souhaitent que ces propositions, volontairement modérées, contribuent à relancer le débat *nécessaire sur l'adaptation de l'orthographe française au contexte culturel et politique actuel.*

Les Français n'ont pas à rougir de leur orthographe, qui est dans l'ensemble regulière et plus cohérente qu'on ne le croit: mais ils risquent de souffrir d'avoir cesse de la moderniser. Il s'agit, en effet, de notre écriture nationale.

On sait l'importance du mode de transcription écrite d'une langue, pour la culture que cette langue exprime, mais aussi dans le dévéloppement de cette langue elle-même. Une écriture ne se fait pas au hasard: elle entretient avec la langue qu'elle transcrit des rapports qui ne cessent d'évoluer. Il convient de rappeler que l'on peut, avec les précautions du savoir et de l'expérience, adapter cette écriture, sans pour autant nuire à la langue. Une langue est vivante, sa graphie également. Les exemples de tels aménagements sont si nombreux qu'ils constituent quasiment la règle. Presque tous les pays européens, et la France parmi eux, ont, à plusieurs reprises, modifié leur façon d'écrire. Les langues, dans leurs spécificités et leur génie propre, n'en ont pas été affectées; elles en ont même amplement profité, tant sont étroits les liens qu'elles ont avec leur transcription.

Ce fut le cas pour l'Allemagne (1900–1920), la Russie (1917), les Pays-Bas (1936–1970), le Portugal et le Brésil (encore tout récemment), l'Espagne et les pays d'Amérique du Sud, les pays de l'Est, etc. La Grèce vient de supprimer certains signes hérités du grec ancien, qu'elle utilisait depuis plus de deux mille ans. Rares sont les pays qui, d'une façon ou d'une autre, ne se préoccupent pas d'adapter leur graphie. En France, du Moyen Age à Rabelais, de Rabelais à Ronsard, des classiques à Voltaire, de Voltaire à Littré, d'édition en édition du dictionnaire de l'Académie, des milliers de mots français ont changé de forme. L'on a écrit *conestre, connoistre* ou *congnoistre*, puis *connaitre, eschole* puis *école, adjouster* puis *ajouter*, sans que la langue en pâtit.

Et l'on peut penser qu'une des qualités de l'orthographe française fut, des siècles durant, sa capacité à se moderniser.

Or cette modernisation que l'histoire nous permet, que la science nous suggère, les défis lancés à notre pays l'exigent.

Défi technique. L'écrit est en pleine expansion, qu'il soit imprimé (les livres du dépôt légal de la Bibliothèque nationale sont passés, en moyenne annuelle, de dix-sept mille à trente-huit mille de 1960 à 1980, et ont plus que doublé depuis) ou qu'il soit électronique. La technologie informatique consomme, produit, stocke et diffuse d'immenses quantités de données: c'est là un trésor de savoir écrit, auquel on ne peut accéder qu'en evitant la défaillance graphique, et l'à-peu-près.

Défi pédagogique. Vouloir conduire 80% d'une classe d'âge au niveau du baccalauréat implique qu'on s'interroge sur l'écart qui se creuse entre les français écrit et parlé, sur une norme devenue en certains points impraticable, et non transmissible au cours d'études raisonnables. Sur l'écart, également, entre la connaissance scientifique de l'orthographe et la pédagogie de cette orthographe, qui doit consacrer beaucoup de temps aux détails sans importance, et à des listes d'exceptions.

Défi politique, en un mot. En cette année du Bicentenaire de la Révolution, il convient de rappeler avec force que savoir lire et écrire, posséder pleinement les possibilités de cet instrument incomparable qu'est l'écriture, est un droit civique,

Défi politique, en un mot. En cette année du Bicentenaire de la Révolution, il convient de rappeler avec force que savoir lire et écrire, posséder pleinement les possibilités de cet instrument incomparable qu'est l'écriture, est un droit civique, et l'accès à la culture écrite un droit des citoyens. Sera-t-elle encore en français demain, cette culture, si nous n'assurons pas à l'ensemble de la nation la transmission, la pratique et la connaissance satisfaisantes de l'instrument forgé pour eux au fil des siècles? Notre langue deviendra-t-elle une langue minoritaire en Europe? Son apprentissage, par le déclin d'une norme désuète, ne risque-t-il pas de décourager nos partenaires européens? L'immobilisme est un handicap pour le développement de la francophonie.

Seule une langue qui vit et se développe, une langue parlée et écrite aisément par tous, peut se défendre et s'épanouir. Il faut donc moderniser la graphie du français.

Une politique de tolérance

Ce qui ne signifie rien de plus qu'aménager l'orthographe, la réviser, comme on dit d'une mécanique, en ôtant ce qui a cessé de servir, et qui est devenu aberrant. Ce qui signifie également avoir davantage d'estime pour la réflexion que pour la mémoire. Prenons l'exemple de l'accent circonflexe. Celui-ci note, en général, un son que l'on ne prononce plus depuis longtemps (ainsi un s devant une consonne: *ile* pour *isle*): c'est donc la mémoire, et non la prononciation, qui nous invite à utiliser cet accent. Si, par expérience, on ôte l'accent circonflexe aux mots du français, on obtient, tout au plus, une trentaine de termes devenus ambigus, et que le circonflexe distinguait (*du* et *dû*, *tache* et *tâche*, etc.). Mais, d'une part, ces quelques termes deviennent ambigus seulement hors contexte; cette ambiguïté, d'autre part, est moindre que celle qui est monnaie courante, et comme fondamentale, dans la langue: qui a jamais protesté contre l'ambiguïté de *je suis* (verbes *être* ou *suivre*), de *je finis* (présent ou passé simple), etc.? Si l'on ajoute que plus du quart des fautes relevées dans les dictées, dans les textes de tous ordres, concernent l'accent circonflexe, il est évident que le coût est disproportionné.

Une modernisation de ce type avait été envisagée par l'excellent rapport que prépara, à l'initiative du ministre de l'éducation nationale, la commission Beslais, de 1960 à 1965. Dans l'immédiat, pourraient être retenues comme prioritaires, outre l'acceptation de graphies sans accent circonflexe, la réduction des consonnes doubles, l'assouplissement des règles d'accord du participe passé, et l'autorisation de doubles graphies (on écrirait, par exemple. *événement*, ou *événement*, *oignon* ou *ognon*, graphies qu'a d'ailleurs acceptés l'Académie française en 1976).

Depuis plus d'un siècle, contrairement à une tradition dans l'histoire de notre langue, aucune initiative tendant à adapter l'orthographie n'a pu être menée à bien. Un arrêté de tolérance avait été promulgué par le ministre de l'éducation nationale en 1901, un autre a été repris en 1977; bien qu'ils soient toujours en vigueur, ils n'ont pas été appliqués. L'Académie française elle-même avait admis certaines simplifications en 1976: ses recommandations n'on pas été suivies d'effet. Le retard pris dans ce domaine est tel qu'il convient, dans un premier temps, de mettre en œuvre une politique de tolérance. Que l'on s'entende: il ne s'agit-pas de tolérer n'importe quoi, mais d'accepter, comme cela a été le cas pour d'autres langues, deux (et seulement deux) graphies possibles, entre lesquelles on hésite d'ordinaire, faute d'avoir mémorisé cette information aléatoire. Ainsi *j'étiquette* et *j'étiquète*, *abime* et *abîme*, etc. Une politique de tolérance est en soi un enseignement de l'orthographe: elle fait comprendre ce qu'est et à quoi sert une norme graphique. Il convient en somme, après l'avoir revue, d'appliquer, de faire connaître, d'enseigner aux futurs maîtres et aux écoliers l'arrêté de 1977.

Certes, il faudra expliquer et informer, choisir avec prudence les points où porteront les aménagements: un comité des sages pourrait être chargé de les recommander. On devra se donner du temps pour leur application, comme à l'époque où l'on est passé des anciens aux nouveaux francs. Mais il importe de commencer aujourd'hui. Les exigences nous pressent, aucune période n'est plus propice que l'année des droits de l'homme, aucune politique ne peut lier plus fortement la culture, la science, et l'amour de la langue française.

(*Le Monde*, 7 February 1989)

Text 2

Orthographe: enfin la cohérence

UN ENTRETIEN AVEC PIERRE ENCREVÉ

'Il entre dans la langue 25,000 ou 30,000 mots nouveaux tous les ans . . . Alors, au lieu de laisser la graphie flotter; nous pensons qu'il vaut mieux la régler'
Le Nouvel Observateur. – *Dans quel but opérez-vous cette réforme de l'orthographe, et de quel droit?* **Pierre Encrevé.** – Il n'y a pas de réforme. Une réforme viserait à changer le système graphique français; il ne s'agit pas de cela, mais seulement de propositions faites par le Conseil supérieur de la Langue française, qui considère au contraire que le système graphique français est bon, mais que l'orthographe présente ici et là des anomalies, des incohérences par rapport à ce système. Le but est clair: il est d'améliorer l'ensemble du lexique, de le régler davantage, en respectant plus le système et l'histoire, de manière que le français se maintienne, se défende le mieux possible. Autrefois, lorsque l'Académie faisait un dictionnaire, on n'avait pas de liste exhaustive de mots, ni d'ordinateurs pour garder en mémoire, quand on en était à la lettre *z*, ce qui avait été décidé pour la lettre *a*. L'orthographe n'est pas une nature, encore moins un objet sacré, c'est une histoire. On est scandalisé par la graphie que nous proposons de *nénufar*; mais sait-on que le *ph* qui déguise en grec ce mot arabe n'a été imposé par l'Académie qu'en 1933? Par ailleurs, il est indispensable de créer et d'emprunter des mots sans cesse. On compte qu'il entre dans la langue 25 000 ou 30 000 mots nouveaux tous les ans. Comment allons-nous les graphier? Il faut des règles de néologie, pour les traits d'union, le pluriel des mots composés, les accents, la jonction entre la racine et le suffixe, et des règles pour l'intégration des mots d'origine étrangère. Bref, au lieu de laisser la graphie flotter, nous pensons qu'il vaut mîeux la régler. Quant au droit de le faire, il est fondé sur la

nécessité d'enseigner le français. L'enseignement suppose des règles. Or relativement peu de graphies sont fixées: la dernière édition du dictionnaire de l'Académie (1933) compte autour de 30 000 mots, et l'on évalue à un million le nombre de formes du français d'aujourd'hui. Les dictionnaristes proposent, décident, mais divergent . . . sur plus de 3 000 mots pour les dictionnaires courants. Par exemple, Larousse et Robert donnent, au singulier et au pluriel, l'un *cache-flamme* et l'autre *cache-flammes*. C'est pourquoi le Premier ministre nous a demandé de faire des propositions sur cinq points [les traits d'union, le pluriel des mots composés, l'accent circonflexe, le participe passé des verbes pronominaux, et *'diverses anomalies'*]; propositions que nous faisons d'abord aux principaux producteurs d'écritures imprimées: les dictionnaristes, les éditeurs, les correcteurs, la presse. On a réuni le Conseil supérieur de la Langue française, qui a crée un groupe de travail, lequel a nommé un groupe d'experts. Les propositions de ces spécialistes ont fait l'objet de discussions avec le Conseil; les décisions prises ont été soumises à l'Académie française, au Conseil de la Langue française du Québec, celui de Belgique, qui les ont agréées. Le Premier ministre a donc donné son accord pour que l'on *propose* ces rectifications. Mais il n'a jamais été question de légiférer.

N.O. – *Ces propositions n'ont donc pas fait l'objet d'un débat public. Vont-elles le faire? Vous êtes conscient, j'imagine, du tollé qu'elles soulèvent.*

P. Encrevé. – Tollé, c'est beaucoup dire. L'interminable débat public, vieux d'un siècle, a eu pour résultat que l'idée d'une réforme phonétique, de 'simplification', a été abandonnée au profit d'une 'harmonisation' et donc d'un renforcement du système orthographique actuel. Les propositions du Conseil sont très modérées, et vous n'avez qu'à lire la presse, l'opinion les a bien accueillies.

N.O. – *La presse n'est pas l'opinion publique. Vous prétendez ne pas 'légiférer'. Pourquoi alors ne pas laisser la langue évoluer toute seule, comme elle l'a toujours fait? Par exemple, 'événement' n'a plus que quelques années à vivre avec son accent aigu. Cela fait belle lurette que 'Libération' l'écrit avec un grave, comme avènement, que Littré donnait encore avec un aigu.*

P. Encrevé. – Il ne s'agit que de suivre l'usage, de l'accompagner, d'accélérer un peu l'unification des dictionnaires. C'était le rôle de celui de l'Académie; mais le ministère de l'Education n'a pas fait suivre d'effet les décisions de l'Académie en 1977: elles n'ont pas été enseignées. Aujourd'hui elles sont reprises.

(*Le Nouvel Observateur*, 3 October 1990)

8

Alternative French

KEN GEORGE

*T'as pas dix balles?, Ça coûte la peau des fesses, I m'est rentré d'dans,
Décrocher un appart aux Invaloches c'est pas évident, Le frangin, il est giga fort
en cunu, il assure un max, Vlà la meuf qui s'est fait péta son keus* ('Tu n'as pas
dix francs?', 'C'est très cher', 'Il s'est jeté sur moi', 'Trouver un
appartement aux Invalides n'est pas facile', 'Mon frère est très fort en
arithmétique, il fait preuve de beaucoup de compétence', 'Voilà la
femme à qui on a volé le sac')

Utterances such as these are more or less immediately identifiable as
non-standard, in the sense that they are not consistent with the
recommendations of the conventional reference grammars and textbooks intended for the language learner, which traditionally have
favoured the long-established patterns of formal written usage. But
exactly what is it that enables us to identify the above as unconventional
in these terms? The many different indicators can be classified under
three main headings:

phonetic – elision: *t'as* (tu as) *i* (il) *d'dans* (dedans) *vlà* (voilà)
syntactic – negation: *t'as pas   c'est pas* (*ne*-deletion)
  – interrogation: *t'as pas dix balles?* (intonation as sole marker)
  – repetition: *le frangin, il* (noun + pronoun)
lexical – colloquialism: *balles   décrocher   frangin   coûter la peau des
  fesses   pas évident   assurer*
  – abbreviation: *appart*/ement *giga*/ntesque ca*l*/*cul* *nu*/mérique
  max/imum
  – resuffixation: *Invaloche*
  – *verlan: meuf* (femme) *péta* (taper = voler) *keus* (sac)

Some of these features are more generally recognisable than others.
Elision, noun + pronoun repetition, omission of *ne*, the use of *balles* for
francs are all common. *Pas évident* and *assurer* became widespread in the
1980s. However *Invaloches* is basically Parisian, *cunu* largely confined to
school slang and *giga* typical of adolescent and young adult usage. As

for *péta* and *keus* age group is again a determining factor: with relatively few exceptions (of which *meuf* is one) *verlan* remains the prerogative of youth.

Such forms are also recognisable as being essentially oral, in particular characteristic of spontaneous informal dialogue. Of course one can be just as formal in spoken as in written French. The great danger has always been the tendency to equate writing with formal register and speech with informal register. Claude Hagège encourages students to be aware of the two basic levels within oral French itself, a distinction which is perhaps blurred by the broadcast media:

> En effet, les médias audiovisuels, du fait qu'ils mettent sur le même plan, dans les programmes et les répartitions d'horaires, les genres oraux très formels, comme les informations ou les discours présidentiels ou ministériels, et les genres informels, comme l'entretien avec un coureur cycliste, pratiquent l'amalgame entre deux niveaux très différents de français non écrit. Autrefois, cet amalgame n'existait pas. On était conscient de deux oppositions: non seulement entre le français parlé et la langue écrite, évidemment, mais encore entre le français parlé et l'oral public, qu'il se manifeste dans l'éloquence de la chaire et du prétoire . . . , dans l'enseignement ou aux tribunes d'assemblées politiques. Proche de l'écrit, l'oral public doit être présenté aux écoliers comme un registre tout à fait différent de leur oralité spontanée, et dont ils doivent apprendre à se servir en cas de besoin.   (Hagège 1987)

Conversely, unconventional usage is increasingly attested in written French, in addition to private correspondence, notably among certain sections of the press (e.g. *Actuel, Le Nouvel Observateur, Libération*; even *Le Monde* has for some years now made a gesture towards linguistic informality in its 'Sur le vif' column), in strip cartoons, advertisements with a popular bias, and the contemporary novel (e.g. Raymond Queneau, René Fallet, Christiane Rochefort, Albertine Sarrazin, Frédéric Dard, Alphonse Boudard, Victoria Thérame).

Developments such as these pose a fundamental problem. Given the constant evolution of usage, and sociolinguistic variation within a language, how can one use 'standard' or 'conventional' as blanket terms? These labels can surely only be attached within a historical perspective and against the background of a more or less abstract norm. Here we must distinguish between the two meanings of the word *norm*, namely 'that which is normative' and 'that which is normal', in other words between the prescriptive and the descriptive approaches to linguistic performance. Like my colleagues I am caught in a dilemma: on the one hand we note that French is continually changing and try to describe these changes through our teaching and research, on the other hand we mark students' language work and therefore have to apply some kind of conventional standards. In this case the synchronic and the diachronic are clearly in conflict. I shall return to this question at the end of the chapter.

As a starting point in the attempt to describe variation in the French language, let us illustrate the basic sub-division into formal, neutral (or sociolinguistically unmarked) and informal usage at the lexical level. The following examples will, I hope, be uncontroversial:

formal	neutral	informal
monsieur	homme	mec
dame	femme	nana
demeure	maison	baraque
disgracieux	laid	moche
se restaurer	manger	bouffer

Of course synonyms of the above could be found to exist within the same register, but what becomes immediately apparent is that the number of informal synonyms far outweighs that of the formal and neutral. Non-standard lexis has always been much richer in alternatives than standard in the Modern French period. Take for instance the distribution of synonyms of the verb *partir*, using the same sub-divisions.

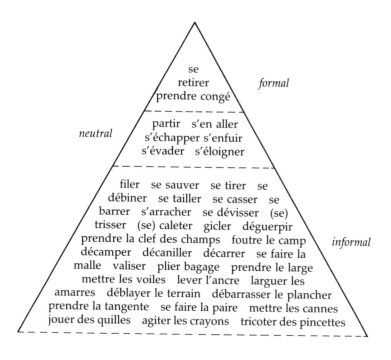

Figure 8.1   Distribution of the synonyms of *partir*

The list is far from exhaustive, and similar distributions could be shown for a large number of other head-words, e.g. *argent, faire l'amour, excellent, femme, homme, être bête, manger* (see Marks et al. 1984: 373–401). It should not however be assumed that the non-standard forms quoted above are fully interchangeable: there are many subtleties *within* informal French, quite apart from chronological discrepancies.

Some of these forms are used by – or at least are familiar to – the majority of French speakers (*Allez, file!, Il s'est sauvé, Fous-moi le camp*). That is to say that together with pronunciations such as *chuis* for *je suis, t'es* for *tu es, aut'chose* for *autre chose, valab* for *valable* and grammatical constructions of the type *Elle, elle vient pas. Tu viens, toi?*, lexical items such as *filer* and *se sauver* simply form part of colloquial French (*le français familier*). Like *balles, bagnole, bouffe, bouquin, boulot, gosse, fric, flic, se marrer, s'emmerder, bosser, dingue, crevant, dégueulasse* (= *francs, voiture, nourriture/repas, livre, travail, enfant, argent, agent de police, s'amuser, s'ennuyer, travailler, idiot, fatigant/amusant, sale*) etc., they make up the common stock of informal vocabulary which the French as a whole use automatically when the situation allows, and which poses no problem whatsoever in terms of recognition and comprehension.

But the rest of the informal synonyms in the triangle are to a greater or lesser extent restricted sociologically, in terms of age group, class, occupation, etc. This restriction indicates that, while it is not possible to assign each and every form to one specific social group, we *are* dealing here with various types of argot. The difference can be represented by the reaction of French readers to contemporary writers: whereas Rochefort's colloquial style generally causes no difficulties, Boudard can present real problems for anyone who is not closely acquainted with criminals' slang – which has not prevented his books from becoming best-sellers.

Not only does it imply a degree of social restriction, argot also represents a more or less deliberate intention to exclude non-members by maintaining and reinforcing internal group identity. It is a kind of linguistic defence mechanism, at the same time exclusive and inclusive. Argot is thus wilfully unconventional, in that it rejects standard vocabulary by creating alternative, parallel sets of words peculiar to specific groups (soldiers, students, stock-brokers, professional cyclists, civilian aircrews, printers, musicians, footballers, prisoners, drug-abusers, etc.).

There is therefore a fundamental difference between argot and jargon, in the sense in which this term is currently used in France ('langage technique utilisé dans une pure intention de transmission d'information', Singy 1986). Whereas the latter is indispensable for intercommunication between colleagues working within the same field and for the development of technological and scientific research, the former is characterised by an element of gratuitousness: it is not strictly necessary to communication. Jargon is a *sine qua non* (for example each plant must have one and only one official name, which is universally accepted and used throughout the botanical world), argot is an adjunct and allows a degree of subjectivity (*nana, julie, gonzesse, frangine, meuf, poupée, pouliche*, etc. are all potentially available as alternatives to *femme*).

Of course argot can exist within a jargon. The surgeon will write in his report about the results of a *nécropsie* (post mortem) but may well use the abbreviated form *nécrops* when chatting informally with a colleague. The medical student's handbook will list *urologie* (study of the urinary system) as an area of specialisation, but among the students themselves it is referred to as *la pisse*.

Pierre Guiraud stressed the essentially oral nature of slang: 'Car c'est bien d'un langage *parlé, familier* et *vivant* qu'il s'agit et dont les caractères se retrouvent dès que l'individu, quelle que soit son origine sociale, cesse de se soumettre aux contraintes de la langue scolaire et académique' (Guiraud 1956). He also pointed to what he called its 'caractère crypto-ludique', meaning that slang is both secretive and playful, experimenting with different forms and creating variants. He does however rightly play down the cryptic aspect. It would appear that the bulk of French slang vocabulary is shared by all kinds of slang within the language. It is only a minority of terms that are exclusive to each individual kind.

Many of the entries in Robert Galisson's 'Liste des items argotiques', representing the slang of professional footballers, are part of current colloquial usage: *recharger les accus* 'recharge one's batteries', *faire du cinéma* 'put on an act', *être dans la confiote* 'be in a sticky position' (literally 'jam'), *tirer la couverture à soi* 'look after number one', etc. (Galisson 1978). This does not in itself weaken the autonomy of the various argots. It is sufficient that there *are* differences, however few, for in-grouping to be maintained.

So in addition to what is – or has become by absorption – merely colloquial, e.g. *mec, pote, jules, piaule, flotte, marrant, sympa, emmerdant, pas con, vachement, avoir ras le bol, avoir de la veine, marcher à côté de ses pompes* (= *individu, camarade, petit ami/mari, chambre/appartement, eau/pluie, amusant, sympathique, ennuyeux, pas idiot, très, en avoir assez, avoir de la chance, se sentir mal (à l'aise)*) there is a relatively limited number of truly cryptic forms. Few people outside the armed forces would know that *sardines* are an NCO's stripes. Those unfamiliar with police work or prison life are unlikely to recognise *passer au piano* as meaning 'have one's fingerprints taken'. At the *Ecole Polytechnique* the *cabinet de service* is referred to as the *binet de ser*. Paris taxi-drivers call a journey made without turning on the meter (i.e. to their benefit) *un toubou*, and the plain-clothes policeman who checks on such illicit practices is *un boer* (pronounced [buʀ]).

Whether shared or restricted, slang provides an abundance of alternatives to the standard lexicon, the use of metaphor being especially striking. Here are just some of the synonyms of *mourir*, as recorded in nineteenth- and twentieth-century slang dictionaries:

> clamser calancher claquer cronir caner quimper faire couic   lâcher la rampe   glisser la pente   passer l'arme à gauche   bouffer des pissenlits par la racine   avaler son bulletin de naissance   casser sa pipe   filer son câble   remercier son boulanger   rentrer ses pouces   déchirer son tablier   fermer son parapluie   retourner sa veste   renverser son café   dévisser son billard   plier son paquet   faire sa malle   crever son pneu   cirer ses bottes   dépoter son géranium   déposer son bilan   éteindre son gaz   souffler sa veilleuse.

Yet the sheer number of alternatives should not obscure the fact that there are certain recurrent patterns, both morpho-syntactic (e.g. verb + possessive adjective + noun above) and semantic (e.g. from the earlier *partir* variants: *lever l'ancre/mettre les voiles/larguer les amarres/prendre le large*).

Unconventional usage – still in the traditional sense – is characteristic too of adolescent speech, which as a particular form of argot, or rather as a group of argots, is often deliberately non-standard (see George 1986). An anti-establishment tone is immediately apparent in the many disparaging expressions for 'adults' or 'parents' over the last few decades: *les amortis, les croulants, les vestiges, les moins de vingt dents, les son et lumière* (i.e. ancient monuments), *les vieux/viocs*, plus the more or less short-lived acronyms *NEB* (= *nuit et brouillard*), *BS* (= *bientôt squelette*), *BSC* (= *bientôt sous chrysanthèmes*), *PPH* (= *passeront pas l'hiver*), etc.

While phonetically and syntactically, adolescent informal speech is largely concordant with adult informal speech (vocalic and consonantal elision, infrequent liaisons, avoidance of inversion, etc.), lexically there are many differences. Certain suffixes, for instance, may be more productive among the young, e.g. *-os* (*calmos, tristos, nullos* – the *s* is pronounced) and *-oche* (*la téloche, bouffer à la cantoche, sac en plastoche*). Abbreviated forms, usually by apocope (final syllable deletion) are more common, and are a regular feature of magazines aimed at the young market. This sentence in *Actuel* (November 1989), from an article on Bob Marley's children, is typical: 'Blouson fluo, survet de foot et bonnet rasta, Ziggy ressemble à sa mère' (= fluorescent, survêtement, football, rastafari). More significantly, words already shortened in colloquial French may be further truncated by the younger generation, thus *dégueulasse > dégueu > deg, maximum > maxi > max, pédéraste > pédé > pèd(e), pattes d'éléphant* 'flared trousers' *> pattes d'éleph > pattes d'eph, santiagos* 'Mexican boots' *> santiags > tiags* (initial syllabic deletion, or aphaeresis, is involved here too).

Another characteristic is the coexistence of hyperbole (exaggeration) and litotes (understatement). Like English *great, fantastic, far out, crucial, wicked,* etc., French has known a large number of alternatives for *excellent* in recent years, including *génial, dément, géant, canon, balaise, béton, flashant, sauvage, sublime,* which have coexisted with such downbeat equivalents as *pas sale, pas cochon, pas triste, pas dégueu, pas pourri, pas craignos.* Occasionally the two opposites meet, as in *vachement pas mauvais.* Hyperbole is reinforced by intensive prefixation: *hypersensass, superclass, mégafoutral* (again merely synonyms of *excellent*).

Lexical borrowing from English, though increasingly frequent in the French population as a whole, has been prevalent among the young particularly in the fields of music: *country, hard, rap, funk, hip hop, new age,* clothes and hair-styles: *baskets, creepers, rangers, dreadlocks, skin, spike hair* and drug-taking: *stick* 'joint', *shit* 'hashish', *junk* 'heroin', *stoned,* and the verbs *flipper* 'be in cold turkey', *se shooter, sniffer* (see Obalk, Sorel and Pasche 1984). Some of these forms are doubly unconventional in that they are not only foreign elements but are non-standard within English usage itself. One might also mention here some of the oddities which arise though borrowing. *Off* can be used in French to mean 'off the record' (*rien n'est off*). The French for *blusher* (cosmetics) and *clapper board* is *blush* and *clap.* On the model of the loan word *golden boy* 'financial whizz kid' they have created *golden papy* to refer to the former's senior equivalent. Derivatives formed by adding a French suffix may appear, temporarily at least, to stand uneasily between the two languages, e.g. *jamer* 'take part in a jam session', *jazzeux* 'jazz player', *nursage* 'nursing', *badgé* 'wearing a badge', *looké* 'stylish', 'eye-catching' (i.e. adopting *un look*), *scoopant* 'newsworthy', *scrabbleur* 'scrabble player', *punkette* 'female punk'. Other examples of imbalance include *un timing record* 'record time' (sport), *un reporting hebdomadaire* 'weekly report', *vélo de home-training* 'exercise bike', *faire son coming out* 'come out' (e.g. homosexuals, cf. the calque *sortir du placard* 'come out of the closet'). *Un best of,* with or without hyphen, is a selection of highlights or album of greatest hits (*un best of de ses chansons*). A *rallye-girl* is a débutante, itself of course a Gallicism.

However the most obvious discrepancy from the morphological point of view is *verlan,* which involves reversing the conventional order of syllables or phonemes, *verlan* (formerly *vers-l'en*) resulting from *l'envers* (see Andreini 1985). Though not a recent phenomenon its spread since the 1970s is due to the creativity of young Parisians who clearly saw it as a useful way of establishing and affirming their identity. *Verlan* has proved to be a highly effective code by means of which non-members can be kept at arm's length. Examples of syllable-switching include *dombi, docra, cécoin, chantmé, tromé, pepons, rima, zessegon, tainpu, Secor, les renpats, déglan, se faire pécho* (= *bidon* 'worthless', *crado* < *crasseux, coincé* 'inhibited', *méchant*, *métro*, *pompes* 'shoes', *mari*, *gonzesse*, *putain*, *Corse* 'Corsican', *les parents*, *glander* 'laze about', *se faire choper* 'get arrested'). More unusually monosyllables are reversed: *ouf*, *iench*, *sub*, *j'ai fait as* (= *fou*, *chien* 'untrustworthy individual', *bus*, *j'ai fait ça*). Other monosyllabic forms presuppose an extra vowel, actual or hypothetical: *feub* 'food' < *feubou* < *bouffe* (**bouffeu*), *feuj* 'Jew' < *feujui* < *juif* (**juifeu*), *keuf* 'cop' < *keufli* < *flic* (**fliqueu*). The few cases of *verlan* attested in the speech of adults (e.g. *ripou* 'corrupt official' < *pourri*, *chébran* 'trendy' < *branché*, *barjot* 'crazy' < *jobard*) are secondhand: 'the wider public is a consumer and not a producer of *verlan*' (Ball 1990).

While recognising the relative autonomy of youth it would be a mistake to suppose linguistic uniformity among the younger generation. The gulf between *les napies* 'neo-Sloanes/Hooray Henries' (< *NAP* = Neuilly, Auteuil, Passy, chic Parisian suburbs) and *les zonards* 'young dropouts from the slum belt' (*la zone*) is as wide as ever, and is automatically reflected in their speech-forms. The skinhead and the yuppie do not exactly use language in the same way. Even within the speech of French students there can be significant differences. Whereas secondary and higher education has almost exclusively practised abbreviation by apocope (*fac*/ulté, *amphi*/théâtre, *philo*/sophie, *Sciences Po*/litiques, *math*/ématiques *spé*/ciales, *restau*/rant *u*/niversitaire, etc.), the *Ecole Polytechnique* has, like military slang, also favoured aphaeresis (ca/*pitaine*, com/*mandant*, com/*missaire*, ca/*binet*, ma/*tricule*, etc.).

Whatever the sociological context, certain lexical patterns are common to all types of alternative usage. Standard words are modified or replaced in a number of ways:

SUFFIXATION

resuffixation – Replacement of standard suffix or word-ending by non-standard suffix: *cinoche* < *ciné(ma)* *valoche* < *valise* *gouvernoche* < *gouvernement* *boutanche* < *bouteille* *niguedouille* < *nigaud* *cradingue* < *crasseux* *furibard* < *furieux* *stupéfax* < *stupéfait* *jalmince* < *jaloux* *la Bastaga* < *la Bastille* *la Villetouse* < *la Villette* *Ménilmuche* < *Ménilmontant*

– Unlike standard French – but in line with Old French usage – variants often exist as alternatives: *Bastaga/Bastoche* *valoche/valouse/valtouse/valdingue* *crad- ingue/ crado(s)/ cradoc/ craspec(t)/ craspignol/ craspouillard/cracra*

gratuitous suffixation – Addition of suffix where none exists in standard: *chérot* 'expensive' < *cher* *duraille* 'difficult' < *dur* *seulabre* 'lonely' < *seul* *salingue* < *sale* *débilos* < *débile* *tristos* < *triste* *chicos* < *chic* *trucmuche* < *truc* *merdouille* < *merde* *pestouille* 'bad luck' < *peste*

ABBREVIATION
- Normally by apocope or right-hand syllabic deletion. Highly productive (see George 1980); *impec/*
cable *dégueu/*lasse *hallu/*cinant *folklo/*rique *déca/*féiné
*calva/*dos *périf/*érique *alloc/*ations *sécu/*rité sociale
*gynéco/*logue *suppo/*sitoire *mob/*ylette *Contrex/*éville
*Cité U/*niversitaire *Prisu/*nic *Boull/*evard (Saint) *Mich/*
el (Boulevard) *Sébasto/*pol *Saint-Trop/*ez *Nouvel Obs/*
ervateur
- Many forms end in non-etymological -*o*: *apéro*
(apéritif) *Amerlo* (Américain) *dirlo* (directeur) *exo*
(exercise) *facho* (fasciste) *gaucho* (gauchiste) *prolo*
(prolétaire) *Montparno* (Montparnasse)

REPETITION

Syllabic
- Identical repetition of syllable, with euphemistic or
hypocoristic function: *coco* (communiste) *gaga*
(gâteux) *nunu* (nudiste) *pas jojo* 'not very nice' (joli)
pas fute-fute 'none too clever' (futé) *bibi* 'kiss' (bisou)
nounou (nourrice) *Nini* (Mélanie) *Nono* (Noël) *Riri*
(Henri)

whole-word
- Identical repetition of word, with intensive function: *mignon mignon* 'really sweet' (of child); *être*
copain-copain 'be close friends' *être boulot-boulot* 'be a
workaholic' *être discipline-discipline* 'be a stickler for
discipline' *pas brillant-brillant* 'not very bright' *pas*
content-content 'not exactly pleased' *pas chaud-chaud*
'not terribly keen'
- Exclamations and oaths: *zut zut zut! merde et merde!*
nom de dieu de nom de dieu! bordel de bordel! vache de
vache! putain de putain!

non-identical
- Euphemistic or hypocoristic function: *bébête* 'silly'
(bête) *sosotte* (sotte) *féfesse* (fesse) *guéguerre* (guerre)
Gaugaulle (de Gaulle) *Fifine* (Joséphine) *Lolotte*
(Charlotte) *Gégène* (Eugène)

INVERSION

verlan
- Syllable or phoneme switching: *narzo* (zonard) *narco*
(connard) *zomblou* (blouson) *larfou* (foulard) *lépoux*
(poulets 'police') *stomba* (baston 'punch-up') *rebier*
[rəbje] (bière) *sclums* (muscles) *euf* (feu 'light for
cigarette')

largonji and **loucherbem**
- Displacing initial consonant of standard word,
substituting *l* and usually adding a suffix, as in
largonji (= jargon) and *loucherbem* (= boucher, i.e.
the butchers' slang of La Villette, variant of *largonji*):
lacsé (sac) *lam(e)dé* (dame) *leudé* (deux) *laubé* (beau) à
loilpé (à poil) *lerche* (cher) *latronpem* (patron) *lissépem*
(pisser) *lutainpem* (putain)

– While *verlan* continues to be practised by the young, the use of *largonji* and *loucherbem* appears to be unproductive and limited to a relatively small number of working-class Parisians. *Javanais*, the only example of lexical infixation in French (the syllable *-av-* is inserted: *un baveau javardin* < *un beau jardin*), is in a similar situation.

ANGLICISMS

– Commonly referred to as *franglais* (see Etiemble 1973, George 1976). The interest here is not so much in 'straight' anglicisms (morphologically and semantically consistent with the original, e.g. *chewing-gum, weekend, baby-sitter*) as in hybrids and pseudo-anglicisms

hybrids
– Part English, part French: *top niveau top modèle block-système crack-pain* 'crispbread' *crédit revolving opéra-rock défilé-show* 'fashion parade' *pipi-room* 'WC' *papy-boom* 'OAP explosion' *autocoat* 'car coat' *pubman* 'ad-man' *perchman* 'boom operator'

pseudo-anglicisms
– Created within French, consisting entirely of English elements but not consistent with English usage: *crossman* 'cross country runner' *tenniswoman* 'female tennis player' *recordwoman* 'female record holder' *baby-foot* 'table football' *baby-star* 'child star' *tip-tap* 'tap-dancing' *horseball* 'type of handball played on horseback' *athletic-foot* 'athlete's foot'

– Ellipsis also produces discrepancies between French and English usage: *pull*/over *sweat*/shirt *bristol*/board 'visiting card' *hard*/ware (computing) *fast*/food *self*/service *living*/room

– There is a break with convention too in that many anglicisms acquire a different meaning in French: *un palace* is not a palace but a 5-star hotel, cf. *building* 'high-rise block', *baskets* 'trainers', 'sneakers', *un jogging* 'tracksuit', *faire jockey* 'go on a strict diet'. *McDo* (McDonald's) has come to mean 'banal', 'functional' ('un design 'McDo' – fonctionnel, aseptique', *L'Express* 19 February 1988)

Combinations of the above devices are common:

domb [dɔb] 'useless', 'lousy' = verlan (*dombi* < *bidon*) + apocope
linguebur 'office' = resuffixation (*burlingue* < *bureau*) + verlan
blackos [-os] 'Black (person)' = anglicism + gratuitous suffixation

The combination of *verlan* and truncation can produce particularly obscure results, *meugre* < *meugra* < *gramme* 'gramme (of cocaine)' being a case in point. Some developments are quite complex. English *grass* 'marihuana' was translated into French as *herbe* (a calque or loan translation). The synonym *gazon* was subsequently used in the same sense. This was then converted by *verlan* into *zonga*.

A fundamental difference between standard and non-standard forms is that the latter, by their very nature, do not always have a recognised, fixed spelling. This is really only a nuisance for the compiler of the slang dictionary, who will frequently offer orthographic variants. Typical examples are words for 'money': *auber/aubère/aubert, flouse/flouze, pèse/ pèze, pésètes/pésettes, pépètes/pépettes* and 'guy': *gnace/gniasse, gonce/gonse/ gonze, gus/guss/gusse, zig/zigue, keum/kem.* Apocopated words often show considerable variation: *aprem/aprem'/aprèm/aprèm'/aprème/après-m* (< *après-midi*). When an internal syllable containing *é* [e] becomes a final closed syllable (i.e. ending in a pronounced consonant) the [e] automatically opens to [ɛ]: *agrégation* > *agreg/agrèg, mathématiques élémentaires* > *math élem/élèm, raide défoncé* 'stoned' > *raide def/dèf*, though sometimes the original *é* will be retained thus creating a discrepancy between the orthographic and phonetic forms. Given that these are essentially oral items there is no real difficulty. It is only if they eventually become standard that the question of a single spelling arises, and the choice will in any case be more or less arbitrary.

Collectively the non-standard vocabulary illustrated in this chapter is available, together with informal pronunciation and grammar, as an alternative to the standard equivalents, social context being the determining factor. However 'alternative' should not necessarily be interpreted in the sense of 'marginal'. For example, *ne*-deletion in negative constructions and avoidance of inversion in the interrogative occur at the rate of some 85 per cent in spontaneous dialogue. The bulk of the words given as illustrations in this chapter will be familiar to native French speakers as a whole, even if they are not part of their active vocabulary. Indeed the twentieth century has seen a kind of linguistic democratisation, as the result of which lexical differences are less marked than previously. Both Mitterand and Guiraud drew attention to this phenomenon in the 1960s:

> Le parler dit 'populaire' conserve sa verdeur, et le style des discours académiques sa pompe, mais l'académicien et le délégué ouvrier, dans les mille situations identiques qui sont imposées à l'un et à l'autre par les formes de la vie moderne, sont astreints à user des mêmes mots. Le vocabulaire qui leur est commun représente une part du vocabulaire de chacun d'eux sans aucun doute plus étendue qu'au début de ce siècle . . . A l'uniformisation des bases matérielles de la vie moderne . . . répond une uniformisation du vocabulaire courant, ou du moins la constitution d'un 'niveau lexical neutralisé' à extension maximale. (Mitterand 1963)

> Nous assistons à une intégration des classes sociales; non qu'elles aient disparu, ni que les signes dont elles sont marquées soient moins significatifs et impératifs, mais ils sont moins différenciés: aujourd'hui la grande majorité de la population mange, s'habille, parle de façon à peu près identique. Aussi les variations linguistiques (et les autres), sans avoir rien perdu de leur réalité et de leur importance, s'inscrivent dans une marge stylistique plus étroite et qui rend leur identification plus difficile.   (Guiraud 1965)

Certainly the pseudo left-wing intellectuals so expertly portrayed by Claire Bretécher in her strip cartoons affect a casual speech-style, even if the motivating factor is often snobbery. But generally, young French professionals do use an informal register which makes it difficult to distinguish them linguistically from non-professionals. Here are a few excerpts from interviews conducted among unmarried professional couples aged between twenty and thirty-five (Chalvon-Demersay 1983): 'On se téléphone, on se fait une bouffe', 'Chacun met sa main à la sauce', 'On vient avec du pinard', 'Quand il y a des amis qui viennent, j'adore ça, je fais des trucs assez compliqués', 'Ils ont demandé si j'avais des trucs pour l'apéro, j'avais rien', 'Quand on fait une bouffe, chacun apporte une bricole, on n'a pas beaucoup de sous', 'L'argent file', 'On claque du fric', 'Dis pas que je suis riche, j'ai rien', 'On n'a pas de télé', 'On a un four qui est foutu', 'J'ai récupéré un frigo dans la rue' (longer extracts at end of chapter).

It is this kind of vocabulary and syntax that the French use constantly in their day-to-day lives, though they tend to disown such usage, condemning it as 'incorrect' ('C'est pas bien', 'Faut pas parler comme ça', 'Attention hein, ça se dit pas, ça'). As Frédéric François put it: 'On ne doit pas considérer comme fautives les constructions comme *qu'est-ce qu'il fait, le garçon? le garçon, il est parti* (sans oublier que ces constructions prohibées sont fréquemment utilisées par ceux mêmes qui les condamnent)' (François 1983).

This bring us back to the question of conventionality, raised earlier. Clearly the idea so fondly cherished until relatively recently that there is only one 'proper' form of the language is misguided. French is multiple, providing alternatives for a variety of social situations. What is normal in one context will not necessarily be appropriate in another. It is perfectly normal for close colleagues in an informal conversation to enquire after each other's *gosses* rather than *enfants*, or for schoolchildren to refer among themselves to their *prof de math* – indeed, use of the full form would be totally incongruous (cf. *my mathematics teacher*). The criterion is consistency: just as the *lycéen* will automatically use *tu* with his fellow students and *vous* with the teachers, so he will greet the former with a *salut*, the latter with a *bonjour*.

Henri Frei's great contribution was to show that even in uneducated usage – *le français populaire* in its traditional definition – there are what he called natural laws as distinct from artificial rules, a kind of spontaneous and unconscious regularisation producing a linguistic system which, though different from educated French, has a cohesion and a simplicity of its own. Thus for example the systematic use of *avoir* as auxiliary, at the expense of *être: il a tombé, je m'ai mis à genoux*, the adoption of *que* as an all-purpose relative: *celui que je pense* (= *à qui*) or the analogical use of *disez* and *faisez* in place of the exceptional *dites* and *faites*. It is only when the Popular French speaker tries to use a formal register that inconsistencies occur, often in the form of hypercorrection or over-compensation: *Voici tous les renseignements dont je m'empresse de vous donner* (= *que*), *dont* being associated with extreme formality (see Frei 1929, Guiraud 1965).

There are therefore several norms within French, depending basically on whether one is writing or speaking the language and whether the situation is formal or informal. Each variety and each register has its own conventions, which is why the term 'unconventional' is in the end unsatisfactory when applied exclusively to non-standard usage.

This becomes doubly apparent in a chronological perspective. Large numbers of expressions come into fashion and are adopted by general implicit consent (i.e. by convention) only to be replaced by another. The concept 'fashionable' itself provides an illustration: *à la page/à la coule/dans le vent/in/branché/chébran/câblé*. Examples of recent vogues have included *à la limite, au niveau de, pas évident, faire problème, quelque part, on se calme, y a malaise* (see Merle 1989). It is of course impossible to predict the lifespan of any individual innovation. Many of the entries in the *Dictionnaire du français parlé* (Bernet and Rézeau 1989) are over a hundred years old, and adolescent speech has resuscitated several elements of nineteenth-century criminal and military slang, e.g. *mec, ras le bol* (on *bol* 'arse'), *balaise* 'great', *fayot* 'swot' (originally 'keen recruit'), *rab* ('second helpings' then 'lots': *y a rab de nanas*). That many more are likely to be relatively short-lived is immaterial.

The important thing for the well-being of the French language is that, just as new forms are constantly being created to meet the ever-changing needs of an increasingly international society, so alternative forms are being generated in parallel to meet more individual, more intimate needs, both through innovation and by the modification of existing usage. It is equally important that such alternatives should be seen as simply non-standard, rather than sub-standard.

Text 1

Entretiens avec jeunes couples, non-mariés, professions libérales

Ma mère, elle est ravie que je sois en couple. Même, avant, quand je vivais avec Pascal, elle voulait absolument me payer un appartement. Elle sait que c'est un vrai couple. Elle nous croit plus heureux en couple que seuls. Elle pense qu'on se stabilise. Elle désire pour nous un cadre bien fermé avec un avenir tracé. Je dis ça ironiquement, mais c'est vachement agréable. Elle nous donne des torchons, des draps, de la vaisselle, de la bouffe. Elle nous reçoit ensemble. C'est vachement sympa. J'aime autant qu'elle soit comme ça. Ce qui m'embête, c'est que si, un jour, je ne suis plus en couple, ça marche moins bien avec elle. J'avais des super-problèmes avec elle. Là, ça va beaucoup mieux. Ça me revalorise parce qu'elle aime bien Marc. J'ai commencé plein de trucs, et j'ai toujours arrêté au milieu. Tout en me filant du fric, elle n'admet pas tellement que je sois comme ça. (22-year-old woman, student teacher)

Je voulais habiter avec Joseph. Seulement Joseph, il habitait nulle part. En fait, il avait un peu frimé, avec des airs mystérieux, mais je crois qu'il logeait tout bêtement chez ses parents. On s'est retrouvé dans la rue. On s'est baladé toute la soirée dans Paris. De bancs publics en bancs publics. On a marché, marché. On n'avait pas un rond. Finalement, à l'aube, on a fini par atterrir chez ma grand-mère. Je pleurais. J'étais désespérée. Je voulais plus rentrer à la maison. Mais je voulais plus vivre avec lui. Elle nous a fait un café. Et puis elle est descendue téléphoner à ma mère qu'elle avait besoin de moi pour quelques jours. Qu'elle m'avait demandé de passer. La pauvre petite dame . . . Elle est morte maintenant. Tu sais, ça fait un fameux bail. (33-year-old woman, trainee).

Je comprends pas. J'ai dix fois plus d'argent que quand j'étais étudiante, mais je ne m'en sors pas. Tous les mois, c'est la dèche. Je suis obligée d'emprunter à mes parents pour payer mes impôts. A la fin du mois, j'ai plus un rond. Je vais bouffer chez eux. Pourtant, je suis pas une fille de luxe. J'ais pas l'impression de faire des excès. Bon, le taxi de temps en temps, mais on n'a pas de bagnole. Je vais au resto, trois ou quatre fois par semaine, mais c'est des petites bouffes pas chères. Je mets tout mon linge au pressing; je vais pas mal au cinéma. Et puis le loyer et la psycha . . . C'est pas parce qu'on gagne un million par mois à deux qu'on est des riches. (25-year-old woman, lawyer)

(From Chalvon-Demersay 1983)

Text 2

Parlez-vous zulu?

'Ici, chaque cité a ses bandes', explique Mohamed. 'Elles sont à base de musique, de sexe ou de violence.' 'Aux 4000', ajoute Nicarson, 'les keums sont branchés funk. C'est des beurs – des racailles – des reurtis (lire lexique) qui vont voler dans le tromé pour la came. Alors que nous, on est zulus.' Et les zulus, en principe, sont 'peace' (non violents). 'Authentique', confirme Colette, 15 ans, d'origine camerounaise. 'Moi, précise-t-elle, je sors qu'avec des renois, même si j'ai des copains beurs. Quant aux gaulois j'en parle même pas. Même si je me rasais la tête, je ne pourrais jamais être skin, parce que ma peau est noire.'

Ils s'appellent: les Black Fist, les Derniers Salauds, Requins vicieux, Esprit criminel, 357 Magnum, NTM 93, Attentat, C. Cassis, etc. Ils sont 'renois' pour la plupart, mais aussi: 'beurs', 'feujs', 'gaulois' et parfois 'tos'. Leur langue: le verlan. Ils ont entre 13 et 25 ans, habitent la banlieue – forcément – dans des cités déglinguées et sans âme. Certains rapent ou taguent, ou bien les deux à la fois. D'autres, minoritaires, – les 'cailleras' – dépouillent et pratiquent plus la baston que l'art du graffiti . . .

Petit lexique à l'usage des non-rapants

B. Boy: Bad boy ou break boy. Jeune de la mouvance hip hop (tout ce qui tourne autour du rap).

Beur (ou reubeu, en verlan): Arabe.

Caillera (péjoratif): Racaille, en verlan. Désigne tout ce qui n'est pas zulu authentique: drogués, voleurs, bastonneurs, etc.

Dépouiller: Agresser quelqu'un pour lui voler des vêtements de valeur (Perfecto, Chevignon).

Embrouille: Provocation, *casus belli*. Exemple: draguer une fille d'une autre cité, dépouiller un type d'une bande rivale.

Feuj: Juif, en verlan.

Foncedé: défoncé, en verlan. Synonyme de 'séca' (cassé), qui veut aussi dire ivre.

Gaulois: Français de souche. Synonyme: saifran.

Ghetto-blaster: Littéralement, exploseur de ghetto. Désigne les énormes magnétophones qui se portent sur l'épaule.

Homeboy: Garçon du quartier, de la cité.

Keuf: Flic. On dit aussi: un 'schmit' ou un 'babylone'. 'Se faire serrer par les keufs': être arrêté par la police.

Keum: Mec, en verlan.

MC: Maître de cérémonie. Rapeur, disc-jockey, celui qui organise une soirée.

Meuf: Fille (femme, en verlan).

Pécho la meuf: Draguer une fille.

Peura: Rap, en verlan.

Posse (prononcer 'possi'): Le groupe, la bande au sens large. S'utilise aussi pour un groupe de rap.

Relou: Lourd en verlan. Synonyme: grave. On dit aussi: 'Y m'prend la teté' (il me prend la tête).

Retourner une rame: Taguer entièrement une station de métro, wagons compris.

Renoi: Noir, en verlan.

Reurti: Voleur à la tire en verlan, pickpocket.

Robocop: La nouvelle brigade de sécurité de la RATP. Allusion à un film américain sous-titré: '50% homme, 50% robot, 100% flic'.

Tarpé (se faire un): Fumer un joint. On dit aussi 'fumer un stick'.

Teboi: Boîte de nuit, en verlan. Les plus fréquentées: le Bobino, rue de la Gaîte (14e), et le Midnight, sur le parvis de la Défense.

Tos (péjoratif): Portugais. En verlan: 'Guétupor'.

Tromé (ou treum): métro, en verlan.

Zonzon: La prison. S'utilise dans l'expression 'être béton en zonzon': être en prison. Popularisé par le chanteur guadeloupéen Daddy Yod avec sa chanson 'Rock en zonzon'.

Zulu: Vient de la Zulu Nation, fondée en 1975 par Afrika Bambaata à New York. Mouvement apolitique qui vise à transformer la violence de la rue en violence créative: tag, rap, smurf. La Zulu Nation est implantée en France sous la houlette de la reine Candy. *F. A. et J. Du.*

(From 'Faut il avoir peur des bandes?' *Le Nouvel Observateur*, 9–15 August 1990)

9

New words for new technologies

STEPHEN NOREIKO

If we grant that the vocabularies of different languages are not nomenclatures in the Saussurean sense (Saussure 1916 I: 1.1) in a one-to-one correspondence with each other, if we accept that French distinguishes *un plan* and *une carte* where English only sees 'maps', or *un horaire* and *un emploi du temps* for what English calls 'timetables', then we might perhaps expect it to go without saying that the vocabulary of a language contains, if looked at from the right angle, a portrait of the culture that uses it.

After all, if we are to talk about objects and actions that are important to us, we need labels for them, and although we should beware of drawing raw conclusions – that English has no ready and generally acceptable translation for the French verb *jouir* in its most common sense (the last in *Harrap*, the first in *Petit Robert*) gives no grounds for supposing Saxon insufficiency in the domain, though the French might like to think so – the basic principle seems firm enough, and it has in fact been said repeatedly from Diderot, 'la langue d'un peuple donne son vocabulaire, et le vocabulaire est une table assez fidèle de toutes les connoissances de ce peuple: sur la seule comparaison du vocabulaire d'une nation en differens tems, on se formeroit une idée de ses progrès' (in the *Encyclopédie*, under the heading 'langue') to Dauzat (1949: 118), 'c'est l'étude du vocabulaire qui permet de saisir le mieux la répercussion des influences sociales sur le langage', but best of all by Meillet (1938: 145): 'tout vocabulaire exprime une civilisation'.

What most obviously marks our 'civilisation' in the last quarter of the twentieth century is the explosion of the technologies by which information is processed and transmitted: twenty years ago I calculated examination marks and averages with a machine that was the last word in electronic wizardry; desk-top size, mains-powered, cumbersome, it could add, subtract, divide and multiply, and there was one for the whole faculty. In examination meetings today, everybody has a solar-powered gadget the size of a credit card. Certainly, if any domains are reflected in the vocabulary, this is one of them: *calculette* is a recent creation, and a glance at the article *calculatrice* in almost any dictionary on the library shelves recalls an earlier stage of technology: dictionaries take some time to catch up.

But rather than simply cataloguing the new words and looking at them in isolation, we should also attempt to see them in the overall context of the vocabulary of the language and relate them to the usual underlying patterns of word creation and derivation in French. It is of course obvious that the new objects had to be named; what is more interesting and instructive about the workings of the French language is how its mechanisms have responded to the demands made of them.

A generation ago, Jacques Dubois and others (1960) examined the general trend of French vocabulary, basing their study on a comparison of successive revisions of the *Petit Larousse*. This dictionary, though it has little academic standing (see Rickard 1978: 502), is an institution in France (see Austin 1977: 368): a new edition appears annually, and is hailed by reviewers as an indicator of change and renewal (*Le Monde*, 7 September 1979: 'les nouveautés du Petit Larousse 1980', or 18 September 1982: 'Le Petit Larousse 1983, reflet du changement'), while at longer intervals fuller revisions and facelifts are undertaken, making the dictionary, if not a reliable indicator, at least one to consider before its indications are argued away. One of the conclusions of the Dubois study was that the overall size of the vocabulary was tending to decrease, with omissions outnumbering new entries. A corollary to this was what they considered to be the increasing technicality of the vocabulary, since the new inclusions belonged overwhelmingly to specialised domains, while items of general vocabulary fell out of use, and relatively few general everyday terms were being introduced.

This analysis is obviously open to question on a number of counts: technicality is an elastic concept (I find cars and telephones dauntingly technical, but cannot understand why most people are mystified by such simple things as computers and their operating systems), and the etymology of such a general term as French *arriver* suggests that it was once a technical mariner's term (*adripare*: 'to put in to (*ad*) the bank (*ripam*)'), while *une IVG* (*interruption volontaire de grossesse*: 'abortion', or 'termination of pregnancy' in doctor's parlance) is obviously medical jargon, though now sufficiently general and everyday for the derived verb 'j'ivégète' to have been heard. Everyday vocabulary feeds on other people's technicalities, and such concepts as *culpabiliser* ('give guilt feelings to') or *cibler* ('target'), formerly limited to psychologists, and sociologists or marketing executives, have become part of the mental furniture of the late twentieth century. Here is another of the ways in which vocabulary does reflect our culture, by the depth to which technical concepts have become part of ordinary people's habits of thought: 'notre époque n'est-elle pas justement caractérisée par la pénétration de vocables spécialisés dans le langage courant' (Bécherel 1981: 120).

What Dubois and his co-authors call everyday vocabulary, the vocabulary which can be assigned to no particular specialised domain, is probably much more likely to grow by expanding existing words, increasing the number of senses, so that the already ubiquitous *faire* extends its usage to telephone ('faire le 19, puis l'indicatif du pays demandé') and petrol consumption or speed ('faire 5 litres au cent kilometres', 'faire du 160 chrono'), while in the technical sphere we might generally expect new things to require new names, so that although typewriter and computer keyboards do simply extend the existing word and are still *claviers*, with the latter including a *pavé numérique* ('numeric keypad'), *le transistor* ('transistor' and 'tranny'), *le synthétiseur* ('synthesiser'), *le décodeur* ('decoder': the black box that sits on top of a television set and unscrambles the signal of Canal Plus, the subscription-only television channel), and many others, get new labels.

But whatever conceptual faults we may find with it, the Dubois conclusion is generally accepted: it fits well enough with the received wisdom about the vocabulary of French and it comforts the prejudices both of the reactionary purist who sees the French tradition declining and the humanist values it embodies withering under the attack of, mainly Anglo-Saxon, technologies, as well as of the libertarian laxist who sees the initiative of the individual speaker stifled by the authoritarian tradition so that the general vocabulary necessarily dwindles, leaving a vacuum to be filled by, mainly Anglo-Saxon, technicalities.

It is of course a commonplace of French that the common speaker is not allowed (or cannot be trusted: it depends on the point of view) to create new words. Martinet (1969: 29) insists that 'on les a dressés à obéir, à respecter le précédent, à n'innover en rien; ils n'osent pas forger un mot composé, utiliser librement un suffixe de dérivation, procéder à des combinaisons inattendues. Les anglicismes contre lesquels fulminent la plupart de nos régents ont la partie belle dans une langue dont on n'ose plus utiliser toutes les ressources', and it is part of the background assumptions of French as a planned language (see chapter 1) that acceptable neologisms are the business of one or other of the ministerial commissions on terminology, set up from 1971 onwards, and which eventually produce lists of replacement terms for the unacceptable neologisms or borrowings that people have been using meanwhile.

Thus, having signed the decree on 24 January 1983, the then Minister of Communication, Georges Fillioud presented to the press on 15 February 'une première liste d'une centaine de termes français, nouveaux ou peu usités, destinés surtout à remplacer des expressions anglo-saxonnes dans le domaine de l'audio-visuel et de la publicité' (*Le*

Monde, 17 February 1983). The list gives, for example, *publipostage* for 'mailing', *(ouverture en) fondu* for 'fade (in)', *égaliseur* for 'equaliser', *(très) gros plan* for '(big) close up', *baladeur* for 'walkman', *sonal* for 'jingle' (see chapter 1). Some of these seem obvious; others however, like *sonal,* appear born to fail: though it does contain *son,* the form gives no further clue to its meaning and the staff at Radio NRJ (= 'énergie') and no doubt elsewhere still refer to 'un djingle'. The real point at issue however is the underlying assumption that creates the apparatus that produces such a list, and produces it in the format: Anglicism followed by French equivalent. If English were not so dominant, French *disc-jockeys* (who may also be called *animateurs* – or *animatrices,* though French media-speak might prefer *disc-jockettes*) could have used the word *scie* ('any piece of speech or song that goes round and round') or, from *un tube* (French for 'hit'), have formed *une tubette.* What French lacks is not the lexical resources, but, if it lacks anything at all, the motivation.

Another commonplace is that French is threatened by the computer. The threat takes a number of forms. First of all, the status of the language and indeed its very essence are called in question by machines that are labelled in English ('Escape', 'Caps Lock') and whose instruction sets are made up of English words: 'GOTO', 'IF . . . THEN', and which reply, when French is typed in, 'Mistake'. There is of course no reason why computer instructions sets ('languages') cannot be recast in whatever human language is wished, and French BASICS and LOGOS are available, with instructions such as GOMME, REPETE, POUR. They are not what is provided as standard however, and the French-made Thomson MO-5 which was the first machine adopted in French schools, though it came equipped with a light-pen (*crayon optique*), had to be programmed in a BASIC not only clumsy, but composed of English words. And then, the form of French is menaced because its character set does not match the computer standard: the accents pose a problem, obvious on the old MO-5, which required three keypresses to put *é* on the screen, and which insisted, if asked (with the English instruction 'LEN'), that *é* was a string of three characters (presumably, *e* + backspace + accent). The same problem seems to be in evidence at the *Bibliothèque nationale,* where, at least for a time, computer-produced lists showed accents floating over empty spaces after their letters (giving, for example, *tre`s*).

Gabriel de Broglie, once vice-president of the *Haut Comité de la langue française,* is one of those who sound the alarm (1986: 271–2):

> Il paraît que l'ordinateur n'aimerait pas les accents et qu'il faudrait bien les supprimer pour harmoniser nos claviers avec ceux des autres langues et ne pas handicaper notre industrie. Que l'on prenne garde! L'ordinateur est une Chimère prête à tout dévorer; après les accents, les doubles consonnes, puis les terminaisons muettes même si elles sont signifiantes, puis les homonymes, surtout les monosyllabes, etc. L'or-

dinateur peut réduire la langue en sabir, mais il peut aussi en assimiler presque toutes les nuances. C'est une question de capacité, de volonté et de principe. Il devrait y avoir une convention internationale de protection des langues contre l'informatique.

A professor at the university of Paris-VII and director of the CNRS linguistics and computing laboratory, Maurice Gross, interviewed by the *Nouvel Observateur* for the special number on 'Les Français malades de l'orthographe' (6–12 September 1985), seems to be saying much the same, but he draws in fact the contrary conclusion, arguing not that French must be defended against the computer, but that the simplification which computers will require in French spelling at least will turn to the advantage of the language:

> le français comporte 25% de signes typographiques de plus que l'anglais, ce qui implique la nécessité d'un équipement spécial. Mais, surtout, ces signes sont régis par des codes internationaux. Les informaticiens français doivent donc détourner certains codes de leur usage standard. D'où des pertes de temps, des risques d'erreur . . . D'où la nécessité d'une réforme pour simplifier l'orthographe, qui nous semble par ailleurs nécessaire pour des raisons pédagogiques.

He goes on to assert that the computer-led simplifications which seem to some to threaten so much of what is seen as quintessentially French and culturally essential, the 'terminaisons muettes' which are the grammar of the verb, would in fact put the language in a stronger position to resist the encroachments of English, pointing out that 'si l'on simplifie l'orthographe, le verbe français ne serait pas plus compliqué que le verbe anglais'.

However, the influence of computers is not wholly negative: vocabulary in the fields of information processing and transmission shows very well that French is creative and capable of invention, that it is reacting. One could argue in fact that the general trend has been reversed and that the vocabulary is now on the increase. Although apparently the anglicism *computer* has been used (and the abbreviation *PC*), and though for example T[élématique] V[idéotex] F[rançaise] has registered the trademark *handtop computer* (*desktop* and *laptop*, for which 'lapheld' makes more sense in English, are found, though a gloss may be needed), French has always preferred the native term *ordinateur*, and thus put the emphasis on the information ordering potential of the computer, which the English term seems to relegate to number-crunching. The French term for the science of computing reflects this, combining *information* with the *-ique* (later re-interpreted as *-tique*) of *botanique, cybernétique, linguistique* and so on to give *informatique*. Even if de Broglie (1986: 101) seems not to like it, 'les applications de l'informatique, cette floraison de *tiques* et de *niques* font craindre pour la langue', the word has gained a foothold in English: there is a professor of Informatics at the University of Ulster. But the real measure of the term's viability in the language is that it supports derivatives: an adjective (*un virus informatique*) a noun (*un(e) informaticien(ne)*), and a very useful verb *informatiser* which gives in turn another noun (*l'informatisation du catalogue*).

Informatique rhymes with *automatique*, and the -*tique* suffix seems to be sufficiently striking and meaningful to produce a new series of creations, of terms generally relating to new technologies and their application. *La mercatique* does not fit well with the others, and accordingly has not replaced *le marketing*, but the field of reproductive technology and genetic experimentation is aptly labelled *la procréatique*; other formations, by now well established, are *la bureautique*, in fact a trade mark for office automation, a specialised application of *informatique*, and another specialised use of this technology, *la télématique*, computer communications. This has become an everyday item in most French offices and many French households since the introduction of *le Minitel* (another trademark become part of the language). Not a miniature telephone, but a cheap and robust terminal that plugs piggyback (*gigogne* has become more common in *prise gigogne*) into the same socket as the household telephone, the *Minitel*, first introduced experimentally in the Paris suburb of Vélizy in 1980 and since extended to the whole of France, like the telephone directory it replaces, is supplied free to all telephone subscribers. It also replaces directory enquiries, since the '11' enquiry service allows searches for phone numbers all over France, and will even extend the search to phonetic approximations: if it can't find the *Dupont* you want, it will suggest trying *Dupond*, or *Cantin* for *Quentin*.

The *Minitel*, with its rubber keys on a keyboard that folds back under the small screen, is the gateway to the largest on-line database in the world, and via '36 15', the *kiosque* system, users can tap in (*taper*) the code words of a variety of services, the charges for which are added to their telephone bills. You can get careers information, look up railway or plane timetables, book tickets, find out about university places and courses or exam results; to enrol at some Paris universities you need a Minitel; it is now possible for a school to have a *serveur sur Minitel* so that parents can get up-to-date information on pupils' progress, ask for an appointment with a teacher, or send a letter of excuse. Or you can just play games or send messages; accordingly, the term *messagerie* has come out of relative obscurity (parcels and press delivery service, though the *service national des messageries* is better known as *Sernam*) for the new sense of computer bulletin boards and electronic mail. Some of these services, those that run large advertisements and use female given names as access codes – *code* has also become more common for these, and, as *code confidentiel* for 'PIN' – are, given the use made of them, known collectively as *le Minitel rose*.

A computer mailbox is quite simply *une boîte aux lettres*, often abbreviated to give a new term: *bal*. In spite of the form, this is feminine, though, as with *HLM*, there is a tendency, once the underlying expressions are forgotten, for such abbreviations to revert to the unmarked ('masculine') gender. On a desk in a *seconde* classroom of a provincial lycée, a pupil had laboriously inscribed details of all the software he had available for exchange via Minitel, putting at the end 'mon bal: 36.14 . . . '. Another hand had queried the use of the '36.14' number, and added 'on dit *une bal*', thus proving that whatever the effects of computers, France is still a nation of grammarians.

Informatique and the other terms show an existing suffix modified and reinterpreted. Another item of computer terminology involved the creation of a new suffix. As computers grew closer to what they are today, the distinction grew up, among English-speaking users, between the 'hardware', the machinery itself, and the instructions needed to make the hardware work: the 'software'. For want of an equivalent, the terms began to make inroads into French usage, and in the sixties, the French, or some of them, were searching for native terms to replace the borrowings. Canadians used a 'calque' from English in their own language and dubbed the machines *quincaillerie*, an unsatisfactory solution since it replaced one of a matched pair with an isolated term (no one was going to call programs *droguerie* or *parfumerie*). In mainland French a more academic but quite natural approach was to extend an existing term: *matériel* can denote any kind of equipment, and to complete its extension to computer hardware it only needed a matching expression for software. The invention of *logiciel*, in which *logique* with the final plosive /k/ harmonised to a fricative /s/ is added to the -*iel* extracted from *matériel*, not only solved the dilemma by providing a pair of words, but proved to be a starting point for further expansion; since -*iciel* now appeared to be the suffix to designate computer programs, different types could be labelled: a game is *un ludiciel*, a teaching program *un didacticiel*. In 1971, the general secretary of the *Comité d'étude des termes techniques français* (Agron 1971: 74) suggested, to replace the English *package* (a suite of related programs usually including *traitement de texte*, *tableur*, and *base de données*), the locution *bloc de programmes*; like a lot of the expressions proposed by official bodies, this one did not catch on, but such programs are in fact now called *progiciels*.

There is, it would appear, a new confidence growing in French. They no longer need *La Banque des mots* (1972: 3, 99) to suggest *photostyle* for what they are happy to call *un crayon optique*, though if they did, *Franterm*, the terminological service of the *Commissariat général de la langue française* is available on Minitel. Rather than attempting to translate 'user-friendly', they speak of *logiciels confortables*, *machine conviviale*: one user remarked of a certain unforgiving *langage de requête* ('query language') that 'il a une convivialité de crocodile'. In this climate, the pronouncements of linguistic purists seem less relevant, and the purists are probably out of their depth. There are signs of this in de Broglie for example, who uses *télé-prompteur* (1986: 92) and *digitaliser* (1986: 104). Idiot-boards and autocues 'prompt', but this anglicism is meaningless in French where the word used in theatres and classrooms is *souffler*: the *Guide des mots nouveaux* (Depecker and Pages 1985) gives *télé-souffleur*. English 'digital', 'digitizer' and so on derive from 'digit', which in French is *chiffre*; French does have an adjective *digital*, but of course it corresponds to *doigt* (as in *empreintes digitales*), and although we can find in catalogues *montre digitale* or *affichage digital*, *affichage numérique* is gaining ground, and the term for converting information into numbers is commonly *numériser*, though it is done with *un scanner*.

There is pressure from English of course (see chapter 8). Terms like *autofocus* or *zoom* are learnt from the labels on imported equipment; the adjective *portable* is becoming more common beside or in place of *portatif*, although the distinction may be made in this way between 'portable' and 'transportable'; the use of international applications software will also have an influence, but there is reaction too in that elements of English are treated as native material. *Un clip* was already established in film usage (it's also an item of jewellery) and although *(bande) promo* was suggested, *clip* has quite naturally been extended to the pop videos which are the staple of the television channel M6. Officially, the continuity person on a film set should be *la scripte* (feminine and with an *e*) rather than the more obviously (but still pseudo-) English *script-girl*, but the credits (*le générique*) of Patrice Leconte's 1981 film *Viens chez moi j'habite chez une copine* listed a *script-boy*. French now possesses a pool of originally English elements of which native creative use can be made: *le zapping* only looks like English, and like *zapper*, *zappeur*, this term for channel-switching with *une télécommande* is an in-hexagon creation; *soft*, as applied, say, to Mylène Farmer's videos, has taken on a rather more specialised sense than its source.

English influence is also evident behind some French expressions: there is hesitation between *CD* and *disque compact*, and the attempt to assimilate *un bug* and *débugger* turns on a relatively obscure term for the spiny outer husk of the chestnut, *bogue*, giving *déboguer*. It is a reasonable conjecture that but for the English term the argotic expressions 'il y a un os', 'tomber sur un os', might have produced *désosser* in this sense. The influence is less obvious in such calques as *saisir*, *saisie* for data capture and loan translations like *temps réel*. *Un frontal* for 'front end', *utilisateur final*, or *L4G* (*langage de quatrième génération*) are also no doubt loan translations, but French enough for any purist; *système d'exploitation*, and *tourner* for 'run' are moving further away, while *mémoire vive* and *mémoire morte*, measured now in *Mo*, or *méga-octets* are convincingly French.

Even more convincingly French is *camembert* which owes nothing to the English 'pie-chart', and where French does make use of its native resources, the first of the methods available is the extension of an existing word. The key term of the computer revolution is *la puce*, used more frequently than its literal English equivalent and so more readily available for metaphorical expansion. Senses can be widened to encompass new developments, with *lecteur* serving for all kinds of *disques, durs, compacts*, or *disquettes*, as well as for *cassettes* (K7 for short), *chaîne* and *enceinte* widen their use, and *platine*, originally extended to record turntables, is now commonly used for *platine laser*, and the word *laser* is also acquiring new uses: witness the slogan 'Hi-Fi laser, c'est le rayon Fnac'. Existing nouns can be extended by combining them in apposition: again, the process looks English, especially when the modifier precedes the head-word, as in *politique-fiction* (in fact a French creation, on the model of the naturalised *science-fiction*), and *mémoire-tampon* is an obvious loan translation, but the process is well-established in French, and the order head-word qualifier is typically French, as in *bande annonce* ('trailer'), *bande son*, and *bande promo*, which was suggested to replace [*video-*]*clip*. The syntax of other compounds such as *radio-cassette, auto-radio, radio-réveil*, is less clear, and this may be why users prefer to make them masculine, although the official sources give *radio-cassette* feminine; *autoroute* is also masculine for many speakers.

It will be clear from examples previously cited that most of the derivational suffixes of French are in fact productive: *-eur* and *-iste* are perhaps most in favour (*pupitreur, publiciste, claviste*), with *-eur* also used for machines, perhaps rather more commonly than *-euse* (*répondeur* [*automatique*], *copieur*, though a printer is *une imprimante-matricielle* or *à marguerite*; *téléviseur* is also gaining ground, leaving *télévision* for the *média*); also in evidence is *-ette* (*sanisette*). Deverbal nouns may be formed with the well-established *-age* (*bruitage, mixage, sondage, pleurage; publi-postage* is suggested for *mailing*, *listage* for *listing*, neither of them with much success), but, though they are not in fact recent formations, it is substantivised past participles, usually masculine, which seem, by the frequency of their use, most typical of contemporary use: *le drapé, le suivi, le fini*, all of these are commonly heard *au niveau du vécu quotidien*.

For verbs, *-er* and *-iser* are common: *médiatiser* represents an important concept, *crédibiliser* is used, while when the slogan says 'avec Carrefour, je positive', one might be at a loss to say what is meant, but the verb is well-formed. In addition to the suffixes which can be used for the formation of nouns as well as adjectives (to which we may add *-ien*, and of course *-tique*: *médiatique*), the *-ble* suffix seems to be usable with most verbs, as was already noted by the Dubois survey (1960: 104 and see also Noreiko 1985: 189); this may explain the ready acceptance of *portable* beside *portatif*.

So far, the main interest has been in noting that lexical enrichment is taking place in contemporary French, though in fact the derivational processes are themselves unremarkable: they have all been documented by Brunot for various stages of the language's history. Where there is significant expansion and indeed a change almost in kind is in the area of recomposition. The term is Martinet's (1960: 135; 1964: 146–7), for the construction of new words out of elements 'extracted by analysis'. As Mitterand puts it, 'les recomposés se caractérisent par le fait qu'un de leurs termes au moins n'existe pas dans la langue à l'état isolé: ou bien c'est un radical d'origine latine ou grecque, ou bien c'est un radical français (éventuellement emprunté autrefois à une langue étrangère moderne), dont la syllabe finale a subi pour les besoins de la composition une modification' (1963: 56).

In fact, the line between composition and recomposition is growing fainter as the elements themselves acquire greater autonomy, becoming polysemantic in the process as they come to stand also for the words they have been extracted from: *télé* in *téléfilm* is the now independent *télé* from *télévision*, in the indispensible *télécarte* it stands for *téléphone*, while in *téléski* (also known commonly as *tire-fesses*, illustrating another productive means of noun-formation) it has been extracted from *téléphérique*; finally, in *télécommande* it is actually the Greek recompositional element meaning 'far' – though the average *zappeur* using one might not realise this. Similarly *auto* in *auto-radio* is the independent 'car'; in *autofocus*, though the word is English, most speakers would understand the root 'self'. There is thus overall a greater fluidity in the use of these elements. Mitterand (1963: 59) gives the example of *bus*, extracted from *omnibus* before achieving independent status (*le bus*), and functioning also as a suffix in *bibliobus*, although the separate analysis proposed is hardly needed, since if *-thèque* signifies 'library' or 'collection', as in *médiathèque*, *ludothèque*, or even *pochothèque*, and *biblio* stands for 'books', then *bibliobus* is simply 'bookbus' rather than *bibliothèque circulante*.

This is in fact the measure of the increased flexibility, since we now have *abribus*, poorly formed from a logical point of view – it is not to shelter buses – though this is not the point: it is nonetheless a successful coinage in that it has passed into general use. It is of course, like *Minitel*, *sanisette*, or *bureautique*, an advertiser's invention, but such inventions not only legitimise themselves by acquiring what French philologists used to call *droit de cité*, they also contribute to the overall climate of inventiveness: if *sanisette*, then why not *caninette* (for a motor scooter adapted to clean up city streets after dogs who can't read)? In such a climate *un mainframe* can become *un ordinateur multiposte*, which will of course be *multitâche*; *fax* my be used, but *télécopie*, *télécopieur* are more usual because more readily understandable. Given *magnétoscope* on the model of *magnétophone*, the way is open to extract *-scope* for *caméscope*. As in *téléspectateur*, the accent at the juncture is not strictly necessary: it serves to maintain the identity of the first element, here recalling *caméra* from which it has been carved.

Mini, maxi, multi can be freely used: *maxi-rock et minibruits* is the title of a guide to the French pop scene, some of which is concerned with the availability of *studio multipistes*, and *ad hoc* creations with these or with *super* are possible; as well as *micro*, more limited in its use, *nano* has made an appearance in *nano-réseau*, the typical school configuration of a *compatible PC* serving a cluster of small machines, and of course sharing *appareils de péri-informatique*.

Computers and the media are pre-eminently the domain of initiates, of cliques and clans and people in the know or people who like to be thought in the know. Accordingly, all the devices of *français non-conventionnel* (see chapter 8) may be seen in operation. Truncation, obviously. 'Le micro qui bouleverse la micro', said an IBM poster (*une pub IBM*). The second might more normally be *la micro-informatique*, but the first is common for *micro-ordinateur*; in another field, *micro* is *microphone*: and broadcasters generally identify themselves or each other with the formula 'au micro, Un Tel'. A guitarist's equipment includes *un ampli* and *une pédale disto*, while keyboards of all kinds are referred to as *synthé*, even though some of them are *machines à sampler*, or *échantillon-neurs*. The complete sound system is *la sono*. Argotic deformations and replacements are used too: collectively all this equipment is *le matos* [matos], and in the old days when computers were fed with *cartes perforées*, these were known also as *brêmes*.

And though what used to be *les PTT* or for a time *les P et T* is now split between *la Poste* on the one hand and *France-Télécom* or *les Télécoms* on the other, *siglaison*, the reduction to initials, spelt out ([petete]) or read as a word (*le SMIG, les TUC*), is another method of reducing long expressions to manageable and familiar proportions. What is called, derisively, *le PAF* (*paysage audio-visuel français: le paf* has several argotic meanings, and *la PAF* is *police de l'air et des frontières*), divided as it is betwen *TF1, A2, RTL, RMC, NRJ* and others, is overseen by the *INA* and the *CSA* (*institut national* and *conseil supérieur de l'audio-visuel*). The growing computerisation of banks, making the *DAB* (*distributeur automa-tique de billets*) obsolete, replaces it with the *GAB* or *guichet automatique bancaire*; among other computer applications are a number of sets of initials: *EAO, CAO, PAO* (respectively *enseignement, conception, publica-tion,* all *assisté(e) par ordinateur*: English uses 'CAL', 'CAD', 'DTP'), and *CDI* (*compact disque interactif*); where English has 'DBMS', French refers to *SGBD* (*système de gestion de base de données*). And of course, the expression may be engineered to produce a fetching *sigle*: the city of Bordeaux is equipped with *gestion électronique du réseau de trafic routier urbain défiant les embouteillages*, known to friends as *GERTRUDE*.

We do seem to be a long way from 'l'apathie terminologique du français' (de Broglie 1986: 196) so often deplored. Television may be the *attrape-mômes* (a nonce-formation used by *Le Monde de l'Education* for the cover feature of issue 161, June 1989), computers may threaten the distinctiveness of French, and both are no doubt jargon-ridden. Their jargon is however showing that even as it absorbs anglicisms, going from *hit-parade* to *le Top 50* (pronounced *cinquante*), it is also using native resources to react. The creations may be inelegant, and it is certain that the derivational chaos of French has not been improved: it is still true, as Guiraud says (1966: 65), that 'la synonymie et la polysémie des suffixes restait une des plaies du vocabulaire français'. Much of this complaining reflects the fact that the centre of influence of French has yet again shifted: where once it was the Court, or, later, the intellectual circles of Paris, the centre of gravity is now with those who process and move the information. Those who are listened to, those who have the ear of a public much larger than it was when French achieved its classical status are those whose concern is with *le look* and *la branchitude*, or with *un matos super-performant* providing *un environnement convivial*. In this climate, language is not an end but a tool. There seems no reason to suppose it will not attain *super-perfomances* of its own.

Text 1
Langages: le règne du Basic english

Le matériel micro-informatique est anglo-saxon. Les claviers français 'Azerty' avec les caractères accentués, comprennent des touches dont le rôle est affiché en anglais: Esc, PrtSc, Caps Lock, Del, etc . . . La synthèse vocale intégrée de l'Amiga s'exprime avec l'accent anglo-saxon. Les éditeurs sont empoisonnés par des problèmes de traduction entre la dizaine de standards de machines utilisés. Adapter un jeu d'une machine à une autre exige de réécrire le programme. Les distributeurs des logiciels tentent de traduire les notices en français. Impossible, en revanche, de traduire les textes qui s'affichent à l'écran sans un travail de reprogrammation du jeu sur chacun des types de machines: l'analyseur syntaxique des jeux d'aventure est propre à chaque langue. Les éditeurs y renoncent. Les analyseurs de syntaxe les plus sommaires et les plus répandus acceptent un verbe (parfois à l'infinitif) suivi d'un substantif. Ce 'petit nègre' n'utilise que les premières lettres des mots: 'Exam(iner) tabl(e)', 'Tuer dra(gon)'. Le vocabulaire limité qui est utilisé revient de jeu en jeu: paresse qui évite au joueur d'errer dans la forêt des mots synonymes, mais qui appauvrit le langage. D'autres analyseurs de syntaxe comprennent un vocabulaire de plusieurs centaines de mots, acceptent des verbes à l'impératif, tolèrent la présence des articles, voire exécutent à la suite une succession de commandes: *'Examine la table, va à l'Est et tue le dragon'*. Plutôt que d'améliorer les analyseurs, les auteurs préfèrent limiter les dialogues saisis au clavier. En effet, pour vendre dans le monde entier, les éditeurs cherchant à éliminer les épineux problèmes de traduction: le joueur conduit son aventure en 'cliquant' le curseur qu'il promène sur l'écran. Ainsi un clic du curseur sur l'îcône 'main' transformera le curseur en une main mobile qui, cliquée à son tour sur certaines zones de l'écran, s'appropriera les objets transportables. D'ailleurs, les consoles de jeu, les bornes d'arcade dans les cafés, ne disposent pas de clavier. Un volant ou une manette munie d'un bouton 'feu' suffit. Or, de plus en plus de programmes tournant sur micro sont des adaptations fidèles des jeux d'arcade développés par les grandes compagnies japonaises . . . D.S.

(From *Le Monde de l'Education*, April 1989)

Text 2

Cent mots peur l'audiovisuel

La néologie, si vivante au Québec, est en France un art inconnu. Puriste à sa façon, le Français préfère généralement adopter un mot étranger plutôt qu'un terme hexagonal tout neuf. Ainsi appelle-t-il un 'baladeur' *Walkman* bien qu'il s'agisse là d'une marque, comme Frigidaire ou Moulinex. Les commissions ministérielles de terminologie créées en 1971 sous l'impulsion du Haut Comité de la langue française ne se sont guère livrées, depuis lors, au 'remue-méninges' que l'on continue donc d'appeler *brainstorming*. Regardant avec gourmandise vers les Etats-Unis, Mme Christine Ockrent, responsable des journaux du soir à Antenne 2, peut déclarer, sans faire sursauter quiconque, que *'le rythme et le ton qu'imprime notre langue à une information filmée sont inadéquats ou style concis et efficace que requiert le journalisme télévisé'*. Pour pallier cette 'inadéquation', on truffe le plus possible le langage médiatique de termes anglo-saxons. Avec un peu de patience nous arriverons à un langage totalement 'adéquat', c'est-à-dire *clean and cool*, et pour tout dire *american*.

Il est peu rassurant qu'aucun des neuf membres de la Haute Autorité de la communicaton audiovisuelle n'ait assisté à la présentation par M. Georges Fillioud de quatre-vingt-dix-sept termes destinés à remplacer autant de mots anglais dans le vocabulaire audiovisuel. M. Alain Savary, ministre de l'éducation nationale, qui a, lui aussi, signé l'arrêté du 24 janvier 1983 relatif à ces expressions et néologismes, s'était fait représenter à leur 'baptême' par un de ses collaborateurs. Comme nous demandions à ce haut fonctionnaire s'il ne conviendrait pas de consacrer à un cours de néologie l'heure de français 'traditionnel' que l'on va sans doute supprimer bientôt dans les écoles, il nous a rétorqué que notre question était *'hors du sujet'* . . .

Souhaitons quand même bonne chance à cette centaine de jeunes mots lâchés dans la jungle franglaise sans aucune garantie de vie en dehors des textes administratifs. Il est clair que chaque mot anglais d'une syllabe ou deux remplacé par une expression française à tiroir ('prêt-à-monter' pour *kit* 'télévision-à-péage' pour *pay-TV*) n'aura guère de mal à se maintenir. En revanche, 'stylisme' devrait pouvoir triompher de *styling elements*, et 'promo' de *video-clip*. On applaudit aussi à la 'stylique' qui succédera à *design* plus facilement qu' 'esthétique industrielle' proposé naguère; 'maquette' devrait sans mal damer le pion à *advanced lay-out*. Mais pourquoi 'achat groupé' et non pas 'groupage' pour expulser *package*? Et quel dommage d'avoir omis de proposer 'listage', ou tout bêtement le bon vieux 'liste', pour l'intrus *listing* qui fait actuellement fureur, en informatique notamment! Les travaux des terminologistes n'auront de franc succès que lorsqu'ils devanceront l'événement linguistique au lieu de le suivre, parfois avec dix ans de retard. J.-P. Péroncel-Hugoz

(From *Le Monde* 17 février 1983)

10

Language and style in politics

JOHN GAFFNEY

In representative democracies (if not in all polities maintained by conventions and practices other than brute force alone) politics is essentially a question of language, that is to say, of thousands upon thousands of linguistic utterances and exchanges which take place in the context of an elaborate set of generally accepted conventions: a civil servant functions as the skilled user of a particular language; a politician, via the framework of an electoral campaign or parliamentary procedure, wins support by means of what he or she says; a diplomat sustains or negotiates international relations by employing a highly charged but very restricted code of euphemisms; and so on (comparative and contrastive claims can be made for lawyers, trade unionists, television reporters, indeed for all political and social actors).

Language acts to maintain, challenge or effect changes within the political status quo; and the relationship between political language, convention and ritual is of crucial importance here. Ritual normally constrains participants who wish to effect change. Occasionally, however, language within ritual can bring about significant change (the brilliant speech in the National Assembly which swings the vote, the emotional appeal at conference which saves the party from scission, and so on).

The codified language of diplomacy is an illustrative example of the potential power of language and of the severe constraints placed upon it in order to control or neutralise its effects. When such constraints are subverted, the effects can be dramatic. Let us mention briefly here one of the most famous of these transgressions in the twentieth century.

In 1967, President de Gaulle of France was on a state trip to Canada, that is as an invited guest of the Canadian federal government. In Montreal, the capital of the French-speaking Canadian province of Quebec, a province where anti-(English-speaking) Canadian feeling was strong, and which, in the 1960s, entertained the idea of secession, de Gaulle unexpectedly ended a speech with the words: 'Vive Montréal!

Vive le Québec! Vive le Québec libre! Vive le Canada français! Et vive la France!'

Let us look at these five short utterances in more detail. The first two, while emotional, are uncontentious – de Gaulle is in Montreal and Montreal is in Quebec. The third utterance should logically be 'Vive le Canada!'. The 'Vive le Québec libre!' veers away from convention, as if spontaneously triggered by the need to repeat the word 'Québec', and celebrates a mythical (unrealised) entity in which actual Quebec is contained: a free Quebec (whose freedom is impeded by a reality, English Canada). The speaker then returns as if to convention: 'Vive le Canada!', but adds the adjective 'français', thus undermining totally actual, and named, Canada, while at the same time denoting an everyday reality (Quebec is known as 'le Canada français' in ordinary language), as well as a transcendent entity to be brought into be-ing – another country. French Canada's apparent justification, distant France itself (there 'in person' in the form of de Gaulle), is then named as the culminating point of this part real, part mythical series of terms. The affront to the Canadian government by a visiting head of state was complete. This is a very good example of how the (mis)use of diplomatic language can have significant effects.

This brief analysis of the breaking of linguistic protocol demonstrates two things. In order to appreciate fully the significance of the role of language in politics, we need to be able to analyse, in this case, first, the rhetoric, that is, the internal structure as well as the development of the linked utterances themselves, the rhetorical effects of repetition ('Vive!'), deviation from convention, convention itself (the cry 'Vive!' is usually only ever used in relation to France or the French Republic), and other qualities of the utterances, such as, paradoxically, what is not said, or what is implied, or how the traditional appeal ('vive!' normally of no consequence) can be charged or recharged with an emotional quality; and, second, the context of the utterances – the situation in Quebec and in Canada generally, the person and reputation of de Gaulle, his relation to French-speaking Canadians, to French national and cultural pride, and so on.

If we understand both of the areas: context and text, or provenance and utterance, we shall be some way towards understanding how politics functions in relation to society and its agencies of communica-tion.

Most political communication takes place in contexts which are freer and less dependable than those dictated by strict diplomatic conven-tions. Most of it is also less dramatic than de Gaulle's in the example given. Daily, in any given society, there is an unimaginable number of political exchanges, and any of them can be chosen for analysis: they can be written (books, tracts, manifestos, posters etc.), or spoken (press conferences, television interviews, Prime Minister's Question Time etc.). Some of these exchanges are 'privileged' in terms of analysis (as well as in reality) in that they offer comparative insights into how politics is functioning at a particular time. They can be dramatic in terms of their context, or they may offer quietly illuminating insights into the workings of a particular government or regime. Let us analyse at some length another French presidential example.

François Mitterrand's *Lettre à tous les Français*, 1988

The context

Mitterrand's *Lettre à tous les Français* constituted his personal manifesto for the presidential elections of 1988 which he won against his second-round rival, Jacques Chirac, by 54 per cent to 46 per cent, a resounding win in French presidential election terms.

Mitterrand had been president since 1981, the year in which he won the presidency for the left (he had been leader of the Socialist Party (PS) since 1971) after nearly a quarter of a century of right-wing rule. After winning the presidential elections he dissolved the National Assembly and called for legislative elections, which saw the PS sweep to power in the Assembly with an absolute majority of seats.

Although Mitterrand remained the symbolic leader of the PS throughout the 1980s (indeed, his stature as their symbolic leader increased), a marked distinction between himself and his own party began to establish itself. The distinction was not the expected developmental one of his outlook becoming more conservative than that of his party (if anything, the opposite happened) but was based, principally, upon the nature of his election: his source of legitimacy was no longer solely his 'socialism' or his claim to membership of the socialist family or tradition, but his attainment of the presidency in an election which involved the whole national electorate. This distinction allowed Mitterrand to cultivate a highly personalised style (already begun before 1981) which meant that 'Mitterrandism' became not only a term which designated a form of allegiance within socialism but also one which designated President Mitterrand's own 'thought', quite apart from his representation or enunciation of a particular form of French socialism.

The point here is that by the time the now unpopular PS lost power in the legislative elections of March 1986, the president and the PS, though still in an important relation to one another, were perceived, and behaved, as quite distinct entities.

The political right, therefore, returned to power in the National Assembly in 1986 and formed the government. Mitterrand's separation from his former party, and his growing personal isolation – exacerbated by the hostility of the new government and his new prime minister, Jacques Chirac – were further emphasised. Gradually, however, Mitterrand moved from this lonely and impotent position to one where he enjoyed a towering popularity, as recorded by the polls, during the two years of increasingly unpopular right-wing government.

As regards our analysis, we can make three contextual points at this stage. First, although anecdotal, it is interesting to note that during the 1986–8 period it became clear that Mitterrand's rival for the presidency was likely to be his own prime minister, Jacques Chirac, that is to say, a man who was not a writer, an intellectual of the old style, a lover of the arts, a thinker, and so on, as was Mitterrand himself; that is, just the kind of man who could *not* write, or be seen to have written, a personal and characteristic, almost loving, letter to 'all the French people'. Interestingly, Jacques Chirac's immediate public response to the publication of Mitterrand's *Letter* was that it was 'well written'. Chirac was here attempting to highlight the work as 'literary' in a pejorative way, that is, the work of an intellectual rather than a politician. The second point is that, for better or worse, it is the nature of the office of the presidency that allows or encourages the idea that the president is in a particular relationship to the people. This trait of closeness between president and people has precedents in the Fifth Republic, the most notable example being de Gaulle's presidency and his many passionate radio and television broadcasts to the nation. It is worthy of note here that some of de Gaulle's most successful establishings of a direct relationship with the people as the source of his strength were moments not of triumph but of extreme vulnerability (cf. Mitterrand's powerless isolation between 1986 and 1988) – the most memorable being his televised plea 'Françaises, Français, aidez-moi', when faced with a military putsch in 1961. Over and above these institutional and historical contexts, a further context of Mitterrand's *Lettre à tous les Français* was the party political one. As we have seen, Mitterrand had a party of his own, the PS. In 1988, moreover, this party had a political manifesto, its *Propositions pour la France*. Mitterrand's *Letter* must also be seen in this context: that of the rejection of the party's own text and its replacement by his message to the people. In fact, seen in this light, Mitterrand's *Letter* is not simply a substitution of the party tradition with a plebiscitary appeal, it is an implicit affirmation that in the political ontology of France, the parties do not exist, or that if they do (which of course is the case) they are structures that can impede the unmediated relationship of a leader to his people.

Mitterrand's *Letter*, therefore, reaches, as it were, over the head of Jacques Chirac, his hostile prime minister and rival, over the government, out past the media even (given that its *form*, a letter, was so unlike anything the modern media was used to in this age of 'TV-bites'), out past the political parties, even his own, to 'The French'. We can see already that the context itself of such an address to the nation, to the people, mythifies not only the sender of the message but also its receiver/s (we shall come back to this strange use of the plural).

The *Lettre à tous les Français* was published in twenty-five newspapers (totalling two-and-a-half million copies), as well as in booklet form, and was given much publicity. It attracted a great deal of comment in the press, on radio and on television. The cost of producing and publicising it has been estimated at twelve million francs.

The text

The *Letter* is about 16,000 words long. The very length of the text (much longer than most political manifestos) suggests the extreme personal effort of the writer, and the concomitant desire to reach out to the people. There is also implied, of course, the assumption that the reader/s were a) capable of reading and b) willing to read this long letter. Whether or not the *Letter* was read in its entirety is irrelevant. What is being established by publication is an ideal relationship between a particular writer and an imagined reader. The text is divided into an introduction and seven sections of unequal length:

1   Introduction;
2   Equilibrer les institutions;
3   Construire l'Europe;
4   Encourager le désarmement, garantir la securité, agir pour la paix;
5   Le développement du tiers monde;
6   Moderniser l'économie;
7   Assurer la cohésion sociale;
8   Multiplier les espaces de culture.

Several of the sections are also divided into titled sub-sections. If we first examine the layout of the sections and sub-sections themselves we can draw out some of the overall significance of the *Letter*.

The text begins with a short introduction (see below and Text 1), which establishes a particular relation between the letter-writer and the reader (an examination of this will constitute the bulk of our analysis). It then moves on to a discussion of the role of the president, that is, the role of the author himself and his relation to the French people (i.e. the reader/s). The next sub-section continues this theme by referring to revisions of the constitution (that is, the protection of the Fifth Republic by the actual president, with the help of the people), and its updating (that is, the actual president's personal stamp upon the contemporary period). This notion of protecting the old and introducing the new continues into sub-section iii which deals with the state, where the discussion becomes more abstract, and demonstrates the personal philosophy of the author, and portrays his deep reflection and historical knowledge. These thoughts are 'shared' with the reader, but the superiority of the writer over the reader (as well as his certainty) is nevertheless established by means of this demonstration of his extensive knowledge.

Interestingly, the next sub-section takes a form very unfamiliar in left-wing discourse in that it treats foreign policy *before* domestic policy, thus conferring by association a further role upon the president, that of the representative of France in foreign affairs. It is also worthy of note here that by taking the discussion out of the, as it were, familiar area of domestic policy, the author is taking the reader (the average French voter) away from the known to the unknown, to the world of diplomacy and international affairs, a world of which most people have only a limited awareness and expertise. Thus, once again, the writer enhances his own status vis-à-vis the reader. It is also worth remembering that this sub-section – where the author 'reveals' foreign policy requirements to the reader – is one of the longest and most complex in the *Letter*. The subsequent three sections dealing with Europe, arms control and the Third World involve further discussions of areas where the reader is likely to be least informed.

It is only in the final three sections, on the economy, society and culture, that the writer brings the reader back to the 'known'; and, of course, the economy, though domestic and of crucial importance to the reader, is a difficult topic. Only in the final two sections is the reader brought to a place which he or she understands – society. The penultimate section is called 'Assurer la cohésion sociale'. The title of this section suggests that a) society is under threat, b) society is not just a disparate and random grouping but a cohesive whole, that is, a community. Its place in the *Letter* suggests that the attainment of social cohesion is like a culmination of the writer's argument: a harmonious, contented, prosperous society is dependent upon the successful outcome and application of the proposals made throughout the *Letter*. The final section on culture is somewhat different from the other sections in that it forms a conclusion to the whole *Letter* as well as being a section in its own right (see Text 2).

It is clear from this brief analysis of the general lay-out of the *Letter* that much implicit and coded information is being transmitted, information which involves the status of the writer and his relationship to (and the status of) the reader.

We can make two points here. The first is that the *form* of the *Letter*, irrespective of its content, by putting the discussion of institutions and foreign policy before discussion of the economy and of society (thereby making the latter subservient to the former), marks a significant departure from the usual pattern of leftist discourse. The second point is that it is not so much the tone of the *Letter* which establishes the hierarchy between the writer and reader – in fact, in spite of his monarchical distance and paternalistic image in French politics (especially in the second half of the 1980s), Mitterrand's discourse in its substance and its style is far less patronising than that of many contemporary French politicians. Rather, the form of the *Letter* (the sections and other sub-divisions discussed above), by taking the reader beyond daily concerns to the grand issues of state and foreign affairs before returning finally to the known and domestic, establishes the hierarchy and, by extension, the status of the speaker.

This very brief overview of the subdivisions within the text gives an illustration of how information is encoded within the text's surface structure. Let us now examine in more detail just one small extract, the 350-word introduction, in order to see how analysis of the content of the *Letter* informs our understanding of the overall significance of the text.

The first sentence of the *Letter* after the address, 'Mes chers compatriotes,' is 'Vous le comprendrez'. Here is an immediate establishing of a relation of 'je' with 'vous'. It valorises 'vous' by making 'vous' the first 'actor' mentioned, it reinforces, even as the letter begins, the reality of the reader, it places trust in the reader (the writer has no doubt that 'vous' will understand), it demonstrates the writer's knowledge of 'vous' (he knows 'vous' will understand), and it forces the reader into the reading (because in fact 'vous' will only understand if she, he or they read on!).

The following sentence, introducing 'je' (again reminding the reader that this is a personal communication and not just a party political tract), demonstrates the modesty of 'je': 'je souhaite, par cette lettre, vous parler de la France'. 'Vous' is firm and knowing. 'Je' is modest. There is also implicitly expressed in these two sentences the need for the writer to reach out across all the obstacles to make contact with the reader as if something, or someone, has impeded such ease of communication. We are reminded here too of the sacred nature of the election of a president: the campaign is the privileged moment when the leader takes the time, finds the time, to talk with his people.

In the first two sentences, the two main actors in the *Letter*, therefore, are introduced: 'vous' ($\times$ 2) and 'je' ($\times$ 1). This frequency relation will soon be reversed with 'je' becoming dominant and informing every sentence.

The *Letter* continues; 'je dois à votre confiance d'exercer depuis sept ans la plus haute charge de la République'. The 'vous' and its importance is stressed again here but is accompanied by the implicit reminder that the writer is in fact the most important person in the Republic, and has the heaviest burden to bear: I am the most important person in France (thanks to you), runs the logic of the sentence.

It goes on: 'Au terme de ce mandat, je n'aurais pas conçu le projet de me présenter de nouveau à vos suffrages si je n'avais eu la conviction que nous avions encore beaucoup à faire ensemble pour assurer à notre pays le rôle que l'on attend de lui dans le monde et pour veiller à l'unité de la Nation.'

We can see that apart from the disclaimer that he had not thought of seeking office again until faced with imperatives which forced him to act in order to protect his country (and the fact that such knowledge is given like a shared secret), the writer is making it clear that it is not the fact of being president that justifies him but the people, to whom he must return for benediction once again before continuing the task of helping France and assuring its unity. This sentence is also significant in that it introduces the third main character in the text, namely, 'France' (note also here and throughout the text, 'pays', 'lui', and 'Nation').

This trio, 'je', 'vous' and 'France', form a kind of interactive triple singularity in the text from here on, that is, they are distinct characters, and yet together constitute a unity.

It is already clear the writer's undertaking is Gaullist or *gaullien* in nature: there is the visionary ('je') who sees that France is threatened, has a task (in the chivalric sense), and needs the support or sanction of 'vous' in order to meet the challenge.

There is a second main reason for writing. As he has stated, his first reason is to talk of France: 'Mais je veux aussi vous parler de vous, de vos soucis, de vos espoirs et de vos justes intérêts.' It is apparent here that 'je' knows 'vous' and understands him/her/them (cf. 'soucis', 'espoirs', 'intérêts') (although we should note that France's needs come before those of 'vous'). We can see also from this that, stylistically and structurally, the introduction foreshadows the structure of the text itself: France and the great issues first, the people's concerns second. We can note also that the emotions of 'vous' are relatively passive ones: hopes, worries, and so on, whereas the verbs which describe 'je' are active: 'souhaiter', 'concevoir', 'avoir la conviction', 'vouloir.' 'Vous' combines quiet vision and anxiousness (both qualities will be exploited: you have wisdom, therefore you will understand me; you have anxiety and I understand you), while 'je' is active, intellectual, and wordly. There is almost, in stereotypical terms, a gender-like division: 'vous' is female – wise, worried and essentially passive; 'je' is male – knowledgeable, active, and 'doing things'.

It is appropriate at this point in our discussion to elaborate a little further on one of the characters in the text, namely, 'vous'. The form of Mitterrand's *Lettre à tous Les Français* allows him to address the whole nation and each individual simultaneously (the *Letter* is, by definition, to all the French, and yet reading a letter is almost invariably a personal, private activity). In this way, the reader is both addressed individually while simultaneously sensing that she or he is part of a wider community. We can also add that this dual identity of the reader (she or he is both singular and plural) is reinforced by the 'vous' form itself which is both singular (polite) and plural.

In the third paragraph, and for the third time, the writer refers to the letter quality of the text: 'j'ai choisi ce moyen, vous écrire'. The form of address is to all the French and, simultaneously, to each person. Each elector is addressed at the same moment as is the whole nation, the reader, therefore, having the status of a kind of collective individual. This, of course, underscores the intimacy of the relation, as does the homely image the writer then uses: 'afin de m'exprimer sur tous les grandes sujets qui valent d'être traités et discutés entre Français, sorte de réflexion en commun, comme il arrive le soir, autour de la table, en famille'. The intimacy, the near-sentimentality here is explicit with the image of Mitterrand who – although president, and used to official banquets and the pomp and circumstance of office – knows also the ordinary life and humble French meal table. Mitterrand is the (implied) head of household of a close, caring, relaxed, and serious-minded family to which the reader also belongs.

In this atmosphere of relaxed discussion, the writer goes on to say that his *Letter* is not a political programme in the traditional sense as was his programme in the 1981 elections when he was leader of the Socialist Party. Programmes and the like remain the province of the political parties: 'Pas du Président de la République ou de celui qui aspire à le devenir'. A strange inversion has therefore taken place within the same paragraph. The logic of the argument runs: I speak to you as a friend in the intimacy of the family table; I do not draw up party political programmes; I am too important for that because I am the president. (There is also the accompanying humility of, I am only a candidate seeking the presidency from you; 'celui qui aspire à le devenir'). The distinguishing of the writer from the parties allows him to underline his singular status as president (and, of course, to highlight the party-based quality of most other candidates).

At this point, the humanity (in both its humble and elevated sense) of the writer is further elaborated: 'L'expérience acquise, là ou vous m'avez mis, et la pratique des institutions m'ont appris que si l'on voulait que la République march bien, chacun devait être et rester à sa place' (i.e. the president above everything, the parties in their confined role). The individual learning process of the writer (humble) and his having learned because of such experience (elevated) add to the depth and singularity of the writer's personality. It is worth mentioning here in passing that such exclusive wisdom portrays the writer as being distinguished not only vis-à-vis both the political parties and the reader, but also vis-à-vis the other candidates, none of whom had been president before, and who therefore could not be privy to the acquired experience mentioned. We can also see that although 'vous' is again valorised here ('où vous m'avez mis'), only 'je' is the active, experienced element in the relation; only he can know.

The writer then describes the political parties' role as being that of managing or sorting out ('régler') the details of daily life via government. The writer/president's role is other (as is the function of the *Letter* itself): 'Mon rôle est de vous soumettre le projet sur lequel la France aura à se prononcer les 24 avril et 8 mai prochains pour les sept années à venir.' He implies two things here. First, that the president's role transcends the mundane, daily grind of politics. And, second, that the writer/president is capable of working, as he indeed had between 1981 and 1988, with governments of different political colours.

In terms of the distinction here between a 'programme', to which we referred earlier, and a 'projet' we can say that one would need to be highly informed to know exactly what the difference was between them. The status of the *Letter*, paradoxically, is increased further by this. First, the 'projet', whatever it entails, is contained in the *Letter* itself; 'Mon rôle est de vous soumettre le projet' = I must write this letter to you. Second, the 'projet', being clearly more intangible than a programme, confers a mystery on the project/letter. Thirdly, there is an urgency introduced by the mention of the two dates; this is not a game – the fate of France for the next seven years (a France whose reality and value have already been conjured up in the *Letter*) depends upon what the reader does on these two dates (and to act properly he/she/they must read the *Letter*).

The writer next establishes the relation between himself and the 'projet' he will undertake (and in so doing, adding further mystery to its function): 'Je le remplirai de mon mieux avec, au coeur et dans l'esprit, une fois dépassés les légitimes contradictions de notre vie démocratique, la passion d'une France unie.' Once again, the chivalric notion of a burdensome though passionate task is implied, and the reader locked into a relationship which implies his or her contribution to an undertaking that goes beyond the normal self-interested reading of political manifestos.

It is probable that the bizarre phrase 'les légitimes contradictions de . . . ' refers to the elections themselves, and that the president, therefore, although he must respect these, situates himself on another plane, a transcendent one involving the uniting of France. It is not so much that the writer is scorning the democratic process (although this could be argued); rather, elections and the like operate in a kind of non-mythic, ordinary time, whereas the relationship between leader and people takes place in mythic time. This way of perceiving things was, it is worth noting, very characteristic of de Gaulle. Such reference to unity suggests, first, that the writer's role is of a different order to that of ordinary people, and, second, that unity, whatever this means, is threatened. He goes on to underline this second point, 'Je m'inquiète parfois des montées de l'intolérance.' His solution? the classical one of the political left, right, and centre: 'rassembler'. Here, within a rally, 'nous', a notional fusion of all the French with the writer is created: 'Nous avons besoin de nous rassembler'. He addresses the readers directly as 'mes chers compatriotes' (a term of address often used by Mitterrand, reminiscent of the beginning of the *Letter* and thereby another reminder that the text is a personal letter), and states that in order to rally, a policy is necessary, the writer's own, which, of course, takes the form of the *Letter* itself: 'je vous propose une politique pour la France'. This personalised offering is the last phrase of the introduction. It is not just any policy, given the foregoing disclaimers concerning political parties and programmes, but a 'projet', in fact, a kind of personal philosophy.

The *Letter* itself does contain much that could be construed as a programme. It therefore is many things: an address to the French people, a project, a programme, and the exposition of a particular personality and his personal philosophy. On this question of personality, the 'je' designating the writer appears throughout the *Letter*, but what is equally important is that it is accompanied by a series of expressed emotions, insights, personal reflections, and so on which, together, constitute the personality of the author (and, one would assume, reflect the true personality of François Mitterrand).

In terms of methodology-related issues involved in analysis we can make three points. The first is that it is clear from our analysis that what is implied, what is 'understood' in the grammatical sense, what is alluded to, and so on, is just as important as what is written, in certain cases, more important.

Second, we can see that the 'rhetoric' of a political text, its structure, its dynamic, its persuasiveness, the tricks and figures it uses, are not dependent upon high oratory or declamatory speeches. The political text should be treated for the purposes of analysis like any other text; dramatic, poetic or prose, with the additional element of there being a real person designated by the text (in this case, the person, François Mitterrand) who may or may not resemble the 'je' of the text but who reinforces it because of the reader's awareness of his physical existence.

Third, we should bear in mind that what appears to be essential to the political text is the creation and development of characters; here, 'je', 'vous', and 'la France' (there are many others throughout the text which constitute the 'universe' of Mitterrand's discourse). And it is the relationship elaborated between them which gives the text its texture and depth and, in a favourable context, its political significance.

Text 1

François Mitterrand
Lettre à tous les français
(Introduction)

Mes chers compatriotes,
Vous le comprendrez. Je souhaite, par cette lettre, vous parler de la France. Je dois à votre confiance d'exercer depuis sept ans la plus haute charge de la République. Au terme de ce mandat, je n'aurais pas conçu le projet de me présenter de nouveau à vos suffrages si je n'avais pas eu la conviction que nous avions encore beaucoup à faire ensemble pour assurer à notre pays le rôle que l'on attend de lui dans le monde et pour veiller à l'unité de la nation.

Mais je veux aussi vous parler de vous, de vos soucis, de vos espoirs et de vos justes intérêts.

J'ai choisi ce moyen, vous écrire, afin de m'exprimer sur tous les grands sujets qui valent d'être traités et discutés entre Français, sorte de réflexion en commun, comme il arrive le soir, autour de la table, en famille. Je ne vous présente pas un programme, au sens habituel du mot. Je l'ai fait en 1981 alors que j'étais à la tête du Parti socialiste. Un programme en effet est l'affaire des partis. Pas du président de la République ou de celui qui aspire à le devenir. L'expérience acquise, là où vous m'avez mis, et la pratique des institutions m'ont appris que si l'on voulait que la République marche bien, chacun devait être et rester à sa place. Rien n'est pire que la confusion. L'élection présidentielle n'est pas comparable à l'élection des députés. Et s'il s'agit de régler, jusqu'au détail, la vie quotidienne du pays, la tâche en revient au gouvernement. Mon rôle est de vous soumettre le projet sur lequel la France aura à se prononcer les 24 avril et 8 mai prochains sur les sept années à venir. Je le remplirai de mon mieux avec, au coeur et dans l'esprit, une fois dépassées le légitimes contradictions de notre vie démocratique, la passion d'une France unie. Je m'inquiète parfois des montées de l'intolérance. Nous avons besoin de nous rassembler, mes chers compatriotes. Pour cela, je vous propose une politique pour la France.

Text 2

François Mitterrand
Lettre à tous les français
(Conclusion)

Multiplier les espaces de culture

En commençant cette lettre j'écrivais que je vous parlerais, comme autour de la table, en famille. Ce dernier mot n'est pas tombé par hasard sous ma plume. Je suis né, j'ai vécu ma jeunesse au sein d'une famille nombreuse. Les leçons que j'en ai reçu restent mes plus sûres références. Nous habitions une petite ville, loin des fureurs du monde, mais elles sont venues jusqu'à nous. Le temps a passé. Les valeurs apprises sans qu'on me les eût enseignées autrement que par une certaine façon de penser et de vivre, je ne m'en suis pas séparé. Tout le monde n'a pas cette chance. C'est peut-être à la mienne que je dois cette certitude: la France sera forte de ses familles et s'épanouira dans ses enfants. Les générations nombreuses sont les générations créatrices. Aussi ai-je encouragé, pendant ce septennat, ceux qui, au gouvernement et ailleurs, ont compris qu'aimer la famille n'était pas rétrograde, que c'était au contraire regarder devant soi. Or, nous sommes pauvres d'enfants dans une Europe plus pauvre encore. On expliquait naguère cette crise de la natalité par la crainte confuse, viscérale, des lendemains, qui s'était emparée de notre société. Et l'on entendait partout répéter: 'Qu'offrir à nos enfants? Le chômage et la bombe atomique? La mort de l'espoir tue la vie'.

Je crois pourtant que les temps changent. Est-ce l'approche de ce troisième millénaire qui ouvre à l'homme les grands chemins de l'univers? Une immense curiosité, un énorme appétit de voir et de connaître, un besoin d'échange et d'amour aiguillonnent notre jeunesse.

On s'en doute, je ne parlerai pas en son nom! La jeunesse n'adhère pas au culte de la jeunesse. Les adultes doivent s'en convaincre. Mais la preuve est là. J'ai voulu que fussent multipliés, semblables aux puits de vie évoqués par Joseph Delteil, les espaces de culture: 1000 bibliothèques nouvelles, 1000 lieux de répétition pour les musiciens, 200 salles nouvelles de théâtre et de musique, 600 de cinéma, 120 musées créés ou rénovés, des dizaines de centres d'art, deux Zénith pour le rock et la musique populaire, le cirque à Châlons-sur-Marne, la danse à Marseille et Nanterre, la photographie à Arles, la bande dessinée à Angoulême, le design industriel à Paris . . . De la plus modeste église de village à la cathédrale de Strasbourg et à la Cour carrée du Louvre, 3 000 chantiers ont entrepris de restaurer le patrimoine. J'ai poursuivi l'œuvre de mon prédécesseur au musée d'Orsay, à la Cité de La Villette et engagé des projets qui s'inscrivent déjà dans notre paysage, Grand Louvre, Opéra-Bastille, Arche de la Défense, Institut du Monde arabe, Théâtre de l'Europe, Grande Halle. Tout est culture en fin de compte, Jack Lang avait raison. Nous avons bâti les espaces mais la jeunesse les a remplis et c'est elle qui invente ses rythmes, ses couleurs, ses désirs, ses exigences et ses rêves, elle qui rassemble ses foules partout en France et en Europe, à l'entrée de l'été, le 21 juin, pour la célébration d'un mystère, la Fête de la Musique.

Mais elle se rend aussi à d'autres rendez-vous: celui de la nature et celui de la science. 'Endommager l'équilibre écologique est un crime contre l'avenir', telle était la première conclusion de l'assemblée des prix Nobel, qui rappelait une évidence: la terre est grande mais bornée; ses ressources multiples mais épuisables; l'homme n'en est pas propriétaire mais seulement l'usufruitier. Je me souviens de l'attention passionnée d'une classe de première écoutant la leçon d'un timide savant venu lui raconter les batailles perdues par l'ozone et par l'eau, par la forêt, par les espèces animales que le progrès condamne à mort.

Que Jacques-Yves Cousteau symbolise aujourd'hui, avant tout autre, comme le montrent les sondages, la belle aventure humaine: découvrir, révéler, sauver des mondes hier encore inconnus, le fond des mers, l'intime relation du fleuve et de la terre, forces irrépressibles et pourtant si fragile, on se sent envahi par des bouffées d'espoir. En vingt ans, non seulement le monde mais l'idée qu'on en a ont inversé leur cours.

La jeunesse entre en religion, je veux dire qu'elle va là où elle croit trouver quelque chose de plus. Se dépasser, c'est vrai du sport, c'est vrai de la recherche, c'est vrai de tout engagement spirituel, c'est vrai de tout échange où, pour vivre mieux, il faut vivre autrement.

Il me semble que cette disposition d'esprit explique le dédain des privilèges, l'horreur des exclusions, le rejet du racisme, qui mobilisent tant de jeunes gens. Dans tous les coins de la planète où l'on bafoue les droits de l'homme, ils sont là. Mais ils n'y sont pas seuls. La chaîne des générations autour des grandes causes n'est pas près de se rompre.

Mes chers compatriotes, la vraie responsabilité politique oblige à prendre en compte les problèmes de société tels qu'ils se posent et se transforment. Elle oblige aussi à rappeler à tous que rien n'est jamais donné, qu'une vie se construit à chaque instant, que l'effort est la loi.

'Aller à l'idéal et comprendre le réel', enseignait Jean Jaurès aux lycéens d'Albi, Jaurès dont je m'inspire.

Vous reconnaîtrez dans ces mots, je l'espère, l'ambition du projet qui m'engage auprès de vous pour les années à venir. Mais quel homme, quel groupe d'hommes y suffirait? La France unie, elle, le pourra.

Croyez, mes chers compatriotes, à mes fidèles sentiments.

François Mitterrand.

11

French and French-based Creoles: the case of the French Caribbean

GERTRUD AUB-BUSCHER

Introduction

Maps of *la francophonie* often include countries where the language most
widely spoken is not French but *Créole*, a French-lexifier Creole. In
places as far apart as Haiti in the Caribbean and Mauritius in the Indian
Ocean, the normal vehicle of communication is a form of language very
different from that of the *Académie française*. Though it is quite clearly
related to French, the nature of that relationship has led to much
discussion and a multiplicity of labels. They range from 'broken French'
or 'French-based Creole', both of which, though using very different
value judgements, assume that the relationship is a very close one, to
Créole à base lexicale française, which takes into account only the un-
disputed fact that the vast majority of its vocabulary does indeed come
from France, but leaves open questions about the source of its grammar
and phonology.

The word *Creole* comes from a Portuguese term referring to a slave
born in the colonies, and it is still used to designate people of mixed race
or, especially in the French West Indies, of European ancestry born in
former colonial territories. In linguistics, it covers a type of contact
language which arises in certain multilingual situations. Where people
speaking several different languages have to live and work together but
can keep their own language for their home-life, the result is often a
pidgin, a stable but reduced language which only covers those areas of
life in which speakers of the different languages have to interact. (An
example of a French pidgin is the *français populaire* of Abidjan, or the *tây
bôy* of Indochina.) During the colonial period it often happened,
however, that children born in the colonies did not have one language
which they could learn as a mother tongue. In order to prevent the
fomenting of rebellion, slave owners frequently separated slaves from
the same tribe, and hence the father and mother of a child born on the
plantation were likely to speak different languages; while the European

master was socially and physically too far removed to serve as a model. Under such circumstances, the language that arose was a Creole, a language which needed to cover the whole of the life experience of its speakers.

The exact processes by which Creole languages develop have been the subject of long and often impassioned debate. Scholars have variously argued that the form of Creoles can be explained by a lack of language learning skills on the part of those who had to learn; by a more or less conscious simplification of their own language on the part of Europeans; by the relexification of a Portuguese trading pidgin possibly related to the Mediterranean *lingua franca*; or as a more or less organic development of the popular spoken language of the colonisers (a case argued particularly for French *Créoles* in Chaudenson 1974). The current controversy opposes particularly on the one hand the partisans of a strong substratum influence (many Creole features have their parallel in the languages spoken by the African slaves who were the first, or parents of the first, Creole speakers), and on the other those who follow Derek Bickerton's hypothesis (Bickerton 1981) of an innate bioprogram which predisposes us all to acquire certain linguistic features.

Where Creoles were formed, they appear to have developed very quickly, within less than a generation, and far from being reduced, they are highly complex languages, as anyone who has tried to learn more than a smattering of them will know. Several different languages have provided the lexical base for Creoles (e.g. most of the vocabulary of Jamaican originated in the British Isles, and Papiamentu, the Creole of Curaçao, derives most of its lexis from the Iberian Peninsula), but there are certain traits common to Creoles whatever their background. (For a very readable overview see Todd 1990.) We shall however concern ourselves here only with French-based Creole and call it by its French name, to distinguish it from the others.

The time of its formation is in most cases the period following the arrival of French settlers in the colonies in the seventeenth or eighteenth centuries, and the model of French brought was that of the time. This explains certain features of *Créole* vocabulary in particular (and, since Canada was settled about the same time and often by people from the same regions in France, it also accounts for certain lexical similarities between Canadian French and *Créole*).

Today, there are about 9 million *Créole* speakers in the world (Prudent 1990: 4). They live mainly in countries which have had or still have a plantation-based economy, places where the majority of the population is descended from slaves uprooted from their original homeland, usually in Africa. With the exception of Trinidad, they are countries which have at some time been French colonies; Trinidad was repopulated by French colonisers and their Creole-speaking slaves at the end of the eighteenth century. They are (the numbers refer to their location on the map below):

In North America:	Louisiana (1)
In the Caribbean:	Haiti (2)
	Guadeloupe with its dependencies of Marie Galante, Les Désirades and Saint Barthélemy (3)
	Dominica (3)
	St Lucia (3)
	Martinique (3)
	Grenada (3)
	Trinidad (3)
In South America:	French Guiana (Guyane) (4)
In the Indian Ocean:	Réunion (5)
	Mauritius and Rodrigues (5)
	Seychelles (6)

(Some listings of Caribbean Creoles also include the French dialect of St Thomas in the US Virgin Islands. While sharing many of the features of *Créole*, however, it does so because it descends directly from the language brought by the French settlers who also influenced the development of West Indian *Créole*. Cf. Highfield 1979.)

Given patterns of migration in the second half of this century, there are also pockets of *créolophones* in countries of Europe and North America: it is possible to hear conversations in *Créole* in Portobello Market in London or parts of New York. It is one of the factors that bind the large West Indian community in France, and provides one important constituent of the speech used among young second-generation Antillais in the suburbs of Paris.

In all the countries on our list, *Créole* coexists with at least one other language, often with several. In the French *Départements d'Outre-Mer* (DOM) of Martinique, Guadeloupe, Guyane and Réunion, the other language is French, and to a lesser degree this is true in Haiti. St Barthélemy is distinctive in that is also has an old French dialect of its own. In Dominica, St Lucia and Grenada, the official language is English and the vernacular increasingly (in Grenada preponderantly) an English-based Creole. This is also true in Trinidad, but here we must add a South American form of Spanish, several Indian languages, and a little French and Chinese. Trinidad shares honours for the most diverse linguistic mosaic with Mauritius, where the mix of languages is similar (except for the Spanish), but the number of bilingual or multilingual households is even higher, with *Créole* the normal language of the majority, used occasionally even in Parliament, French the language of a large elite, English that of the civil service, English, French and sometimes *Créole* used in education, and Indian languages not only in

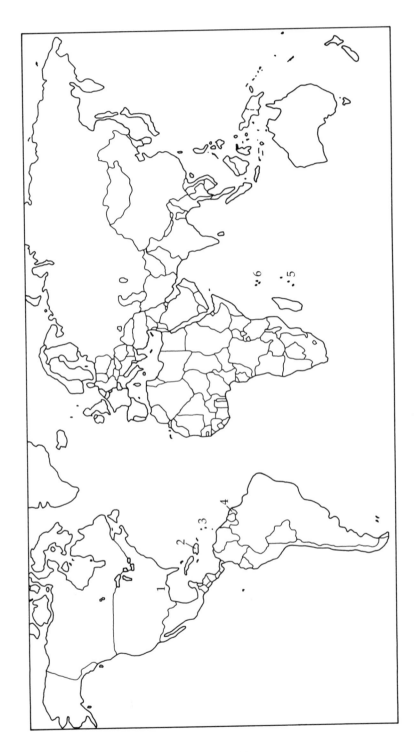

Map 2   Creole distribution (see p. 201 above)

many homes but also in Hindu or Moslem worship. In Louisiana, *Créole* (or *gumbo* or Negro French) is one of four languages, the others being the French dialect brought in by settlers from Canada known as Cajun, the local French, and American English (see H. Phillips in Valdman ed. 1979). In the Seychelles, *Créole* has achieved the status of an official language: it is the first of the three official languages, the others being English and French.

The position in Haiti, the country which accounts for more than half the *Créole* speakers in the world, was one of the classic cases of diglossia discussed by Ferguson in his 1959 article, though the position has changed somewhat since then, and some linguists (e.g. Valdman 1988: 68–9) question whether the term is, or ever has been, appropriate here. French is the *de facto* official language, used in official documents and on most official occasions (the nominal elevation of *Créole* to the status of co-official language having had little effect), but it is not the native language of any but a small handful of Haitians, only about 5 per cent of the population being bilingual in French and *Créole*. For 90 per cent of the inhabitants *Créole* is the only vehicle for normal communication, and even the bilingual elite will usually use it at home and among friends, for the telling of jokes and for political meetings. Until relatively recently it was excluded from schools and little Haitians had to learn the three Rs in a language which for the vast majority was not their own. This is no longer always the case, and teaching in the early years of schooling is now often done in *Créole*, though French is still the medium of instruction at higher levels. While newspapers have carried some articles in *Créole* for some time and there has been some writing in the language since the eighteenth century, until the last decades even the most nationalist of writers have expressed themselves in French; now there is the slow but steady development of a body of literature written in *Créole*, including not only poetry, which goes back over two centuries, and plays, a number of which were written in the 1950s notably by F. Morisseau-Leroy, but also full-length novels. Earlier novelists such as Jacques Roumain used *Créole* words, expressions and especially rhythms in their work; the first novel, *Desafi*, entirely in *Créole* was published by Franketienne in 1975.

French and *Créole*

The coexistence with French is usually a complex and often a fraught one. In most places, *Créole* does not enjoy very high prestige. While there are now probably few cases of children getting a whipping if they are caught speaking it at school, as still happened earlier this century, the attitude of a father in the French West Indies, quoted by Dany Bebel-Gisler (1976: 191), almost certainly still exists:

Mes parents ont mis trois générations pour me sortir du créole et vous voudriez que mes enfants retournent à la sauvagerie en parlant créole. Le créole, c'est ma langue secrète, mais je punis mes enfants quand ils le parlent.

Dany Bebel-Gisler is one of a growing number of linguists in the French West Indies fighting for proper recognition of *Créole* and a halt to the process of decreolisation which it undergoes under the influence of the official language.

They have recently had some success, in that in 1983 *Créole* was admitted as one of the regional languages which can be used as a medium of instruction in schools under the *loi Haby*. To prepare teachers for such teaching, there are now even classes in *Créole* at the *Université Antilles-Guyane* at Schoelcher (Carrington 1988: 29). It is also increasingly used as a vehicle for political protest, in speeches and articles, by those seeking greater autonomy or independence for the French Caribbean. *Créole* appears in the media, especially in local radio and television, and in the literary works not only of those engaged in the independence movement, such as the late Guadeloupian poet Sonny Rupaire, but for example in the plays of Ina Césaire. The success of Euzan Palcy's film of Zobel's *La rue Cases-Nègres* has brought *Créole* to audiences world-wide.

There are several reasons for the disparagement of *Créole* or *patois* as it is known in some islands. One is its perceived relationship to French. To many, even among native speakers, it seems like a bastardised form of standard French: its grammar especially is seen as lacking the finer points of French. Those making such comparisons seldom reflect upon the fact that they are comparing an essentially spoken language with the written French of their grammar books; a comparison between *Créole* and spoken French would be much more appropriate, and would show rather fewer differences, for example in the morphology of the present tense of the verb. Another reason given for denying *Créole* a higher status is that there is no *Créole* orthography. The answer to this has come from various linguists and practitioners of the language, who have devised spelling systems, some of which are now widely used within different creolophone countries, though there is as yet no standard system for all *Créoles*. A third purported reason is that it lacks the vocabulary to express complex abstract thought. This is a somewhat circular argument, since if *Créole* were called upon to express scientific or philosophical ideas, the necessary terminology would be created or borrowed, just as happened in the late Middle Ages when French had to take over functions until then fulfilled by Latin. Probably the most important reason for the lowly position of *Créole* in countries where it coexists with French is a purely social one, viz. that it is the language of the masses rather than the elite. In the French overseas departments, a good command of French is an essential attribute for anyone wishing to achieve a higher social status.

The form of that French will depend very much on particular circumstances. In the context of the school, the model is the Parisian standard, but in many others a third entity enters the linguistic forum, viz. the local form of French, *le français local*. This will be characterised by phonetic and especially prosodic features (the best known and most parodied being the articulation of /R/), some differences at the morpho-syntactic level (e.g. paratactic constructions such as *boudin cochon*, or the use of [fin] as a mark of perfective aspect in the Indian Ocean *Créoles* leading to a similar use of *finir* in the local French), and a great number of local expressions, usually dubbed *créolismes*, in the lexicon. They will include not just terms for aspects of local life such as customs, plants and animals, but also turns of phrase, French words with local meanings (e.g. in the West Indies *serrer* for 'to put away' or *savane* for any open space covered with grass; *connaître* instead of *savoir*, *baiser* for 'to deceive' in the Indian Ocean), and terms taken from *Créole* such as *driver* for 'to loiter', *lolo* for a small general store.

One of the characteristic features of the local French is its lack of some of the familiar registers found in the metropolitan language. There is little need for them: in situations where the Parisian or Bordelais would change to *français familier*, the average Martinican or Mauritian can turn to *Créole*, either switching codes completely or increasing the proportion of *créolismes*. This no doubt in part explains why the French of some people from Haiti or the French West Indies appears stilted or excessively formal to speakers from France.

The case of Martinique

Let us get some more precise details about the relationship between French and *Créole* by looking more closely at Martinique. Geographically it is a part of the West Indies, and its linguistic history is closely tied up with that of neighbours such as Haiti, but as one of the *Départements d'Outre-Mer*, it is technically a part of France. This has its visible cultural manifestations – the latest Paris fashions, supermarkets whose shelves differ little from those in Grenoble or Toulouse – and also profoundly affects the linguistic situation.

French is the official language of the island. It is the language of newspapers (a large number of which come directly from France), of most radio and television programmes, of almost all literature written by Martinicans, and, most importantly and despite the *loi Haby*, of the school. The level of schooling in the French West Indies has been high for many years, and hence, in contrast to earlier periods and to present-day Haiti, there are now very few Martinicans who do not have at least a reasonable command of (Martinican) French. There is even some doubt that the assumption that *Créole* is the mother tongue of nearly all Martinicans still holds. It has recently been shown (March 1990) that for members of the younger generation, French may be the first language they learn: since success in school and social advancement are conditional on a good command of French, some Martinican mothers use French with their small children in order to give them a 'good start in life'.

One result of this preponderance of French in Martinique and the other DOMs is that the *Créole* is undergoing a process of decreolisation. This is a phenomenon found in the life cycle of many Creoles existing side by side with the original lexifier language. In the French West Indies this movement of *Créole* towards the French its speakers constantly hear, read, and use is very marked. It affects the phonology (e.g. use of front rounded vowels – see below, p. 208), syntax and vocabulary, and reinforces the difference between the *Créole* of the French territories and that of Haiti, where the position of French is much less strong, or countries such as Dominica or St Lucia, where the French model was almost completely withdrawn when these islands became British.

Scholars disagree on whether the French West Indies have ever had a full linguistic continuum such as has been described for other Creole societies, with a basilect or deep Creole at one end, French, or something very like it, as an acrolect at the other, and mesolects as stages in between; traditionally one has tended to speak rather of four layers – *créole, créole francisé, français créolisé and français*. What is certain is that the basilectal form of *Créole* is disappearing fast if it has not already done so. (See Bernabé 1983.)

And yet there is no doubt that the majority of Martinicans feel that *Créole* is their language. The same mothers who think they must use French with their babies to equip them for a successful life will show a very positive attitude to *Créole*, argue that it has a place in school, and use it to express strong emotions even with the babies whom they are otherwise addressing in French. Writers who publish in French speak of the conflict within themselves between the language which has formed their thinking and the French in which they have to write. (Cf. for example Glissant 1981.)

What then is the role of *Créole* in present-day Martinique? As has always been the case, it is still very largely the language of the masses: the higher up one goes on the social scale, the less likely one is to use *Créole* in situations other than those outlined by Ferguson (1959), e.g. for intimate conversation, for jokes, to tell folktales or in proverbs. But a recent study (Coadou 1990) has shown that the use of *Créole* obeys very complex rules or tendencies even among those who use it for a large proportion of their communication. Older people are more likely to use it than the young; young people are more likely to use it to speak to their friends than to persons in authority or older persons, even if, as is often the case, those persons address them in *Créole*; it is used more in the home than outside, though for most people it is the only language to be used in the market; men use it among themselves more regularly than in talking to women, while women also prefer to use French to talk to members of the opposite sex but seem undecided what language is appropriate for conversation among themselves; young men between twenty and thirty follow different rules and codes of behaviour from other groups. Hesitation about which language is appropriate for certain circumstances and interlocutors characterised many of the responses in Coadou's survey, and Martinicans will frequently use both French and *Créole* in similar circumstances, often within the same utterance or sentence.

In recent years the use of *Créole* has become part of the political campaign of those opposed to the impact of France on Antillean culture. Whereas the *autonomistes* of the older generation, such as Aimé Césaire, felt that the most effective way to express themselves was in impeccable French, whereas Edouard Glissant (1981), deploring the effects of French cultural domination, maintains at the same time that 'la source principale de notre préjugé est que nous voyons bien . . . qu'en Martinique aujourd'hui la langue créole est une langue dans laquelle nous ne produisons plus rien' (1981: 345) and writes in French, the younger thinkers grouped around the *Université des Antilles et de la Guyane* feel that *Créole* is a basic element of the Caribbean cultural heritage. Their aim is not only to raise the status and use of *Créole*, but to revitalise or 'recreolise' it by a return to its basilectal form. While they acknowledge that this deep *Créole* is not spoken spontaneously by anyone now, they feel that this is the model which should be aimed for, to save the language from the danger of being increasingly influenced by French and hence losing its specificity (Bernabé 1983: 1494).

Despite their efforts, however, it seems very improbable that the situation will change radically in the future. The movement is seen by many as the preoccupation of intellectuals who have nothing to lose by promoting *Créole*, and as long as the French West Indies remain DOMs, as long as the national capital is Paris rather than Fort-de-France or Basseterre, there is no doubt that French will be an essential tool for anyone wanting to progress in society. At the same time, the French spoken in Martinique is unlikely to lose its local characteristics, and the *Créole* will continue to underlie much of what is said and written, even if the surface form is French.

Some characteristic features of *Créoles*

Although all the different *Créoles* have their distinctive features (it would be surprising if it were otherwise, given their geographical distribution and different histories), they also share common characteristics, and some writers refer to them collectively as *Créole* (e.g. Vintilǎ-Rǎdulescu 1976, Valdman 1978). Many of these traits are considered to be typical of *Créoles*. They appear at all levels of language, e.g. the sound system is characterised by a typical CONSONANT + VOWEL (+ CONSONANT) syllable structure (e.g. French *force, jour, cercle*, *Créole* [fòs, ʒu, sɛk]); and most *Créoles* lack the French front rounded vowels (hence [pis] not *puce*, [pe] not *peux*, [pɛ] not *peur*).

At the grammatical level *Créoles* are marked by features which they share not only with each other but also with other Creole languages which have little or no connection with French. Many of the features discussed below are illustrated in text 1 at the end of the chapter, to which reference will be made.

(a)   They are all highly analytical languages. There are examples of this in the lexis: e.g. the notion of 'tears' is expressed by [dlo zje] or 'eye water' in the West Indies; serial verbs may convey concepts expressed by a single verb in French ([pote vini] for *apporter*, [pote ale] *emporter*) or in English (Jamaican *carry come* for 'to bring'). The phenomenon is however particularly noticeable in the morpho-syntax. Grammatical functions are marked by separate particles, rather than finding their expression in complex synthetic forms. This is true of English-based Creoles when compared even with English, which itself is an analytical language (cp. Jamaican *Me ben tell you* 'I told you', where *ben* marks the past). The difference between *Créole* and French is still more striking, e.g. in the Martinican sequence

[mwẽ te ka mãʒe]

[te] expresses the notion of past, [ka] durative aspect, and [mãʒe] that of eating, whereas in French the three notions are synthesised into *mangeais*; while, at the extreme opposite of the spectrum in this respect, in Latin the single form *edebam* also includes the information that the eating was being done by the first person. Where French distinguishes the male from the female of a species, either by completely different lexical forms (*taureau/vache*) or by different endings (*chat/chatte*), *Créole* usually expresses creature and sex separately ([papa bɛf/mamã bɛf], [mal bɛf/fimɛl bɛf], similarly with [ʃat]; cp. Jamaican *man cow* 'bull'). Where French has simple interrogatives, *Créoles* have a composite form: [ki lɛ?] = *quand?*, [ki manjɛ?] = *comment?*

(b)   Most words are invariable. This is to some extent true of spoken French as well, of course, since in most contexts we cannot hear the difference between *chapeau* and *chapeaux*, between *il chante* and *ils chantent*, but the phenomenon is much more marked in *Créole*. Nouns do not change for number (e.g. [ʃuval] can be the equivalent of French *cheval* or *chevaux* according to the context, [zje] is both *œil* and *yeux*), nor adjectives for gender (e.g. [piti gasõ, piti fij]; [bɛl gasõ, bɛl fij]). Grammatical gender does not exist at all: there is only one form of each of the articles and of the third-person personal pronouns (cf. *yo* in the text, the third-person plural pronoun referring sometimes to groups of women, sometimes to an unspecified *ils*). Sex differentiation is routinely expressed only for humans ([nom ≠ fãm], [nɛg ≠ negwɛs]), but even here most nouns are epicene (a [dirɛktɛ] can be a *directeur* or *directrice*); and for animals sex is only specified where relevant: the generic term [bɛf] can be a cow, an ox or a bull. In most (though not all) *Créoles*, pronouns do not vary for case, as seen with the first-person singular pronoun [mwẽ] in the following sentences from the eastern Caribbean:

[mwẽ ẽmẽ u]	*je t'aime*
[u ẽmẽ mwẽ]	*tu m'aimes*
[baj mwẽ laʒã]	*donne-moi de l'argent*
[ʃapo mwẽ]	*mon chapeau*

Verbs do not vary for person, which is indicated by the subject pronoun, nor for tense or mood. In most *Créoles* there is only one form of the verb; it may be derived from the French infinitive, past participle or present indicative, but in *Créole* will function simply as the invariable base form. (c)   The verbal system is based on distinctions of aspect much more than on tense, i.e. the cardinal distinctions are not between present, past and future but, for example, between punctual and durative, or between *realis* and *irrealis*. Both aspect and tense are marked by a system of particles. This is a feature of Creoles so typical that it is sometimes included in the very definition of this type of language. In our text four of the particles are illustrated: *ka* the durative/habitual, *ké* the prospective, an optative *sé*, and the past marker *té*. The particles may be combined, in fixed order, illustrated in our text by the sequence of past and durative *té ka* in *mwin té ka viv épi kanmarad mwin = je vivais avec mes camarades*. A distinction is made between stative and non-stative verbs, the former not taking durative *ka*, hence *té ni = il y avait* (rather than **té ka ni*). The durative of stative verbs is expressed by the simple base form of the verb (e.g. *man pa sav = je ne sais pas*), whereas for non-stative verbs this form expresses perfective aspect. (d)   In many contexts there is apparently no copula, hence the *Li bon* 'it good', advertisement for a certain Caribbean product which used to adorn French billboards. Far from lacking a basic equational verb, however, some *Créoles* have a tri-partite system where French has the one verb *être*. There is one form used sentence-finally (e.g. [sa sa je?]

literally 'what that is?', 'what is that?'), another for the expression of inherent, essential qualities (e.g. [mwẽ se fãm] 'I am a woman'), and a third, which does not have any surface manifestation (e.g. [mwẽ las] 'I am tired'). This feature illustrates well that *Créole*, rather than being a simplified form of French, is in fact sometimes more complex in its syntax.

(e)   Word order is fixed and in some respects rather different from that of French, e.g. the negative particle [pa] precedes the verb, while the object, whether noun or pronoun, always follows it, as in [mwẽ pa ẽmẽ u] *je ne t'aime pas*. Both possessives and definite determiners are post-posed in most *Créoles*: *ti-anmay-mwin* = *mes enfants*, *bagay-la* = *la chose*.

(f)   The system of determiners is very different from that of French in both form and function. The invariable indefinite (*an* in our text) is preposed, but it does not appear when a noun is truly indefinite, and there is no partitive (*pé jwinn travay* = *peut trouver du travail*). The postposed definite in the West Indies varies according to the final phoneme of the noun: in Martinican it is [a] after an oral and [ã] after a nasal vowel, [la] after an oral and [lã] after a nasal consonant, hence in our text *lavi-a, sitiyasyon-an, bagay-la, fanm-lan*. It is used only to particularise, not to generalise.

(g)   The reflexive and reciprocal are expressed by a word meaning 'body': *nou té ka antann kò-nou* = *nous nous entendions*.

(h)   The use of prepositions is much more restricted than in French, e.g. they do not usually occur in adjectival phrases (*léta sé fanm péyi-a* = *l'état des femmes du pays*), nor to mark an indirect object (*ba moun lison* = *donner une leçon aux gens*), nor in locative expressions with certain nouns (*lékòl= à l'école, kay larivyè* = *aller à la rivière*).

(i)   Subordinate clauses and subordinating conjunctions are relatively rare. This is again a feature of many spoken languages, but parataxis is a regular feature of *Créole*, e.g. [i di i ke vini] *il a dit qu'il viendrait*, or in our text *lanmannyè mwin té ka viv* = *la manière dont je vivais*.

(j)   A typical focusing mechanism is that known as 'double predication' (Baker and Corne 1982: 85), illustrated in our text by (a not wholly typical use of it) *sé alé i ka alé kochi*, or in Jamaican by *a tief im tief it* 'he stole it'.

(k)   There is very little redundancy. Whereas in *les chevaux sont partis* the notion of plurality is expressed four (in the spoken form three) times, *Créole* [se ʃuval la pati] is distinguished from its singular equivalent only by the plural marker [se].

It is in their lexis that the *Créoles* are closest to French, hence their designation as *créoles à base lexicale française* or 'French lexifier Creoles'. If we take the Swadesh list of 100 basic terms (the vocabulary list used to study relationships between languages – see for example Swadesh 1972:

283) and insert the appropriate *Créole* items, we find that the vast majority, if not all, are of French or at least Gallo-Romance origin. This does not mean that they are identical to modern French words. There will not only be phonetic differences, but also items whose meaning differs from that in standard French (e.g. [pje] 'tree', as well as 'foot'; or a form from *connaître* for *savoir*), and above all nouns which show agglutination of part or all of an article (e.g. [lanwit, zje, dlo], which are equivalent to *nuit*, *yeux* or *œil*, and *eau* respectively, not *la nuit*, *les yeux* or *de l'eau*), as well as verbs which show the opposite phenomenon of deglutination (e.g. [tãn] for *entendre*).

Other typical divergences from the lexicon of modern standard French do not show up in the Swadesh list. They include examples of the retention of seventeenth- and eighteenth-century forms and meanings, e.g. [balje] not *balai*, [bwɛt], [zetwɛl] etc., where /wɛ/ corresponds to a modern /wa/ (*boîte*, *étoile*), or [espere] meaning 'to wait' as well as 'to hope'. Since the settlers who came to the colonies were for the most part not Parisians, they also brought with them terms from their own regional dialects (e.g. northern and western [krɛp] where French has *crête (de coq)*, [kãni] 'mouldy' from Normandy, [mare] with a general dialect (Norman and Loire region) sense of 'to tie' rather than the more specific maritime sense of French *amarrer*). If these features can be traced back to France (and incidentally also occur in Canada, which was settled about the same time and largely by persons from the same regions in the west and north of France), there are also developments which appear to have taken place in the *Créole*-speaking territories, such as the almost universal use of a derivative of *case* for the notion of 'house', as well as borrowings from other languages present in the various colonies to designate local *realia*, beliefs and customs brought by the slaves. The languages in question included notably Malagasy in the Indian Ocean, Amerindian languages and Spanish in the Caribbean, Indian and African languages and English in both areas.

Although *Créoles* share a great many features, however, this does not necessarily mean that they can legitimately be considered as a unitary language. If the morphosyntax of different *Créoles* is comparable for a linguist working in the abstract, speakers of *Créole* in different parts of the world are probably more conscious of the points that distinguish them from one another. Mutual intelligibility is hampered by differences of prosody, to a lesser extent phonetics and morphosyntax, and above all vocabulary, not only between *Créoles* of different areas (Indian Ocean as against Caribbean), but to some degree also between different islands of the same area (Baker reports that Réunionnais on holiday in Mauritius cannot readily make themselves understood there by using *Créole* – see Baker and Corne 1982: 140), and there are clearly perceptible dialectal differences within Haiti. By no means all the features illustrated by text 1 below would therefore be familiar to *créolophones* from Mauritius, Haiti or even Guadeloupe.

The extract presented in text 1 is taken from *Grif an tè*, a weekly paper entirely in *Créole* which appeared in Martinique in the late seventies and early eighties. The organ of a group seeking greater autonomy for the French West Indies, it treated mainly local issues and carried a column teaching a spelling system for *Créole*. The text below is taken from a reportage on the situation of women, entitled *viv epi goumin, lavi epi lespwa*, 'Living and struggling, life and hope'.

The writing system used differs slightly from that advocated by the linguists of the *Université Antilles Guyane*. Both use some of the conventions of French orthography, in particular accents for distinguishing open and closed /E/, and vowels followed by *n* to indicate nasals; a double *n* indicates a nasal vowel before a nasal consonant.

The text is an example of mesolectal *Créole*, with several features derived from French in the lexis (e.g. *divini* rather than *vini* for 'to become') as well as in the syntax (e.g. the use of a connector *ki*).

It is followed by a fairly close translation into French.

Text 1

Ki léta sé fanm péyi-a? Ki divini-yo? Dé-o-twa manmay ka palé. Yo pa ka frazé, yo pa ka ba moun lison. Dapré sa yo viv, dapré sa yo santi èk sa yo sipôté kivédi dapré lèspéryans-yo, yo ka èsplitché ki jan yo ka wè bagay-la.

'Lavi-a asé kritik. Primyé pwoblinm nou ni sé travay. Anpil fanm pa ka travay. Mwin minm mwin adan an ti travay min sé pa sa. Sé pa sa ou pé kriyé vréman ni an travay . . . pou di pa rété la san fè anyin. Kon yo ka di: simyé ou an ranyon pasé ou tou tou-ni. Sa mwin ka ginyin adan an mwa pa ni asé pou sa mwin ka dépansé adan an siminn.

'An vil ou pé mèyè jwinn travay min mwin ni 6 ti-anmay, ès mwin ké kité ti-anmay-mwin pou désann an vil? Tout bagay ka ôgmanté. Chak siminn fôk mwin ni 50 fwan pou mwin vréyé sé ti-anmay-la lékôl, èk byin dé lè, yo ka pwan-ï a pyé. Mwin ka santi sitiyasyon-an vréman kritik.' MATNIK . . .

'Lavi lontan té pli byin ki atchèlman. Atchèlman ni plis lajan min lavi-a, i pli rèd. Mwin ka wè lanmannyè mwin té ka viv épi kanmarad-mwin, lanmannyè nou té ka antann kò-nou. Atchèlman, sé pa minm bayay-la. Mannyè nou té ka viv antan lontan té diféwan. Nou té ka antann kô-nou pou ay larivyè èk yonn té ka rédé lôt. Atchôlman chak moun pou lo-yo. Si ou wè ta-la ginyin an bagay, yo jalou. Si ou wè i pa ni-ï, yo ka palé-ï mal. Abiyé yo ka pòté-ou jalouzi, pa abyé yo ka kriyé-ou malpwòp.

'Ki divini sé fanm-lan nan péyi-a? Man pa sav. Sa mwin ka wè sé ki bagay-la pa-a woulé byin, sé alé i ka alé kochi. Mwin sé anvi bagay-la maché kon lontan, pou nou viv kon nou té ka viv lontan.

'Antan-lontan, lè ou wè nou té kay larivyè, ta-a ka minnin limonnad, ta-a ka pôté diri, ta-a ka pôté zalimèt, ta-a ka pôté pwéson, epi nou té ka viv kô-nou, nou té ka fè ti manjé-nou ant kanmarad. Pa té ni pyès konparézonnri. Sé nou minm ki té ka najé kanno-a pou nou ay larivyè . . . '(AN MANMAN YICH KI NI 47 LANNE)   (From *Grif an tè* liméwo 12, 4/1/78 pou 11/1/78)

Translation

Quel est l'état des femmes du pays? Que deviennent-elles? Quelques personnes parlent. Elles ne font pas de belles paroles, elles ne donnent pas des leçons aux gens. Selon ce qu'elles ont vécu, selon ce qu'elles ont senti et ce qu'elles ont supporté, c'est-à-dire selon leur expérience, elles expliquent de quelle manière elles voient la chose.

'La vie est assez critique. Le premier problème que nous avons est le travail. Beaucoup de femmes ne travaillent pas. Moi-même je suis dans un petit travail, mais ce n'est pas ça. Ce n'est pas ce que vous pouvez vraiment appeler un travail . . . pour dire ne pas rester là sans rien faire. Comme ils disent: il vaut mieux être en haillons plutôt que d'être tout nu. Ce que je gagne en un mois, il n'y a pas assez pour ce que je dépense en une semaine.

En ville on peut mieux trouver un travail mais j'ai 6 enfants, est-ce que je vais quitter mes enfants pour descendre en ville? Tout augmente. Chaque semaine il faut que j'aie 50 francs pour envoyer les enfants à l'école, et c'est bien deux heures qu'ils mettent à pied. Je sens que la situation est vraiment critique.' MARTINIQUE . . .

'La vie autrefois était meilleure qu'actuellement. Actuellement il y a plus d'argent mais la vie, elle est plus dure. Je vois la manière dont je vivais avec mes camarades, la manière dont nous nous entendions. Actuellement ce n'est pas la même chose. La manière dont nous vivions dans le passé était différente. Nous nous entendions pour aller à la rivière et l'une aidait l'autre. Actuellement c'est chacun pour soi. Si vous voyez quelqu'un obtenir quelque chose, ils sont jaloux. Si vous voyez qu'il ne l'a pas, ils en disent du mal. Habillé ils vous apportent de la jalousie, pas habillé ils vous appellent malpropre.

Que deviennent les femmes dans ce pays? Je ne sais pas. Ce que je vois c'est que les chosent ne roulent pas bien, qu'elles vont de travers. Je voudrais que les choses aillent comme autrefois, pour que nous vivions comme nous vivions autrefois.

Dans le passé, quand vous voyez que nous allons à la rivière, l'une amène de la limonade. une autre apporte du riz, l'autre apporte des allumettes, l'autre apporte du poisson, et nous nous amusions ensemble, nous faisions notre petit manger entre camarades. Il n'y avait point de rivalité. C'est nous-mêmes qui ramions le canot pour aller à la rivière . . . ' (UNE MÈRE DE FAMILLE DE 47 ANS)

(From *Grif an tè*, no. 12, 4/1/78–11/1/78)

Text 2

Situation sociolinguistique des Antilles Françaises

GUY HAZAËL-MASSIEUX

Les accidents de l'histoire font qu'aujourd'hui, le français aux Antilles a parfois disparu des lieux où il s'était tout d'abord implanté, qu'il est présent dans des terres de souveraineté française mais aussi dans des pays qui relèvent d'autres souverainetés: Haïti, St-Thomas; et qu'enfin, il n'a survécu ailleurs que dans de nouveaux parlers, modernes versions des jargons et baragouins du XVIIe siècle: les créoles (c'est le cas de la Dominique, de Ste-Lucie et de Trinidad).

Mais cette diversité de situation à la fois historique et géographique peut se résumer de façon exemplaire dans le tableau de l'usage actuel des Petites Antilles: on y trouve le français et le créole comme pôles opposés d'un continuum aboutissant à une diglossie. Il faudra pour compléter l'ensemble simplement prendre en compte ce qui s'inscrit dans la tradition de la 'colonisation officielle', l'impact d'une scolarité diversement efficace suivant les territoires.

La distinction entre français et créole a été délicate à établir: dès le XVIIe siècle, le Père Raymond Breton parlait de 'notre français des Iles', opposé à l'usage métropolitain. Il s'agissait sans doute de ce 'français créole', au sens premier du mot créole, c'est-à-dire français des *vieux-habitants*, non indigènes, c'est-à-dire non-amérindiens, mais dans le même temps, nés aux îles de parents importés. La première opposition se fit avec l'usage des nouveaux arrivants. Mais il est probable que la frontière entre le parler populaire des marginaux (sociaux, culturels, économiques, religieux, politiques: cadets, provinciaux, pauvres engagés sans feu ni lieu, protestants, déserteurs ou réfugiés) héritiers des voyages de l'avant et le 'jargon' ou 'français corrompu' des non-français (Caraïbes, esclaves noirs, Hollandais), faute d'une norme sociale très consciente, n'était pas bien nette. Les cadres supérieurs de la colonisation – maintenant le rapport avec Versailles – pouvaient noter l'écart entre Paris et les îles; les gens des îles, comme les missionnaires, suivant la situation et le besoin de communication, suivant la condition de l'interlocuteur, pour reprendre l'expression du R. P. Pelleprat, se conformaient à l'usage de leurs partenaires divers sans toujours percevoir qu'ils s'éloignaient de la norme du français. Cette inconscience explique qu'on doive attendre la seconde moitié du XVIIIe siècle pour que les voyageurs (Girod-Chantrans, par exemple) s'attachent à noter un 'langage créole' quelque peu différent du français et qui ne deviendra le créole et non plus simplement un 'patois nègre' qu'avec Moreau de St Méry (1798).

(From *La francophonie*, ed. D. E. Ager and J. R. French (Association for French Language Studies and Portsmouth Polytechnic, 1986))

12

French in Africa

SUZANNE LAFAGE

Introduction

It seems to be increasingly accepted that the survival of French as an international language depends on its development in Africa. Is this indeed so? Can one say that in the year 2000 most French speakers will be African? And is such a geographical and demographical extension taking place without causing radical changes to the French language, now that it is being adapted to a new African context and used by Africans, whose conceptual universe is not the same as that of the French?

I shall endeavour to give a concise answer to these questions by describing the current state of the French language in Africa. In a few pages it is not possible to deal fully with all aspects of the language, so I shall only deal with the analysis of lexicon to illustrate my remarks.

An optimistic vision

This vision of an African destiny for the French language has been outlined in many recent documents produced for summit meetings of heads of state and government that have in common the use of French (Paris: 1986; Quebec: 1987; Dakar: 1989). The vision is based on three factors.

The role of French as an official language

The first factor is the status of official language afforded (*de jure* or *de facto*) to French and the functions which are a consequence of this. This is the case in twelve Sub-Saharan countries: Benin, Burkina-Faso, the Central African Republic, the Congo, the Ivory Coast, Gabon, Guinea, Mali, Niger, Senegal, Togo and Zaïre. French shares this role with other languages in a few other states: Burundi (with Kirundi), Cameroun (with English), Rwanda (with Kinyarwanda), the Comoros, Djibouti, Mauritania and Chad (with Arabic). It is also the foreign language with preferred status in certain Portuguese-speaking African countries (Guinea-Bissau, Cape Verde etc.) and is the first foreign language taught in most English-speaking African countries to the south of the Sahara. This is why French, together with English and Arabic, was chosen for OUA (*Organisation de l'Unité Africaine*) publications.

French is of course a legacy of French or Belgian colonisation. However, it has survived the crisis of Independence and there does not appear to be any challenge in the foreseeable future to the role of French in the functions for which it is used: administration, international relations, teaching, the media, trade, transport, tourism, science and technology, literature and so on, despite sociolinguistic and socioeconomic situations and political options being very different (cf. *Politique africaine* 1985–6; Rapport Confémen 1986; CILF, 1988). This position is very probably reinforced by the role played in black Africa by not only French and Belgian but Canadian cultural and technical cooperation, and, to a much lesser extent, by that of the Swiss.

Some further points must, however, be made. A large part of the population of these countries remains non-French-speaking, especially in rural areas. Thus in 1980 'non-francophones' represented at least 88.9 per cent of the people in Chad, 81.80 per cent in the Central African Republic, 46.86 per cent in the Congo and 36.88 per cent in Gabon (Couvert, 1984b).

The official language is a second language which exists alongside the many local languages, with the possible exception of a minority urban fringe in some countries such as the Ivory Coast, the Congo, Gabon or Senegal. It is mainly learnt at school, although in certain urban contexts there is a relatively large degree of learning by contact at an early age. Yet nowhere is French a truly foreign language as in Ghana or Angola. The relationship that French has with local languages differs from one 'francophone' nation to another, depending on the number of native languages and the status afforded them: whether the languages are considered 'national' or not, whether they are taught or not, whether the vehicular language is widespread or simply regional or a vernacular language and so on.

French schooling and demographic growth

Two further linked factors are thought to guarantee the survival of French in most studies. The hypothesis is that the population explosion and the increase in schooling (and therefore in the diffusion of French) will go hand in hand. We will see below in the next section that this is not necessarily the case. Furthermore, those who receive an education and are classified as 'francophones' have widely different levels of command of the French language. One should therefore read with caution statistics quoted in official documents (such as appeared in the *Journal Officiel de la République Française, Avis et Rapports du Conseil Economique et Social*, 29–30 March 1989). Thus, for the number of those taught French (that is the percentage of people taught French in relation to the total school population in a geopolitical area), 'French-speaking' Africa is top of the league (75.96 per cent) ahead of the Maghreb (69.6 per cent) and Western Europe, including France (36.6 per cent).

In the 1985 report on 'l'état de la Francophonie dans le monde', published by the Haut Conseil de la Francophonie (in *Bull. FIPF*, June 1986: pp. 10–12), the following figures are given:

A   Total number of people taught French, *in all sectors of education* (my emphasis):
    1. Western Europe (including France)   24,135,000
    2. French-speaking Africa   21,241,000
B   Total number per French-speaking country: *as a language taught and as the language used in teaching*. (We shall only mention the main Sub-Saharan countries and their order in the list.)
    5th: Cameroun   1,730,000
    6th: Ivory Coast   1,470,000
    7th: Senegal   1,281,000
    9th: Zaïre   1,035,000
    13th: Rwanda   768,000
    14th: Congo   560,000
    15th: Benin   550,000
    16th: Mali   386,000
    17th: Central African Republic   344,000
    18th: Burkina-Faso   311,000 etc.

It can be seen, for example, that in this list Rwanda (where primary schooling is given in Kinyarwanda and where French is only introduced towards the end of the primary cycle) appears next to the Congo (where the whole of schooling is in French). And comment could be made on the Cameroun, where teaching is either in French or in English depending on the region.

C   Percentage of people taught French (i.e the percentage of the number of people taught French in relation to the total population of a geopolitical area):
    1. French-speaking Africa: 18.9%

When one sees the whole range of linguistic competence presented in such a way, one can understand R. Chaudenson's criticisms (1984: 46–53), when he writes

La plupart des élèves même en fin du primaire, entrent, non dans la catégorie des francophones mais dans celle des 'francophonoïdes', frottés au français, quelques années durant, dans des classes souvent surchargées . . . sans livres ni matériel scolaire, instruits par des maîtres dont la compétence en français n'est pas toujours ce qu'on pourrait croire, ayant reçu non pas un réel enseignement *du* français mais un enseignement *en* français, langue qu'ils ne maîtrisent nullement . . .

In these same official documents (*Journal Officiel*, 1989: 33) the very sharp increase in Africa's population is referred to in the following terms: 'La population vivant dans les pays d'Afrique noire d'expression officielle française passera de 102 millions en 1980 à plus de 180 millions de personnes en 1'an 2000 avec un taux de croissance de 2.5 à 3%.' And on this basis they estimate that black Africa's 'francophone' population will approach 25 million (ibid.: note 4).

As things stand at present, are our assessments more realistic?

IRAF (Institut de Recherches sur l'Avenir du Français) has carried out a series of much-debated studies (Couvert 1982–6; Perrin 1983–7) in the majority of the countries concerned. These studies distinguish five levels of language competence in 'francophones', ranging from a basic and exclusively oral knowledge, to different oral and written levels depending on the level of schooling reached. If the threshold at which a sufficiently stable knowledge of the oral and written language can be considered to have been reached is fixed at the end of the first cycle of secondary education (i.e. after ten or eleven years of schooling in French), then this data provides us with less optimistic but more credible information:

- In relation to the population of a country aged six years or over, the number of 'real francophones' is very small. The percentage varies very noticeably between different countries: for example, only 1.92 per cent of the population in Chad, 3.59 per cent in the Central African Republic, 7.5 per cent in Gabon, 19.7 per cent in the Congo etc.
- The numbers of francophones are made up, throughout Africa, by speakers who have only an approximate knowledge of French.
- In certain countries, the proportion of francophone illiterates is much higher. Thus in the Central African Republic the figure is 6.83 per cent, but in Gabon 32.35 per cent (Couvert 1984b) and in the Ivory Coast 33.5 per cent (Perrin 1985: 167).
- The percentage of francophones (including 'francophonoids' – see Chaudenson 1989) is higher in towns than in rural areas, especially in the large coastal centres. Thus in Abidjan in 1978 there were 73.7

per cent francophones but only 24 per cent in rural areas of the Ivory Coast (Perrin 1985).
- This imbalance between towns and rural areas is a consistent feature. If one moves away from the coastal areas, the percentage of 'francophones' in relation to the whole of the population aged six years or over is lower. In comparison with the data given for the Ivory Coast above, the figures for Mali in 1976 are: towns – 36.7 per cent, rural areas – 8.2 per cent (Perrin 1984: 59).
- Most francophones are male: 1980, Ivory Coast: men 58.9 per cent, women 33.6 per cent (Perrin 1985: 167); 1976, Mali: men 17.5 per cent, women 4.9 per cent (Perrin 1984: 59).
- Most francophones are young: 1979, Benin: 52 per cent of ten–fourteen year-olds compared to 10.7 per cent of those aged twenty-five or above (Perrin 1986: 128).
- There is a marked variation according to occupation: 1975, Ivory Coast: 90.8 per cent of 'francophones' amongst senior civil servants and in the professions; 83.7 per cent in the government services' 72.1 per cent in the service sector; 70.3 per cent of technicians and manual workers; 41.6 per cent of shopkeepers; 15 per cent of farmworkers and fishermen (General Population Census quoted in Lafage 1979: 209–10).

Whatever criticisms linguists may level at some of these surveys, the trends that emerge from them nevertheless confirm the results of work done in the field.

Looking forward to the year 2000

Are we to expect in French-speaking black Africa a qualitative and quantitative change in the use of French, comparable to that which can be forecast for the Maghreb, where schooling is being progressively and intensively arabicised because of the desire to reduce the role of the former colonial language? According to C. Sauvageot (1984: 45), in Algeria, Morocco and Tunisia 'la part des francophones d'éducation et de culture est vouée à décroître même si le nombre de locuteurs francophones augmente . . . par le résultat de l'essor démographique et de la généralisation de la scolarisation'.

All the Sub-Saharan states are of course endeavouring to promote their main national languages and to ensure their use as a medium of written communication. This has already been achieved for the whole of primary schooling in Burundi and Rwanda, and for its first few years in Togo and Zaïre. Extensive experimentation is taking place in Niger, Mali and in the Ivory Coast. However, although the political decision to introduce these national languages into education has been taken, it has not always been systematically carried out (Benin, Congo etc.). There is even sometimes a return to a 'francophone' system that had been virtually abandoned: for example, in Guinea, where between 1958 and 1984, under the Sékou Touré regime, French had been replaced by eight of the national languages.

If there is a consensus of opinion between all states that have in common the use of French (and with the exception of any political upheaval that the current disastrous economic crisis might bring about), it is certainly to do with exploiting this bilingualism of national languages and French 'afin qu'il soit un facteur d'équilibre intellectuel et psychologique des personnes . . . pour une plus saine ouverture sur la modernité'. (Houis and Bole-Richard: 1978, 20–22). Indeed, in societies that are generally multilingual and heterogeneous and in which interethnic, religious and social tensions are latent, French may appear as the lesser evil. 'Il arrive que les représentations et les attentes liées au français et les comportements langagiers qu'elles déterminent soient tout ce qu'ont en commun les citoyens d'un même état. On s'explique bien que les gouvernements hésitent à remettre en cause un aussi fragile équilibre' (Manessy 1986: 13).

Throughout Africa there have been complaints about the deterioration of the educational system which is criticised by the World Bank in its recent report (1988) in strong terms. It was in the eighties that French became threatened, precisely because people's expectations of French schooling were being increasingly frustrated. For a very long time families considered the sacrifices that they were prepared to make for their children's education as a sort of investment for the future, so convinced were they, after Independence, that l'école des Blancs would be the guarantee of rapid and often spectacular upward social mobility. But much disillusionment was caused by the high cost of schooling, the excessive dropout rate in an education system of mediocre quality, which although open to nearly all in the early stages, later becomes frighteningly restrictive with its succession of bottlenecks (competitive examinations for entry into the first year of secondary schools, then again in the fifth year, the baccalauréat, rigorous selection for entrance into university etc.). Moreover, it becomes virtually impossible for those who have had to leave school after a few years of study to readapt to their own milieu, and, to make matters even worse, the saturation of the job market in most areas is causing increasing unemployment amongst young people with qualifications (Lange 1984, Politique Africaine 1987, Jeune Afrique 1990). The result of this is an increasingly noticeable rejection of l'école des Blancs, further reinforced, moreover, in Muslim areas by the upsurge of fundamentalism: less schooling for girls, the strengthening of the position of Koranic schools etc. Thus, for example, between 1960 and 1984 in the Ivory Coast:

- the primary sector increased from 200,000 children to 1,159,800 (+ 7.6 per cent per year on average)
- the general secondary sector increased from 8,300 to 229,900 (+ 14.8 per cent per year on average)
- the university sector increased from 48 to 11 400 (+ 25.6 per cent per year on average)   (Perrin 1985: appendix III.2)

In this same country, however, whereas the number of children of school age is increasing, the admission rate of newly enrolled pupils (six years old), which was 72 per cent between 1977 and 1980, fell to 65 per cent in 1983 (Perrin 1984: 10). And it seems that this decline is continuing. In Togo the admission rate of 72.1 per cent in 1980 fell to 52.3 per cent in 1985 (Anzorge 1988: 53). In Senegal, the *Etats Généraux de l'Education*, referring to the expansion of Islam and the Arabic language, requested that the latter be given a status in the educational system more in keeping with the sociocultural realities of the country (Perrin 1984: 44).

Looking forward to the year 2000, what will be the real significance of all these facts? It is very difficult to tell, but it seems that it would be wise to temper the official optimism.

One French language or several?

In Europe, the French language has had to adapt to very different sociocultural contexts. Its diffusion has varied according to different factors, of which only the most significant will be mentioned.

The length of French presence in Africa

French has only been present in Sub-Saharan Africa for a relatively short time, with the exception of part of Senegal, where, according to old documents (De Saint Lô [1637] 1967: 220–1), a kind of pidgin French is said to have existed in the area where Captain Lambert of the *Compagnie Normande* founded in 1638 the first permanent French settlement which was to become, in 1659, the town of Saint-Louis. Despite many setbacks, this settlement established itself and expanded, as is witnessed in two historical events. This region sent a *Cahier de Doléances* to the 1789 *Etats Généraux*, and the inhabitants of the *quatre communes* (St Louis, Gorée, Rufisque and Dakar) were granted French citizenship in 1876, although the French presence was then restricted to a very few forts, trading posts or missions on the African coast.

The annexation of the colonies took from 1878 to 1885 in Gabon and in the Congo and until 1900 in Chad. In 1919, the former German colonies Burundi and Rwanda came under Belgian mandate, and the area that corresponds to present-day Cameroun and Togo under French mandate. But this 'pacification' only came to an end in 1918 in the Ivory Coast, in 1931 in Ubangi-Shari (Central African Republic) and in 1934 in Mauritania.

Linguistic options in the colonial era

During the pre-colonial era, the French language spread by contact with the sailors who plied the coast, with the traders in the trading stations or with the soldiers in the forts and their native auxiliaries who spoke *français tiraillou* or 'infantry French' (Manessy 1984: 113–26). The missionaries set up schools for the native population and usually gave importance to local languages – and they were the first to describe these languages – for teaching and evangelisation purposes. At the beginning of the twentieth century, French teaching was very rare, except in Senegal. French decrees outlining proposals for teaching the language in French West Africa were signed in 1903. Use of the native tongue was proscribed. The aim was to provide African auxiliary administrators to be intermediaries between the colonial administration and the native population. The gradual extension of this education system was to confirm France's intention: in 1944, the Brazzaville Conference modelled Africa's embryonic educational system on that of France (Biarnes 1987). The inadequacy of such a system has been criticised at length and ridiculed both by contemporary teachers and by francophone black African literature; we need not dwell on it here. Belgium, on the other hand, decided that children between the ages of six and eleven should be taught in the local vehicular languages since the emphasis in this mass education programme was more on manual work than on a general education.

But this system was criticised just as much as the French one, resulting as it did in deeply felt frustrations: for during the period of Belgian colonisation, the only people 'à faire de véritables études et à maîtriser suffisamment le français, sont les séminaristes' (Picoche and Marchello-Nizia 1989: 95).

Sociolinguistic locations

The frontiers of the young states that were inherited from colonisation are quite arbitrary, even if there is agreement to consider them as inviolable. They carve out heterogeneous areas which only rarely coincide with historical or cultural entities. We shall schematise the relationships between the local African languages and the French language by taking as points of reference two opposing theoretical poles, with each nation known as 'francophone' being closer to one or the other of these theoretical poles.

Most communication at a national level takes place in the dominant African language. The dominance of this language may date back many years (Kinyarwanda/Kirundi for Rwanda/Burundi, Wolof for Senegal, Mande for Mali and a large part of West Africa etc.) or may have appeared more recently (Sango in the Central African Republic, for example). In larger countries, different languages share the role of *lingua franca* at a regional level (in Zaïre: Swahili in Shaba and the east of the Republic, Lingala in Kinshasa and Equatorial Africa, Ciluba in the east and west of Kasai, Kikongo in Lower Zaïre and Bandudu).

French is in these cases in functional complementarity with the dominant native language, according to the opposition modernity/ tradition, international (or interprovincial) exchanges/ local exchanges. The acquisition of the imported official language is essentially made at school and affects few people as it may start at a late stage (at the end of primary school or at the beginning of secondary school). The risk of pidginisation is reduced for French since its vehicular role is restricted to 'élites' who have received extensive schooling for use in formal situations. However for those bilingual people who know French and the dominant language, informal exchanges sometimes reveal mixed speech patterns (code-switching within the same utterance using lexical elements originating from one or other of the speeches in contact):

> Mont Ngaliema efungwami mpo na peuple zaïrois à partir du samedi ler février, c'est-à-dire à partir d'aujourd'hui.
> 'Le mont Ngaliema est ouvert au peuple zaïrois à partir du samedi ler février, c'est-à-dire à partir d'aujourd'hui.' (extract from a Lingala/ French speech by President Mobutu, quoted in Sesep 1978: 5)

But young people who live in the towns often resort to a hybrid language, with the morphology of one language affecting the lexis of the other:

> Badirecteur mingi penseke ti i faut kisalu commencé na sept heures.
> plural + directeur plusieurs penser + durative past il faut travail commencer à sept heures.
> 'Plusieurs directeurs pensaient qu'il fallait commencer le travail à sept heures.' (Zaïre, Kituba/French)

Lexically, the adaptation of oral or written French seems to be distinguished more by substratum loans than by neologistic formations (derivation, composition etc).

In a second model, there is no African language which is genuinely dominant on a national level. Multilingualism is very common (for example, it is said that there are more than two hundred vernacular languages in Cameroun). Because of natural obstacles such as virgin forests, rivers and mountains, languages have split up into numerous dialects which are sometimes only understood by a very few people. Yet a modern state requires intercommunication. Of course, for a part of a country or for a precise sector of activity (trade, for example), the local language may fulfil the role of a vehicular language.

But the official language (or two official languages in the case of Cameroun) assumes the function of *lingua franca* on a national level by virtue of there being two different varieties:

a) for those who have received the most schooling, in the form of a variety of the standard language which is hardly regionalised at all (pronunciation and lexis etc.), or of a more marked variant when the shorter length of schooling makes it more difficult to acquire the standard level. Nevertheless reference to the 'academic' norm remains present at all levels of this continuum and there is usually complete understanding with other French speakers.

b) for those who have received little or no education, by extremely approximative local varieties with no reference to the norm. So as not to be completely marginalised, a varying proportion (cf. pp. 226–7 below) of the working classes endeavour to achieve national intercommunication. The aim is to provide for their daily needs in face-to-face exchanges without ambiguity. But the interlanguage (that is the reconstruction of the various systems of rules of the target language by the development of a succession of approximative intermediary states) becomes fossilised very quickly once these limited needs are met: there is 'pidginisation' – 'réduction de la structure profonde et simplification de la structure de surface, au profit de l'établissement d'une compétence communicative rudimentaire mais suffisante pour des contacts interlinguistiques transitoires' (Manessy 1975: 3–14).

However, in some urbanised environments that are linguistically extremely heterogeneous but homogeneous as far as lifestyle and living conditions are concerned, the pidginised basilect tends to establish itself as the usual means of expression, sometimes even within the home. In certain areas of this 'French' speech there then appear some features of 'creolisation' (the expansion of the deep structure and increased complexity of the surface structure) which often develop idiosyncratically, distinct from both the African 'mother' tongue and from French. These distortions affect all fields and it becomes difficult, if not on occasion impossible, to achieve mutual understanding with a 'francophone' who is not local.

Example 1 Cameroun
An approximate utterance that is incomprehensible out of context (Manessy 1978a: 3–32):

Mon femme tu connais pidgin y a pas.
'Aucune de mes épouses ne parle pidgin (English).'

Example 2 Ivory Coast
Français Populaire d'Abidjan (henceforth referred to as 'FPA'): complex approximative utterance:

[la vi la sɛ sɛr avɛk nu. Si depyi ɔ̃ na
La vie la c'est sèr avec nous. Si depuis on a
kɔ̃tinyje kom sa, zɔ pø pa eleve mɔ̃ lezãfã
continué comme ça, ze peux pas élever mon les zenfants
zyska ɔ̃ gRã zyska ɔ̃ vijẽ ne le zotR]
zusqu'à on grands, zusqu'à on vient né les zautres.
'Cette vie est trop chère pour nous. Si ça continue encore comme ça, je ne pourrai pas élever mes enfants jusqu'à ce qu'ils soient grands, jusqu'à ce que d'autres naissent.'

In such a context, the teaching of French poses particular problems since 'street French' affects the French taught at school far more frequently and permanently than African languages do.

Highly complex and very varied communication networks are assigned to different social hierarchies because the variety of French used serves as a differentiating parameter of social status. Indeed, those who have received the most schooling may, depending on the competence they attribute to their interlocutor, use a different lect, even though this may entail imitating the structures of the popular language that are furthest from French; the same is not true of the genuine speakers of the vehicular language who, in French, have no other means of expression.

Admittedly, one 'pidginised' idiolect can vary greatly from another. It can vary in its phonology, prosody, morphology, syntax, semantics etc. Its lexicon is distinguished by sociosemantic adaptations (Lafage et al. 1984a: 103–12): changes of denotation, connotation, collocation and various transfers, and by the abundance of neology: derivation, composition, hybridisation and so on.

The situation described above could, to varying degrees, be applied to the Congo, Gabon, Cameroun etc. The Ivory Coast is without doubt the most advanced case of this, probably because of a further parameter that is of particular importance in this country.

Inter-African immigration

For various reasons, after Independence some countries witnessed rapid economic development (for example in the seventies there was talk of the 'Ivory Coast miracle'). There was intense urbanisation. On top of the rural exodus, which threw together all the different ethnic groups of the state in huge urban centres, there was widespread African immigration, which attracted an influx of largely illiterate African migrants from a variety of regions.

Such a phenomenon exerts a considerable influence on the spread of French, both in quantitative terms (an increase in the number of speakers since, in the host country, the French language affords access to the job market and is often the only means of communication between immigrants and natives), as well as in qualitative terms (a speeded-up development of the pidginised variety of the vehicular language).

Abidjan is probably the most significant example of this. According to the 1975 General Census, 41.3 per cent of the inhabitants of this rapidly expanding city were of Sub-Saharan origin: people from Upper Volta (now Burkina-Faso), Malians, Guineans, Togolese, Ghanaians, Senegalese, Zaïrois etc. More recent data show that the influx continues despite the Ivory Coast's serious economic crisis. And the democratisation of the country's education system has no effect on the adult newcomers who often come from countries with very high rates of illiteracy.

What are the likely, longer-term linguistic consequences of this potentially explosive population mix? There seem to be two possible scenarios:

a) The political, economic and social climate will remain unfavourable for a fairly long time. The effect of this might be 'que le F.P.A. se coupe de tout contact avec la norme tout en restant un instrument de communication pour les populations . . . On aboutirait alors vraisemblablement à un parler très proche (voire identique en certains points due système) des créoles "conservateurs" tels ceux de l'Océan Indien' (Hattiger 1983: 298).

b) Or socioeconomic and political conditions will remain much the same as those that prevailed in the seventies, with French retaining its prestige and exerting pressure on FPA, and with increased schooling. It might be that 'on aboutisse à un état de langue' that could be considered 'comme une variété du français standard, d'un statut proche de celui de français parlé à Montréal, dans les milieux populaires' (ibid).

Varieties of French and attitudes

For all the 'French-speaking' African countries, the only form of French which is likely to survive and develop is 'standard' French as it is used internationally. Popular local varieties of the *lingua franca* such as FPA, where they exist, have no openings onto the outside world. Specialists think that these varieties should gradually disappear as the teaching of national languages is further developed. Of course, the users of this *français façon* (i.e. bad French) are themselves aware of its shortcomings and its divergence from the prestigious variety. For in their eyes:

> frãsē Musa ty mwajē mãʒe travaje, frãse tubabu ty mwajē tú
> 'avec le "français de Moussa" tu peux manger et travailler. Avec le "français des Toubabous" tu peux tout!'

> with Moussa's French (a pastiche of FPA which appears in the 'chroniques de Moussa' in the weekly *Ivoire Dimanche*, and which the population mistakes for the FPA which it endeavours to imitate) you can eat and work. With the *Toubabous* French (school French, literally 'white man's French') you can do everything! (Lescutier 1985: vol. 1, p. 107)

Despite all this, a need is beginning to make itself felt for a form of French that is 'correct' in its morphosyntax but that retains certain African features.

Thus a Paris accent (*parler chocobi*, as they say in the Ivory Coast) is mocked and the speaker is not considered to 'belong' (*un pied dedans un pied dehors*, as they say in Togo). He who uses *gros français* or 'posh' French is a *en haut d'en haut* – a snob, a *been to* (a show-off).

It can even sometimes happen that the local popular varieties act as a rallying for social discontent (Lafage et al. 1983, 1987–8). Pastiches of these varieties appear in the humorous pages of the weeklies, in cartoon strips (Ivory Coast, Burkina-Faso etc.), in songs (Congo, Zaïre etc.), in advertising, in satirical radio and television programmes.

The first African writers to write in French treated the language with awe, but others soon expressed their doubts about the adequacy of French to express the African soul. Thus Senghor (1948, xviii), talking about the African writer, acknowledges that: 'cette syntaxe et ce vocabulaire forgés en d'autres temps, à des milliers de lieues, pour répondre à d'autres besoins et pour désigner d'autres objets, sont impropres à lui fournir les moyens de parler de lui . . . , de ses soucis, de ses espoirs.' The writer Ahmadou Kourouma from the Ivory Coast is one of the first to illustrate in *Le soleil des Indépendances* what we call the 'appropriation' of French. In an interview with a journalist (1970) he explains: 'Le français classique constituait un carcan qu'il fallait dépasser . . . Qu'avais-je donc fait? Simplement donné libre cours à mon tempérament en distordant une langue trop rigide pour que ma pensé s'y meuve. J'ai donc traduit le malinké en français en *cassant* le français' (my emphasis). Other equally important writers will go even further, playing on the oppositions of varieties which coexist, using an approximative basilect to characterise certain characters and to give as life-like a social picture as possible (see texts below). This is shown by Chemain in a forthcoming article 'La littérature africaine se ré-africanise' which subtly draws on elements of the mother tongues (using loan words, calques, rhythm), and of the different varieties of African French (with their own neologisms, images, tropes and so on) thereby creating an original style.

This African contribution to the enrichment of the French language which is so striking in recent literature can also be observed in the daily language on the lexical level, for it is in its vocabulary that the specificity of African French is most plainly evident.

Lexis as a reflection of the dialogue between cultures

The research done so far

After some isolated studies carried out by previous researchers (Mauny 1952; Flutre 1958, 1961; Van der Vorst and Pohl 1961, amongst others), research into African French lexis has evolved mainly around the IFA project (*L'Inventaire des particularités lexicales du Français en Afrique noire*), under the aegis of AUPELF and ACCT (see chapter 1). The first stage (1974–83) covered a dozen states. Teams were formed to draw up a joint research methodology which aimed to be synchronic, non-normative, differential but not ethno-centred. There was a dual aim: to make an inventory of the particular lexical features of the spoken and written French of each country and to provide an overview of the sample based on a certain number of selection criteria. The plan was to go further than just identifying those 'deviations' which can be attributed to inadequacies of learning or to communication strategies peculiar to the interlanguage; they in fact aimed to distinguish 'un ensemble de traits dotés d'une relative spécificité, d'une fréquence élevée, d'une dispersion assez grande et qui n'étaient pas ressentis comme des fautes ni comme des singularités par des locuteurs possédant une bonne maîtrise du français' (W. Bal, *IFA* introduction, 1988: xiii). A second stage, begun in 1990, will build on studies carried out from 1983 on, in order to further refine existing surveys and extend them to all French-speaking Sub-Saharan countries. In the longer term, research along more normative lines and with a view to the compilation of a dictionary, should result in the integration of the African data in the *Trésor informatisé des vocabulaires francophones*, an ambitious programme adopted and backed by the conference of heads of state and government 'ayant en commun l'usage du français'.

Some general observations

In the first stage, the IFA considered more than 12,000 specific lexical features, although the total collected was infinitely greater than this. Of course, IFA 2 will have to make some corrections and revisions, but a certain number of observations can nevertheless be made:

a)   Contrary to what might be thought in France where the diversity of African cultures is not fully appreciated, particular lexical features common to the whole of the French-speaking Sub-Saharan area are relatively few in number. Curiously, the extension of certain words owes much to the widespread distribution of reading books such as *Mamadou et Bineta* created in principle for the AOF (the old French West Africa) but used, in the colonial era, more or less everywhere. One has the proof of this when one comes across loan words from Mande such as *daba* ('short-handled hoe'), from Wolof such as *hilaire* ('a ploughing implement with a blade in the shape of a wing') in countries where these languages have never been a local reality.

b)   For reasons already given (cf. pp. 225–6 above) some countries are more 'productive' than others. The more a 'francophone' population uses French, the more it tends to appropriate it and adapt it to its needs. However 'local' lexical items are not frequently present in the French spoken by educated Africans, except from certain specific lexical areas.

c)   When the geographical distribution of a specific local feature goes beyond the frontiers of a state, it is often bound by former colonial borders: French West Africa/French Equatorial Africa/Belgian territories. Hence the 'servant in charge of the household linen' will be called *boy-blanchisseur/lavadère/lavandier* respectively. Of course for local reasons other synonyms may appear here or there: *washman* in Togo where this job was for a long time confined to the 'anglophones' of the Gold Coast (Ghanaians), *fannico* in the Ivory Coast where the distinction is made between 'a sort of worker looking after the linen of poor, working-class clients' and the 'family servant' or the 'launderette'.

d)   The geographical extension of a term is often accompanied by a semantic shift, for example: *maquis* (Ivory Coast: 'a small semi-clandestine *bar-restaurant* where poached game can be eaten') is in Senegal 'a bar, a dance-hall, a hotel of ill repute' and even in Mali 'all of the disreputable places in a town'.

e)   Mesolectal varieties where there is a great difference between the cultures in contact are more 'productive' than either the acrolect which respects the explicit norm or the basilect which has a limited lexicon. If varieties such as FPA often give the impression of an intense proliferation of neologisms, this is because non-linguists confuse them with pastiches such as the *français de Moussa* in which writers give free rein to their imagination. But these innovations do of course subsequently contaminate other varieties. They can be recognised by their playful, familiar character: *gramoxon* (Ivory Coast: 'low-quality red wine', an allusion to a powerful weed-killer), *faire coup d'état* (Ivory Coast: 'to steal a friend's girlfriend') and so on.

f)   The part which is most affected by particular local features is regularly used, everyday vocabulary: words which designate realia, food, the environment, customs, beliefs, ways of life. This is why many local features are polylectal (that is, likely to appear in contexts which reveal different degrees of proficiency in French). Some, however, are of limited distribution – technical vocabulary, for example: *écabosseuse* (Ivory Coast: a machine for opening the cacao-pod (*cabosse*) and extracting the cocoa beans) and its derivatives: *écabosser, écobossage*. Others are basilectal (apart from when used playfully by writers): *bouffement* (Ivory Coast: from *bouffe*, a colloquial expression for food), and yet others are slang: *agrégé* (Ivory Coast: prisoners' slang for a habitual offender (whereas in French the word denotes the successful candidate in the *agrégation*).

g)   There are important lexical traces of the history of the continent which vary according to the region.

– Loans from Portuguese by coastal languages which subsequently passed into French: *capita* (*capitão*, Zaïre: 'a foreman'), *matabiche* (*matar o bicho*, Zaïre, Congo: 'a tip, a bribe'); from Brazilian Portuguese: *caldérade* (*caldeirada*, Zaïre, Togo: a sort of dish); from English: *coconotte* ('coconut', Zaïre), *wharf, beach, pool, com* (comb, Senegal: 'a long-toothed wooden comb') and so on; African English: *been to* (as in 'I have been to England', Togo, Ivory Coast: 'a show-off'), *sekeni* (second-hand, Rwanda: 'second-hand clothing'); from Arabic: *hadj* (all Islamised countries: the title of any Muslim who has been on a pilgrimage to Mecca), *medersa, moud* (Mali: a unit of measurement for cereals), *alcati* (Senegal: 'a policeman') and from Arabic from the Maghreb: *mehari* (Mali: a dromedary specially trained for fast races).

– There are loan words from regional varieties of French – Belgian French: *farde* (Rwanda, Zaïre: 'a file or dossier'), *drache* (Rwanda, Zaïre: 'a shower') *dracher, athénée, bourgmestre* etc.; from Canadian French: *budgéter* (Rwanda, *budgétiser*), *accommoder* (Rwanda) and so on.

– Technical terms lose their specialised sense. From the army: *tinettes* (all countries, military slang: 'latrines'), *vaguemestre* (West Africa: the person in charge of the post in a firm), *planton* (all countries: 'a clerk'), *solde* (all countries: 'pay'). From the navy: *amarrer* (Senegal: 'to tie or attach'), *faubérer* (Senegal, from *fauber*, a broom made of old pieces of rope for drying the deck of a ship: 'to mop') amongst others.

– Exotic words from elsewhere are 'adapted': *agouti* (from Tupi-Guarani *acuti* designating a South-American rodent similar to a hare, and applied to a different rodent, the aulacode, on the coast of Benin), *toucan* (from the Tupi *tucano* applied to another large-beaked bird, the calao or hornbill).

Concise functional typology

Three types of specific local features can be distinguished schematically:

1.   differences in usage,
2.   semantic shift,
3.   specific local features (neologisms etc.).

In certain complex cases, several phenomena may be combined.

Differences in usage

a) Change in frequency   In view of their tropical or equatorial context, certain words which are relatively common in France will virtually never be used in Africa: chilblain (*engelure*) for example. The opposite is equally possible: *pian, onchocercose, kwashiorkor*, are accessible to the average African speaker because of the campaigns to make the public aware of these diseases, but in Europe they are restricted to a highly specialised medical field.

b) Archaisms   Some words that contemporary dictionaries consider as archaic or obsolete are still very much alive in Africa: *honnir* (West Africa), *chambre* (all countries: 'room'), *se gêner* (West Africa), *portefaix* (Senegal), *tympaniser* (Senegal) and so on.

c) Confusion of registers   Some words that, according to dictionaries, are vulgar or vernacular, or on the contrary *recherché* or sophisticated, are locally quite neutral as shall be seen in the following quotations: 'Vous risquez de *trépasser* comme un poulet' (Guinea, *Horoya*, 17 May 1985); 'Vexé d'être éconduit, il la traite de *belle de nuit*' (Senegal, *Soleil*, 22 February 1977); 'Est-ce que le gouvernement a la possibilité de débarrasser les modestes passants de la bande d'*emmerdeuses* . . . qui ne cesse d'importuner tout ce qui bouge' (Cameroun, *Messager*, 9–25 July 1986. *Emmerdeuse* is here a euphemism for prostitute).

d) Change of collocation   The case of the set phrase has been selected for illustration here. The set phrase can be modified
   – by adding an element: *faire la mafière* (Zaïre), or by fusing two similar expressions: *demander la main d'une fille en mariage* (Burkina-Faso: *demander la main d'une jeune fille/demander une jeune fille en mariage*).
   – by suppressing an element: *avoir un oeil en beurre* (Ivory Coast: *avoir un oeil au beurre noir*).
   – by substitution: *gagner son mil* (all countries: *gagner son pain*); *vendre sous les boubous* (= *vendre sous le manteau*).
   – by permutation of elements: *faire des mains et des pieds* (Burkina-Faso, Ivory Coast: *faire des pieds et des mains*); *être les oreilles et les yeux de quelqu'un* (Ivory Coast: *être les yeux et les oreilles*).

Semantic shift
In this case, the word or expression is in the dictionary, but the African usage has undergone some sort of semantic shift.

1. There is a change in the relationship between *signifiant* and *signifié*

a) by restricting the meaning   *graine* (Senegal: 'peanut'; Ivory Coast: 'palm nut'); *charbon* (all countries: 'charcoal' (*charbon de bois*)).

b) by extending the meaning   *frère* (all countries: brother, half-brother, cousin, any man of the same generation with whom one feels one has common ties such as origin, district, village, tribe, ethnic group, religion, race etc.); *beaux-parents* (Burkina-Faso: 'the whole of one's family by marriage'); *goudron* (all countries: 'a street or a tarmacked road').

c) by transfer   *écritures* (Senegal: *inscription*), *film* (all countries: 'cinema'); *théâtre* (all countries: a play), *accueil* (West Africa: 'reception in honour of the arrival of a VIP').

2. There is a change at the level of connotation or denotation:

a) connotation   In Burkina-Faso, a *grincement* is 'the melodious sound of a stringed instrument'.
   In Togo, an *accoutrement* is 'an elegant outfit showing good taste'.
   In West Africa, a *charlatan* is 'a soothsayer and faith healer in whom one has complete trust'.
   The symbolism of the human body and of animals are African and different from that which the French words convey in France. *Son ventre est comme une forêt* (Ivory Coast, calque from Kwa languages) means: 'his thoughts are inpenetrable'. Throughout the Kwa area, along the coast of Benin, *l'araignée* (a male character in tales of the forest) incarnates craftiness, *la tortue* 'perfidy', *la pintade* 'laziness', *l'hyène* 'stupidity' and so on . . . different images from those of the tales of the savannah.

b) denotation   *Faux amis* or 'false friends' are extremely common for various reasons and the intricacies of their derivations have to be carefully followed. *Etal* being a table, a *vendeur à l'étalage* is *un tablier* (West Africa); *Gros* denotes riches and power – *gros français* (*recherché* French) is in opposition to *petit français* ('gibberish, approximative French'). A *gros mot* can therefore only be 'a very elegant word' (West Africa). *Pardon* accompanies a request, a shift in meaning, by contiguity, to that of any polite phrase conveying a situation of inferiority. By metonymy, in Burkina-Faso, *une berceuse* is a nanny. In Mali, *une gourde* does not evoke foolish behaviour but the 'buxom curves of a lady'. In the Ivory Coast, *l'accélérateur* is an aphrodisiac . . . These are like metaphors *in absentia* in which it is not always easy to discover the relationship between the two parts.

Specific local features (neologisms etc.)
Neologisms can originate from any of the following:

a) a change in grammatical class   The preposition *depuis*, said in a long high-pitched note [depyííí] (all countries) becomes an adverb meaning *depuis très longtemps*. The adverb *longtemps* (Cameroun) becomes a noun: *vieille fille*. The noun *acharnément* (Zaïre) becomes an adverb *avec acharnement*. The noun *façon* (Ivory Coast) becomes an adjective: *bizarre*, or an adverb *d'une drôle de façon*. The adjective *provisoire* (Togo) becomes a noun: *costume masculin sans doublure et à manches courtes*, the noun *moyen* (Mali, basilect) becomes the verb: *pouvoir*, and so on.

b) an abbreviation   A *filtrée* is more or less everywhere *une cigarette à bout filtre*. The apocopes *hippo, soutien, palu* are more usual than *hippopotame, soutien-gorge* and *paludisme*.

   Sapoti (Senegal) is *sapotille* and *GD* (Zaïre) is an example of both syncope and apocope: *gendarme*.

   Aphaeresis is less common: *gnon* (Ivory Coast, student slang) is *pognon*. *Traper son coeur* (Ivory Coast basilect, splitting *attraper son coeur*) means *tenter de reprendre son calme*.

c) reduplication   In some African languages, reduplication suggests distribution.

   Combien, combien (Ivory Coast, Mali, Zaïre) means *combien chaque unité?* *Cinq francs-cinq francs* means *cinq francs chaque unité*.

   But for many local languages reduplication is an intensifier: *un peu un peu* means *très peu, à peine un peu*; *chaud-chaud* when referring to an examination means *très difficile* and to a teacher means *extrêment sévère* (heat is locally more a source of annoyance than of pleasure!).

d) a derivation   This process is very productive and virtually knows no bounds. Whole families are developed. In the Ivory Coast, *griot* (a term mentioned in dictionaries) generates *griote, griotage, griotique, grioticien, griotège, grioticité* etc. And from *marabout* (also in the dictionary) are generated *maraboutage, maraboutal, maraboutique, maraboutisme* as well as the parasynthetics *démarabouter, démaraboutage* etc. (West Africa).

   French models are used – suffixation as in *hêtraie* from *hêtre: bamboussaie, teckeraie, ananeraie, avocateraie* etc. (Ivory Coast: *lieux plantés de bambous, de tecks, d'ananas, d'avocatiers . . .*). Prefixation is less common: *coépouse* (all countries: *l'une des épouses d'un polygame par rapport aux autres*), *contreveste* (Zaïre: *chemise, veste* etc.). Parasynthetics: *dévierger* (all countries: *déflorer*); *détribaliser* (Zaïre: *enlever le caractère tribal*). There are also some cases of regressive derivation. *Alphabète* (all countries, from *analphabète: personne qui sait lire et écrire*); *carent* (Senegal, Ivory Coast, from *carence*: *incompetent*) *compétir* (West Africa, from *compétition*: *concourir*, *participer à une compétition*) etc.

e) compounding   This is the process which is the most constructive. Hence we find numerous popular terms for flora and fauna (c.f. Lafage et al. 1987–8) *arbre à beurre, à calebasse, à cola, à encens, à farine, à fauve, à pain, à palabre* and so on. The process of compounding may also be straightforward juxtaposition: *arbre-miracle, arbre-parasol, arbre-parapluie* etc. (It is therefore often a sort of metasemesis by comparison.)

Popular terminology states firstly the generic and adds a specific characteristic: form, colour, use, place of origin etc.: *oiseau-lunettes, poisson-ceinture, singe vert, mangue-ananas, herbe à paillottes, cerise du Cayor, ver de Guinée, ananas de brousse* etc. At other times the adjective *faux* is placed in front of a commonplace noun in order to draw attention to a possible confusion: *faux-baobab, faux-cotonnier* for example. In some compositions there is a kind of *in praesentia* metaphor: *arachide de mer* (intersection: form, colour) – a marine animal of the sponge family; *fourmi-cadavre* (intersection: putrid smell) – *Palthothyreus tarsatus*, a large black ant which gives off a nauseating smell when crushed; *dollar des sables* (intersection: form, value) – a gold or silver pendant in the shape of the skeleton of a sea-urchin (*Radiorotula*), the size of a gold coin.

Some compound formations are more familiar: *madame-bagages* (Mali: porter), *madame-panier* (Central Africa: 'a street-urchin, a hooligan'), *deux doigts* (Ivory Coast: 'shoplifter'), *tiens pour toi* (Zaïre: 'a bonus'), *fais-nous-fais* (Ivory Coast: 'if you give us some money, we will do what you want' – a formula making it plain to someone that the service requested will not be entirely free of charge).

There is also an abundance of phrases inspired by, or adapted from, what is said in a group of languages without being the faithful calque of any precise language in particular: *donner la route* (all countries: a phrase whereby a host allows his guests to leave), *boire le feu* (Burkina-Faso: 'to lose face'), *avoir une mémoire de poule* (Cameroun, Mali: 'to have a short memory'), *refroidir son coeur* (Ivory Coast, basilectal variant: *froidir son coeur*, re- being interpreted as a repetition of the action, 'to try to calm one's temper or violent emotion').

f) borrowing   We have seen examples of loan words taken from non-local languages – English, Portuguese, Arabic etc (see above, p. 230). There are few loan words from African languages which are found all over Africa. If they are, then they will often already have been integrated into French: *boubou, balafon, banco, karité, néré* etc., and will generally originate from languages such as Wolof (with which they have been in contact for a very long time) or Mande (functioning as a *lingua franca* for the greater part of western Africa). Usually, there will be a great many loan words and they will reveal the dominant languages in a country or a region. Thus, virtually all loan words from African languages of the Ivory Coast come from the four national languages – Dioula/Mande firstly, then Agni/Baoulé, with Bété and Tyembara (Sénoufo) not being very common at all. A common African reality will carry different denominations from one country to another, the link being established by a French neologism. The famous *jeu à douze cases* is called: *adji* (Benin, from Fon), *a kidada* (Togo, from Ewe), *awalé/walé* (Ivory Coast, Kwa languages), *wouri* (Senegal, Mali, from Mande), *dara* (Niger, from Hausa), *dili* (Niger, from Zerma), *igisoro* (Rwanda, from Kinyarwanda) etc. The *bois blanc* of *Antiaris africana*, which is used as commonly as pine is in France, is called: *ako* (in the Ivory Coast) and *wawa* (in Togo). 'Palm wine alcohol' is *koutoukou* (Ivory Coast), *sodabi* (Togo, from the name of the infantryman who, in 1918, introduced the still into this area), and *patassi* (Burkina-Faso).

In the same country, loans from different languages may compete with each other: in Togo, millet beer: *tchapalo* (*tyapalo, kyapalo, kyap* etc., from various Voltaic languages), but also *dolo* (from Mande).

g) hybridisation   Two elements from different languages are associated to form a neologism (by derivation or by composition).

– An English word with a French suffix: *boyesse* (all countries: 'a nanny'), *boyerie* (all countries: 'living accommodation for household staff').

– An African word with a French suffix: *banabanisme* (West Africa: from the Wolof *banabana*, a pedlar, meaning 'a pedlar's activities', often used pejoratively).

Few African morphemes are added to French lexemes, except in hybrid varieties. Prefixion resulting in a hybrid is rare: *antitoubab* (Ivory Coast: *anti-blanc, anti-français*) and most parasynthetics cannot be considered as hybrids because the original foreign word which serves as the base is generally acknowledged in French dictionaries (cf. *démarabouter*).

Hybrid compound formation is common: *faux-iroko* (*Antiaris africana*, Togo), *fourmi-magnan* (association of the French generic and the Mande word for *Annoma nigricans*), *taxi-mbar* (Senegal: from the Wolof *mbar* 'tent, shelter', meaning a van with a covered platform for the transport of passengers), *rat-toto* (Mali, Ivory Coast, Mande: *toto* designates the Gambia rat, *Cricetomys gambianus*, also called *rat-voleur*).

Faire le nnam (Cameroun, Bamileke: 'to show favouritism towards certain tribes'), *faire kpakpato* (Ivory Coast, colloquial, from the Baul: 'to deceive someone with flattery and lies'), *faire le upeye* (Cameroun, pidgin English: 'to abuse one's position of superiority').

h) a calque   We shall use the term calque when comparison with the language of origin shows irrefutably that there is literal translation and not free interpretation or allusion, and for this reason all our examples will be taken from Togo (Ewe language; Lafage 1985):

> *gâter l'oreille* (egble to na m: il a gâté oreille pour moi – donner de mauvais conseils), *couper le sein* [eɖe anɔ lè ɖevi-sí]: elle a coupé sein à son enfant – sévrer), *penser dans sa tête* [ebu ta–me]: il a pensé tête-dans – réfléchir), *rester calebasse* (etsi tre: il est resté calebasse – rester célibataire), *manger la tête du chat* ([eɖû awi–ta]: il a mangé chat-tête – être enroué, avoir un chat dans la gorge).

Conclusion

The study of popular African varieties provides a laboratory situation (in C. Hagege's words) in the sense that it enables one to understand, as they are developing, some of the processes which can result in a creole. The analysis of particular lexical features of French in Africa is neither complete nor perfect. We have to wait and see what is revealed by the extension of the survey to the Congo, to Gabon, to Guinea, Mauritania, Djibouti and the Comoros. The study of loan words needs to be taken further; we need research with a diachronic dimension, standardised transcriptions, an examination of cryptotypes and broader study of sociosemantics. A comparison with recent and current surveys, in the Indian Ocean, the Caribbean, the Maghreb, the Pacific and elsewhere where French was a colonial language, should enable us to establish areas of divergence and areas of consensus within French.

It must be stressed that the research in which both African and European researchers have been engaged is linguistic description; they are not dealing only with humour, folklore or 'third-rate French' as some purists have apparently feared. All the attested processes of change are the same (metaplasms, metataxes, metasememes, metalogisms) as those by which the spoken and written French language has gradually been formed and has evolved over the centuries.

Openness towards the outside world, enrichment through a dialogue of cultures and adaptation to the language of other civilisations seem the only way, nowadays, that any language can claim to be an international language.

Text

Monnè, outrages et défis

AHMADOU DOUROUMA

Béma entra dans la campagne électorale comme son totem l'hippopotame plonge dans le bief: de grands ploufs et plafs éclaboussèrent et secouèrent tout le pays; des fromagers des volées de vautours et de gendarmes se levèrent. La tête enrubannée, drapé dans un grand boubou amidonné, suivi par une foule de griots, de tam-tamistes et de balafonistes, il sortait de son palais après la troisième prière, s'arrêtait sur la petite place attenante au Bolloda. Ses joueurs organisaient un cercle et tambourinaient. Au centre, Béma faisait caracoler le cheval, lui faisait exécuter des écarts, des courbettes et des cabrioles en réponse aux dithyrambes des griots. A la fin la bête se cabrait, Béma faisait interrompre le vacarme et le spectacle, se dressait sur les étriers, invectivait les déhontés de la case de l'agonie en montrant du doigt la case de Mariam.

'Je vous défie tous et vous attend. Qu'un seul sorte du repaire et vienne pour que dans un duel franc au sabre et dans un franc concours hippique nous montrions au peuple qui est le meilleur, lequel mérite le mieux la confiance des Malinkés.' Un instant de silence: personne ne paraissait. Il criait, triomphant: 'Lâches, tous des fils de lâches. Pas un seul parmi vous n'a du solide entre les jambes. Les gens de chez nous jamais n'écouteront un côtier, jamais ils ne voteront pour un *boussman* inféodé à un autre côtier, Houphouët, un petit bonhomme chef d'un minuscule canton. On dit que Houphouët fait trembler les Blancs, jamais un vrai Keita, un incirconcis, un croyant, un authentique Keita comme Béma ne le craindra.' Il injuriait les deux maudits de notre race qui soutenaient la candidature d'un cadre comme Touboug inféodé à un infidèle comme Houphouët.

Avec sarcasmes, il disait pourquoi il ne parlerait pas des travers de son grand frère, tout le monde les connaissait. Brusquement il pouffait, le rire se communiquait aux auditeurs: il annonçait la brouille prochaine, très prochaine entre son frère et ses associés dans la débauche: comment partager quelque chose avec celui qui ne se rassasie pas?

Avec indignation et colère, il parlait de la petite non incisée qui se livrait à la honterie et transgressait les interdits. C'est elle et ses semblables qui ont amené la sécheresse et les autres manques qui nous fatiguent. 'Nous serons toujours dans le malheur tant que de telles filles ne seront pas brûlées sur les immondices, les hommes qui les consomment déshabillés, flagellés et promenés avec les pantalons sur les têtes jusqu'à ce qu'ils renoncent publiquement à leur péché.'

Il quittait le cercle de danse; les badauds, les tam-tams et les griots se levaient et le suivaient: le spectacle recommençait avec les mêmes défis et injures au prochain arrêt.

Un jour, dans les invectives contre les incirconcis, les non-incisées, les cafres, les ennemis du Tout-Puissant, il commanda aux collecteurs de la capitation et recruteurs d'interdire les chemins de nos montagnes et des villages aux propagandistes des *boussmen* étrangers. Les collecteurs et les recruteurs se heurtèrent à des résistances aux abords des villages: il y eut des coups de feu et aussi des morts, les premiers de la nouvelle ère qui s'annonçait pour notre pays de peine.

Les derniers jours de la campagne électorale, Béma abandonna le cheval et se fit conduire dans la voiture que les colons toubabs du Sud lui avaient envoyée afin qu'il paraisse aussi riche que Touboug qui, des semaines durant, avait parcouru les circonscriptions de la colonie en grosse Buick rouge. La veille des élections, Béma organisa un grand festin sur la place du marché pour tous ceux qui dans la vie n'avaient jamais, une seule fois encore, mangé à leur faim, c'est-à-dire pratiquement nous tous. Il nous offrit d'avaler du riz bien cuit et pimenté aux oignons et *soumara*, de déchirer de la viande avec nos canines. Nous nous sommes ballonnés au point que nos ventres ont retenti comme la peau de tam-tam bien tendue et longuement chauffée; la générosité ne troubla point, ne changea rien à nos décisions: nous n'avons jamais eu la reconnaissance du ventre.

(From Ahmadou Kourouma, *Monnè, outrages et défis*, Paris: Seuil, 1990)

Pas de note de l'auteur. Deux mots seulement sont écrits en italique: c'est-à-dire *boussman* pl. *boussmen*: *littéral*, les hommes de la brousse, expression péjorative par laquelle les peuples de la savane comme les Malinkés désignent les populations forestières du Sud. *Soumara*: mot bambara désignant un condiment odorant à base de graines de néré, appelé aussi *moutarde de néré*.
totem: animal protecteur d'un groupe ethnique et qui fait donc l'objet d'un interdit, *fromager*: grand arbre de la famille des Bombacées à contreforts caractéristiques, *gendarmes*: petits passereaux destructeurs des récoltes, *grande boubou*: tenue traditionnelle masculine d'apparat, en basin blanc décoré à l'encolure de broderies, *tamtamistes*: batteurs de tam-tam, *balafonistes*: joueurs de balafon, *Bolloda*: palais royal, *déhontés*: personnes considérées comme la honte du royaume, *agonie*: femme couverte d'opprobes, *avoir du solide entre les jambes*: être un homme véritable, *côtier*: personne originaire de la côte ivoirienne, *cafre*: païen, *non incisée*: non excisée et cousue, selon la coutume, *honterie*: débauche, *fatiguer*: détruire, anéantir, *incirconcis*: homme qui n'a pas subi la circoncision, soit parce qu'il est encore trop jeune soit parce qu'il est étranger au groupe, équivalent masculin de *non-incisée*, colons-*toubabs*: colons français.

13

French in Canada
MICHEL BLANC

Introduction

By the Official Languages Act (1969) Canada recognised English and French as having equal status in Parliament and the Canadian government, in the federal administration, judicial bodies and crown corporations. This 'institutional bilingualism', which is not to be confused with individuals' ability to operate in these two languages, has since been extended to one province, New Brunswick, which is officially bilingual in English and French, and to some institutions, notably in the areas of law and education, in other provinces. Quebec, however, while being institutionally bilingual in federal matters, recognises only French as the official language of the province (Bill 101 or Charter of the French Language; see Tetley 1986). Before examining the implications of institutional English–French bilingualism and of the presence of speakers of other languages (allophones) for the French language in Canada, it is first necessary to look briefly at the history, the geographical distribution, and the main linguistic characteristics of Canadian French. In what follows I will adopt an interdisciplinary approach, looking at Canadian French from the standpoints of linguistics, sociolinguistics, and the sociology and social psychology of language.

A brief history of French settlements in Canada

In the early seventeenth century France founded two colonies in North America: Acadia, on the Atlantic seaboard, roughly corresponding to today's Nova Scotia, New Brunswick and Prince Edward Island; and New France, at one time covering most of the North American continent, the strip of land extending along the banks of the St Lawrence being loosely known as Canada, and its French population calling themselves *canadiens* or *habitants*. By the Treaty of Utrecht in 1713 France surrendered Acadia to England: in 1755 the English dispossessed and

239

deported two-thirds of the Acadians to New England (*le grand dérange-ment*), some of whom found their way to Louisiana, whose descendants are still called Cajuns /kadʒɛ̃/). Many of the exiles later returned and settled in Acadia. According to the 1981 census (Statistics Canada 1981) 273,550 Acadians (or 16.6 per cent of the population of the three provinces) claimed French as their mother tongue.[1]

The French population of Canada, which was less than 13,000 in 1695, had risen to 70,000 in 1763 when, by the Treaty of Paris, it became a British colony. The break with the 'mother country' was catastrophic for the *habitants* and their language. The power vacuum left by the depar-ture of French elites was filled by British colonials, and English became the language of government, administration and commerce. English domination was to be reinforced by successive waves of diverse anglo-phone immigration, which threatened the space, the culture and the language of the *canadiens*. The Constitutional Act of 1791 divided Canada into anglophone Upper Canada and francophone Lower Can-ada but, following the *patriotes*' rebellion of 1837, the Act of Union (1840) established the Province of Canada with a single Assembly made up of equal representation from Upper and (the more populated) Lower Canada, making English the only official language, thus 'minorising' the French population and language. By the 1867 British North America Act, however, Canada became a Dominion composed of four provinces, Ontario, Quebec, Nova Scotia and New Brunswick. French was made official in federal laws and in the federal Assembly, but anglophone districts were set up in Quebec with representatives in the provincial assembly. In the towns the French intelligentsia became bilingual, while the new urban proletariate spoke a more and more anglicised form of French, especially at the lexical level. Rural Quebec, the majority of the province, withdrew into itself, its conservative elites extolling the virtues of (Roman Catholic) faith, family, farming and French. Only a very high birthrate (65 per 1000), the so-called *revanche des berceaux*, enabled francophones to survive in large numbers, despite emigration to western Canada and the United States provoked by overpopulation and shortage of land or labour at home. In the 1981 census, 150 years later, 6,176,215 people declared French as their mother tongue in the whole of Canada (or 25.6 per cent of the total population) of which 5,248,440 lived in Quebec (or 82.4 per cent of the province) and 651,550 in Ontario and western Canada (4.2 per cent) (Statistics Canada, 1981). We will return to geo- and demo-linguistic issues later in this chapter (below, pp. 248ff.).

Geographical distribution of French speakers

The early settlers of Acadia and New France came chiefly from western France and the dialects they spoke reflected the linguistic situation prevailing in the seventeenth and eighteenth centuries. Over half the Acadians came from south of the Loire, whereas half the Canadians originated north of the Loire, which accounts for many of the differences between today's two closely related varieties, Acadian and Canadian French. However, these settlers did not establish linguistically distinct communities: as a result, there was convergence of the regional dialects (Dulong 1973) and, ultimately, formation of an 'immigrant koine' (Siegel 1985), not unlike Standard French, but independent of the latter's influence after immigration from France had stopped. However, this colonial French was in turn subject to the normative influence, at first of the local elites, later of educational standardisation. From 1763 on, the French language in both Acadia and Canada was in contact and conflict with Canadian English. (On the first hundred years of French–English contacts see Bouthillier and Meynaud 1972; Noel 1990; for the relationships between French varieties in Canada see Haden 1973 and figure 13.1.)

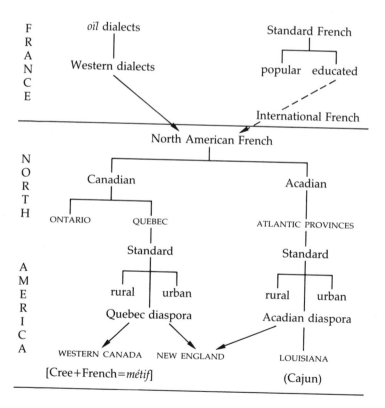

Figure 13.1 Origins and relationships of French language varieties in North America

In Canada today, it is convenient to distinguish four main linguistic regions where French is used in varying degrees of contact with, and interference from English.

(i) In the Atlantic Provinces of New Brunswick (where it has official provincial status), Nova Scotia and Prince Edward Island (where it survives in a few isolates), Acadian French is the direct descendant of Acadian dialects. In rural and fishing communities it is characterised by many archaic forms. (For a linguistic treatment see Massignon 1962 and Péronnet 1989; for a study of the relationship of Acadian to other French dialects in North America, see Valdman 1980; Prujiner et al. (1984) explore French–English contact; and for illustrations, see texts 12 and 13 below). In the towns, Acadian is closer to Canadian French (see below), ranging from an educated variety to a vernacular called *chiac* (from the place-name Shediac), spoken by adolescents who wish to express their cultural distinctiveness from, on the one hand, traditional Acadians and, on the other, Quebec or French models, which are perceived as alien: it is a mixed code with strong lexical and syntactic borrowings from English (Blanc 1982).

(ii) West of Ontario live minority French-speaking communities (French mother-tongue population: 183,675) who are descendants of immigrants from Quebec: they are facing assimilation to English Canada, except in areas of heavy concentration, where they are fighting for cultural and linguistic survival through the *Fédération des Francophones hors Québec* (Federation of Francophones outside Quebec 1978). A unique group are the Métis, of mixed American–Indian and French descent, who speak a mixed Cree–French code called *métif* (pronounced /mItʃIf/). Papen (1987) has described its syntax as 'half French' and 'half Cree', the noun group following French *métis* dialect grammatical rules, the verb group following Cree rules. This mixed syntactic structure raises fundamental questions for linguistic theory.

(iii) Franco-Ontarians (French mother-tongue population 467,885 in 1981) have lived in Ontario since the beginning of the French regime in (Upper) Canada. In counties where they are in the majority (eastern Ontario bordering on Quebec) and have institutional support, they are more likely to use French in the home and, as a result, attrition is low. At school pupils use French and their French contains fewer anglicisms. Elsewhere, where francophones are in a minority, acculturation to English is pervasive, the shift to English increases in the home. Children communicate with each other in English in French-medium schools and anglicisms (of form and meaning) begin to creep into their French, which is characterised by a tendency to morphological simplification and regularisation (e.g. generalisation of *avoir* as sole past tense auxiliary, deletion of reflexive pronoun in pronominal verbs, etc. (See Mougeon and Beniak 1991.)

(iv) Finally, in Quebec where francophones are in a majority of 4 to 1, the French language varies along a number of interacting dimensions: geographically, there is a distinction between rural and urban French, the former more archaic, the latter more 'advanced' and open to the influence of English; socially, it varies according to age and gender, the educational level of the speakers, and the importance of language in their professional activity, as measured by the 'linguistic market index' (Sankoff and Laberge 1978); and according to register (medium, level of formality, situation, topic, and so on). According to these parameters Quebec French varies from a standard close to Standard Educated (SEF) or International French to an archaic rural dialect or an advanced urban sociolect more or less influenced by English. A characteristic behaviour of many educated Quebecers who come from a rural or urban background is their ability to switch from standard to vernacular and back again as a sign of identification with one group or another in a given situation. On rural speech the reader should consult Dulong and Bergeron (1980); on urban speech there are two main corpus-based sociolinguistic studies: Deshaies (1981) on the speech of working-class and middle-class adolescents in two districts of Quebec City; and Thibault (1980) and Lemieux and Cedergren's (1985) variationist analysis of Montreal French, the last two being diachronic as well as synchronic in their approach to social variation.

Quebec French has been the main object of study by linguists under the name of Canadian French (Walker 1979). We will now briefly sketch the main defining characteristics of Canadian French in its popular urban variety. To date, phonology and lexis have been the main focus of attention.

Chief characteristics of urban Canadian French (CF)

Phonology

Important defining characteristics are:
– the affrication of dental plosives before close front vowels:
  /t/ + /i, y/ → [ts] e.g. [pətsi] *petit*. [tsy] *tu*
  /d/ + /i, y/ → [dz] e.g. [dzi] *dis*. [dzy] *du*
– the reduction of final consonant clusters (categorial rule):
  simp(le), probab(le), aut(re), touris(me), jus(te)
– the elision of /l/ and /r/, with vowel lengthening, can have morpho-phonemic implications, e.g. compare:
  [sa:tab] *s(ur l)a tab(le)* with [satab] *sa tab(le)*
This affects the phonotactic and rhythmic quality of CF.

– the opening of vowels in closed syllables, with medial vocalic elision (syncope) in polysyllabic words, e.g.:

[pɪp] *pipe*, [tʊt] *tout*, [dzɪfsɪl] *difficile*, [lɪtsratsYr] *littérature*

– diphthongisation of long vowels, e.g.:

[ʃawr] *char* (car), [ʃæiz] *chaise*, [ʃɔwz] *chose*, [pɪjr] *pire*

– /wa/ → [we] in *moi, toi, bois, doigt*, etc.

– nasalised vowels have undergone a systematic shift, rotating in a clockwise direction compared to SEF:

/ẽ ← ɛ̃ ← æ̃ ← ã ← ɔ̃ ← õ/

– vowel lengthening in pretonic position gives CF its basic rhythm with two stresses, initial and final, and syncope.

(For a more thorough treatment see Gendron 1966.)

Morphology

The main defining characteristic is the analogical regularisation of the morphology, e.g.:

– differentiation of feminine and masculine forms of the adjective: *avare–avarde, pointu–pointuse, pourri–pourrite*

– regularisation of plural markers: *mal–mals, cheval–chevals*

– extension of auxiliary *avoir* to all verbs in perfect tense

– levelling of vocalic alternation in present tense, e.g. *bois–boivons*, or of the stem final /z/: *disez, faisez, ils s'assisent*

– different gender from SEF: *escalier, été, hiver, hotel* are feminine, while *erreur, auto, oie*, are masculine: English loans are often feminine: *une gang, une job*

On the feminisation of professions see Martin and Dupuis (1985).

Syntax

Among the many differences between CF and SEF are:

– use of emphatic particle *là* [lɒ] suffixed to a phrase or clause, but pronounced on a lower tone, e.g. *tu l'as, là*

– use of periphrastic verb phrases, e.g. *être à faire, être après faire*, in the sense of *en train de faire*

– tense usage: conditional for subjunctive, or after *si*

– insertion of interrogative marker *ti* [tsɪ] in both polar and wh-questions: *tu vas-ti bien? où c'est-ti que tu vas?*

– word order in imperative phrase: *dis-moi-le-(pas)*

Some of these morphological and syntactic features are also found in popular French in France.

Lexis

This is the best-researched aspect of CF (Juneau and Poirier 1979). The lexicon is defined by three main characteristic features: archaisms: neologisms and loan words.

a) *Archaisms*. Canadian French has inherited a large vocabulary from its western French dialectal origins, which either no longer exists in SEF (e.g. *pinte*; *poudrerie* = *tempête de neige*) or else exists but with a different meaning from SEF: *espérer* ('to wait'); *la porte est barrée* ('locked').

b) *Neologisms*: the enormous effort by the *Conseil de la Langue Française* to produce a French-based scientific and technological vocabulary (see p. 246 below) has resulted in great terminological innovations, which are the envy of the French themselves. It is also to be noted that, because CF is less under the influence of normative pressures than SEF, it has exploited lexical derivation more freely, using such suffixes as *-able, -eux, -erie, -age* and so on, to create many new words.

c) *Anglicisms*: apart from English loan words, e.g. *fun, chum, gang, brakes, checker* ('control'), etc., and loan translations or calques (*fin de semaine, chien chaud, annonces classées*, compared to *week-end, hot dog, petites annonces*, in France), CF has many loanshifts, e.g. *voteur, éducationnel, les politiques, actuel*, in the sense of 'actual', *faire une application*, etc. (On Quebec lexis see Paquot 1988; on anglicisms Edwards 1973.) The use of anglicisms in speech varies widely as a function of the social dimensions already referred to; its extension has been greatly exaggerated.

No domain is more indicative of the vitality, expressiveness and creativity of the spoken language than the use of swear-words or *sacres* (based on religious vocabulary) with which Quebecers pepper their informal speech. It is a phenomenon so pervasive that it passes almost unnoticed in ordinary circumstances. The list is endless, but the most frequent basic words are *calice, Christ, ciboire, hostie, sacrement, tabernacle*, usually modified, sometimes euphemistically disguised (there exist conversion tables of *sacres* into numbers, e.g. *Christ = dix*). They can be uttered together in a string of interjections, linked or not by *de* (*hostie de criss de ciboire de tabernak!*: *il l'a crissé* ('struck') *là, l'hostie!*), relexified as nouns, adjectives, verbs and adverbs (of intensity); they are highly productive by means of derivation (e.g. *desaintciboiriser*). The use of *sacres* has been seen as an expression of an individual's sense of identity (see Vincent 1982; Légaré and Bougaieff 1984; and texts 7 and 8 below, for examples).

The existence of several varieties of French in Canada and the impact of English on the language, especially in the lexical field, raise the controversial question of which French should be chosen as a standard: in other words the question of the 'norm'.

The issue of a sociolinguistic norm[2]

Ever since the conquest of New France by Britain two fundamental issues have confronted francophones with respect to their language: the survival of French in contact and conflict with English, on the one hand, and its relationship with the French of France in their search for a standard, on the other. Although these are twin issues, the first will be examined separately in the next section on language planning. Here we will consider the much-debated question of a French Canadian 'norm'. As expected, the debate has raged between the supporters of linguistic unity predicated upon the legitimate educated French of France (Standard Educated French) or of a supranational standard (*le français international*), and the partisans of linguistic variety, most of whom opt for the choice of a French Canadian standard rooted in native soil.

The dominance of 'hexagonal' French norm prevailed well into the 1970s. Quebec's 'cultural revolution', for all its ideology of liberation, was accompanied by an ethnolinguistic mobilisation which included the 'revalorisation' of a hitherto stigmatised language; this led to demands for the modernisation, standardisation and 'purification' of French. Set up by the Charter of the French Language in 1977 (Bill 101) the *Conseil* and *Office de la Langue Française* not only promoted veritable 'industries de la langue' (producing new terminologies for all sectors of the economy, for example), but also fought for the 'qualité de la langue' in every walk of life ('bien parler, c'est se respecter' was the slogan of two decades), but more especially in education and the media. Nothing is more symptomatic of this attitude than the publication of the *Dictionnaire correctif du français au Canada* (Dulong 1968), a twentieth-century *Appendix Probi* ('Do not say, say . . . '), banning anglicisms and hundreds of native (*canayens*) words, sparing only 'canadianismes de bon aloi'. It remains, paradoxically, a good guide to the real lexical usage of that period. Contrast with that impoverished lexicon the *Dictionnaire de la langue québécoise* (Bergeron 1980), published twenty-two years later, which claims to include 'tout le français moderne' plus 'des milliers de mots . . . qui sont propres au français du Québec, sans parler de toute la créativité quotidienne dont font preuve les Québécois pas trop influencés par un conformisme stérilisant' (Préface; compare Poirier 1985).

Throughout the period another battle was joined: that between the purists and the users and/or defenders of that illusive popular variety known as *joual* (popular transliteration of *cheval*; see Jean Marcel

(Paquette)'s ironic *Le Joual de Troie*, 1973, and texts 10 and 11 below). The political existence of *joual* goes back to the decision of the 'Parti Pris' group of writers in the early 1960s to repatriate Quebec culture from France. For some of its users its main characteristic is the accent or the pronunciation; for others it is the presence of bad speech and anglicisms (see texts 10–11 below). To its detractors this jargon is a sign of low class, vulgarity, lack of education, corruption, of degeneracy even: 'Autorisa-tion, pour deux ans, de tuer à bout portant tout fonctionnaire, tout ministre, tout professeur, tout curé, qui parle joual', exclaims (tongue in cheek) the pseudonymous author of *Les Insolences du Frère Untel*. For its defenders, 'parler joual, écrire joual, chanter joual' became a rallying cry, the language of anger for some Quebec nationalists and writers, synonymous with a Quebec in search of an identity (see, for example, Michel Tremblay's use of Montreal working-class French and May 1985).

But what of Quebecers' attitudes to their own and other people's speech?[3] A number of surveys were conducted by sociolinguists and social psychologists of language in the 1970s. D'Anglejan and Tucker (1973) found that 243 subjects (students, teachers and factory workers) did not perceive SEF as more attractive than CF and were less ready to accept criticism of their own speech from a European than from a Quebecer. Nevertheless they rated EF higher on personality traits and professional occupation. Three years later, in a similar investigation, educated CF speakers were rated more highly than SEF speakers on personality traits. In another experiment (Bourhis et al. 1975) Montreal schoolchildren approved a Quebecer interviewee when she used CF to answer two journalists (one speaking CF, the other SEF), while they strongly disapproved when she switched to SEF to answer the SEF journalist, thus accommodating to his speech. This would seem to indicate that, although SEF might still be perceived as more prestigious, it was becoming less attractive than CF in terms of personality and speaker-accommodation.

In a sociolinguistic investigation by in-depth interviews of adolescents in Quebec city, drawn from two different districts, one (Sainte-Foy) socially higher than the other (Saint-Sauveur), Deshaies (1981) and her team found interesting differences in their subjects' attitudes to their own and others' ways of speaking (see texts 1 to 8 for examples). For the Sainte-Foy adolescents the reference group was Quebec society as a whole; they perceived their own speech as 'ordinaire', 'normal', 'comme tout le monde' and their betters as not different from themselves, except teachers of French, whose speech was 'better' than their own. The Saint-Sauveur subjects, on the other hand, had two reference groups, Quebec society and their in-group. Relative to the former they speak badly ('mal'), but in terms of their own group they speak correctly ('correct'). In relation to society, therefore, they seem to suffer from linguistic insecurity: but not all of them: some reject correct speech, even for themselves (text 8).

However divided these social groups are on their attitudes to what constitutes 'good', 'bad', or 'normal' speech, it would appear from the preceding investigations, and others, that there is now a consensus on the question of 'which standard: French from France or Canadian?' It can only be a Canadian one. A decade later the official *Bulletin du Conseil de la Langue Française* writes: 'Il y a maintenant consensus au Québec: il existe un français standard d'ici et sa description constitue la prochaine étape obligée du projet collectif québécois d'aménagement de la langue' (Summer–Autumn 1990, p.3). The guardians of the quality of the French language in Quebec have come a long way since 1975 when one of their leading members could write: 'La forme officielle de la langue française au Quebec doit être le plus près possible du français de France' (Corbeil 1975, p.33). To what extent this change in attitudes to the 'norm' reflects Quebec's new language-planning policies is a question we examine in the next section.

Language planning in Canada, with special reference to Quebec[4]

Ever since their conquest by the British (see above) the francophones in Canada in general, and in Quebec in particular, have felt that they were members of an ethnolinguistic minority threatened by the economic, demographic and cultural domination of English-speaking Canada. During and after World War II the rapid industrialisation of Quebec society forced French speakers to leave the land and compete for jobs in anglophone-dominated cities. But while they were becoming involved in the modernisation of their society, they felt increasingly resentful of their subordinate status in a country where they were in a majority. The 'Quiet (economic) Revolution' had been accompanied by the emergence of a distinctive *québécois* cultural, linguistic, literary, artistic revival. It raised high expectations, which were not realised, and this led to the emergence of an independence movement which rallied round the language question. The French language was the last bastion of Franco-Canadian and *québécois* identity. But it was threatened, first by the isolation and the decline in numbers of the francophones outside Quebec, who were being assimilated to English in spite of improved bilingual services provided by the federal government. Second, by demographic changes within Quebec itself: the catastrophic fall in their birthrate meant that francophones could no longer rely on the rural-based *revanche des berceaux* to compensate for the growth of the anglophone population, swollen by the immigration of allophones, who spoke neither French nor English, but assimilated to the anglophone community. Third, these immigrants were granted the freedom to choose the language of instruction for their children and, for the majority of them, this meant English-medium schools. Fourth, in Quebec as in the rest of Canada, English was the dominant language of the economy, which was in the hands of Anglo-Canadians. Moreover, the Report of the Royal Commission on Bilingualism and Biculturalism (1967) had shown that francophones were discriminated against in industry and commerce. English, not French, was necessary for advancement and upward social mobility (Gendron 1972). As we have seen (pp. 242–3 above) some 90 per cent of all French-speaking Canadians lived in an area 1,500 kilometres long, from eastern Ontario to New Brunswick, with Quebec at the centre. Beyond this area, east and west, there were scattered francophone communities. Gone was the nineteenth-century pattern of English and French communities intermingled within the same region. Such a pattern remained only in the 'Bilingual Belt' around the borders of Quebec (Cartwright and Williams 1982); but contrary to what had happened before, when the French assimilated small communities of Irish, Scottish and even English origin, the shift was now towards English (Vallee and Dufour 1974). As Joy (1972) has shown, linguistic assimilation to English is a function of ethnic density, the type of environment (rural versus urban), age, and exogamy. Anglicisation coincides with the period of early adulthood, when young francophones seek work in an anglophone-dominated urban environment and marry an English-speaking spouse. English will almost invariably be spoken in the home and be the mother tongue of the next generation.

Canada was witnessing a growing geographical concentration and separation of the two official language communities. This territorial polarisation has crucial implications for language planning. The state, whether federal or provincial, has two possible solutions: it can either guarantee individual rights, e.g. the right to education in the language of one's choice; or it can separate the two communities, each with its own language, with guarantees for linguistic minorities. The first option was, and still is, the federal institutional response. The second was Quebec's solution: making French the sole official language of the province and the language of work by a series of Bills (Bill 63 in 1969; Bill 22 in 1974; Bill 101, also known as the Charter of the French Language, in 1977). Thus, French became not just a means of communication; it became an instrument of power, a way of gaining control of the economy and education by securing its future and that of French culture in Quebec. Language-planning was implemented through three governmental agencies: (1) the *Office de la Langue Française* (OLF) was given a mandate to define policy and carry out research in sociolinguistics, neology and terminology; it was also empowered to issue or cancel 'francisation certificates' which firms required for doing business in Quebec. As the lack of French terminology in the world of work was the main obstacle to the francisation process, it set up terminology committees. (2) The OLF's role was also to monitor difficulties encountered in the implementation of Bill 101. (3) The *Commission de Surveillance et des Enquêtes* was set up to deal with violations of the language laws.

Let us now consider whether the Charter of the French language has fundamentally modified the use of French, English and other languages by the various communities in Quebec. In particular, has it halted the trend of assimilation to English? What has been its impact on schooling in French? What has been its influence on the status of the French language? Although it is too early to come to firm answers and reach definite conclusions, recent censuses and surveys suggest certain trends and directions. We will examine macro-studies first.

Censuses

The 1981 and 1986 census figures suggest that Quebec continues to become more French and the rest of Canada more English, thus confirming earlier trends (see figure 13.2, which gives for 1981 a graphic picture of the degree of assimilation to English by province; see also de Vries 1986, Lachapelle 1987 and Henripin 1988). French just manages to hold its ground overall, increases slightly in Quebec (where its losses to English are exactly compensated for by the gains made at the expense of third languages). In the other provinces its vitality varies from weak to very weak, except in New Brunswick, where its strength is remarkable, and in Ontario, where, after falling between 1971 and 1981, the numbers of francophones increased very slightly in 1986. The slight increase of French mother tongue and home language speakers in Quebec since 1971 cannot be attributed with any degree of certainty to the language legislation, but is encouraging. So is the probable effect of official bilingual policy in New Brunswick.

Use of French by francophones and anglophones

Since Bill 101 guarantees the right of customers to be served or informed in French, the language of client/salesman interactions was investigated in experiments in Montreal (Bourhis and Genesee 1980). The results showed that, Bill 101 notwithstanding, the salesman was expected to follow the situational norm, that is, he should respond in the language in which he is addressed by the customer, whether in French or in English; in other words, 'the customer is always right'. Bourhis (1984) discovered from field studies in Montreal that anglophone students

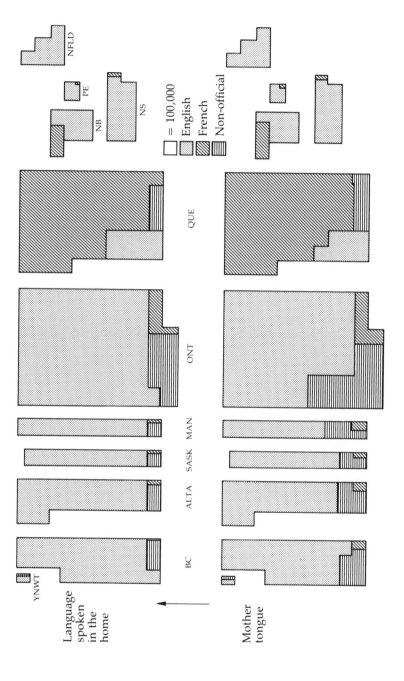

Figure 13.2 Relative demographic strength in 1981 of official and non-official language groups for each of the provinces of Canada showing shift from mother tongue to language spoken in the home (Blanc 1986)

were more likely to be helped in English by francophones than were francophones to be helped in French by anglophones. He tentatively concluded that by increasing the status of French in Quebec Bill 101 may have made francophones more secure in their linguistic and cultural identity and made English a less threatening language (cf. Berry et al. 1977). In a more recent study, Cartwright (1987) showed that young anglophones have greater ability in French and use it more frequently at work and with friends than do older anglophones. Their attitudes towards greater participation in Quebec society have improved and their interactions with francophones have increased. This progress has been confirmed by the president of the English rights lobby group, Alliance Quebec, who concludes that the increasing bilinguality of young anglophone Montrealers might slow down the outward migration of Anglo-Quebecers. It should be added that, according to the 1981 census, 53 per cent of Quebec anglophones declared a knowledge of French, compared to less than 38 per cent in 1971. This is no doubt the result of 'immersion programmes', for which there is a growing demand. Finally, between 1974 and 1984 the proportion of allophone immigrant children in French schools has increased from 20 per cent to 65 per cent (Bourhis and Sachdev, 1989), a situation directly attributable to the language legislation.

French as the language of work

Although most Quebec firms now seem to have obtained their 'Francisation Certificate', the progress of French as the language of work has been slow (on the use of French in firms see Deshaies and Hamers 1982 and de Villers 1990). English is still the language of business in North America, and the advancement of Quebecers is dependent on French–English bilingual competence.

Conclusion

Who could have predicted that after four centuries, the French language would have survived in Canada, in spite of English and Anglo-Canadian domination in the economic and political domains? It owed this survival first to its relative rural and cultural isolation as well as one of the highest birthrates in the world. Second, when this isolation ended and the birthrate fell dramatically after World War II, it survived thanks to provincial language-planning policies, which made it the only official language in Quebec, and one of the two official languages in New Brunswick. In both these provinces the vitality of the French language is very 'high'. In Quebec, since the *révolution tranquille* of the 1960s it has been a dynamic force, at once the symbol and the instrument of national cultural identity. It has produced a vigorous literature. It has managed to develop its own standard, independent of, but in close association with the French language of France and *francophonie* without a levelling of the geographical and social dialects which continue to enrich it. It competes with English, on which it is far less dependent for its vocabulary. It can face the future with confidence, especially as the Quebec birthrate is rising again. But in the rest of Canada the survival of the French language is threatened with assimilation to English; it only survives in small pockets, where it is struggling without adequate services and against discriminatory practices. With the failure of the Meech Lake Accord to reintegrate Quebec into the constitutional fold, Canada is again entering a crisis of identity. If Quebec separates from the Federation, it will strengthen its French language legislation and, provided that it can maintain its French-speaking population growth, the future of French is assured in that country. But this might mean the demise of French outside Quebec, as its speakers would then be in a helpless minority in the rest of Canada.

Notes

1. In the Canadian census 'mother tongue' refers to the first language spoken in childhood and still understood by the respondent: 'home language' refers to the specific language spoken in the home by the respondent (if more than one language is spoken, it is the one used most often).
2. On the general question of 'norm' in French, see Valdman (1983).
3. For a review, see Hartley (1986).
4. On this whole question see Bourhis (1984), Blanc (1984, 1986), Maurais (1987) and Bourhis and Sachdev (1989).

Texts

Samples of urban and rural Canadian French

Samples from Quebec City corpus (Deshaies 1981)

Adolescent schoolchildren from Sainte-Foy ('Haute-Ville')

(1) Je trouve qu'elle [ma façon de parler] est correcte, c'est ben ordinaire.
(2) J'essaie de parler, ben de parler normalement.
(3) E'(= elle est) normale. Je parle comme tout l'monde, i'm'semble.
(4) Comme tout l'monde . . . Ben ordinaire. Ben je choque peut-être moins que d'autres par exemple.

Adolescent schoolchildren from Saint-Sauveur ('Basse-Ville')

(5) La façon que je parle. Ben moi je parle, moi par rapport à moi je parle correct parce que je le parle tout le temps de même. Mais si je parle avec un gars de la haute-ville (Sainte-Foy), pour moi je parle mal, la manière qu'eux autres parlent.

(6) C'est une façon de parler comme une autre, t'sais. Je parle bien. Ya des affaires (topics) que j'vas parler bien, ça va dépendre. Mais la plupart du temps, j'parle mal.

(7) J'parle comme j'ai entendu parler. Si j'avais entendu parler avec des *moi*[*], pis des *toi*, j'aurais parlé avec des *moi* pis des *toi*. J'ai entendu parler *moé*, *toé*[**], *crisse* pis *tabarnak, crisse ton camp.*[***] Je parle de même. C'est normal pour moé.
    [*][mwa] [**][mwe] [***]*sacres* or swear words

(8) J'changerai pas ma façon de parler à cause que j'suis avec un aut' monde: m'a été porte à moins sacrer, mais *toé* pis *moé*, j'irai pas dire *toi*. I(ls) ont l'air à être snob. J'les ai jamais vus. Si i'disent qu'on parle mal, i'viendront nous l'dire dans face[*]. On va leur montrer qu'on parle peut-être mal, mais on tape bien. I(ls) auront beau s'penser n'importe quoi, j'suis capable de les égaler quand j'voudrai, *hostie*[**].
    [*]*to our face* [**]*sacre*

Samples from Montreal corpus

(9) Moé[*], je suis un vrai. Je suis comme ça, je suis comme ça, c'est tout. Toi[**], tu es un vrai. Si tu parles bien, euh, tu parles bien. Moi, je parle mal, je parle mal. D'après lui, moi je parle pas le vrai euh le vrai français. On est pas des Français, on est des Canadiens. Il y a une différence. Québécois, c'est ça . . . Bien vous, vous parlez mieux que moi.
    [*]*25-year-old baker* [mwe] [**]*the interviewer, a student* [twa]

(10) Parler joual c'est peut-être avoir un . . . disons une façon, un accent . . . le joual, c'est dans la prononciation . . . le joual pour moi, c'est pas l'anglais mêlé au français. (20-year-old student)

(11) (Le joual) c'est un mélange d'anglicismes avec des phrases qui sont pas françaises. Le gars que je sors avec . . . il va dire 'passe-moi telle affaire . . . place ça sur ça' . . . au lieu du mot juste . . . J'ai travaillé un été pour la Canadian International Papers . . . Ils ont décidé pour un mois d'utiliser que du vocabulaire français . . . pour faire un essai . . . alors la *pitoune* . . . vous connaissez ça? En français, c'est quoi? C'est des billots de seize pieds. Puis les gars disaient des *logs* . . . et puis un *boom*? C'est tous des billots qu'on attache . . . Hein? *Estacade.* Mais personne savait ce que c'était qu'une estacade. Puis tout le monde connaît, ce que c'est qu'un boom hein? (51-year-old woman with medical training)

(12) Example of literary prose from rural Acadian dialect

C'est pas toute. Parce qu'y a sus leux listes une question* encore ben pus malaisée . . . Ta natiounalité, qu'ils te demandont. Citoyenneté pis natiounalité. C'est malaisé à dire.

Je vivons en Amarique, ben je sons pas des Amaricains. Non, les Amaricains, ils travaillont dans des shops aux Etats, pis ils s'en venont se promener par icitte sus nos côtes, l'été, en culottes blanches pis en parlant anglais. Pis ils sont riches, les Amaricains, j'en sons point. Nous autres je vivons au Canada; ça fait que je devons putöt être des Canadjens, ça me r'semble.

Ben ça se peut pas non plus, parce que les Dysart, pis les Caroll, pis les Jones, c'est pas des genses de notre race, ça, pis ça vit au Canada itou. Si i' sont des Canadjens, je pouvons pas en être, nous autres. Par rapport qu'ils sont des Anglais, pis nous autres, je sons des Français.

Non, je sons pas tout à fait des Français, je pouvons pas dire ça: les Français, c'est les Français de France. Ah! pour ça, je sons encore moins des Français de France que des Amaricains. Je sons plutöt des Canadjens français, qu'ils nous avont dit. Ça se peut pas non plus, ça. Les Canadjens français, c'est du monde qui vit à Québec. Ils les appelont des Canayens, ou ben des Québécois. Ben coument c'est que je pouvons être des Québécois si je vivons point à Québec? Pour l'amour de Djeu, où c'est que je vivons, nous autres?

En Acadie, qu'ils nous avont dit, et je sons des Acadjens. Ça fait que j'avons entrepris de répondre à leu question de natiounalité coume ça: des Acadjens, que je leur avons dit. Ça, je sons sûrs d'une chouse, c'est que je sons les seuls à porter ce nom-là. Ben ils avont point voulu écrire ce mot-la dans leu liste, les encenseux. Parce qu'ils avont eu pour leu dire que l'Acadie, c'est point un pays, ça, pis un Acadjen c'est point une natiounalite, par rapport que c'est pas écrit dans les livres de Jos Graphie.

Eh! ben, après ça, je saviouns pus quoi trouver, et je leur avons dit de nous bailler la natiounalite qu'i' voudriont. Ça fait que je crois qu'ils nous avont placés parmi les Sauvages.

(Antonine Maillet, *La Sagouine*, Montreal: Leméac, 1971)
*i.e. population census which includes questions on ethnic origin and language.

(13) Example of literary Acadian vernacular poetry

Acadie rock
Bouctouche by the sea
Cocagne in the bay
Shédiac on the rocks
Northumberland
Straight
pi un jardin de patates
du côte d'la mer.
Un jardin de
Kent Homes

au côte d'la Highway
cultivay par:
Irving Plus.
Farewell
Kent homes.
Ta maison
cé ton ché vous.
Shédiac by the sea
Cocagne in the bay
Bouctouche sur mer
pi le bas d'la trac
comme tiriac.
pi la senteur
pi la chaleur
du bon bois d'érable brulé
cé pas pareil comme
la senteur
pi la chaleur
d'un poêle à l'huile
Ta maison
cé ton ché vous
Shédiac by the sea
Bouctouche sur mer
J'ai faim de l'Acadie
et jai soif de Parole

(Guy Arsenault, *Acadie Rock*, Moncton: Editions d'Acadie, 1973)

14

Sociolinguistic variation and the linguist

JACQUES DURAND

Introduction[1]

Although we know that a thousand years ago when Hugues Capet was elected king of France (987), 'French', the vernacular of the Ile de France was only one dialect among many and remained so for centuries, French is undeniably the language of most people living in France today and in many francophone countries throughout the world. The various *coups de force* which have led to the imposition of French as a national language in France and elsewhere have been well documented in a variety of works and will not be discussed here (cf. Balibar and Laporte 1974, Vermes and Boutet 1987).[2] Whether royal or republican, the agents of the state (the schools, the universities, the law, the police, the army), supported by strata of the local populations wishing to increase their social and economic standing, have successfully completed their task. We speak of 'success' here in the sense that, despite many repressive measures which have led to this situation, the vast majority of citizens in 'hexagonal' France at least would unhesitatingly describe French as their mother tongue.

A component of this spread of French is the belief in the unity of the language. This belief is carefully nurtured by what I called above the 'agents' of the state. It is aided and abetted by popular belief in the superiority of the written system over the oral system as witnessed in the passion for orthography in France which leads thousands of French speakers to punish themselves by doing the 'concours de dictées' organised until recently by the television personality Bernard Pivot. H. Walter in *Le français dans tous les sens* speaks aptly of 'Prestige de la langue écrite, oui, mais aussi prestige de son complément diabolique l'orthographe qui, pour la plupart des gens, a fini par se confondre avec la langue elle-même' (1988: 249).

In the following paragraphs, we will see that the 'unity' of French is a problematic notion. What seems to face us is rather diversity and variation, and a major problem is how to account for the multi-faceted linguistic reality we are confronted with. We will start with geographical variation within French and then move on to variation based on other dimensions such as class or gender. The presentation will be selective and move on progressively to a general discussion of sociolinguistic methods and their significance for a theory of language structure and language use.

Geographical variation

It is patently obvious that individuals who describe themselves as French speakers, and indeed for whom French may be the only language that they know, do not use this language in a uniform way. The most obvious example of variation that can be observed is due to geographical differences and occurs at all levels (phonological–phonetic, morphological, syntactic, lexical). For instance, from a phonological point of view, while most speakers of mainland France make a distinction between /w/, /ɥ/ and /j/ as in:

(1)   oui   [wi]   huit   [ɥit]   bière   [bjɛr]
       enfouir [ãfwir]   enfuir [ãfɥir]   fiole   [fjɔl]

Belgian speakers do not make the distinction between /w/ and /ɥ/ and use /w/ for both lexical sets so that *enfuir* and *enfouir* are pronounced identically as [ãfwir]. If we compare Canadian French with European French, we notice that while the two consonants /t/ and /d/ are invariably pronounced [t] and [d] in Europe, in Quebec the pronunciation of these consonants varies in a striking way according to the vowel that follows. Consider the representative examples from Canadian French given below (adapted from Kaye 1989: 29):

(2)   Words   Phonetic transcription
       typer   [tˢipe]
       tu   [tˢy]
       thé   [te]
       taux   [to]
       dis   [dᶻi]
       du   [dᶻy]
       doux   [du]
       dé   [de]
       deux   [dø]
       date   [dat]

In Quebec French, the high front vowels /i/ and /y/ trigger an affrication or assibilation of /t/ and /d/ (represented here as [tˢ] and [dᶻ]) whereas some other specialists use [ts] as in *cats* and [dz] as in *cads*). Interestingly, this phenomenon is not as widespread in Ontario French and does not apply to the speech of the Acadians who are now scattered over various parts of Canada as well as in Lousiana under the name of Cajuns (see Walter 1988: 205 for some remarks and, for a phonological discussion of this phenomenon, Kaye 1989: 28–32, 51–3 *et passim*).

From a morphological point of view, we observe that some processes of word-formation immediately identify speakers as belonging to a given part of the French-speaking world. Thus, on hearing a speaker saying *Elle est encore petitoune* (where *-oune* is a diminutive added to *petite*) and, even more strikingly, suffixing *-ette* to this complex word yielding *petitounette* (a redoubled diminutive), we would identify the speaker as *méridional*.

From a syntactic point of view, there are also obvious differences between varieties of French. For instance, the *passé surcomposé* (e.g. *je l'ai eu connu*) is still alive in Midi French but rare, or perhaps even non-existent, in other varieties of French (cf. Walter 1988: 170–2). Another example is the presence in Canadian French of constructions such as the following (King and Roberge 1989):

(3)   a. Quelle heure qu'il a arrivé à?
      (What time did he arrive at?)
   b. Quoi-ce que tu as parlé à Jean de?
      (What did you speak to John about?)

These examples illustrate a phenomenon often referred to as 'preposition stranding'.

At the lexical level, differences between varieties of French abound and we shall content ourselves with a single example. The French spoken in Switzerland shares many features with the French varieties of eastern France and Belgium. But Walter (1988: 197–8) cites as specific to Swiss French words such as *panosse* for 'serpillière', *relaver* for 'faire la vaisselle', *poutser* for 'nettoyer, faire le ménage' and *lavette* for 'carré de tissu éponge pour se laver' and adds 'Est-ce un hasard si ce choix, tout à fait aléatoire, s'est porté sur l'une des qualités qui font la réputation des Suisses: la propreté?'.

Much of the above is the subject of classical dialectology (with titles such as *Le Français parlé à Marseille/Bruxelles/Montréal*, etc.). One traditional explanation for much of this variation has been in terms of *substratum* (or *substrate*). This term refers to a language or linguistic variety which is seen as exercising an influence on the structure or use of a more dominant language or linguistic variety. Thus, in the south of France, the author knows older speakers near Toulouse who use a palatal *l* ([ʎ]) in words such as *vieille* (pronouncing it [vjɛʎə] versus 'standard' [vjɛj]). As these speakers have the phoneme [ʎ] in Occitan (e.g. in the word *vielha* [bjɛʎa] 'vieille'), Occitan would be said to be the substratum which underlies their French. Undeniably, for speakers who use two languages concurrently or two very different varieties of a language (a situation described as 'diglossia'), awareness of the pressure exercised by one variety on the other (and perhaps in both directions) can be relevant to the analysis. But it is important to see that notions such as 'substratum' (or 'language mixture') have limited explanatory power. Thus, in Occitan, as in Spanish, there is no opposition between [v] and [b]. But, in French, Occitan speakers (to the knowledge of the author) invariably make a contrast between [v] and [b]. Moreover, one can have a Midi accent without speaking Occitan! This is why the phenomenon of preposition stranding in Canadian French which has been mentioned above was not directly related to English in our presentation. It may well have emerged under the influence of English in the speech of francophone Canadians, but it has to be appreciated that young speakers of Canadian French may learn these forms without necessarily having any knowledge of English. Since such forms can become the norm within a variety without a necessary link to another variety, reference to the historical origin of a dialect-internal norm does not have the explanatory power that many people attribute to it.

In fact, even if we leave aside the previous argument, appealing to the concept of 'substratum', or simple interference, to explain preposition stranding in Canadian French raises problems. Mainland varieties of spoken French also illustrate preposition stranding in examples such as:

(4)   a. Cette valise, je voyage toujours avec.
       b. A: Ton fils, il a vu la Sainte Chapelle?
          B: Oui, pendant que nous visitions Notre Dame, il est passé devant

As pointed out in Roberge and Vinet (1989: 71) the notion of syntactic borrowing from English is not satisfactory since a close examination of such examples and their ramifications in French show that this pheno-menon is organised in a very different way from English. As partial evidence, they cite examples such as the following which are either ungrammatical or far less natural if translated literally into English:

(5)   a. Mitterand, J'ai voté pour
          * Mitterand, I voted for
       b. Parler avec a toujours été difficile
          * Talking with has always been difficult

(where the asterisks do not indicate the historical source of a word but a sequence of dubious acceptability).

Of course, all the examples given in this section could be rejected as not belonging to 'standard' French. But such a rejection would be based on a normative concept of the language not corresponding to usage. A sociologist, who is professionally interested in the way people really behave within social systems, does not start by excluding 'undesirable' subjects from the data-base. To do so would be equivalent to letting religious, moral or political prejudices interfere with observations and thus make results unreliable. In the same way, the banishment of forms such as the above as non-French is a political judgement. As linguists we are interested in the language as it really functions and cannot start from prescriptive exclusions. In any case, as we shall see presently in the next section, even the notion of 'standard' is not without its problems.

Non-geographical variation

The notion of geographical variation may seem obvious to the reader but one of the striking results of contemporary work in sociolinguistics, often confirming older intuitions, has been the demonstration that even linguistic communities which, at first sight, appeared relatively homogeneous turned on closer inspection to be heterogeneous along a variety of dimensions. To be more specific, work in sociolinguistics has been concerned with the correlation between areas of variation and extra-linguistic dimensions such as class, gender, age, education, ethnicity, style and register and the interpretation of this correlation. I will concentrate on two examples: one from syntax, the other one from phonology.

Our first example of variability will concern the presence or absence of negation *ne* within verb phrases. In written French, the prescribed way of indicating negation is by means of discontinuous markers such as *ne . . . pas, ne . . . jamais, ne . . . plus* as in the following examples:

(6)   a. Les Méridionaux ne sont pas comme nous
        b. On ne vous connaît pas
        c. Mon mari n'a jamais voulu
        d. Ils ne fichent plus rien

In spoken French, however, speakers oscillate between pronouncing *ne* and dropping it, so that the above would often be pronounced as:

(7)   a. Les Méridionaux sont pas comme nous
        b. On vous connaît pas
        c. Mon mari a jamais voulu
        d. Ils fichent plus rien

In a well-known study, Ashby (1981) demonstrated that the deletion or retention of *ne* was far from random but was correlated, not only with linguistic factors, but also with non-linguistic factors such as age, class and gender as summarised in table 14.1.

To point out the existence of a correlation between linguistic variables and extra-linguistic dimensions is not altogether surprising since we are all aware of the social significance of the use of language. But, what such

Table 14.1 *Correlation of 'ne' deletion with non-linguistic factors*

Factor	Observed frequency	% of 'ne' dropped
Age		
14–21 years	1104/1379	81
51–64 years	683/1439	48
Class		
lowest	719/853	84
middle	389/737	53
highest	679/1228	55
Sex		
female	999/1445	69
male	788/1373	57

studies have shown is that many areas of variation such as *ne* deletion/ retention characterise all speakers. It is not just 'working-class' or 'uneducated' speakers who drop *ne* in sentences such as the above but, given an appropriate context (e.g. an informal family situation), even the most 'educated' speakers will use variants without *ne*. Such facts had been suspected before but sociolinguistic studies have demonstrated their application to large populations.

Just as crucially, studies of various phenomena in a naturalistic environment have sharpened our perception of the data. Despite claims to the contrary, it is not uncommon for linguists to work from observations which are just handed down by tradition: witness the influence of such authorities as Fouché, Grevisse or Grammont in the field of French pronunciation. As wisely pointed out by Morin (1987), this would be acceptable if these descriptions of 'standard' French offered a reasonable model of language use. But, in fact, a comparison of various authors shows surprising divergences as to what the standard is supposed to consist of (compare any two randomly chosen authors or dictionaries with respect to the representation of the /a/–/ɑ/ opposition in such pairs as *patte–pâte*). With respect to phonetics, for instance, Fouché describes his work as based on 'la prononciation en usage dans une conversation "soignée" chez les Parisiens cultivés . . . à égale distance de la Comédie française ou du Conservatoire ou même celle de la conférence, du sermon ou du discours, d'une part, et la prononciation familière, surtout la prononciation populaire, de l'autre' (1956: 11), but he gives no information about the method followed to reach this 'average' careful and cultivated pronunciation. In the light of the important study by Martinet and Walter, *La prononciation du français dans son usage réel* (1973), where it is shown how diverse and variable the formal pronunciation of a group of seventeen highly educated Parisians can be, serious doubts can be expressed on the empirical (as opposed to normative/pedagog-ical) nature of 'standard' French (see further Morin 1987: 816–17). I, for one, would totally concur with Morin's judgement that 'standard' French is no more than a 'linguistic Frankenstein' and I will speak of 'standardised French' to emphasise the fictitious and ideological nature of the system in question.[3]

Having stressed the importance of 'authentic' observations and re-jected 'standard' French as a possible escape route in favour of the 'unity' of the language, let us examine one well-known phenome-non – that of liaison – in more detail from a sociolinguistic standpoint. In a nutshell, French liaison involves the pronunciation of the final 'latent' consonant of a word when the word in question is followed by a word closely connected to it and beginning with a vowel. The phonetics and phonology of liaison are in fact quite complex and will not be examined here (see Durand 1986, 1990a, Encrevé 1988, among many). Three contexts are traditionally distinguished and exemplified below: (a) those where liaison is said to be obligatory, (b) those where liaison is optional and (c) those where liaison is forbidden. Three examples are given in table 14.2.

Table 14.2 *Examples of French liaison*

(a) DETERMINER + NOUN			
les amis	[lɛzami]		*[lɛami]
(b) AUXILIARY + COMPLEMENT			
est ici	[ɛisi]	or	[ɛtisi]
(c) NOUN PHRASE + VERB PHRASE			
les amis arrivent	[lɛzamiariv]		*[lɛzamizariv]

Various studies of French liaison have argued that, for most varieties of French, one could establish a set of obligatory liaisons which was stable and could be described as 'categorical'. Obligatory liaisons include Determiner + Noun, Personal Pronoun + Verb, Verb + Pronoun as well as a number of frozen expressions (*tout à coup*). Cases where a speaker might say [lɛami] for *les amis* or [vuave] for *vous avez* are attested but are statistically insignificant. They are clear examples of 'lapses' or performance errors. At the other extreme, liaisons in contexts of type (c) are also extremely rare and can be classified as erratic. In between these two extremes we find an area of choice – the optional realisations which are labelled 'variable' in sociolinguistic approaches – where the choice is far from random. The variability is first of all associated with linguistic dimensions. Other things being equal, for instance, liaison is more likely after a monosyllable than after a polysyllable (e.g. liaison after *est* is more frequent than after *seront*). Secondly, the higher the social class the more likely are we to find optional liaisons realised. Thus, the corpus of recordings of Villejuif working-class teenagers studied by Laks (1980, 1983) contains 1,082 possible cases of liaison, 508 of these are examples of obligatory liaison and they are all realised. On the other hand, out of 576 cases of optional liaison, only 17 are actually realised (i.e. 3 per cent). If we compare this corpus with the results of Encrevé's study of liaison among seventeen political leaders (including François Mitterand and Valéry Giscard d'Estaing) the difference is striking. Out of 5,787 cases of optional liaison, Encrevé found that 2,815 (i.e. 48.6 per cent were realised. And it hardly seems surprising that out of all these leaders, the one with the lowest number of optional liaisons is Georges Marchais (18.8 per cent) the leader of the Communist Party whose role is traditionally to represent the 'working class'. Thirdly, the higher the style or register the more liaisons we encounter. Comparing, on the basis of his corpus, the use of liaison by Mitterand and Giscard d'Estaing in various situations, Encrevé points out:

> Ces résultats confortent l'opinion courante que le taux de liaisons facultatives réalisés croît pour chaque locuteur avec la 'hauteur' du style: les taux les plus bas sont obtenus pour les deux locuteurs dans le même débat télévisé où les discours étaient spontanés et où l'enjeu politique majeur (l'élection présidentielle) détournait relativement l'attention des locuteurs de la forme phonétique de leur langage au profit du sens de leurs paroles; les taux les plus hauts sont obtenus pour les deux locuteurs dans des interventions monologuées assurément écrites et apprises par coeur: toute improvisation étant bannie et le style visant à traduire la hauteur de la fonction (les deux locuteurs ici ne sont pas candidats à la présidence de la république, mais présidents en exercice), les locuteurs surveillent le plus possible leur élocution – ils 'l'élèvent'. (p. 61)

The same results have been obtained from studies more closely modelled on the seminal work of Labov (1966, 1972) where an independently established social classification is correlated with the occurrence of liaison in various contexts. Booij and de Jong (1987) base their tabulation on the Tours corpus of de Jong et al. (1981), where the figures correspond to percentages of attested liaisons (see table 14.3). The Tours corpus is a study of thirty-eight informants divided into five classes according to criteria elaborated by the INSEE (*Institut National de la Statistique et des Etudes Economiques*): A = *professions libérales et cadres supérieurs*, B = *cadres moyens*, C = *employés*, D = *contremaîtres, ouvriers qualifiés*, E = *ouvriers spécialisés, manoeuvres*. The study was based on conversations, the reading of a text (RS = Reading Style) and the reading of short sentences containing a liaison context (classified above as WLS = Word List Style). As is clear from this table, the higher the

Table 14.3 *Liaison correlated with social classification*

	Class	A	B	C	D	E	Style
débâcles_inattendues		88	67	17	50	25	RS
certains_exécutants		100	100	67	50	50	RS
moins_important		100	100	75	67	40	WLS
fort_intéressant		100	100	58	67	20	WLS

social class the more occurrences of liaison. Moreover, the Word List Style which in all studies provides the most formal style (the degree of self-monitoring is highest) triggers more occurrences of liaison than the reading of a text with respect to the same word sequences.

From a linguistic point of view, the work by the authors mentioned here and others shows that variation in optional liaison is not a function of rigidly separate speech styles as posited by various specialists (Fouché, Selkirk) but rather an example of 'inherent variation' in the sense of Labov: the variation is irreducible and two variants (e.g. [ɛisi] and [ɛtisi] for *est ici*) often occur within the same utterance in the same speech style and situation.

The data in studies of this type can also be tabulated as shown in figure 14.1 (Booij and de Jong 1987: 1018) typical in the work inspired by Labov.

The advantage of such figures is to provide a good visual illustration of various phenomena. Unexpected correlations and discrepancies are easy to spot and help us to examine more thoroughly the link between language use and social systems. Sometimes a given group will be seen to be leading or lagging and the data can sometimes be read as providing information about ongoing language change (in apparent time): see the next section. From a general point of view, the picture of a community that emerges is a complex one: for most variables, it seems that all speakers participate in the variation and that there is no sharp break between various classes or other types of groupings. As Guy (1988: 41) puts it: 'The distribution of socially symbolic characteristics such as sociolinguistic variables should from this standpoint, be relatively gradient, finely stratified, without the sharp breaks in the social fabric that Marx perceived.' On the other hand, certain variables show a sharp stratification: one group (say A) uses a variable which is absent from the speech of other groups (say B and C). For instance, in a study of diphthongisation in Montreal French by Santerre and Millo (1978) it is pointed out that the diphthongisation of /aʒ/ is a characteristic of working-class speakers only.

The two types of result produce conflicting views of society: in the first one, society will be seen as relatively homogeneous, all speakers

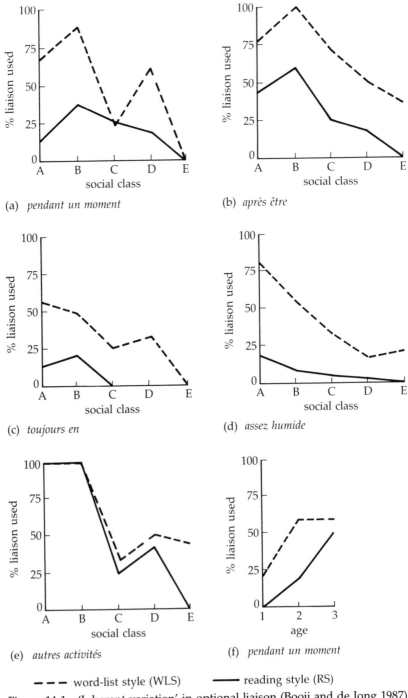

(a) *pendant un moment*

(b) *après être*

(c) *toujours en*

(d) *assez humide*

(e) *autres activités*

(f) *pendant un moment*

$-\,-\,-$ word-list style (WLS)   —— reading style (RS)

Figure 14.1 'Inherent variation' in optional liaison (Booij and de Jong 1987) seeking the same goal and displaying the same aspirations. In the second one, society will be seen as made up of groups which are in conflict and vie with one another for economic and cultural power. It is quite common in France for linguists interested in language and society to reject Labovian sociolinguistic studies on the grounds that they espouse a politically naive (consensual) view of society. A proper discussion of this issue would take us too far afield (see Guy 1988 for an interesting discussion and further references). But, at the very least, it must be realised that well-constructed sociolinguistic work offers a testing ground for the checking of various hypotheses concerning social stratification by opposition to speculation about language and society based on purely qualitative judgements. This has been recognised by at least one famous French sociologist – Pierre Bourdieu – who says in a discussion with William Labov:

> Cela dit, il y a un point où les travaux des sociolinguistes, notamment les vôtres, à Philadelphie aussi bien qu'à Foussais, me paraissent en avance sur les travaux des sociologues: montrer comment une variable sociale quelconque, linguistique ou autre, subit des changements continus, imperceptibles, qui finissent par créer des discontinuités pertinentes, me semble constituer un apport très important à la sociologie du changement social.   (see Labov 1983: 71)

And it is indeed to the subject of change, but linguistic change, that we are going to turn now.

Linguistic change: are women the leaders?

Apart from providing information about language in use within social contexts, an important contribution of studies on variation has been to provide a window on linguistic change. Our knowledge of the history of languages, and French is no exception, is limited by the need to work from written sources, and the often limited number of available documents and social information about the speakers prevents a detailed study of the way linguistic changes originate and spread within a community. One of the claims made by sociolinguists is that by paying attention to differences between various groups and particularly age groups we may be able to observe and chart changes in progress. Thus, Ashby (1981) claims that the difference in age distribution in the dropping of *ne* illustrated above, coupled with other considerations (e.g. the fact that *ne*-retention is linked to a high register) reflects an ongoing change in the language. If this change is untrammelled – there could be a strong social reaction leading to an increased use of *ne* – the prediction is that at some point in the future *ne* would no longer be present in the speech of French speakers. If so, a cycle would have been completed leading from the marking of negation by *ne* alone in Old French (or its historical source derived from Latin *non*), through the progressive reinforcement of this *ne* by 'pleonastic' elements such as *pas, plus, jamais*, to the use of these elements as the sole markers of negation.

Although this particular claim has been challenged by some scholars (see below), the overall thesis that variation can indicate change in progress seems a compelling one and there are many examples in the literature of this kind of phenomenon. One of the advantages of these studies is that the question of how linguistic changes spread through a community can be raised in a more objective way. There is a wide agreement among sociolinguists that innovations are not adapted uniformly and simultaneously across a society. Rather, some groups are innovators and early adopters and others lag behind. Changes can be in several directions: some changes may be towards a perceived external norm. For instance, some features of sociolinguistic variation in Midi French can be perceived as trends towards the 'Parisian' norm (see Durand et al. 1987). Other changes can be purely dialect-specific and even go against the national norm. One of the claims often made has been that in many societies women use speech variants closer to the standard and spearhead changes in the direction of a supra-dialectal norm. To quote Bourdieu:

> En Béarn, comme en Algérie, j'ai constaté qu'en matière de langue, et cela est vrai plus généralement en matière de culture, les femmes étaient plus disposées et plus aptes à adopter le modèle standard. On peut poser comme hypothèse que les femmes étant dominées dans les sociétés masculines, ne pouvant monter socialement que par le mariage et la conformité aux normes dominantes, ont une disposition socialement acquise à se conformer. Cela peut se retraduire plus trivialement en disant que les femmes sont socialement plus dociles que les hommes. (p. 69)

That there are differences in language use between male and female speakers is borne out by the study of many variables: see the data in table 14.1 and figure 14.2. To give another example, in the French spoken in North Africa, male speakers tend to pronounce the phoneme /R/ as [r] – a rolled alveolar sound – whereas women always pronounce it as a uvular [ʁ] (Walter 1988: 215). There is an historical explanation for this (see Walter 1988: 215) but clearly, in so far as the observation is correct, this is now a distinction characterising the North African community as a whole. The women are closer to the supra-dialectal norm of mainland France where [ʁ] is the prestige realisation. Moreover, we know independently that, throughout Europe, in languages which have an /R/ phoneme, the uvular realisation has been steadily gaining ground over the rolled [r] variant (see Chambers and Trudgill 1980: 187–90). Were the [ʁ] realisation to end up as the sole variant in North

African French, we would have some evidence for women having spearheaded this change.

Assuming that, in many cases, women are closer to the norm and may be leaders in changes towards the norm, an explanation is needed. Usually, the explanation has been in terms of the power structure of society. Most societies in the world are dominated by males and females' language practices will reflect this domination as argued by Bourdieu in the quote cited above. This thesis can even be refined by giving a pragmatic interpretation of its consequences (see Deuchar 1987: 305–9). But prudence in the interpretation of the data referred to in this section is required in various directions. First of all, one must beware of erecting observed correlations into an absolute norm concerning women's behaviour which might even be seen as biologically triggered. Labov (1983) points out that, in studies of India and Iran, women have been shown to be lagging behind in various changes and he adds:

> si, dans la plupart des enquêtes sociolinguistiques . . . les femmes sont en avance, dans des situations sociales spécifiques elles peuvent être en retard. La conclusion qu'il faut tirer de cette contradiction, c'est que, comme l'a souligné Goffman, ce n'est pas la caractéristique sexuelle qui peut expliquer le comportement linguistique. Au contraire, il faut rechercher des explications à la différenciation sexuelle en dehors des caractéristiques purement biologiques.

Secondly, women can lead in directions away from the supra-dialectal norm as demonstrated in relation to Belfast speech (see Milroy 1980) and if we look at the data concerning *ne* deletion/retention, it could be argued that women are leading away from the norm (assuming that *ne* retention is more 'proper' than its deletion). More generally, the study of any community will reveal many competing directions taken by speakers and a unitary explanation is perhaps not possible.

Finally, the notion of 'apparent change' must be used carefully. For instance, Blanche-Benveniste and Jeanjean (1987) have argued that *ne* deletion/retention has been a characteristic of French for many centuries. And, as part of this thesis, it might be argued that the fact that older speakers differ from younger speakers may simply reflect the fact that as people grow older they adopt speech habits – such as using more liaisons – which conform to their age group (a phenomenon known as age grading). As pointed out above, the notion of change in apparent time is an interesting one (see Ashby 1991). Given that many changes are slow and may take centuries to unfold, the study of linguistic variation gives an interesting perspective on the diffusion of changes through society. Nevertheless, each case must be studied on its merit and one must avoid facile conclusions about who is the leader. An apparently objective account of language variation in relation to women may end up with formulations which just reinforce societal prejudices about male/female orientations within the social space.

The formalisation of variation

One of the questions which arise from results such as the ones reported above is how to formalise such variation in relation to the language system of individual speakers. Early studies of variation often posited the notion of dialect mixture. The idea was that speakers might have integrated the systems of two or more dialects and would be shifting between these dialects in their speech. But this notion of dialect mixture is not fully satisfactory: as we have seen, for many variables, we are dealing with inherent, irreducible variation and not with a shift between two or more dialects (or styles). Therefore most sociolinguists have abandoned the notion of dialect mixture and, in much research inspired by the work of Labov, variation has been dealt with in terms of what are called 'variable rules'. The idea of rules is one which is familiar from classical generative grammar. Let us take an example from Midi French. For many speakers of Midi French, words such as *page, faire, rose* contains a schwa in final position. The phonemic representation of a word like *page* will be /paʒə/ whereas in Parisian French there is at least a *prima facie* case for assuming that the underlying form of this word is /paʒ/ (but see Dell 1973, Durand 1986). In conservative varieties of Midi French this schwa is sometimes said to be always pronounced. It is however categorically deleted when the next word within a breath-group begins with a vowel. Thus, a Midi French speaker will say [lapaʒadrwatə] for *la page à droite* and not [lapaʒəadrawat] (unless there is an intentional pause or hesitation between *page* and *à*). We can formalise this deletion by means of a rule of the following form:

(8)   Prevocalic schwa deletion (categorical rule)
       ə → 0 / — — # V

This can be read as follows: schwa, /ə/, becomes zero when followed by a vowel from which it is separated by a word-boundary.

One characteristic of generative grammars is that when a rule is not categorical its application is merely specified as optional. Thus, in many modern varieties of Midi French, schwas are in fact deleted in other contexts than the prevocalic environment considered above. And some speakers oscillate between [turnelapaʒ] and [turnelapaʒə] for *Tournez la page!*. In a micro-sociolinguistic study of speakers from Hérault, Durand et al. (1987) have shown that the deletion in question was sensitive to a variety of linguistic and extra-linguistic parameters and not random. From a sociolinguistic point of view, it has therefore been objected that it is not sufficient to posit a rule and say of it that it is optional (which seems to imply a random choice on the part of speakers). The formulation of the rule, it is argued, should reflect in a direct manner all the parameters which will influence the choice of one variant over the other. The suggestion has therefore been that we should allow numerical variables to be attached to specific variable constraints, whether these are linguistic or non-linguistic.

Good exemplification of this type of approach is provided in the work done on Canadian French by the Sankoffs and their associates which, to my knowledge, is unmatched by work on *français hexagonal*. We will consider one example from the work of Cedergren and Sankoff (1974), which is clearly presented in Deuchar (1987), on whom the following remarks are based. This example concerns the deletion of the relative pronoun *que* in Montreal French. In this variety of French, *que* can be deleted in the same way as *that* in English. That is, we observe *Elle dit tu es là* as well as *Elle dit que tu es là* in the same way as in English we find *She says you are here* beside *She says that you are here*. It can be shown that the deletion of *que* is a typical variable rule. It is sensitive to linguistic variables (e.g. it is more frequent in the environment of sibilant sounds such as [s, z, ʃ, 3] than non-sibilant sounds) and extra-linguistic variables (it is more common in the speech of workers than professionals). The variable rule reached on the basis of extensive corpus investigation would look as follows:

(9)   *Que* – deletion (variable rule)
       $que \rightarrow <0> / <[sibilant]>$ ——————— $<[sibilant]>$
       $<[consonantal]>$ [complementiser] $<[consonantal]$

where the angled brackets indicate that the zero realisation is dependent on the linguistic factors on the right. And the constraints on the application of the rule would be derived from table 14.4.

The overall probability of *que*-deletion applying is worked out by multiplying the three effects: $p1 \times p2 \times p3$. Thus, in a sentence such as

Table 14.4 *Values for constraints on the deletion of 'que' (after Cedergren and Sankoff, 1974). See Deuchar 1987: 299.*

Preceding environment:	[+sib]	$\begin{bmatrix} +cns \\ -sib \end{bmatrix}$	[−cns]
Effect (p1):	1	0.85	0.37
Following environment:	[+sib]	$\begin{bmatrix} +cns \\ -sib \end{bmatrix}$	[−cns]
Effect (p2):	1	0.5	0.1
Occupational class:		workers	professionals
Effect (p3):		1	0.35

Marie dit (que) Marc doit partir/mari di [kə] mark dwa partir/ the presence
of a non-consonantal sound to the left of *que* (the vowel of *dit*) gives a
value of 0.37 for p1. The word following *que*, i.e. *Marc*, begins with
consonantal, non-sibilant /m/, which gives a value of 0.5 for p2. If the
sentence is uttered by a speaker of professional occupational class
(p3 = 0.35), the overall probability of *que* being deleted will be 0.37 ×
0.5 × 0.35 (p1 × p2 × p3), that is 0.06, which is a low rate of deletion.
Once this abstract probability has been worked out it can be confronted
with actual corpus frequencies of deletion to see how close a fit there is
between theory and data.

Despite its initial appeal, the conversion of corpus-based frequencies
into probabilities attached to rules has been seen by many researchers as
a blind alley. Ever since the inception of such sociolinguistic methods, it
has been objected that variable rules related to performance data and not
to the competence system underlying speakers' productions as is
familiar in generative grammar (see below pp. 275–80). A response to
this has been that we should see the probabilities as giving an abstract
specification of a system of 'pragmatic competence': speakers do not just
know the rules of the language but they have also internalised mechanisms for linking rules and situations. But, it is rather odd to see speakers
as carrying probabilities in their heads: if a rule applies 33 per cent of the
time, do we need to keep a tally of all applications to make sure that our
behaviour matches the constraints on the application of the rule? A
familiar move in sociolinguistics is to deny the psychological relevance
of variable rules and to see them as characterising group grammars (see
particularly the work of Labov in this respect). However, as I will argue
below, the assumption that there are group grammars is a dubious one.
If this is correct, it raises the question of whether there is any invariance
at all within linguistic systems and what the probabilities established in
sociolinguistics mean.

On the notion of group grammar

In the previous section, the notion of a group grammar, a kind of system
shared by all speakers was mentioned. The idea of a supra-individual
system is by no means new. Saussure (1916), for instance, views
language as a 'trésor' shared by all the speakers of a community. And
the same assumption is implicitly made in a great deal of sociolinguistic
work, i.e. that there is a vernacular characterising all speakers of a given
community. Perhaps, indeed, there is a system used by all French
speakers which is what unites them. It is clear that all speakers of French
share a great deal but there is no evidence that there is a *unique* system
which underlies the performance of *all* speakers. It is easy to see the
problem by reference to phonology. The phonemic vowel system of

many varieties of northern French – including standardised French – is usually described as shown in table 14.5.

Table 14.5 *Oral vowels of standardised French (excluding /ə/)*

	front		back	
	non-round	round	non-round	round
high	i	y		u
mid high	e	ø		o
mid low	ɛ	œ		ɔ
low	a		ɑ	

Apart from /i, y, u/, which seem to be stable in varieties of French known to the author, the presence of the other sounds in this table is based on minimal pairs such as the *thé–taie, jeûne–jeune, côte–cote, patte–pâte*. But many studies have shown that such oppositions are by no means uniform even in the speech of individuals that one might qualify as speakers of the standard variety. Moreover, many Midi accents do not possess such oppositions. We might therefore posit a *noyau dur* or minimal system (as is very often done in work of the functionalist school inspired by Martinet) as shown in table 14.6. But, what does this system represent? It may be the system of a speaker of Midi French but it is certainly not the system of speakers who do use some or all the oppositions mentioned earlier. At best, it may be a kind of perceptual grid that speakers who distinguish eleven oral vowels use in decoding the speech of speakers with fewer oppositions but this is no more than speculation.

The point which has been made above is not that speakers of French do not share a number of features but that the features which they have in common do not make up one overarching system. Obviously, sociolinguists would heartily endorse this idea and point out that they are the first to underline that a language is, as the phrase goes, a dialect with an army and a navy. But surprisingly they often cling to the notion of 'dialect' as incorporating a hard nucleus – the group gram-

Table 14.6 *Minimal system of French oral vowels*

	front		back
	non-round	round	round
high	I	Y	U
mid	E	OE	O
low		A	

mar – shared by all speakers. Unfortunately, the notion of uniform dialect grammar is no clearer with respect to a dialect. As a simple example, consider most urban varieties of northern French. Within the same variety, we will often find speakers who distinguish three nasal vowels and speakers who distinguish four nasal vowels. Between these speakers there is simply a discontinuity in the underlying phonemic system. Of course, the closer and the smaller the community the more convergence we can expect. But children, as has been often argued in the study of creoles, do not merely internalise the system which is most immediately available to them but, in a sense, reinvent the language anew.

The above examples are quite simple and deal with the phonemic inventories which can be expected to characterise all speakers of the same language or dialect. We can further strengthen our observation if we note that within an approach based on variable rules, a group or community grammar can be defined as one where (a) the variable rules are shared, (b) the linguistic and social constraints on rules are shared, (c) the constraints are independent of one another. This is often referred to as a 'prototype variable rule community'. Now, a number of researchers have pointed out that, in fact, putative variable rule communities do not seem to behave in line with assumptions (a) to (c) (see Guy 1977, Deuchar 1987, Romaine 1982a and b). Guy (1977), for instance, in ground-breaking work on English showed that within one group of speakers who share a rule of t/d deletion in forms such as *last* or *told* (so that e.g. *last night* will be pronounced as [lasnait] or [lastnait] and *told so* as [toulsou] or [touldsou]), the constraints on the application of the rules are not the same. Extra-linguistic factors appear not to be what differentiates these two sub-groups of speakers. Rather, for some speakers the most important constraint is the presence of a monomorphemic form (e.g. *last*) whereas for other it is the presence of the irregular past tense verb form (e.g. *told*). Yet, the process of t/d deletion appears to be stable and not undergoing change.

To my knowledge, the kind of evidence adduced by Guy against 'variable rule communities' in the sense just established can be unearthed in every community which has been tested. We shall limit ourselves to two examples only in relation to French. First, variable rules are not always shared by all speakers. My own observations on the variety of Midi French described in Durand et al. (1987) show the existence of a variable [wã]–[wẽ] (*soin* being pronounced [swãŋ] or [swẽŋ]). Yet this variation does not exist uniformly in the speech of the eight Midi speakers belonging to a same close-knit family studied in the article just mentioned. Secondly, the way the constraints on rules interact shows that they are not independent of one another. Thus, in a study by Santerre and Millo of diphthongisation in Montreal French

(1978: 180)), the authors observe that 'Within the working class it is only the older speakers who favor the larger range variants, the younger ones preferring the smaller one. Among the middle-class speakers, the small range variant is used by both the old and, overwhelmingly, the young speakers.' This is a clear example of interaction between age and class which offers a serious challenge to the notion of group or community grammar based on variable rules.

In so far as it is correct to deny that linguistic communities do not exist in the strong sense of a 'prototype variable rule community', we rejoin the intuitions of the famous French dialectologist Gauchat who demonstrated the non-existence of homogeneous speech communities. In his study of the small village of Charmey where apparently all conditions were fulfilled for finding unity he found that some fluctuations divided the speakers into sharp sets. One example was the variation between [ʎ] and [j] which had the following shape (Gauchat 1905: 205):

Data from the study of three generations of speakers
Generation I (90–60 years)   II (60–30 years)   III (under 30)
        ʎ   ʎ–j   j

This study, which probably offers the first record of language change in progress (according to age), lead Gauchat to assert 'L'unité du patois de Charmey, après un examen plus attentif, est nulle' (1905: 222).

Of course, I am not denying that there may be speech communities but that the criteria for calling them so cannot be purely linguistic. Indeed, I would go as far as to claim that no satisfactory qualitative or quantitative definition of the linguistic conditions which have to be fulfilled for a group of speakers to constitute a linguistic community has ever been put forward. But, if what we are saying above is correct, does it mean then that there is no invariance in language at all and is this a counsel for despair? Are we condemned to studying ever changing, unpredictable patterns of variations in fictitious communities? In the next section, I would like to show briefly that in at least one tradition – that of Chomskyan generative grammar – the claim is made that invariance can be found in language, but at an abstract level, provided we are prepared to countenance a universalist perspective.

Invariance in generative grammar

Recent work in the foundations of generative grammar has been based on a critique (see Chomsky 1986) of the traditional view of language as 'the totality of utterances that can be made in a speech-community' (Bloomfield) or as 'a pairing of sentences and meanings . . . over an infinite range, where the language is "used by a population" when certain regularities "in action and belief" hold among the population with reference to the language, sustained by an interest in communication' (Lewis, as described by Chomsky 1986: 19). Language viewed like this is what Chomsky (1986) called externalised language (E-language) which should not be the object of linguistic investigation. The goal of linguistic theory should be the study of the abstract system internalised by speakers which, once put into use, allows them to produce and understand an indefinite number of utterances. Chomsky refers to this as internalised language (I-language), another term for the concept of 'competence' used in other work. There is no need to assume that languages such as French, English, German or Hindi exist in an objective sense. As we argued above, there are no group grammars and, in fact, it can easily be shown no two speakers are identical in the total linguistic systems they internalise. Think of variations in lexical knowledge as simple evidence for this claim.

However, this is not a reason for thinking that the task of language description becomes impossible. Barring certain disabilities, all human beings have the ability to produce and understand an unbounded number of utterances and all human children learn the language to which they are exposed (i.e. reach a knowledge sufficiently similar to that of other speakers to count within the community as speaker of language or dialect X). Given that there is now ample demonstration in the literature on first language acquisition that explicit training and teaching play a marginal role in the acquisition of the basic structure of a language, the major goal of the study of language is seen by linguists of the Chomskyan generative school as the discovery of the principles and parameters common to all languages. These principles and parameters are part of the biological endowment of individuals and will guide the children in the acquisition of a first (and arguably a second) language (see e.g. Radford 1990). Among the principles of the grammatical system, we can cite for example the phonological hypothesis that every language will have a constituent such as the syllable and that this syllable will obey certain inviolable constraints. For instance, no language will allow liquids ([l] or [r]) as syllabic elements but not vowels (see e.g. Durand 1990a: ch. 6). Let us now turn to the notion of parameter.

In every language we can identify categories which function as heads and categories which function as complements. Traditionally, only verbs are assumed to have complements. But consider the following examples which could easily be extended:

(10)   Head + Complement
        ouvrir les portes   Verb + Noun Phrase
        parler de ses remarques   Verb + Prepositional Phrase
        objecter qu'elle est malade   Verb + que + Sentence
        l'ouverture des portes   Noun + Prep Phrase

l'objection qu'elle est malade	Noun + que + Sentence
déçu de ses remarques	Adjective + Prep Phrase
déçu qu'elle soit malade	Adjective + que + Sentence
depuis la guerre	Preposition + Noun Phrase
depuis avant la guerre	Preposition + Prep Phrase

It is clear that all the categories listed here (Verb, Noun, Adjective, Preposition) exhibit complements and that there is a great deal of parallelism between them. One of the claims of generative grammar is that the order Head–Complement is a parameter which will be fixed in each language: in English and French the head precedes the complement, the opposite order would be followed in Japanese. When we say in French, we mean that most varieties of contemporary French which have been described, and to my knowledge all, exhibit the order Head + Complement.

The kind of research we are alluding to here is based on the notion of grammar internalised by native speakers which constitutes their knowledge of a language system or competence in traditional Chomskyan terminology (I-language in the sense described earlier). The competence cannot be confused with the performance which is affected by factors such as memory lapses, excitement, tiredness or drunkenness. As mentioned above, the distinction is often criticised by sociolinguists but it is difficult to see how one can avoid making it altogether, for fear of confusing the product of language activity with the system underlying this activity.

The work in generative grammar is ideally done with native speakers as informants or even oneself as informant. This is often attacked in sociolinguistics. But consider the following sentences:

(11)   a. Marie est partie quand elle a vu Pierre arriver.
        b. Elle est partie quand Marie a vu Pierre arriver.
        c. Quand elle est partie, Marie a vu Pierre arriver.

In my system and that of all other French speakers I have consulted, in (11a) the pronoun 'elle' could refer to 'Marie' or to some other person. In (11b), on the other hand, the pronoun 'elle' cannot refer to 'Marie'. 'Of course', the reader will point out, 'It is surely well-known that a pronoun cannot precede its antecedent.' But now look at (11c): 'elle' can either refer to 'Marie' or to some other person. In the study of many other languages, including English, it has been shown that the features of 'co-reference' (the link between the reference of pronouns and that of their antecedents) exhibited in the above sentences were not accidental but recurred and had the same shape. This has led to some groundbreaking work on conditions on the reference of pronouns (under the heading of anaphora), including promising work in the field of first language acquisition. We could clearly devise some tests to objectivise the intuition: we could for instance select twenty subjects and make them act out the situation with dolls, two of which will be called Marie and Pierre. This is exactly what is done with children to verify their acquisition of such forms (see Roeper 1988 on this type of study) but it seems an utter waste of time with adult grammar when all informants can make sharp and clear judgements on the data.

It is moreover clear that such intuitions can hardly be influenced by tradition given that descriptive or pedagogical grammars have generally said little about the conditions under which co-reference is possible or impossible. Consider as another example the formation of Qu-questions in French (that is, questions which involve *qui, que, quand*, etc.). The three following sentences pose no problem:

(12)   a. Tu as vu qui? (echo question)
        b. Qui as-tu vu?
        c. Tu as vu Marie et qui?

But, while *qui* can be moved from its complement position in (12a) to the front of the sentence as in (12b) above, if we try and do the same with respect to (12c), the result is unacceptable:

        d. *Qui as-tu vu Marie et?

Again, such facts are part of the native speakers' competence but, to my knowledge, have never been pointed out in traditional grammars. Out of the range of examples some will exhibit (tentative) universal constraints on what is and is not possible, others will be known to be specific to French. In studying principles and parameters of the type we have mentioned, it has been common in generative grammar to abstract away from variation and concentrate on the speaker's grammar outside its use in particular social contexts. As Chomsky points out:

> By making these idealisations explicit and pursuing our enquiry in accordance with them, we do not in any way prejudice the study of language as a social product. On the contrary, it is difficult to imagine how such studies might fruitfully progress without taking into account the real properties of mind that enter into the acquisition of language, specifically, the properties of the initial state of the language faculty characterized by UG [= Universal Grammar, JD].   (1986: 18)

A full debate on the matters discussed here would take us too far afield,[4] but it is worth pointing out one consequence of adopting a Chomskyan point of view. There is invariance but at an abstract level and variation can be attributed to a different setting of parameters. This point of view potentially offers a fruitful line of enquiry for the study of variation within and across languages (see e.g. Roberge and Vinet 1989).

However, the Chomskyan approach requires that we take seriously the construction of competence systems as an unavoidable task since language use and language systems do not fully coincide. Language use is the result of the interaction of several modules: some of them are psychological (e.g. memory and processing constraints), some of them are social or pragmatic (e.g. the ritualisation of some situations such as weddings and funerals), some of them are paralinguistic (e.g. modulating your speech with Gallic shrugs of the shoulders).

There isn't a single point of view on this issue within sociolinguistics. Many sociolinguists deny the validity of the competence–performance distinction. If so, it seems to me that the observations of sociolinguists on the corpora they study will tell us something about the data and perhaps its link with social systems but do not address the issue which I think is fundamental, i.e. how do speakers internalise the knowledge which allows them to cope with an indefinite number of utterances in context? There are also serious difficulties in the construction of a theory of language based on inductive generalisations from corpora which we cannot go into here but which are worth mentioning given that the Bloomfieldian tradition foundered precisely on this issue (see Lyons 1970: 27–35 among many).

On the other hand, some sociolinguists would claim that their aim is by no means antagonistic to the Chomskyan tradition in that they are attempting to specify that portion of linguistic knowledge which allows speakers to use language appropriately in its social setting (sometimes this is referred to as 'pragmatic competence'). There is no reason to deny that there is much information in sociolinguistic work – some of which has been reported in earlier sections – about the link between language and society. What seems to me problematic is the nature of the quantitative data of the type reported here in the construction of a theory of language use. We saw earlier that frequencies (even erected into probabilities) do not make much sense as competence rules, and changing the label to 'pragmatic competence' does not help. I think that what is needed, if we take the construction of a sociolinguistic theory seriously, is the setting up of an abstract model of language performance (for well-delimited groups) where linguistic and social knowledge would interact and from which the probabilities would derive, so to speak, as 'theorems' (numerical consequences). As they stand, the frequencies are no more than what they are: a quantification of data whose statistical significance is often not brought out (for a negative assessment of figures in linguistics, see Smith 1989).

Sociolinguists frequently criticise the generative tradition for its reliance on intuitions. I have tried to defend above the use of intuitions although I would not deny that recourse to informants in generative linguistics has often been informal, indeed sloppy. But it must be stressed that there is nothing preventing the generative linguist from using corpora (see Encrevé 1988 as a good example of this), or psycho-linguistic tests or whatever other sources of information may be available. Ideally, a thoroughly Chomskyan approach should characterise the system of one speaker but, in practice, there are practical difficulties in operating with one informant only. We therefore deal with idealised systems with information coming from various sources (e.g. dictionaries in studying word formation). If the idealisaton leads to linguistic Frankensteins (as standardised French is) then it should be criticised. On the other hand, many studies in generative grammar have tested properties (e.g. co-reference, question formation) which are shared by many speakers and on which there is wide agreement on the nature of the data. In a sense, theory-construction is difficult for all. The counter-part of the 'bad intuitions' of generative grammar in sociolinguistics is the reliability of the data. As a teacher of phonetics, I often have doubts about studies which are based on subtle distinctions between vowel qualities which are judged on auditory grounds and where the analysis has been applied to a very large database. Experimental analyses of phoneticians' judgements have shown too many inconsistencies to render us immune to doubts in this area (see e.g. Ladefoged 1967).

Conclusion

In this study I first of all presented some results of sociolinguistics concerning French. I then moved on to a brief consideration of one tradition in sociolinguistics – that based on variable rules or large quantitative surveys. I have tried to show that there were difficulties in the interpretation of numerical data from a linguistic point of view. There are, of course, other approaches to sociolinguistics and it was not my purpose to put forward an account – let alone a critique – of all work in sociolinguistics. Indeed, I don't think the reader should go away with a negative picture of the sociolinguistic data presented earlier. One way of interpreting its significance is that it gives an idealised snapshot of the sort of data available to a child within a given community and from which the learner will project a language system. Furthermore, as I have pointed out above, this data is useful in a variety of respects. It gives us information about the link between language and society, although in many cases this link awaits an interpretation within a theory of social systems. It offers an additional tool to the investigation of linguistic change. It helps sharpen observations and provides better information about varieties of French than normative grammars which have often been taken at face-value. This is particularly important in the construc-tion of pedagogical materials where the choice of data and description can easily give a distorted picture of 'norms' within various dialects of

French. The recognition of the diversity of French is essential in a pedagogical context since, as stressed earlier on, there is no such thing as 'the French language today' from a linguistic point of view. French, like other languages and many other concepts such as that of 'a nation', is a social construct.[5] And as such it has a reality – which is simultaneously political, juridical, symbolic, etc. – for people using the language. This reality is not the property of linguistics or sociolinguistics alone and I see no conflict between pursuing on the one hand a universalist approach to the definition of the language faculty which all humans share and recognising, indeed stressing, that a language in its institutional sense, is not generally a *trésor commun* but the locus of complex alliances and conflicts.

Notes

1. I am grateful to Carol Sanders, Gertrud Aub-Buscher, Tony Lodge and an anonymous Cambridge University Press reader for providing me with comments on an earlier version of this article, which have allowed me to rectify a number of errors. All remaining errors are mine and these colleagues are absolved of all responsibility for any perverse ideas defended in this article. A version of this paper was presented at the Third Meeting of the North West Universities Seminar in French at Burton Manor, Wirral. I wish to thank all the participants for an entertaining and enlightening discussion.
2. Tony Lodge points out that I adopt a rather *volontariste* approach in the sense that economic factors (e.g. the growth of a single market in goods) are arguably more powerful as a linguistic unifier than teachers or legislators. But in talking of the imposition of French here I have in mind the ruthless policy pursued in France against *langues régionales* over the centuries. For one example among many, see the fascinating discussion of 'L'école et la culture française' in nineteenth-century Languedoc in Fabre and Lacroix (1973: ch. 12).
3. On the notion of standardisation from an historical point of view, see Lodge (1991) and the references therein.
4. The arguments given here in favour of a Chomskyan approach to language are developed, with fuller references, in Durand (1990b).
5. On this matter, see further Bourdieu (1982).

Text

Ce que parler veut dire

P. BOURDIEU

La langue *standard:* un produit 'normalisé'

A la façon des différentes branches de l'artisanat qui, avant l'avènement de la grande industrie, constituaient, selon le mot de Marx, 'autant d'enclos' séparés, les variantes locales de la langue d'oïl jusqu'au XVIIIᵉ siècle, et jusqu'à ce jour les dialectes régionaux, diffèrent de paroisse à paroisse et, comme le montrent les cartes des dialectologues, les traits phonologiques, morphologiques et lexicologiques se distribuent selon des aires qui ne sont jamais parfaitement superposables et qui ne s'ajustent que très accidentellement aux limites des circonscriptions administratives ou religieuses[8]. En effet, en l'absence de l'*objectivation* dans l'écriture et surtout de la *codification* quasi juridique qui est corrélative de la constitution d'une langue officielle, les 'langues' n'existent qu'à l'état pratique, c'est-à-dire sous la forme d'habitus linguistiques au moins partiellement orchestrés et de productions orales de ces habitus[9]: aussi longtemps qu'on ne demande à la langue que d'assurer un minimum d'intercompréhension dans les rencontres (d'ailleurs fort rares) entre villages voisins ou entre régions, il n'est pas question d'ériger tel parler en norme de l'autre (cela bien que l'on ne manque pas de trouver dans les différences perçues le prétexte d'affirmations de supériorité).

> Jusqu'à la Révolution française, le processus d'unification linguistique se confond avec le processus de construction de l'État monarchique. Les 'dialectes', qui sont parfois dotés de certaines des propriétés que l'on attribue aux 'langues' (la plupart d'entre eux font l'objet d'un usage écrit, actes notariés, délibérations communales, etc.) et les langues littéraires (comme la langue poétique des pays d'oc), sortes de 'langues factices' distinctes de chacun des dialectes utilisés sur l'ensemble du territoire où elles ont cours, cèdent progressivement la place, dès le XIVᵉ siècle, au moins dans les provinces centrales du pays d'oïl, à la langue commune qui s'élabore à Paris dans les milieux cultivés et qui, promue au statut de langue officielle, est utilisée dans la forme que lui ont conférée les usages savants, c'est-à-dire écrits. Corrélativement, les usages populaires et purement oraux de tous les dialectes régionaux ainsi supplantés tombent à l'état de 'patois', du fait de la parcellisation (liée à l'abandon de la forme écrite) et de la désagrégation interne (par emprunt lexical ou syntaxique) qui sont le produit de la dévaluation sociale dont ils font l'objet: abandonnés aux paysans, ils sont définis en effect négativement et péjorativement par opposition aux usages distingués ou lettrés (comme l'atteste, parmi d'autres indices, le changement du sens assigné au mot patois qui, de 'langage incompréhensible', en vient à qualifier un 'langage corrompu et grossier, tel que celui du menu peuple'. Dictionnaire de Furetière, 1690).
>   La situation linguistique est très différente en pays de langue d'oc: il faut attendre le XVIᵉ siècle et la constitution progressive d'une organisation administrative liée au pouvoir royal (avec, notamment, l'apparition d'une multitude d'agents administratifs de rang inférieur, lieutenants, viguiers, juges, etc.) pour voir le dialecte parisien se substituer, dans les actes publics, aux différents dialectes de langue d'oc. L'imposition du français comme langue officielle n'a pas pour effet d'abolir totalement l'usage écrit des dialectes, ni comme langue administrative ou politique ni même comme langue littéraire (avec la perpétuation sous l'ancien régime d'une littérature); quant à leurs usages oraux, ils

restent prédominants. Une situation de bilinguisme tend à s'instaurer: tandis que les membres des classes populaires, et particulièrement les paysans, sont réduits au parler local, les membres de l'aristocratie, de la bourgeoisie du commerce et des affaires et surtout de la petite bourgeoisie lettrée (ceux-là mêmes qui répondront à l'enquête de l'abbé Grégoire et qui ont, à des degrés divers, fréquenté ces institutions d'unification linguistique que sont les collèges jésuites) ont beaucoup plus souvent accès à l'usage de la langue officielle, écrite ou parlée, tout en possédant le dialecte (encore utilisé dans la plupart des situations privées ou même publiques), ce qui les désigne pour remplir une fonction d'*intermédiaires.*

Les membres de ces bourgeoisies locales de curés, médecins ou professeurs, qui doivent leur position à leur maîtrise des instruments d'expression, ont tout à gagner à la politique d'unification linguistique de la Révolution: la promotion de la langue officielle au statut de langue nationale leur donne le monopole de fait de la politique et, plus généralement, de la communication avec le pouvoir central et ses représentants qui définira, sous toutes les républiques, les notables locaux.

L'imposition de la langue légitime contre les idiomes et les patois fait partie des stratégies politiques destinées à assurer l'éternisation des acquis de la Révolution par la production et la reproduction de l'homme nouveau. La théorie condillacienne qui fait de la langue une *méthode* permet d'identifier la langue révolutionnaire à la pensée révolutionnaire: réformer la langue, la purger des usages liés à l'ancienne société et l'imposer ainsi purifiée, c'est imposer une pensée elle-même épurée et purifiée. Il serait naïf d'imputer la politique d'unification linguistique aux seuls besoins techniques de la communication entre les différentes parties du territoire et, notamment, entre Paris et la province, ou d'y voir le produit direct d'un centralisme étatique décidé à écraser les 'particularismes locaux'. Le conflit entre le français de l'intelligentsia révolutionnaire et les idiomes ou les patois est un conflit pour le pouvoir symbolique qui a pour enjeu la *formation* et la *ré-formation* des structures mentales. Bref, il ne s'agit pas seulement de communiquer mais de faire reconnaître un nouveau discours d'autorité, avec son nouveau vocabulaire politique, ses termes d'adresse et de référence, ses métaphores, ses euphémismes et la représentation du monde social qu'il véhicule et qui, parce qu'elle est liée aux intérêts nouveaux de groupes nouveaux, est indicible dans les parlers locaux façonnés par des usages liés aux intérêts spécifiques des groupes paysans.

C'est donc seulement lorsque apparaissent les usages et les fonctions inédits qu'implique la constitution de la nation, groupe tout à fait abstrait et fondé sur le droit, que deviennent indispensables la langue *standard*, impersonnelle et anonyme comme les usages officiels qu'elle doit servir, et, du même coup, le travail de normalisation des produits des habitus linguistiques. Résultat exemplaire de ce travail de codification et de normalisation, le dictionnaire cumule par l'enregistrement savant la totalité des *ressources linguistiques* accumulées au cours du temps et en particulier toutes les utilisations possibles du même mot (ou toutes les expressions possibles du même sens), juxtaposant des usages socialement étrangers, voire exclusifs (quitte à marquer ceux qui passent les limites de l'acceptabilité d'un signe d'exclusion tel que *Vx., Pop.* ou *Arg.*). Par là, il donne une image assez juste de la langue au sens de Saussure, 'somme des trésors de langue individuels' qui est prédisposée à remplir les fonctions de code 'universel': la langue *normalisée* est capable de fonctionner en dehors de la contrainte et de l'assistance de la situation et propre à être émise et déchiffrée par un émetteur et un récepteur quelconques, ignorant tout l'un de l'autre, comme le veulent les exigences de la prévisibilité et de la calculabilité bureaucratiques, qui supposent des fonctionnaires et des clients universels, sans autres qualités que celles qui leur sont assignées par la définition administrative de leur état.

Dans le processus qui conduit à l'élaboration, la légitimation et l'imposition d'une langue officielle, le système scolaire remplit une fonction déterminante: 'Fabriquer les similitudes d'où résulte la communauté de conscience qui est le ciment de la nation. 'Et Georges Davy poursuit avec une évocation de la fonction du maître d'école, maître à parler qui est, par là même, un maître à penser: 'Il (l'instituteur) agit quotidiennement de par sa fonction sur la faculté d'expression de toute idée et de toute émotion: sur le langage. En apprenant aux enfants, qui ne le connaissent que bien confusément ou qui parlent même des dialectes ou des patois divers, la même langue, une, claire et fixée, il les incline déjà tout naturellement à voir et à sentir les choses de la même façon; et il travaille à édifier la conscience commune de la nation[10]. 'La théorie whorfienne – ou, si l'on veut, humboldtienne[11] – du langage qui soutient cette vission de l'action scolaire comme instrument d' 'intégration intellectuelle et morale', au sens de Durkheim, présente avec la philosophie durkheimienne du consensus une affinité au demeurant attestée par le glissement qui a conduit le mot *code* du droit à la linguistique: le code, au sens de chiffre, qui régit la langue écrite, identifiée à la langue correcte, par opposition à la langue parlée (*conversational language*), implicitement tenue pour inférieure, acquiert force de loi dans et par le système d'enseignement[12].

Le système d'enseignement, dont l'action gagne en étendue et en intensité tout au long du XIXe siècle[13], contribue sans doute directement à la dévaluation des modes d'expression populaires, rejetés à l'état de 'jargon' et de 'charabia' (comme disent les annotations marginales des maîtres), et à l'imposition de la reconnaissance de la langue légitime. Mais c'est sans doute la relation dialectique entre l'École et le marché du travail ou, plus précisément, entre l'unification du marché scolaire (et linguistique), liée à l'institution de titres scolaires dotés d'une valeur nationale, indépendante, au moins officiellement, des propriétés sociales ou régionales de leurs porteurs, et l'unification du marché du travail (avec, entre autres choses, le développement de l'administration et du corps des fonctionnaires) qui joue le rôle le plus déterminant dans la dévaluation des dialectes et l'instauration de la nouvelle hiérarchie des usages linguistiques[14]. Pour obtenir des détenteurs de compétences linguistiques dominées qu'ils collaborent à la destruction de leurs instruments d'expression, en s'efforçant par exemple de parler 'français' devant leurs enfants ou en exigeant deux qu'ils parlent 'français' en famille, et cela dans l'intention plus ou moins explicite d'accroître leur valeur sur le marché scolaire, il fallait que l'École fût perçue comme le moyen d'accès principal, voire unique, à des postes administratifs d'autant plus recherchés que l'industrialisation était plus faible; conjonction qui se trouvait réalisée dans les pays à 'dialecte' et à 'idiome' (les régions de l'Est exceptées) plutôt que dans les pays à 'patois' de la moitié nord de la France.

Notes

8. Seul un transfert de la représentation de la langue nationale porte à penser qu'il existerait des dialectes régionaux, eux-mêmes divisés en sous-dialectes, eux-mêmes subdivisés, idée formellement démentie par la dialectologie (cf. F. Brunot, *Histoire de la langue française des origines à nos jours*, Paris, A. Colin, 1968, pp. 77–78). Et ce n'est pas par hasard que les nationalismes succombent presque toujours à cette illusion puisqu'ils sont condamnés à reproduire, une fois triomphants, le processus d'unification dont ils dénonçaient les effets.
9. Cela se voit bien à travers les difficultés que suscite, pendant la Révolution, la traduction des décrets: la langue pratique étant dépourvue de vocabulaire politique et morcelée en dialectes, on doit forger une langue moyenne (comme font aujourd'hui les défenseurs des langues d'oc qui produisent, en particulier par la fixation et la standardisation de l'orthographe, une langue difficilement accessible aux locuteurs ordinaires).
10. G. Davy, *Élements de sociologie*, Paris, Vrin, 1950, p. 233.
11. La théorie linguistique de Humboldt, qui s'est engendrée dans la célébration de l'authenticité' linguistique du peuple basque et l'exaltation du couple langue-nation, entretient une relation intelligible avec la conception de la mission unificatrice de l'Université que Humboldt a investie dans la fondation de l'université de Berlin.
12. La grammaire reçoit, par l'intermédiaire du système scolaire, qui met à son service son pouvoir de certification, une véritable efficacité juridique: s'il arrive que la grammaire et l'orthographe (par exemple, en 1900, l'accord du participe passé conjugué avec le verbe *avoir*) fassent l'objet d'arrêtés, c'est qu'à travers les examens et les titres qu'elles permettent d'obtenir, elles commandent l'accès à des postes et à des positions sociales.
13. Ainsi, en France, le nombre des écoles, des enfants scolarisés et, corrélativement, du volume et de la dispersion dans l'espace du personnel enseignant s'accroissent de façon continue, à partir de 1816, c'est-à-dire bien avant l'officialisation de l'obligation scolaire.

(From Bourdieu 1982)

BIBLIOGRAPHY

Adamczewski, H. 1991. *Le français déchiffré: clé du langage et des langues*, Paris: A. Colin

Aebischer, V. 1983. 'Bavardages: sens commun et linguistiques', in V. Aebischer and C. Forel (eds.), *Parlers masculins, parlers féminins?* Paris: Delachaux et Niestlé

1985. *Les femmes et le langage*, Paris: Presses Universitaires de France

Ager, D. 1990. *Sociolinguistics and contemporary French*, Cambridge University Press

Ågren, J. 1973. *Etude sur quelques liaisons facultatives dans le français de conversation radiophonique. Fréquences et facteurs*. Acta Universitatis Upsaliensis, 10

Agron, P. 1971. 'Le comité d'étude des termes techniques français et les langues des spécialistes', *La Banque des Mots* 1: 67–75

Allaire, S. 1973. *La subordination dans le français parlé devant les micros de la Radiodiffusion*, Paris: Klincksieck

Andreini, L. 1985. *Le Verlan: petit dictionnaire illustré*, Paris: Veyrier

d'Anglejan, A. and Tucker, G. R. 1973. 'Sociolinguistic correlates of speech style in Quebec', in R. W. Shuy and R. W. Fasold (eds.), *Language attitudes: current trends and prospects*, Washington: Georgetown University Press, pp. 1–27

Anzorge, Ir. 1988. 'Le parler français du Togo aujourd'hui: étude lexicale', Université de Paris III, Mémoire de DEA

Aristide. (1984). 'Les verts ont vu rouge!', *Le Figaro*, 26 September

Ashby, W. J. 1981a. 'French liaison as a sociolinguistic phenomenon', in W. Cressey and D. J. Napoli (eds.), *Linguistic Symposium on Romance Languages* 9: 46–57

1981b. 'The loss of the negative particle *ne* in French. A syntactic change in progress', *Language* 57: 674–87

1985. 'L'élision du /l/ dans les pronoms clitiques et dans les articles définis en français', *Actes du XVIIe. Congrès International de Linguistique et Philologie Romanes, Aix-en-Provence*

1991. 'When does variation indicate linguistic change in progress?', *Journal of French Language Studies* 1 (1): 119–37

Atelier Parisien d'Urbanisme, Population et Logements 1984. *Analyse des Résultats de Recensement de 1982*, Multigr. Janvier

Atlas des Parisiens 1984. Paris: Masson

Austin, L. J. 1977. 'Review of *Petit Larousse en couleurs*', *French Studies* 31: 368–9

Bailey, C. J. 1973. *Variation and Linguistic Theory*, Arlington, VA: Center for Applied Linguistics

1987. 'Variation theory and so-called "sociolinguistic grammars"', *Language and Communications* 1: 39–66

Baker, P. 1972. *Kreol. A description of Mauritian Creole*, London: C. Hurst & Co.

Baker, P. and Corne, C. 1982. *Isle de France Creole. Affinities and origins*. Ann Arbor: Karoma Publishers

Bal, W. 1988. 'Mélanges W. BAL, africana romanica, préparés par Dieter Kremer', Romanisk in Geschichte und Gegenwart, vol. 22, Hamburg: Helmut Buske Verlag

Balibar, R. 1985. *L'institution du français: essai sur le colinguisme des Carolingiens à la République*, pp. 423, Paris: PUF

Balibar, R. and Laporte, D. 1974. *Le français national*, Paris: Hachette

Ball, R. V. 1990. 'Lexical innovation in present-day French: "le français branché"', *French Cultural Studies* 1: 21–35

Bally, C. 1965. *Linguistique générale et linguistique française*, 4th edn, Berne: Franke

Banque des Mots (La) 1971. Revue semestrielle

Banque Mondiale. 1988. *L'éducation en Afrique sub-saharienne*

Baraduc, J., Bergounioux, G., Cartellotti, V., Dumont, C. Lansari, M.-H. 1989. 'Le statut linguistique des voyelles moyennes', *Langage et Société*, 49: 5–24 (September)

Batchelor, R. and Offord, M. 1982. *Guide to contemporary French usage*, Cambridge University Press

Battye, A. and Hintze, M.-A. 1992. *The French Language today*. London: Routledge

Bauche, H. 1920. *Le langage populaire: grammaire, syntaxe et dictionnaire du français tel qu'on le parle dans le peuple, avec tous les termes d'argot usuel*, repr. Paris: Payot, 1946

Bazylko, S. 1981. 'Le statut de [ə]', *La Linguistique* 17: 91–101

Beaujot, J. 1981. 'Les statues de neige', *Langue Française* 54, 40–55

Bebel-Gisler, D. 1976. *La langue créole, force jugulée*, Paris: L'Harmattan

Bec, P. 1973. *La langue occitane*, Paris: PUF

Becherel, D. 1981. 'A propos des solutions de remplacement des anglicismes', *Linguistique* 17: 119–31

Behnstedt, P. 1973. *'Viens-tu, est-ce que tu viens?'* – *Formen und Strukturen des direkten Fragesatzes im Französischen*, Tübinger Beiträge zur Linguistik 41, Tübingen: Günter Narr Verlag

Bennett, W. 1991. *Not so much economy*, History of the French language workshop, Association for French Language Studies, Oxford

Bergeron, L. 1980. *Dictionnaire de la langue québécoise*. Montreal: VLB Editeur

Bernabé, J. 1983. *Fondal-natal. Grammaire basilectale approchée des créoles guadeloupéens et martiniquais*, 3 vols., Paris: L'Harmattan

Bernardo, D. 1988. 'La problématique nord-catalane', in Vermes (ed.) vol. 1, pp. 133–49

Bernet, C. and Rézeau, P. 1989. *Dictionnaire du français parlé*, Paris: Seuil

Berrendonner, A. 1982. 'L'éternel grammairien. Etude du discours normatif', Berne: Peter Lang, coll. *Sciences pour la communication*, 1

Berrendonner, A., M. Le Guern and C. Puech. 1983. *Principes de grammaire polylectale*, Lyon: Presse Universitaire de Lyon

Berry, J. W., Kalin, R. and Taylor, D. M. 1977. *Multiculturalism and ethnic attitudes in Canada*, Ottawa: Supply and Services Canada

Biarnes, P. 1987. *Les français en Afrique noire, de Richelieu à Mitterand*, Paris: A. Colin

Bickerton, D. 1971. 'Inherent variability and variable rules', *Foundations of language* 7: 457–92

1981. *Roots of language*, Ann Arbor: Karoma Publishers

Bidot, E. 1925. *La clef du genre des substantifs français* (Méthode dispensant d'avoir recours au dictionnaire), Poitiers: Imprimerie Nouvelle

Blanc, M. 1982. 'Social networks and bilingual behaviour: the Atlantic Provinces Project', paper presented at the Sociolinguistics Symposium IV, University of Sheffield

1984. 'Canada's changing geolinguistic issues', *The London Journal of Canadian Studies* 1: 22–29

1986. 'Canada's non-official languages', *The London Journal of Canadian Studies* 3: 46–56

Blanche-Benveniste, C. and Jeanjean, C. 1987. *Le français parlé. Transcription et édition*, Paris: CNRS/Didier Erudition

Blanche-Benveniste et al. 1990. *Le français parlé. Etudes grammaticales*, Paris: CNRS/Didier Erudition

Bloch, O. and Wartburg, W. von 1932. *Dictionnaire étymologique de la langue française*, Paris: PUF

Bonnard, H. 1981. *Code du français courant*, Paris: Magnard

1982. *Procédés annexes d'expression*, Paris: Magnard

Booij, G. and de Jong, D. 1987. 'The domain of liaison: theories and data', in Wenk, Durand and Slater (eds.), pp. 1005–25

Borrell, A. and Billières, M. 1989. 'L'évolution de la norme phonétique en français contemporain', *La Linguistique* 25: 2

Bosmajian, H. 1972. 'The language of sexism', *ETC: Review of General Semantics*, 29(3): 305–13

Bourcelot, H. 1973. 'Le français régional haut-marnais dans ses rapports avec la langue nationale', *Ethnologie Française* 3: 221–8

Bourdieu, P. 1977. 'L'économie des échanges linguistiques, *Langue Française* no. 34

1982. *Ce que parler veut dire. L'économie des changements linguistiques*, Paris: Fayard

Bourdieu, P. and Boltanski, L. 1975. 'Le fétichisme de la langue', *Actes de la Recherche en Sciences Sociales* no. 4

Bourhis, R. Y. (ed.) 1984. *Conflict and language planning in Quebec*, Clevedon, Avon: Multilingual Matters 5

Bourhis, R. Y. and Genesee, F. 1980. 'Evaluative reactions to code-switching strategies in Montreal', in H. Giles, W. P. Robinson and P. M. Smith (eds.), *Language: social psychological perspectives*, Oxford: Pergamon, pp. 335–43

Bourhis, R. Y., Giles, H. and Lambert, W. E. 1975. 'Social consequences of accommodating one's speech style. A cross-national investigation', *International Journal of the Sociology of Language* 6: 55–71

Bourhis, R. Y. and Sachdev, I. 1989. 'Two decades of language planning in Quebec: issues and controversies', *The London Journal of Canadian Studies* 6: 36–46

Bouthillier, G. and Meynaud, J. 1972. *Le choc des langues au Québec: 1760–1970*, Montreal: Presses de l'Université du Québec

Bouvier, J. C. 1973. 'Les paysans drômois devant les parlers locaux', *Ethnologie Française* 3: 229–34

Broglie, G. de. 1986. *Le français, pour qu'il vive*, Paris: Gallimard

Bronckart, J.-P. 1988. 'Présentation', in Schoeni, Bronckart and Perrenoud (eds.)

Brown, G. and Yule, G. 1983. *Discourse analysis*, Cambridge University Press

Brown, R. and Gilman, A. 1960. 'The pronouns of power and solidarity', in T. Sebeok (ed.), *Style in language*, Cambridge, MA: MIT Press

Brunot, F. 1966–72. *Histoire de la langue française*, 13 vols. Paris: A. Colin

Bulletin de l'Académie Royale de langue et de littérature française 1978. 'Le genre et le sexe', 56(1): 59–76

Bulletin de l'Association Générale des Usagers de la Langue Française (AGULF) 1983. 'La France et son français', bimestriel, no. 4/5

1984. 'La France et son français', bimestriel, no. 3/4

1986. 'La France et son français', bimestriel, no. 15/16

Bulletin de Liaison de la Fédération Internationale des Professeurs de Français (FIPF) 1986. no. 80, juin

Butters, R. 1972. 'Competence, performance and variable rules', *Language Sciences* 20: 29–32

Cadrot, P. 1976. 'Relatives et infinitives "déictiques" en français', *DRLAV* 13

Calvet, L.-J. 1987. 'Des marchés et des langues', in *La guerre des langues et les politiques linguistiques*, Paris: Payot, ch. 7

Caput, J.-P. 1972 and 1975. *La langue française, histoire d'une institution*, 2 vols., Paris: Larousse

Cardinal, M. 1975. *Les mots pour le dire*, Paris: B. Grasset

Carrington, L. D. 1988. 'Creole discourse and social development', manuscript report 212e, Ottawa: International Development Research Centre

Carton, F. 1973. 'Usage des variétés de français dans la région de Lille', *Ethnologie Française* 3: 235–44

1981. 'Les parlers ruraux de la région Nord-Picardie: situation sociolinguistique', *International Journal of the Sociology of Language* 29: 15–28

Carton, F., Rossi, M., Autesserre D. and Léon, P. 1983. *Les accents des Français* (book and audio cassette), Paris: Hachette

Cartwright, D. G. 1987. 'Accommodation among the anglophone minority in Quebec to official language policy: a shift in traditional patterns of language contact' *Journal of Multilingual and Multicultural Development* 8: 187–212

Cartwright, D. C. and Williams, C. H. 1982. 'Bilingual districts as an instrument in Canadian language policy', *Transactions of the Institute of British Geographers*, 7: 474–93

Catach, N. 1968. *L'orthographe française à l'époque de la Renaissance (Auteurs, Imprimeurs, Ateliers d'imprimerie)*. Thèse, Geneva: Droz (ed.) 1974. *La structure de l'orthographe française*, Actes de la Table ronde internationale CNRS-HESO de 1973, Klincksieck (Histoire, Système, pédagogie, informatique, réforme)

1988. *L'orthographe*, Paris: PUF, Que sais-je?

1985. 'La bataille de l'orthographe aux alentours de 1900' in *Histoire de la langue française, 1880–1914*, vol. 14, G. Antoine and R. Martin (eds.), (continuation of F. Brunot: *l'Histoire de la langue française*), pp. 237–51

1987. 'New linguistic approaches to a theory of writing', Actes du Colloque GURT 1986, Georgetown University, Washington, USA, pp. 162–74

(ed.) 1988. 'Pour une théorie de la langue écrite', Actes du Colloque international CNRS-HESO de 1984, Paris: Presses du CNRS, pp. 300

1989. *Les délires de l'orthographe, en forme de dictioNaire*, Paris: Editions Plon

1989. Interview dans le revue *Révolution* no. 4979, vendredi 5 mai

1991. *L'orthographe en débat*, Paris: Nathan

Catach, N., Golfand, J. and Pasques, L. 1976–92. Dictionnaire historique de l'orthographe française (RENA), 2000 mots, suivis de Lexique général des modifications de l'Académie et des principaux dictionnaires qui l'ont précédée (DAC); 1er fascicule 1976, 213 articles; 2e fascicule, 1986; avec Introduction générale et analytique, Bibliographie, Index général des noms, des mots et des graphies (forthcoming)

Cedergren, H. J. and Sankoff, D. 1974. 'Variable rules: performance as a statistical reflection and competence', *Language* 50: 333–5

Cellard, J. 1986. *Histoire des mots*, eds. La Découverte/Le Monde, vol. 1 (1985), vol. 2 (1986)

Cellard, J. and Rey, A. 1980. *Dictionnaire du français non-conventionnel*, Paris: Hachette

Chaker, S. 1988. 'Le berbère. Une langue occultée en exil', in Vermes (ed.), vol. 2, pp. 145–64

Chaliand, G. and Rageau, J.-P. 1989. *Atlas des Européens*, Paris: Fayard

Chalvon-Demersay, S. 1983. *Concubin concubine*, Paris: Seuil

Chambers, J. and Trudgill, P. 1980. *Dialectology*, Cambridge University Press

Charmeux, E. 1989. *Le 'bon' français et les autres*, Milan: Education

Chaudenson, R. 1974. *Le lexique du parler créole de la Réunion*, 2 vols., Paris: Champion

1979. *Les créoles français*, Paris: Nathan

1989. *Créoles et enseignement du français*, Paris: L'Harmattan

1989. *1989, vers une révolution francophone?*, Paris: L'Harmattan

Chaurand, J. 1968. *Le parlers de la Thiérache et du Laonnais*, Paris: Klincksieck

1972. *Introduction à la dialectologie française*, Paris: Bordas

Chioclet, F. and Dupré La Tour, S. 1983. *Les français des Français* (book and audio cassette), Paris: Sermap

Chomsky, N. 1986. *Knowledge of language, its nature, origin and use*, New York: Praeger

Chomsky, N. and Halle, M. 1968. *The sound patterns of English*, New York: Harper and Rowe

Cixous, H. 1986. *Entre l'écriture*, Paris: Des Femmes

Coadou, M. 1990. 'A la recherche des règles d'étiquette sociolinguistique: une enquête de terrain en Martinique', *Nouvelle Revue des Antilles*, 3: 37–51

Cohen, M. 1967. *Histoire d'une langue: le français*, Paris: Editions sociales

Cole, R. A. (ed.) 1980. *Perception and production of fluent speech*, Hillsdale, NJ: Erlbaum

Commissariat général à la langue française. 1985. *Guide des mots nouveaux*, Paris: Nathan

    1988. 'Dictionnaire des néologismes officiels', *Journal Officiel de la République française*, no. 1468, 5th edn

    1991. 'Dictionnaire des termes officiels', *Journal Officiel de la République française*, no. 1/2, 7th edn

Conseil de l'Europe. 1988. 'Résolution 192 sur les langues régionales ou minoritaires en Europe'

Conseil international de la Langue française (CILF) 1988. 'La solidarité entre le français et les langues du tiers-monde pour le développement', Colloque pour le XXème anniversaire du CILF, Paris, 9–10 December 1987

Conseil de la Langue française. 1984. *Bulletin du Conseil de la langue française*, Québec

Corbeil, J.-C. 1975. *L'aménagement linguistique du Québec*, Quebec: Conseil de la Langue française

Corbett, G. 1991. *Gender*, Cambridge University Press

Couvert, C. 1982a. *La langue française en République populaire du Congo*, Paris: Haut Comité de la Langue française, IRAF

    1982b. *La langue française en République populaire Gabonaise*, Paris: Haut Comité de la Langue française, IRAF

    1983a. *La langue française en République populaire au Tchad*, Paris: Haut Comité de la Langue française, IRAF

    1983b. *La langue française en République populaire Centrafique*, Paris: Haut Comité de la Langue française, IRAF

    1983c. *La langue française en République populaire Cameroun*, Paris: Haut Comité de la Langue française, IRAF

    1984a. *La langue française en République populaire Comores*, Paris: Haut Comité de la Langue française, IRAF

    1984b. *La langue française: synthèse de l'Afrique Equatoriale francophone*, Haut Comité de la Langue française, IRAF

    1985a. *La langue française en République populaire Burundi*, Paris: Haut Comité de la Langue française, IRAF

    1985b. *La langue française en République populaire Rwanda*, Paris: Haut Comité de la Langue française, IRAF

    1986. *La langue française en République populaire Djibouti*, Paris: Haut Comité de la Langue française, IRAF

Coveney, A. 1990. 'Variation in interrogatives in spoken French: a preliminary report', in J. Green and W. Ayres-Bennett (eds.) *Variation and change in French; essays presented to Rebecca Posner on the occasion of her sixtieth birthday*, London: Routledge and Kegan Paul

Crystal, D. 1991. *A dictionary of linguistics and phonetics*, 3rd edn, Oxford: Blackwell

Culioli, A. 1983. 'Pourquoi le français parlé est-il si peu étudié? *Recherches sur le français parlé* no. 5, Université de Provence

Damourette, J. and Pichon, E. 1911–39. *Essai de grammaire de la langue française*, 7 vols., Paris: D'Artrey (2nd edn 1968)

Dauzat, A. 1927. *Les patois*, Paris: Delagrave

1949. *Précis d'histoire de la langue et du vocabulaire français*, Paris: Larousse

Decamp, D. 1971. 'Implicational scales and sociolinguistic linearity', *Linguistics* 73: 30–43

Délégation générale à la langue française 1991. *Les brèves. Lettre de la Délégation générale à la langue française*

Dell, F. 1973. *Les sons et les règles*, Paris: Hermann

Delomier, D. 1985. 'Remarques sur certains faits d'intonation accompagnant des relatives explicatives', *Langue Française* 65: 41–51

Denetz, P. 1988. 'La langue bretonne. Mémoire pour la répression', Vermes (ed.), vol. 1, pp. 105–32

Denis, M. N. and Veltman, C. 1989. *Le déclin du dialecte alsacien*, Presse Universitaire de Strasbourg

Depecker, L. and Pages, A. 1985. *Guide des mots nouveaux*, Paris: Nathan

De Saint Lô, rev. P. A. 1967. *Relation du voyage du Cap Verd* (1657) Paris: F. Targa; Rouen: P. Ferrand

Deshaies, D. 1981. *Le français parlé dans la ville de Québec: une étude sociolinguistique*, Quebec: CIRB, G-1

Deshaies, D. and Hamers, J. F. 1982. *Etude des comportements langagiers dans deux entreprises en début de processus de francisation*. Quebec: CIRB, G-3

Désirat, C. and Hordé, T. 1976. *La langue française au 20e siècle*, Paris: Bordas

Deuchar, M. 1987. *Sociolinguistics*, in J. Lyons et al. (eds.), *New horizons in linguistics*, vol. 2, pp. 296–310, Harmondsworth: Penguin Books

Deulofeu, J. 1981. 'Perspective linguistique et sociolinguistique dans l'étude des relatives en français', *RFP* no. 8

1986. 'Syntaxe de *que* en français parlé et le problème de la subordination, *RFP* no. 8

Deyhime, G. 1967. 'Enquête sur la phonologie du français contemporain', *La Linguistique* no. 1

Dictionnaire du français plus, à l'usage des francophones d'Amérique. 1988. Paris: Hachette

Dictionnaire du notre temps, Le. 1990. Paris: Hachette

Dittmar, N. 1976. *Sociolinguistics*, London: Edward Arnold

Dreyfus, M. 1986. *Le multilinguisme des enfants à Dakar, DEA sous la direction de L. J. Calvet*, Paris: Université René Descartes

Dubois, J. 1965. *Grammaire structurale du français: nom et pronom*, Paris: Larousse

1967. *Grammaire structurale du français: le verbe*, Paris: Larousse

Dubois, J., Guilbert, L. Mitterand H. and Pignon, J. 1960. 'Le mouvement général du vocabulaire français de 1949 à 1960 d'après un dictionnaire d'usage', *Le Français Moderne* 28: 60–106 and 196–210

Dulong, G. 1968. *Dictionnaire Correctif du Français au Canada*, Quebec: Presses de l'Université Laval

1973. 'Histoire du français en Amérique du Nord', In T. Sebeok (ed.), *Current Trends in Linguistics 10: Linguistics in North America*, 407–21, The Hague: Mouton

Dulong, G. and Bergeron, G. 1980. *Le parler populaire du Québec et de ses régions voisines. Atlas Linguistique de l'Est du Québec*, Quebec: Editeur Officiel du Québec, 10 vols.

Dumais, H. and Violette M. et al. 1988. *Pour un genre à part entière: guide pour la rédaction des textes non-sexistes*. Quebec: Coordination à la Condition Féminine

Duneton, C. 1973. *Parler croquant*, Paris: Stock

Dunoyer, J. M. 1979. 'La vie de la langue française: les nouveautés du Petit Larousse 1980', *Le Monde*, 7 September

1982. 'Le Petit Larousse 1983, reflet du changement', *Le Monde*, 18 September

Durand, J. 1986. 'French liaison, floating segments and other matters in a dependency framework', in J. Durand (ed.), *Dependency and non-linear phonology*, pp. 161–201, Beckenham: Croom Helm

1990a. *Generative and non-linear phonology*, London: Longman

1990b. 'Language: is it all in the mind?' Inaugural lecture. Department of Modern Languages, Salford: University of Salford

Durand, J. and Slater, C. (eds.). *French sound-patterns: changing perspectives*, London: AFLS/CILT

Durand, J., Slater, C. and Wise, B. 1987. 'Observations on schwa in Southern French', in B. Wenk, J. Durand and C. Slater (eds.), pp. 983–1004

Edwards, J. and Jacobsen, M. 1987. 'Standard and regional standard speech: distinctions and similarities', *Language in Society* 16: 369–80

Edwards, V. 1973. *Anglicization in Quebec City*, Quebec: CIRB, B-36

Emmorey, K. D. and Fromkin, V. 1988. 'The mental lexicon', in F. J. Newmeyer (ed.), *Linguistics: the Cambridge Survey*, vol. 3 *Language: psychological and biological aspects*, pp. 124–49, Cambridge University Press

Encrevé, P. 1976. Preface to Labov (1972) *Sociolinguistique*, Paris: Editions de Minuit

1983. 'La liaison sans enchaînement,' *Actes de la recherche en sciences sociales* 46: 39–66

1988. *La liaison avec ou sans enchaînement. Phonologie tridimensionnelle et usages du français*, Paris: Seuil

Escoffier, S. 1976. 'Aspects du français régional stéphanois', *Revue de Linguistique Romane* 40: 365–72

Etiemble, R. 1973. *Parlez-vous franglais?* Paris: Gallimard, Edition revue

Evans, H. 1985. 'A feminine issue in contemporary French usage', *Modern Languages*, 66(4): 231–6

Evans, H. 1987. 'The government and linguistic change in France: the case of feminisation', *ASMCF Review* 31: 20–6

Fabre, D. and Lacroix, J. 1973. *La vie quotidienne des paysans du Languedoc au XIXe. siècle*, Paris: Hachette

Fantapie, A. and Brûle, M. 1984. *Dictionnaire des néologismes officiels*, Paris: Nathan

Fasold, R. 1990. *Sociolinguistics of language*, Oxford: Blackwell

Fasold, R. and Schriffin, D. (eds.) 1989. *Language change and variation*, Amsterdam: J. Benjamins

Federation of Francophones outside Quebec 1978. *The heirs of Lord Durham: manifesto of a vanishing people*, Ottawa: Fédération des Francophones hors Québec

Ferguson, C. A. 1959. 'Diglossia', *Word* 15: 325–40

Field, T. 1980. 'The sociolinguistic situation of modern Occitan', *French Review* 54: 37–46

Fishman, J. 1972. *Language and nationalism: two integrative essays*. Rowley, MA: Newbury House

Flutre, L. F. 1958. 'De quelques termes usités aux XVIIe. et XVIIIe. siècles sur les côtes occidentales d'Afrique et qui ont passé dans les récits des voyageurs français du temps', *Etymologica* 209–38 (Festschrift W. von Wartburg), Tübingen: Max Niemeyer Verlag

1961. 'De quelques termes de la langue commerciale utilisée sur les côtes de l'Afrique Occidentale aux XVIIe et XVIIIe, siècles, d'après le récits des voyageurs du temps', *Revue de Linguistique Romane* 25: 274–89

Fodor, I. 1959. 'The origin of grammatical gender', *Lingua*, 8: 1–41, 186–214

Fouché, P. 1959. *Traité de prononciation française*, Paris: Klincksieck, 2nd edn

François, D. 1973. 'Sur la variété des usages linguistiques chez les adultes', *La Pensée*, December, p. 190

1974. *Français parlé. Analyse des unités phoniques et significatives d'un corpus recueilli dans la région parisienne*, 2 vols., Paris: SELAF

1977. 'Langage et situations de communication', *Etudes de linguistique appliquée* 26: 5–8

François F. (ed.) 1983. 'Bien parler? bien écrire? qu'est-ce que c'est?' in *J'cause français, non?* Paris: La Découverte-Maspéro (ed.) 1983.

(ed.) 1983. 'Norme orale et norme écrite: l'exemple de *c'est* et *il y a*', *Etudes de grammaire française descriptive*, Heidelberg: J. Groos, pp. 64–8

Frei, H. 1929. *La grammaire des fautes*, repr. Geneva: Slatkine Reprints 1971

Fromkin, V. A. 1980. *Errors in linguistic performance: slips of the tongue, ear, pen and hand*, London: Academic Press

Gadet, F. 1971. 'Recherches récentes sur les variations sociales de la langue', *Langue Française* 9

1989. *Le français ordinaire*, Paris: A. Colin

Gadet, F. and Mazière, F. 1986. 'Effets de langue orale', *Langages* 81

Gallison, R. 1978. *Recherches de lexicologie descriptive: la banalisation lexicale*, Paris: Nathan

Gardette, P. 1955. 'Deux itinéraires des invasions linguistiques dans le domaine provençal', *Revue de Linguistique Romane* 19: 183–96

Gardin, B. 1975. 'Loi Deixonne et langues régionales: représentation de la nature et de la fonction de leur enseignement', *Langue Française* 25: 29–36

Gardy, P. 1985. 'Langue(s), non-langue(s), lambeaux de langue(s), norme', *Cahiers de Linguistique Sociale* no. 7, Publications de l'Université de Rouen, pp. 60–3

Gardy, P. and Lafont, R. 1981. 'La diglossie comme conflit, l'exemple occitan', *Langages* (Larousse) 61: 75–91

GARS (Groupe Aixois de Recherches en Syntaxe) *Recherches sur le français parlé*, nos. 1–11, 1977–91, Université de Provence. (*RFP*)

Gauchat, L. 1905. 'L'unité phonétique dans le patois d'une commune', in *Aus romanischen Sprachen und Literaturen: Festschrift Heinrich Morf*, Halle: Max Niemeyer, pp. 175–232

Gauthier, X. 1974. 'Existe-t-il une écriture de femme?' *Tel Quel*

Gendron, J. D. 1966. *Tendances phonétiques du français parlé au Canada*. Paris: Klincksieck/Quebec: Presses de l'Université Laval
1972. *Rapport de la Commission d'Enquête sur la Situation de la Langue Française et sur les Droits Linguistiques au Québec. Livre I: La Langue du Travail*. Quebec: Editeur Officiel du Québec
Genouvrier, E. 1986. *Naître en français*, Paris: Larousse
George, K. E. M. 1976. 'Anglicisms in contemporary French', in *Modern Languages* 57: 6–11 and 63–8
1980. 'L'apocope et l'aphérèse en français familier, populaire et argotique', *Le Français Moderne* 48: 16–37
1986. 'The language of French adolescents, *Modern Languages* 67: 137–41
Gesner, B. E. 1985. *Bibliographie annotée de linguistique acadienne*, Quebec: Centre International de Recherches sur le Bilinguisme
Giacomo, M. 1975. 'La politique à propos des langues régionales: cadre historique', *Langue Française* 25: 12–28
Giles, H. and Powesland, P. 1975. *Speech styles and social evaluation*, London: Academic Press
Giordan, H. 1982. 'Démocratie culturelle et droit à la différence', rapport au Ministre de la Culture, Paris: La Documentation française
Glissant, E. 1981. *Le discours antillais*, Paris: Seuil
Goffin, P. 1984. 'Interview de Marina Yaguello à propos de la sortie de son livre *Le sexe des mots'*, *Terminologie et Traduction* 2: 147–53
Goosse, A. 1975. *La néologie française d'aujourd'hui*, Conseil international de la langue française
Gordon, D. C. 1978. *The French language and national identity: 1930–1975*, The Hague: Mouton
Green, J. and Ayres-Bennett W. (eds.) 1990. *Variation and change in French: essays presented to Rebecca Posner on the occasion of her sixtieth birthday*, London: Routledge and Kegan Paul
Gregory, M. and Carroll, S. 1978. *Language and situation*, London: Routledge and Kegan Paul
Grévisse, M. 1987. *Le bon usage*, Paris: Gembloux Duculot
Grif, 1976. 'Parlez-vous français?', *Les Cahiers du Grif*, June
Grillo, R. 1989. *Dominant languages: language and hierarchy in Britain and France*, Cambridge University Press
Groupe des Atlas 1978. 'Régionalismes de France', *Revue de Linguistique Romane* 42: 149–94
Groupe IFA de l'AELIA (1983) J. Blonde, G. Canu, J. P. Caprile, J. R. Deltel, P. Dumont, R. Efoua-Zengue, S. Faik, D. Gontier, F. Jouannet, S. Lafage, G. Mendo-Ze, G. Ni-Diaye-Correard, A. Queffelec, D. Racelle-Latin coord., J. L. Rondreux, J. Schmidt. *Inventaire des particularités lexicales du français en Afrique noire*, Quebec, AUPELF/ACCT EDICEF, 1988
Guespin, L. and Marcellesi, J. B. 1986. 'Pour la glottopolitique', *Langages (Larousse)* 83: 5–34
Gueunier, N. Genouvrier, E. and Khomsi, A. 1978. *Les français devant la norme*. Paris: Champion (A shorter version in E. Bédard and J. Maurais (eds.), 1983. *La norme linguistique*, Paris: Robert, 1983)

Guillon, M. and Taboada-Leonetti, I. 1986. *Le triangle de Choisy: un quartier chinois à Paris*, Paris: L'Harmattan/CIEMI

Guiraud, P. 1956. *L'argot*, Paris: PUF, Que sais-je? 700

1965. *Le français populaire*, Paris: PUF, Que sais-je? 1172

1966. *Le moyen français*, Paris: PUF, Que sais-je? 1086

1968. *Patois et dialectes français*, Paris: PUF

1969. 'Français populaire ou français relâché', *Le Français dans le Monde* 69: 23–7

1978. *Les mots savants*, Paris: PUF, Que sais-je? 1325

Guy, G. R. 1977, 'A new look at -t, -d deletion', in R. Fasold and R. Shuy (eds.), *Studies in language variation*, Washington, DC: Georgetown University Press, pp. 1–2

1988. 'Language and social class', in F. J. Newmeyer (ed.), *Linguistics: the Cambridge Survey*, vol. 4 *Language: the socio-cultural context*, Cambridge University Press, pp. 37–63

Haden, E. 1973. 'French dialect geography in North America', in T. A. Sebeok (ed.), *Current Trends in Linguistics 10: Linguistics in North America*, The Hague: Mouton, pp. 422–39

Hadjadj, D. 1981. 'Etude sociolinguistique des rapports entre patois et français dans deux communautés rurales du centre de la France en 1975', in Tabouret-Keller (ed.)

Hagège, C. 1985. *L'homme de paroles*, Paris: Fayard

1987. *Le français et les siècles*, Paris: Odile Jacob

Halliday, M. 1978. *Language as a social semiotic*, London: Edward Arnold

Hanse, J. 1983. *Nouveau dictionnaire des difficultés du français moderne*, Paris: Gembloux Duculot

Haritschelhar, P. 1988. 'Le basque. Une langue résistante', in Vermes (ed.), vol. 1, pp. 87–104

Hartley, A. F. 1986. 'Attitudes to varieties of French in Quebec' in D. E. Ager and J. R. French (eds.), *La Francophonie*, Portsmouth: Association for French Language Studies, 31–53

Hattiger, J. L. 1983. *Le français populaire d'Abidjan, un cas de pidginisation*, Abidjan: ILA, publ. no. 87

Haugen, E. 1966. 'Dialect, language, nation', *American Anthropologist* 68: 922–35

Hazaël-Massieux, G. 1978. 'Approache socio-linguistique de la situation de diglossie français-créole en Guadeloupe', *Langue Française* 37: 106–18

Henripin, J. 1988. 'The 1986 census: some enduring trends abate', *Language and Society* 24: 6–9

Heredia, C. de 1989. 'Le plurilinguisme des enfants à Paris', *Revue internationale des migrations européennes* 5(2), Poitiers

Highfield, A. R. 1979. *The French dialect of St Thomas, US Virgin Islands. A descriptive grammar with texts and glossary*, Ann Arbor: Karoma Publishers

Houdebine, A.-M. 1977. 'Français régional ou français standard? A propos du système des voyelles orales en français contemporain', in Walter (ed.)

1979. 'La différence sexuelle et la langue', *Langage et Société* 7: 3–30

1984. 'La féminisation des noms de métiers ou les femmes devant la langue', *Bulletin du centre de recherches de réflection et d'information féministes* 5: 17–37

Houdebine-Gravaud, A.-M. 1989. 'Une aventure linguistique: la féminisation des noms de métier, titres et fonctions en français contemporain', *Terminolo-gie et traduction* 2: 91–145

Houis, M. and Bole-Richard, R. 1978. *Intégration des langues africaines dans l'enseignement*, Paris: ACCT

Hymes, D. 1971. *On communicative competence*, University of Pennsylvania Press

Institut d'Etudes Occitanes. 1981. *Pour l'occitan et pour l'Occitanie*, Toulouse: Institut d'études occitanes

Irigaray, L. (ed.) 1978. 'Le langage "de" l'homme', *Revue Philosophique de la France et de l'étranger* 4: 495–504

Irigaray, L. (ed.) 1987. 'Le sexe linguistique', *Langages*, 85

Jerab, N. 1988. 'L'arabe des maghrébins. Une langue, des langues', in Vermes (ed.), vol. 2, pp. 31–59

Jeune Afrique 1990. Hebdomadaire international-indépendant (February/March)

Jochnowitz, G. 1973. *Dialect boundaries and the question of Franco-provençal*. The Hague: Mouton

de Jong, D., Poll, E. and Woudman, W. 1981. 'La liaison: l'influence sociale et stylistique sur l'emploi de la liaison dans le français parlé à Tours', unpublished Master's Thesis, University of Groningen

Joseph, L. J. and Taylor, T. (eds.) 1990. *Ideologies of language*, London: Routledge

Journal Officiel de la Republique Française 1984. (Question tabled at the Assemblée Nationale by an R.P.R. Member of Parliament), *JO* for 17 December

1988. *Dictionnaire des néologismes officiels*, Commissariat général de la langue française, 5th edn

1989. Avis et rapports du Conseil économique et social, session de 1989, séances du 29 at 30 mars 1989. 'L'utilité économique et commerciales de la langue française', rapport présenté par B. Renouvin

1991. *Dictionnaire des termes officiels*, Délégation général à la langue française, 7th edn

Joy, R. 1972. *Languages in conflict: the Canadian experience*, Toronto: McClelland and Stewart Ltd

Judge, A. and Healey, F. 1983. *A reference grammar of modern French*, London: Edward Arnold

Juneau, M. and Poirier, C. 1979. *Le TLFQ (Trésor de la Langue française au Québec): une approche d'un vocabulaire régional*, Quebec: Presses de l'Université Laval (Langue Française au Québec, 4e section: Travaux de Linguistique Québécoise)

Kaye, J. 1989. *Phonology: a cognitive view*, London: Lawrence Erlbaum Associates

King, R. and Roberge, Y. 1989. 'Preposition stranding in Prince Edward Island French', MS. York University (Canada) and University of Toronto (to appear in *Probus*)

Kourouma, A. 1970. 'Entretien avec A. Kourouma', *L'Afrique littéraire et artistique* no. 7

Kremnitz, G. 1983. *Français et créole: ce qu'en pensent les enseignants. Le conflit linguist-ique à la Martinique*, Kreolische Bibliothek, 5, Hamburg: Helmut Buske Verlag

Labov, W. 1966. *The social stratification of English in New York city*, Washington, DC: Georgetown University Press

1972. *Sociolinguistic Patterns*, Philadelphia: University of Pennsylvania Press

1976. *Sociolinguistique*, Paris: Les Editions de Minuit (translation of Labov 1972)

1983. 'Le changement linguistique. Entretien avec William Labov' (participants: Pierre Bourdieu and Pierre Encrevé) *Actes de la Recherche en Sciences Sociales* 46: 67–72

Lachapelle, R. 1987. 'The strengthening of majority positions', *Current demographic analysis: report on the demographic situation in Canada 1986*, pp. 109–33

L'Actualité terminologique. 1983. (contains article published jointly by *Le Bureau des traductions du secrétariat d'Etat, La Classification canadienne descriptive des professions* and in agreement with *Le Manuel de la politique administrative du conseil du Trésor du Canada*), February/March, pp. 1–7

Ladefoged, P. 1967. *Three areas of experimental phonetics*, London: Oxford University Press

Lafage, S. 1979. 'Rôle et importance du français populaire dans le continuum langues africaines/français en Côte d'Ivoire', *Français Moderne* 47 no. 3 (July): 208–19

Lafage, S. with Bal, W. and de Barreteau, D. 1978. 'La langue française en Afrique noire et à Madagascar: éléments pour une bibliographie' in Barreteau (ed.), *Inventaire des études linguistiques sur les pays d'Afrique noire et sur Madagascar*, Paris: CILF, pp. 547–77

1983. 'Petite enquête sur la perception du français populaire ivoirien en milieu estudiantin', *Bulletin Observatoire de français contemporain en Afrique noire* (OFCAN), Paris: INaLF, CNRS 4: 15.57

1984a. 'Note sur un processus d'appropriation sociosémantique du français en contexte ivoirien', *Cahiers de l'Institut de Linguistique de Louvain* 9: 3.4, 103.112

1984b. 'Terminologie populaire et floristique africaine: de quelques difficultés liées à l'élaboration de dictionnaires pour l'Afrique' *Bulletin OFCAN*, no. 5 CNRS. InaLF/Abidjan ILA: 159–77

1985. *Français parlé et écrit en pays éwé: Sud-Togo*, Paris: Ministère des Relations Extérieures, SELAF

1985–6. 'Premier inventaire des particularités lexicales du français en Haute Volta (1977–1980)'. Bulletin OFCAN, no. 6. Didier-Erudition/CNRS INaLF

1987–8. 'Terminologie populaire et floristique ivoirienne', *Bulletin OFCAN*, no. 7, CNRS. INaLF/Didier Erudition, 101.136

1989a. 'Französisch in Afrika' (334) in *Lexikon des Romanistischen Linguistik* (LRL) ed. Gunther Holtus, Michael Metzeltin, Christian Schmitt, Tübingen: Max Niemeyer Verlag

1989b. 'Métaboles et changement lexical du français en contexte ivoirien' in *Actes du colloque UREF 'Visages du français, variétés lexicales de l'espace francophone*, UREF, Fès, 20–22, February 1989

Lafont, R. 1971a. 'Un problème de culpabilité sociologique: la diglossie franco-occitane', *Langue Française* 9: 93–9

1971b. *Clefs pour l'Occitanie*, Paris: Seghers

1974. *La revendication occitane*, Paris: Flammarion

1982. 'Espace et norme linguistique, ou l'Occitanie en question de langage', *Amiras* 3: 3–18

Lafont, R. and Anatole, C. 1970. *Nouvelle histoire de la littérature Occitane*, Paris: PUF

Lafont, R., Gardès-Madray, F. and Siblot, P. 1983. 'Pratiques praxématiques', *Cahiers de Linguistique sociale* 6

Laks, B. 1977. 'Contribution empirique à l'analyse socio-différentielle de la chute des /r/ dans les groupes consonantiques finals', *Langue Française*, 34: 109–25

1980. 'Différenciation linguistique et différenciation sociale: quelques problèmes de linguistique française', Thèse de 3ème cycle. Université de Paris VII

1983. 'Langage et pratiques sociales. Etude sociolinguistique d'un groupe d'adolescents', *Actes de la Recherche en Science Sociales* 46: 73–97

Lambert, W. and Tucker, G. R. 1976. *Tu, vous, usted: a social-psychological study of address patterns*, Rowley, MA: Newbury House

Lamérand, R. 1970. *Syntaxe transformationnelle des propositions hypothétiques du français parlé*, Brussels: AIMAV

Lange, M. F. 1984. *Contribution à l'étude du phénomène de déscolarisation*, Lomé: ORSTOM

1987. 'Le refus de l'école' in *Politique Africaine* (October) 27: 74–86

Langue et administration, 1979–80. UGA no. 173–9, Namur

Lanly, A. 1973. 'Le français régional de Lorraine (romane)'. *Ethnologie Française* 3:305–8

Leclerc, A. 1974. *Parole de femme*, Paris: Grasset

Lefebvre, A. 1988. 'Les voyelles moyennes dans le français de la radio et de la télévision', *La Linguistique* 24 (2), 75–91

Lefebvre, A. and Morsley, D. 1990. Présentation, *La Linguistique* 26 (2), special no. 'Linguistique et "facteurs externes"?'

Légaré, C. and Bougaieff, A. 1984. *L'emploi du sacre québécois. Etude sémio-linguistique d'un intensif populaire*, Sillery: Presses de l'Université du Québec

Lemieux, M. and Cedergren, H. J. 1985. *Les tendances dynamiques du français parlé à Montréal*, Quebec: Office de la Langue française, 2 vols (Langues et Sociétés)

Lenning, M. 1979. 'Une étude quantitative du changement linguistique dans le système vocalique parisien' in Thibault (ed.), pp. 29–39

Léon, P. 1966. 'Apparition, maintien et chute de 'e caduc'', *La Linguistique* 2: 111–22

1970. 'Chez le marchand de journaux, conversations prises sur le vif', *Le Français dans le Monde* 76: 53

Lepelley, R. 1975. 'Le français régional de Basse-Normandie', *Le Français Moderne* 43: 1–11

Lescutier, J. M. 1985. 'Recherches sur le processus de réactivation. Cas singulier d'un idiolecte relevant du français populaire d'Abidjan', Université de Nice, thèse du 3ème cycle, 2 vols.

Lindenfeld, J. 1972. 'The social conditioning of syntactic variation in French', in J. Fishman (ed.), *Advances in the sociology of language*, vol. 2, The Hague: Mouton

1978. 'Communicative patterns at French marketplaces', *Semiotica* 23 (3/4): 279–90

Lodge, A. 1991. 'Authority, prescriptivism and the French standard language', *Journal for French Language Studies* 1 (1): 93–111

Lucci, V. 1983. *Etude phonétique du français contemporain à travers la variation situationnelle*, Publications de l'Université des Langues et lettres de Grenoble

Lyons, J. 1970. *Chomsky*, Glasgow: Fontana

Madray, F. and Marcellesi, J. B. 1981. 'Langues de France et Nation', *La Pensée IRM, Paris*, 221/222: 18–31

Magnan, S. 1983. 'Age and sensitivity to gender in French', *Studies in Second Language Acquisition* 5 (2): 194–212

Malécot, A. 1972. 'New procedures for descriptive phonetics', *Papers in Linguistics and Phonetics to the Memory of Pierre Delattre*, Paris–The Hague: Mouton

Manessy, G. 1975. 'Pidgin et créole, pidginisation, créolisation', *Bulletin du Centre d'Etude des Plurilinguismes* (CEP) 2: 3–14 (Nice: IDERIC)

  1978. 'Observation sur un corpus de français oral recueilli dans le sud du Cameroun', *Bulletin du CEP* 5: 3–32 (Nice: IDERIC)

  1984a. *Le français en Afrique noire, tel qu'on le parle, tel qu'on le dit*, Paris: L'Harmattan

  1984b. 'Français tirailleur et français d'Afrique', *Cahiers de l'Institute de Linguistique de Louvain* 9, 3.4, 113.126

  1986. 'Le français en Afrique de tradition coloniale française: statut géopolitique, usages et caractéristiques', *Actes du Congrès des Romanistes de Trèves* (forthcoming)

Marcel, J. 1973. *Le Joual de Troie*, Montreal: Editions du Jour

Marcellesi, J. B. 1979. 'Quelques problèmes de l'hégémonie culturelle en France: langue nationale et langues régionales', *International Journal of the Sociology of Language* 21: 63–80

  1985. 'Pour une politique démocratique de la langue', *Editions de Terre Corse*, Impasse Bertin 20000 Ajaccio

  1986. 'Actualités du processus de naissance de langues en domaine roman', *Cahiers de Linguistique Sociale* 9, 21–9

  1989. Interview dans la revue *Révolution*, no. 479, 5 May

March, C. 1990. 'L'attitude des mères martiniquaises dans le processus de minoration linguistique', *Nouvelle Revue des Antilles* 3: 53–63

Marchello-Nizia, C. 1979. *Histoire de la langue française aux XIVe and XVe siècles*, Paris: Bordas

Marks, G., Johnson, C. B. and Pratt, J. 1984. *Harrap's Slang Dictionary*, London: Harrap

Martel, P. 1987. 'Vingt-cinq ans de luttes identitaires', in Boutet and Vermes (eds.), vol. 1, pp. 125–42

Martin, A. and Dupuis, H. 1985. *La féminisation des titres et les leaders d'opinion: une étude exploratoire*, Quebec: Office de la Langue française (Langues et Sociétés)

Martinet, A. 1945. *La prononciation du français contemporain*, Paris: Droz

  1958. 'C'est jeuli, le Mareuc!' *Romance Philology* 2: 345–55 (reprinted in *Le français sans fard*, 1969, Paris: PUF, coll. SUP, pp. 191–208)

  1960. *Elements de linguistique générale*, Paris: A. Colin

  1969. *Le français sans fard*, Paris: PUF

Martinet, A. and Walter, H. 1973. *Dictionnaire de la prononciation française dans son usage réel*, Paris: France Expansion

Massignon, G. 1962. *Les parlers français d'Acadie: enquête linguistique*, 2 vols. Paris: Klincksieck

Mauny, R. 1952. *Glossaire des expressions et termes locaux employés dans l'ouest africain*, Dakar, IFAN, IX: 38–60

Maurand, G. 1981. 'Situation linguistique d'une communauté rurale en domaine occitan', in Tabouret-Keller (ed.)

Maurais, J. (ed.) 1987. *Politique et aménagement linguistique*, Quebec and Paris: Conseil de la Langue française et Le Robert

May, C. 1985. *Breaking the silence: the literature of Quebec*, University of Birmingham: Regional Canadian Studies Centre

Meillet, A. 1928. *Les langues dans l'Europe nouvelle*, Paris: Payot
    1938. *Linguistique historique et linguistique générale*, vol. 2, Paris: Payot

Mel'cuk, I. A. 1974. 'Statistics and the relationship between the gender of French nouns and their endings', in V. Ju Rozencvejg (ed.), *Essays on lexical semantics 1*: 11–42, Stockholm: Skriptor

Merle, G. et al. 1985. *Les mots nouveaux apparus depuis 1985*, Paris: Belfond

Merle, P. 1989. *Dictionnaire du français branché, suivi du Guide du français tic et toc*. Paris: Seuil (Point virgule)

Mettas, O. 1971. 'Etudes sur le A dans deux sociolectes parisiens', *Revue Romane*, 5(1): 94–105
    1979. *La prononciation parisienne. Aspects phonétiques d'un sociolecte parisien (du faubourg Saint-Germain à la Muette)*, Paris: SELAF

Milroy, L. 1980. *Language and social networks*, Oxford: Blackwell
    1987. *Observing and analysing natural language*, Oxford: Blackwell

Mitterand, H. 1963. *Les mots français*, Paris: PUF, Que sais-je? 270

Mochet, M. (ed.) 1986. *Discours en situation d'entretien: construction et premières exploitations d'une pré-enquête*, Cahiers du français des années quatre-vingt, ENS St Cloud/Crédif

Mok, Q. I. 1968. *Contribution à l'étude des catégories morphologiques du genre et du nombre dans le français parlé actuel*, La Haye–Paris: Mouton

Molard, E. 1810. *Le mauvais langage corrigé*

Morel, M. A. (ed.) 1985. 'L'oral du débat', *Langue Française* no. 65
    1991. *Situation linguistique du dialogue oral*, Paris: Presses de la Sorbonne Nouvelle

Morin, Y.-C. 1987. 'French data and phonological theory', in Wenk, Durand and Slater (eds.)

Mougeon, R. and Beniak, E. 1991. *Linguistic consequences of language contact and restriction: the case of French in Ontario, Canada*, Oxford: Clarendon Press

Muller, B. 1985. *Le français d'aujourd'hui*, Paris: Klincksieck

Nisard, C. 1872. *Etude sur le langage populaire*, Paris: Franck

Noel, D. 1990. *Les questions de la langue au Québec: 1759–1850*, Quebec: Conseil de la Langue française no. 32

Noreiko, S. F. 1983. 'Review of *Petit Larousse 1983*', *French Studies* 37: 504–5
    1985. 'Making room: words and senses excluded from Petit Larousse A–AYME between 1968 and 1983', *Quinquereme* 8: 188–95

Nouvel Observateur, Le. 1985. 'Informatique: le poids des mots', 6–12 September

Obalk, H., Sorel, A. and Pasche, A. 1984. *Les mouvements de mode expliqués aux parents*, Paris: Laffont

Office de la Langue française, Québec. 1986. *Titres et fonctions au féminin: essai d'orientation de l'usage*

Offord, M. 1990. *Varieties of contemporary French*, London: Macmillan

Paltridge, J. and Giles, H. 1984. 'Attitudes towards speakers of regional accents of French': effects of regionality, age and sex of listeners', *Linguistische Berichte* 90: 71–85

Pang, Y. 1989. 'Le bilinguisme franco-chinois dans le 13e arrondissement à Paris', Thèse de doctorat, Université René Descartes, Paris

Papen, R. 1987. 'Le métif: Le nec plus ultra des grammaires en contact', *Revue Québécoise de Linguistique Théorique et Appliquée* 6: 57–70

Paquot, A. 1988. *Les québécois et leur mots. Etudes sémiologiques et sociolinguistiques des régionalismes lexicaux du Québec*. Quebec: Conseil de la Langue française/ Presses de l'Université Laval

Paulston, C. B. 1987. 'Catalan and Occitan: comparative test cases for a theory of language maintenance and shift', *International Journal of the Sociology of Language* 63: 31–62

Peretz, C. 1977. 'Aspects sociolinguistiques du parlé parisien contemporain', in Walter (ed.)

Péronnet, L. 1989. *Le parler acadien*, Berne: Peter Lang

Perrin, G. 1983. *La langue française en Mauritanie*, Paris: Haut Comité de la langue française, IRAF

1984a. *La langue française au Mali*, Paris: Haut Comité de la langue française, IRAF

1984b. *La langue française au Burkinie*, Paris: Haut Comité de la langue française, IRAF

1984c. *La langue française au Sénégal*, Paris: Haut Comité de la langue française, IRAF

1985. *La langue française en Côte d'Ivoire*, Paris: Haut Comité de la langue française, IRAF

1986a. *La langue française au Bénin*, Paris: Haut Comité de la langue française, IRAF

1986b. *La langue française au Niger*, Paris: Haut Comité de la langue française, IRAF

1988. 'La population francophone de Côte d'Ivoire: données statistiques et estimation pour 1980', *Bulletin ROFCAN* no. 7, CNRS-INaLF/Didier Erudition, 7.24

Petyt, K. 1980. *The study of dialect*, London: André Deutsch

Peytard, J. 1970. 'Oral et scriptural: deux ordres de situations et de descriptions linguistiques' *Langue Française*, 6: 35–47

Philipp, M. 1985. 'L'accent alsacien' in G.-L. Salmon (ed.), *Le français en Alsace*, Paris: Champion-Slatkine

Picoche, S. and Marchello-Nizia, C. 1989. *Histoire de la langue française*, Paris: Nathan

Poche, B. 1987. 'La construction sociale de la langue', in Vermes and Boutet (eds.) vol. 1, pp. 79–105

Poirier, C. 1985. *Dictionnaire du français québécois*, Quebec: Presses de l'Université Laval

Politique Africaine, Centre d'Etudes d'Afrique noire, Association des chercheurs de politique africaine, Paris: Karthala

Prudent, L. F. 1980. *Des baragouins à la langue antillaise*. Paris: Editions Caribéennes

Prudent, L. F. 1990. 'La difficile construction de la linguistique créole aux Antilles', *Nouvelle Revue des Antilles* 3, 3–12

Prujiner, A., Deshaies, D., Hamers, J. F., Blanc, M., Clément, R. and Landry, R. 1984. *Variation du comportement langagier lorsque deux langues sont en contact*, Quebec: CIRB, G-5

Queneau, R. 1965. *Bâtons, chiffres et lettres*, Paris: Gallimard

Radford, A. 1990. *Syntactic theory and the acquisition of English syntax*, Oxford: Basil Blackwell

Rapport Confémen (Conférence des Ministres de l'éducation des états d'expression française). 1986. *Promotion et intégration des langues nationales dans les systèmes éducatifs, bilan et inventaire, ACCT, MRE.M.Ed. Québec*, Paris: Champion

Reichstein, R. 1960. 'Etudes des variations sociales et géographiques et faits linguistiques', *Word*, 16 April, pp. 55–99

Repères nos. 61, 67 and 72, Institut National de Recherche Pédagogique, Paris

Rézeau, P. 1984. *Dictionnaire des régionalismes de l'ouest: entre Loire et Gironde*, Sables d'Olonne: Editions Le Cercle d'Or

Rickard, P. 1968. *La langue française au seizième siècle. Etude suivie de textes*. Cambridge University Press

1974. *A history of the French language*, London: Hutchinson

1978. 'Review of Logos', *French Studies* 32: 502–4

Rindler-Schjerve, R. 1985. 'Le code régional alsacien: grammaire de transition', in G.-L. Salmon (ed.), *Le français en Alsace*, Paris: Champion-Slatkine

Roberge, Y. and Vinet, M.-T. 1989. *La variation dialectale en grammaire universelle*, Montreal: Presses Universitaires de Montréal

Robinson, O. F., Fergus, T. D., Gordon, W. M. 1985. *An introduction to European legal history*. Professional Books Ltd.

Roeper, T. 1988. 'Grammatical principles of first language acquisition: theory and evidence', in F. J. Newmeyer (ed.), *Linguistics: the Cambridge Survey*, vol. 2 *Linguistic theory: extensions and implications*, Cambridge University Press, pp. 35–52

Romaine, S. 1982a. *Socio-historical linguistics: its status and methodology*, Cambridge University Press

1982b. *Sociolinguistic variation in speech communities*, London: Edward Arnold

Roudy, Y. 1984. 'Plus qu'une simple affaire de langage', *Médias et Langage* 19–20: 26–30

Royal Commission on Bilingualism and Biculturalism (1967–70) *Reports 1–4*, 4 vols. Ottawa: Queen's Printer

Salmon, G.-L. (ed.) 1991. *Variété et variantes du français des villes états de l'est de la France*, Paris–Geneva: Champion–Slatkine

Sankoff, D. (ed.) 1978. *Linguistic variation: models and methods*, New York: Academic Press

(ed.) 1986. *Diversity and diachrony*, Amsterdam: John Benjamins

Sankoff, D. et al. 1989. 'Montreal French: language, class and ideology', in Fasold and Schriffin (eds.)

Sankoff, D. and Laberge, S. 1978. 'The linguistic market and the statistical explanation of variability', in Sankoff (ed.), pp. 239–50

Sankoff, D. and Vincent, D. 1977. 'L'emploi productif du *ne* dans le français parlé à Montréal', *Le Français Moderne* 45 (3): 243–56

Sansen, J. 1988. 'Le flamand. Une langue-frontière mal connue', in Vermes (ed.), vol. 1, pp. 169–87

Santerre, L. and Millo, J. 1978. 'Diphthongization in Montreal French', in Sankoff (ed.)

Saussure, F. de. 1916. *Cours de linguistique générale*, Paris: Payot

Sauvageot, A. 1978. *Français d'hier ou français de demain?* Paris: Nathan

Sauvageot, C. 1984. *Etude statistique sur les perspectives de la langue au Maghreb de 1980 à 2000*, Paris: Haut Comité de la Langue française, IRAF

Sauzet, P. 1988. 'L'occitan, langue immolée', in Vermes (ed.), vol. 1, pp. 208–60

Schmidt, J. 1984. 'Quelques aspects du lexique des textes anciens en français sur l'Afrique noire', *Bulletin OFCAN* no. 5, Paris, INaLFD, CNRS/Abidjan ILA, 91–157

Schoeni, G., Bronckart, J. P. and Perrenoud P. (eds.) 1988. *La langue française est-elle gouvernable?* Neuchâtel–Paris: Delachaux and Niestlé

Schon, J. 1975. 'En langue aussi, le sexe c'est la femme. La notion de genre en français et les nécessités de la communication', *Actes du deuxième colloque de linguistique fonctionnelle*, Clermont-Ferrand, 22–5 July, pp. 73–5

Séguy, J. 1951. *Le français parlé à Toulouse*, Toulouse: Privat

Selinker, L. 1972. 'Interlanguage', *International Review of Applied Linguistics* 10: 209–31

Sesep N'sial, B. N. 1978. 'Le métissage français lingala au Zaïre: essai d'analyse différentielle et sociolinguistique de la communication bilingue', Université de Nice, Thèse de 3ème cycle

Siegel, J. 1985. 'Koines and koineization', *Language in Society*, 357–78

Singy, P. 1986. 'Le vocabulaire médical: jargon ou argot?', *La Linguistique* 22: 63–74

Smith, N. 1989. *The twitter machine: reflections on language*, Oxford: Basil Blackwell

Spence, N. 1982. 'Another look at the loi des trois consonnes', *French Studies* 36: 1–11

Statistics Canada 1981. *Census of Canada, 1981*, Ottawa

Stourdzé, C. and Collet-Hassan, M. 1969. 'Les niveaux de langue', *Le Français dans le Monde* 65: 18–21

Stubbs, M. 1983. *Discourse analysis. The sociolinguistic analysis of natural language.* Oxford: Basil Blackwell

Swadesh, M. 1972. *The origin and diversification of language*, London: Routledge and Kegan Paul

Swiggers, P. 1990. 'Ideology and the "clarity" of French', in Joseph and Taylor (eds.)

Tabouret-Keller, A. (ed.). 1981. 'Regional languages in France', *International Journal of the Sociology of Language*, 29

Tetley, W. 1986. *Les droits linguistiques et scolaires au Québec et au Canada*, Quebec: CIRB, B-152

Thibault, P. (ed.) 1980. *Le français parlé: études sociolinguistiques* (Current inquiry into language and linguistics 30), Edmonton: Linguistic Research Inc.

Thibault, P. (ed.) 1980. *Le français parlé: études sociolinguistiques* (Current inquiry into language and linguistics 30), Edmonton: Linguistic Research Inc.

Träger, G. L. 1944. 'The verb morphology of spoken French', *Language* 20: 131–41

Tranel, B. 1987. *The sounds of French*, Cambridge University Press

Tuaillon, G. 1983. 'Régionalismes grammaticaux', *RFP* no 5

Tucker, G. R., Lambert, W. E. and Rigault, A. A. 1977. *The French speaker's skills with grammatical gender: an example of rule-governed behavior*, The Hague: Mouton

'Un débat à l'Académie: les mots au féminin' 1983. *Presse*, 19 February, p. 3

Valdman, A. 1978. *Le créole: structure, statut et origine*, Paris: Klincksieck

  (ed.) 1979. *Le français hors de France*, Paris: Champion

  1980. 'L'Acadie dans la francophonie nord-américaine', *Journal of the Atlantic Provinces Linguistic Association* 2: 3–18

  1982. 'Français standard et français populaire: sociolectes ou fictions?' *The French Review* 56: 2

  1983. 'Normes locales et francophonie', in E. Bédard and J. Maurais (eds.), *La norme linguistique*, pp. 667–706, Paris: Le Robert

  1988. 'Diglossia and language conflict in Haiti', *International Journal of Society and Language* 71: 67–80

Vallée, E. G. and Dufour, A. 1974. 'The bilingual belt: a garotte for the French?', *Laurentian University Review* 6, 18–31

Valli, A. 1981. 'Notes sur les constructions dites "pseudo-clivées" en français', *RFP* no. 3

Van de Craen, P. and Baetens Beardsmore, H. 1987. 'Research on city language' in A. Ulrich, N. Dittmar and K. Mattheier (eds.), *Sociolinguistics*, Berlin/New York

Van der Vorst, G. and Pohl, J. 1961. 'Le français tel qu'on le parle à Elizabethville' *Vie et Langage*, pp. 87–94

Varda One, 1971. *Everywoman*, 22 January, p. 15

Vecchio, S. 1989. 'Langue de la liberté et liberté de langue' à propos de glottophagie et de démocracie', *Français Moderne*, April 1/2, pp. 99–108

Vendryes, J. 1921. *Le langage*, Paris: La Renaissance du livre

Vermes, G. (ed.) 1988. *Vingt-cinq communautés linguistiques de la France*, 2 vols., vol. 1: *Langues régionales et langues non-territorialisées*, vol. 2: *Les langues immigrées*, Paris: L'Harmattan

Vermes, G. and Boutet, J. 1987. *France, pays multilingue: logiques sociales*, 2 vols., vol. 1: *Les langues en France, un enjeu historique et social*, vol. 2: *Pratique des langues en France*, Paris: L'Harmattan

Villanova, R. de. 1987. 'La circulation des langues dans les familles portugaises', in Vermes and Boutet, vol. 2, Paris: L'Harmattan

  1988. 'Le Portugais', in Vermes (ed.) vol. 2

Villers, de M. E. 1990, *Francisation des entreprises (1870–89). Analyse de l'activité terminologique québécoise*. Quebec: Conseil de la Langue française 74

Vincent, D. 1982. *Pressions et impressions sur les sacres au Québec*, Quebec: Office de la Langue française (Langues et sociétés)

Vintila-Radulescu, I. 1976. *Le créole français*, The Hague and Paris: Mouton (Janua Linguarum, series critica 17)

Vries, J. de 1986. *Towards a sociology of languages in Canada*, Quebec: CIRB, B-153

Walker, D. 1979. 'Canadian French', in J. K. Chambers (ed.), *The languages of Canada*, Montreal: Didier, pp. 133–67

Walter, H. (ed.) 1977. *Phonologie et société*, Paris: Didier

Walter, H. 1988. *Le français dans tous les sens*, Paris: Laffont

Wandruszka, M. 1975. 'Plaidoyer pour le plurilinguisme', *Revue de Linguistique Romane* 39: 108–21

Wardhaugh, R. 1986. *An introduction to sociolinguistics*, Oxford: Blackwell

Warnant, L. 1973. 'Dialects du français et français régionaux', *Langue Française* 18: 100–25

Wartburg, W. von. 1946. *Evolution et structure de la langue française*, Berne: Francke

Weber, M. H. 1987. *Le yiddish. Cahiers de Linguistique Sociale* n. 10, Université de Rouen

Wenk, B., Durand, J. and Slater, C. (eds.) 1987. *French phonetics and phonology, Linguistics*, 25

Wittig, M. 1964. *L'Opoponax*, Paris: Les Editions de Minuit

1969. *Les Guérillères*, Paris: Les Editions de Minuit

Yaguello, M. 1978. *Les mots et les femmes*, Paris: Payot

1989. *Le sexe des mots*, Paris: Belfont

1991. *En écoutant parler la langue*, Paris: Seuil

Yule, G. 1985. *The study of language*, Cambridge University Press

INDEX